THE STUDIA PHILONICA ANNUAL

SBL

Society of Biblical Literature

THE STUDIA PHILONICA ANNUAL
Studies in Hellenistic Judaism

Editors
David T. Runia
Gregory E. Sterling

THE STUDIA PHILONICA ANNUAL
Studies in Hellenistic Judaism

Volume XXVII

2015

EDITORS
David T. Runia
Gregory E. Sterling

ASSOCIATE EDITOR
Sarah J. K. Pearce

BOOK REVIEW EDITOR
Ronald Cox

SBL Press
Atlanta

THE STUDIA PHILONICA ANNUAL
Studies in Hellenistic Judaism

The financial support of
C. J. de Vogel Foundation, Utrecht
Queen's College, University of Melbourne
Yale University
Pepperdine University
is gratefully acknowledged

ISBN: 9780884141273 (hardcover: alk. paper)
ISBN: 9780884141266 (electronic book)
ISSN : 1052-4533

The cover photo, *Ezra Reads the Law*, is from a wall painting in the Dura Europos synagogue and used with permission from Zev Radovan (www.BibleLandPictures.com).

Printed on acid-free paper.

∞

THE STUDIA PHILONICA ANNUAL
STUDIES IN HELLENISTIC JUDAISM

Contributions should be sent to the Editor, Prof. G. E. Sterling, Yale Divinity School, 409 Prospect Street, New Haven, CT 06511, USA; email: gregory.sterling@ yale.edu. Please send books for review to the Book Review Editor, Prof. Ronald Cox, Religion Division, Pepperdine University, 24255 Pacific Coast Highway, Malibu, CA 90263-4352; email: rcox@pepperdine.edu.

Contributors are requested to observe the "Instructions to Contributors" located at the end of the volume. These can also be consulted on the Annual's website: http://divinity.yale.edu/philo-alexandria. Articles which do not conform to these instructions cannot be accepted for inclusion.

The Studia Philonica Monograph series accepts monographs in the area of Hellenistic Judaism, with special emphasis on Philo and his *Umwelt*. Proposals for books in this series should be sent to the Editor, Prof. Thomas H. Tobin, S.J., Theology Department, Loyola University Chicago, 1032 West Sheridan Road, Chicago, IL 60660-1537, U.S.A.; email: ttobin@luc.edu.

CONTENTS

BOOK REVIEW SECTION

NOTE. The editors wish to thank the typesetter Gonni Runia once again for her tireless work on this volume. They wish to express their thanks to Dr Lisa Marie Belz, OSU, Ph.D., Rev. Paul Adaja and Cory Louie, for meticulously proof-reading the final manuscript. As in previous years we are deeply grateful to our publisher, SBL Press, and to its staff, with a special mention of Nicole Tilford.

ABBREVIATIONS

The abbreviations used for the citation of ancient texts and modern scholarly literature generally follow the guidelines of the Society of Biblical Literature as published in *The SBL Handbook of Style*, second edition (SBL Press: Atlanta, GA, 2014) §8.4. In addition to the abbreviations listed in the Instructions to contributors at the back of the volume, please note the following:

Primary Source Abbreviations

Ar.	*Introductio arithmetica*, Nicomachus of Gerasa
Contr.	*Controversiae*, Seneca the Elder
Hex.	*Homiliae in Hexaemeron*, Basil of Caesarea
In metaph.	*In Aristotelis Metaphysica commentaria*, Syrianus
In. Nic.	*In Nicomachi arithmeticam introductionem*, Iamblichus
In R.	*In Platonis rem publicam commentarii*, Proclus
In Tim.	*In Platonis Timaeum commentaria*, Proclus
Theon Sm.	*De utilitate mathematicae*, Theon of Smyrna

Secondary Source Abbreviations

BT	Rosenzweig, Franz. *Briefe und Tagebücher. Band 1: 1900–1918. Der Mensch und sein Werk. Gesammelte Schriften 1.* ed. Rachel Rosenzweig and Edith Rosenzweig-Scheinmann. Haag: Martinus Nijhoff, 1979.
NBHL	*Nor bargirk' haykazean lezowi*
TvR	*Tijdschrift voor Rechtsgeschiedenis*

The Studia Philonica Annual 27 (2015): 1–26

INTERMARRIAGE AND THE ANCESTORS OF THE JEWS: PHILONIC PERSPECTIVES

SARAH PEARCE

The laws of the Torah include a clear and unambiguous prohibition of intermarriage between the followers of Moses and the other peoples of the promised land: Hittites, Girgashites, Amorites, Canaanites, Perizites, Hivites, and Jebusites (Deut 7:1–4). There must be no relationship, no "covenant" with them. Prefacing a sequence of prohibitions, culminating in the forbidding of intermarriage, the law enjoins only one positive command with respect to the treatment of these peoples: to exterminate them. The reason for the prohibition of intermarriage in this context is spelled out in terms of the inevitability of apostasy from the God of Israel, the Israelite turned by the non-Israelite towards the worship of "other gods" (cf. Exod 34:16), and the divine punishment that will swiftly follow: the extermination of the Israelites themselves. Alongside this absolute prohibition and its stark warning of the fatal consequences of intermarriage, the Torah also presents intermarriage between Israelites and non-Israelites as beginning with the patriarchs and continuing with the example of Moses himself. For Philo of Alexandria, the interpreter of Moses, these are the fundamental traditions that form the starting point of his most substantial reflections on the subject of intermarriage.

Within Jewish traditions of the Second Temple period, questions about intermarriage between Israelites and non-Israelites begin early in the era of Persian rule with the radical demands of the books of Ezra and Nehemiah for the reconstruction of Jerusalem's people through enforced separation from foreign spouses. In these books, the prohibition of intermarriage is extended to forbid the unions of Jerusalemite Jews with non-Jews; the "holy seed" of the Israelites must not be contaminated.[1] The influence of these traditions manifests itself across a range of Jewish writings from the Hellenistic and early Roman period, and results in some striking adaptations of the traditions of the Torah about intermarriage, especially with regard to

---

[1] Ezra 9:1–10:44; cf. Neh 13; Mal 2:10–12.

the unions of the patriarchs.[2] Within the broad context of Second Temple Judaism, however, the strict ideology of the Ezra-Nehemiah traditions by no means represents the only Jewish perspective on intermarriage with outsiders. From the Persian period onwards, other Jewish sources present a more positive picture of relationships between Israelite ancestors and non-Israelites. These traditions inscribe the fundamental place of the outsider in the history of the Jews, underlining the complex nature of Jewish/non-Jewish relations in antiquity.[3]

Through his work as an interpreter of Scripture, Philo offers some important, but often neglected contributions to questions about inter-marriage within Jewish tradition. Most of this material belongs to the Exposition of the Law and the closely related *Life of Moses*, in which Philo's commentary on the books of the Torah is concerned above all with demonstrating the unrivalled superiority of Moses and the supremely rational and universally significant character of his teaching. In this context, Philo's commentary on the "special laws" includes a major restatement and justification of the prohibition of intermarriage between Israelites and non-Israelites (*Spec.* 3.29). But the most substantial body of evidence for Philo's thinking about intermarriage appears in his treatment of the ancestral narratives, presented in the form of biographies of Abraham, Joseph, and Moses; and in his discussions of biblical figures as exemplary models of virtue. Philo's work as an interpreter of Scripture is almost exclusively concerned with the books of Moses and he rarely refers to other books of Scripture. One consequence of this is that Philo does not mention the unions of Israelite kings, including David and Solomon, with non-Israelite wives; nor does he deal with other examples of intermarriage in Jewish traditions from outside the Torah.[4]

---

[2] Important examples include the following: Jub. 20.4; 22.16, 20; 25.1–3; 27.10; 30.7–17; T. Levi 9.10; 14.6; Pseudo-Philo, LAB 18.13; 43.5; Tob 4.12; *Aramaic Levi Document* 17–18; 4QMMT.

[3] Important examples include the book of Ruth, the story of the Moabite ancestor of King David (Ruth 4:17–22), and the genealogy of the tribe of Judah according to 1 Chro-nicles; cf. Gary N. Knoppers, "Intermarriage, Social Complexity, and Ethnic Diversity in the Genealogy of Judah," *JBL* 120.1 (2001): 15–30. On later Second Temple sources and intermarriage: Shaye J. D. Cohen, "From the Bible to the Talmud: The Prohibition of Intermarriage," *HAR* 7 (1983): 23–39; Idem, *The Beginnings of Jewishness: Boundaries, Varie-ties, Uncertainties* (Berkeley, CA: University of California Press, 1999), 241–262; Michael L. Satlow, *Jewish Marriage in Antiquity* (Princeton: Princeton University Press, 2001), 133–161; Christine E. Hayes, *Gentile Impurities and Jewish Identities: Intermarriage and Conversion from the Bible to the Talmud* (Oxford: Oxford University Press, 2002), 70–91.

[4] Some biblical passages that might be deemed relevant for a discussion of inter-marriage, including Deut 21:10–14; 23:8–9 are not treated as such by Philo. With the exception of the examples to be discussed below, other biblical references to intermarriage

In the wider context of scholarship on intermarriage in Jewish antiquity, Philo is cited in support of quite different conclusions. For some, Philo is a severe interpreter of the prohibition of intermarriage, not so far in some respects from the ideology of the Ezra and Nehemiah traditions.[5] Others treat Philo as relatively tolerant and even "lax" in his thinking on intermarriage.[6] Philo's evidence is also interpreted in strikingly different ways in the context of historical questions about Jewish intermarriage in his era, and specifically among the Jews of Egypt. For a minority of scholars, Philo's allegedly infrequent mention of intermarriage, and "surprisingly gentle tone" in discussing it, represents important evidence that Jewish intermarriage was "not frequent" in Ptolemaic and early Roman Egypt.[7] In

---

among the patriarchs receive relatively little comment in Philo's works. He comments directly on the ancestors' instructions to their sons not to marry Canaanite wives (Gen 24:3, 37; 28:1, 6, 8; 36:2) in *QG* 5.88 (Gen 24:3); *QG* 6.241–242; *Post.* 76; *Fug.* 48–52 (Gen 27:46–28:2); and, referring to Esau's marriages to outsiders, *QG* 6.245 (Gen. 26:34; 28:6–9); in all cases, Philo takes an allegorical approach to the significance of such unions, in which the foreign women represent the passions, the absence of reason, and false doctrines about God. The birth of a son to Judah's son Manasseh by a "Syrian" concubine (Gen 46:20 LXX; cf. 1 Chr 7:14) represents the "forgetfulness" associated by Philo with the Hebrew name Manasseh ("out of forgetfulness") (*Congr.* 41). Philo's extensive comments on the Israelites who "profaned themselves by prostituting themselves" with Moabite women, and who agreed to sacrifice to the gods of those women (Num 25), are often cited in discussions of his treatment of intermarriage. But while Philo's comments on apostasy in this context (e.g. *Mos.* 1.298; *Spec.* 1.56; *Virt.* 40) do indeed connect to elements in his discussion of intermarriage, he does not treat this episode, which results in the immediate slaughter of the offenders, as an example of marriage (cf. *Mos.* 1.296–304; in the Allegorical Commentary, the Moabite women represent the passions and false doctrines that must be eradicated from the soul).

[5] Cohen, "From the Bible," 26; Sebastian Grätz, "The Question of "Mixed Marriages" (Intermarriage): the Extra-biblical Evidence," in *Mixed Marriages: Intermarriage and Group Identity in the Second Temple Period*, ed. Christian Frevel (London: Bloomsbury, 2011), 192–204 (202); cf. Hayes, *Gentile Impurities*, 70.

[6] Consider, for example, the view that Philo sees intermarriage as "detrimental to Jews but only because of the immorality of the Gentiles," by contrast with the much stricter Ezra traditions: Hannah Harrington, "Intermarriage in Qumran Texts: The Legacy of Ezra-Nehemiah," in *Mixed Marriages*, 251–279 (257). On Philo's "laxness" on the subject of intermarriage: Alan Mendelson, *Philo's Jewish Identity* (Atlanta, GA: Scholars Press, 1988), 74, and the discussion in the later part of this study.

[7] Louis H. Feldman, *Jew and Gentile in the Ancient World* (Princeton, NJ: Princeton University Press, 1993), 77–78. Feldman's description of Philo's "surprisingly gentle tone" follows Mendelson (*Philo's Jewish Identity*, 73), but draws very different conclusions as to its significance. While carefully avoiding conclusions about whether Second Temple period Jews actually did intermarry, in view of the absence of reliable data, Satlow interprets both Philo and Josephus as appearing "as if they would prefer to pass over Jewish intermarriage in silence, [thus buttressing] Tacitus's assertion that Jews at least had a reputation for not marrying non-Jews": *Jewish Marriage*, 146; cf. Tacitus, *Hist.* 5.5.2 in which

contrast, other studies treat Philo's comments on intermarriage as evidence that the intermarriage of Jews with non-Jews actually was, or is likely to have been, a substantial reality in Philo's Egypt,[8] or at least of major concern to Philo's Jewish community.[9] This lack of consensus leaves wide open the question of Philo's views on intermarriage and their significance for the history of the Jews of Egypt. For historians, this is clearly an unsatisfactory situation: Philo is our main source of evidence for ideas about intermarriage among the Jews of Egypt, the best-attested Jewish diaspora community of the ancient world.[10] While papyri and inscriptions provide rich evidence for many aspects of Jewish life in Hellenistic Egypt, they tell us very little—and offer very little clarity—about whether Egyptian Jews practised or abstained from intermarriage with non-Jews.[11]

---

the Roman historian alleges that Jews abstain from sexual relations with non-Jews but that among themselves "there is nothing unlawful."

[8] Note, in particular, the comments of Victor A. Tcherikover, *Hellenistic Civilization and the Jews* (Philadelphia, PA: The Jewish Publication Society of America; Jerusalem: The Hebrew University, 1959), 353–354, on the "cultural climate" of Philo's Egypt, illustrated by Philo's interpretation of the biblical prohibition of intermarriage, among other things: "We shall not be far wrong in stating that intermarriage was frequent, particularly among the rural population, which lived in direct proximity to the natives…There is no special need to study the various causes of the assimilationist movement in the ancient world, for they have not altered with time and we all know them from present day life in the Diaspora." On "mixed marriage" as "a phenomenon perhaps not unusual in Alexandria though wholly disapproved by Philo" see Victor A. Tcherikover and Alexander Fuks, *Corpus Papyrorum Judaicarum,* 3 vols. (Cambridge, MA: Harvard University Press, 1960), 2:2–3.

[9] Shaye Cohen, *The Beginnings of Jewishness,* 245, suggests that Philo's exegesis was "determined by the anti-traditional behavior of some of the Jews" in his environment, and that "Philo knew many Alexandrian Jews who intermarried or committed other forms of rebellion against the Jewish community." See also Harry A. Wolfson, *Philo: Foundations of Philosophy in Judaism, Christianity, and Islam,* 2 vols. (Cambridge MA: Harvard University Press, revised ed, 1968), 1:73–85; Stephen G. Wilson, *Leaving the Fold: Apostates and Defectors in Antiquity* (Minneapolis, MN: Augsburg Fortress, 2004), 37.

[10] In his comments on assimilation among Egyptian Jews, John Barclay states that "Philo is our chief source of information" on intermarriage or, at least, "Jews who married Gentiles and raised their children as Jews": John M. G. Barclay, *Jews in the Mediterranean Diaspora: From Alexander to Trajan (323 BCE – 117 CE)* (Edinburgh: T&T Clark, 1996), 107–108, cf. 324–325. His examples, all drawn from Philo's biblical commentary, include the prohibition of intermarriage in *Spec.* 3.29.

[11] See further Gideon Bohak, "Ethnic Continuity in the Jewish Diaspora in Antiquity," in *Jews in the Hellenistic and Roman Cities,* ed., John R. Bartlett (London: Routledge, 2002), 175–192 (185): "we are really in the dark when it comes to the marital preferences of Egyptian Jews." There is no unambiguous evidence for the existence of intermarriage among the Jews of Egypt, though a handful of papyri may point in this direction. An example of the difficulties of interpretation is illustrated by *CPJ* 1:128: it is not clear whether this fragmentary complaint brought by Helladote, daughter of Philonides, against

Can Philo's evidence bring greater clarity to this question? And what conclusions does Philo himself draw from the traditions of the Torah on intermarriage? These are questions that I began to explore in an earlier study of Philo's treatment of the prohibition of intermarriage in the setting of the 'special laws' (*Spec.* 3.29).[12] In that context, I argued that Philo's account of the Mosaic prohibition of intermarriage does not in fact help us to answer questions about how far, if at all, the Jews of Philo's era practised intermarriage with non-Jews. On the other hand, in my view, Philo's interpretation of the prohibition does give us a very clear insight into the purpose of the prohibition of intermarriage and its meaning for the followers of Moses. Philo presents the prohibition in the following terms:

> But also, [Moses] says, do not enter into a marriage-partnership with a foreigner, in case one day you are led on [by your partner] and give yourself up to customs in conflict with your own. And, without noticing it, you stray far from the road that leads to piety and you go off course towards places with no roads at all. And perhaps you yourself will be able to hold out, ballasted by the excellent instructions instilled into you from infancy, which your parents, by always repeating them, laid down as the sacred laws. But there is much reason to fear for your sons and daughters. Because, no doubt, enticed by bastard

---

the Jew Jonathas represents a dispute resulting from intermarriage since, as Tcherikover observes, "the Greek name [Helladote] is not sufficient evidence" to prove her non-Jewish identity: Victor A. Tcherikover, *CPJ* 1:237. Other relevant evidence for Jewish intermarriages includes *CPJ* 1:19; 2:144; *BGU* XIV.238; *P.Polit.Iud.* 4, cf. Sylvie Honigman, "The Jewish *Politeuma* at Heracleopolis," *Scripta Classica Israelica* 21 (2002): 251–266 (258–259). The absence of clear-cut evidence for intermarriage has often been interpreted as evidence for Jewish loyalty to the prohibition against intermarriage; cf. Joseph Mélèze-Modrzejewski, *The Jews of Egypt*, trans. Robert Cornman (Princeton, NJ: Princeton University Press, 1995), 71–72, 76–77. But Bohak is right to insist that the documentary evidence supplies almost no conclusive data about inner-Jewish marriage either. With regard to Hellenistic Egypt, Bohak concludes that "the only unambiguous evidence for inner-Jewish marriages is found in *CPR* XVIII, 8 and 9" (Bohak, "Ethnic continuity," 185). The evidence referred to belongs to a collection of papyrus documents, published in 1991, which once formed part of a register of contracts from the Fayum village of Theogonis (232 BCE). The collection contains records of several contracts relating to men and women who are formally identified as Jews. *CPR* XVIII.8 deals with the case of Diagoras son of Diokles, a Jew (ʾIουδαῖος), and his receipt of a dowry from Nikopole daughter of Theodotos, a Jewess (ʾIουδαία). *CPR* XVIII.9 records the acknowledgement by Philoumene, daughter of Diokles, a Jewess, of the return of a dowry for her daughter, returned by Philoumene's erstwhile son-in-law, Menestratos, son of Ionathas, a Jew of the epigone. The document preserves neither the name nor the ethnic label of Philoumene's daughter, but it is reasonable to presume that she too was a Jew. See further Bärbel Kramer, *Das Vertragsregister von Theogonis (P. Vindob.G.40618), Corpus Papyrorum Raineri Archeducis Austriae XVIII*, Griechische Texte XIII (Vienna: Hollinek for Österreichische Nationalbibliothek, 1991).

[12] Sarah Pearce, "Rethinking the Other in Antiquity: Philo of Alexandria on Intermarriage," *Antichthon* 47 (2013): 140–155.

customs that they prefer to the legitimate ones, they risk unlearning the honor due to the one God, and that is the beginning and end of the deepest misfortune. (*Spec.* 3.29)

Philo formulates the prohibition—"do not enter into a marriage-partnership with a foreigner"—in terms that fit his understanding of the universal and comprehensive qualities of the laws of the Torah. In contrast to the laws of Deuteronomy 7 and Exodus 34, in which the ban on intermarriage relates specifically to marriages with the indigenous peoples of the promised land, Philo places the prohibition of intermarriage outside any specific historical context: it applies in all contexts, at any time, and in any place. Furthermore, Philo does not limit the forbidden partners to the particular peoples listed in Deuteronomy 7 and Exodus 34; instead, following Philo's conception of the comprehensive application of Mosaic laws, the prohibition of intermarriage governs relationships with all possible examples of other peoples, and therefore forbids marriage with any "foreigner." Philo's most pronounced concern in his account of the prohibition of intermarriage is with its explanation and justification. He takes his starting point from the warnings against apostasy of Deuteronomy 7 and Exodus 34, expressed here in characteristically Philonic terms as a reverse spiritual migration and as unlearning of the education on which Jewish piety is founded. Philo is also able to draw positive lessons from scriptural prohibitions. Here he emphasises the importance of education in sustaining the existence of the community, rooted in the service of the one God; this vital education may be lost to the next generation if they are the children of intermarried parents. As for the penalty for intermarriage, Philo does not follow Deuteronomy in speaking of the divine wrath and extermination that will surely follow the community of the intermarried (Deut 7:4). Instead, Philo concludes, the children of the intermarried "risk unlearning the honor due to the one God, and that is the beginning and end of the deepest misfortune." Comparison with similar statements in Philo's writings suggests that he is here envisaging the risk of intermarriage in terms of the death of the soul: the "deepest misfortune" that is the condition of those who have abandoned, or who have never known what it is to practice true piety in the service of the one God.[13]

Several scholars have been struck by the fact that Philo avoids speaking of physical extermination as the inevitable punishment for intermarriage

---

[13] Pearce, "Rethinking the Other," 152–155. On the death of the soul see Dieter Zeller, "The Life and Death of the Soul in Philo of Alexandria," *SPhiloA* 7 (1995): 19–55 and Emma Wasserman, *The Death of the Soul in Romans 7*, WUNT 2.256 (Tübingen: Mohr Siebeck, 2008).

and that he does not spell out precisely what punishment awaits those who abandon the service of the one God on account of their non-Israelite relations. Erwin Goodenough suggests that, since Philo mentions no penalty here, "the prohibition of intermarriage was more an advisory than a legal matter."[14] In a brief but valuable study of this question, Alan Mendelson suggests that Philo's "failure" to specify any punishment in *Spec.* 3.29, in contrast to the extreme punishment prescribed in Deuteronomy, should be seen as part of the bigger picture of Philo's interpretation of intermarriage as represented by the lives of the ancestors and their unions with outsiders. Based on Philo's interpretation of Abraham with Hagar, Jacob with Bilhah and Zilpah, and Moses with Zipporah, Mendelson argues that, in each case, "Philo either minimizes the foreign element in the marriage or ennobles the pagan partner."[15] Overall, Mendelson concludes that Philo's discussion of biblical intermarriage represents a "surprisingly gentle tone," particularly with regard to the severity of Deuteronomy, and that Philo's "laxness" on the question may reflect the realities of intermarriage in Alexandria, "a sign that such unions were not unknown and that the better part of wisdom was to hope for the conversion of the non-Jewish partner."[16] In what follows, I explore further the approach taken by Philo with regard to the unions of the ancestors with outsiders, looking not only at the cases of Hagar, Bilhah and Zilpah, and Zipporah, but also two additional examples, namely, the relationship of Tamar with Judah and the marriage of Aseneth to Joseph. Part of my purpose is to probe the extent to which Philo's representation of these unions does indeed treat the "foreign" element in these relationships as either unproblematic or even positive. Where it is clear that Philo "ennobles" the foreign partner, why has he done so? Should this, as Mendelson appears to suggest, be seen as a reflection of Philo's tolerance with regard to intermarriage among Alexandrian Jews, or are there other possible explanations? In each case, particular attention will be given to Philo's use of his fundamental text for interpretation in the Greek Torah.

---

[14] Erwin R. Goodenough, *The Jurisprudence of the Jewish Courts in Egypt: Legal Administration by the Jews under the Early Roman Empire as Described by Philo Judaeus* (New Haven: Yale University Press, 1929), 85.

[15] Mendelson, *Philo's Jewish Identity*, 73.

[16] Ibid, 71–74. Louis Feldman follows Mendelson in describing Philo's "surprisingly gentle tone" with regard to intermarriage, and with Philo's failure to specify a punishment. Feldman's argument, however, implies that Philo mentions no punishment because there was no need for it; Philo's "silence" is used to support the view that intermarriage was a rare phenomenon in the diaspora: Feldman, *Jew and Gentile in the Ancient World*, 78.

1. *Abraham and Hagar*

As is well known, the figure of the Egyptian woman Hagar (LXX Αγαρ) plays a central role in the biblical account of Abraham, the founding patriarch of the people of Israel.[17] In the Book of Genesis, the story of Abram/Abraham (LXX Αβραμ/ Αβρααμ) focuses from the very beginning on the question of his descendants—will there be any, and by whom? The genealogy of Shem, son of Noah, introduces the figure of Abram for the first time, representing him as the eldest son of the present generation, but his wife (LXX γυνή) Sarai (LXX Σαρα), it is emphasised, was "barren, she had no child" (Gen 11:29–30). Will Abram represent the end of the line? In commanding Abram to journey to a new land (12:1-2), the Deity also promises Abram offspring and that he will be the founder of a great nation;[18] and, as the elderly Abram looks set to die childless, the promises of an heir are repeated more intensively;[19] but, ten years on in the land of Canaan, still Sarai remains childless.[20] To this point, the divine promises had not stated who was to be the mother of the "great nation" to be born to Abraham. Interpreting her infertility as God-given, Sarai attempts to produce a son by other means: she commands Abram to have intercourse with her Egyptian servant (LXX παιδίσκη Αἰγυπτία) Hagar, and gives her to him as a "wife" (LXX γυνή).[21] Following the Hebrew, Greek Genesis makes no distinction in terms between Hagar and Sarai as Abram's "wife." The plan succeeds. Hagar conceives, and gives birth to Ishmael, who is also to be the founder of a great nation;[22] but, as the narrative progresses, it makes clear that the heirs to God's promises to Abram will not be through Hagar, but through Sarai who, at the age of ninety, will give birth to Isaac.[23] This transformative moment in the fulfilment of God's promises is accompanied by the gift of new names: "Abraham," interpreted as "father of a multitude of nations" (Gen 17:1–5) and "Sarah" (LXX Σαρρα; cf. Hebrew *sārāh*, "princess"),[24] who, according to the divine promise, is to "give rise to nations,"

---

[17] Erich Gruen usefully explores this episode in the broader context of early Jewish reflections on relations with Ishmaelites and Arabs in his *Rethinking the Other in Antiquity* (Princeton: Princeton University Press, 2010), 299–300.

[18] Cf. Gen 13:15-16; 15:5, 14, 18; 17:2, 4–22; 18:18.

[19] Gen 15:1–21.

[20] Gen 16:1, 3.

[21] Gen 16:1–3.

[22] Gen 16:10; 17:20; 21:14–21.

[23] Gen 17:15–21; 18:10–14; 21:1–21.

[24] Cf. *HALOT* Vol. 3:1354.

and from whom will come "rulers of peoples" (Gen 17:5–16).[25] The union of Abraham and Hagar comes to an end, as he obeys Sarah's command to eject the Egyptian Hagar and her son from the household after the birth of Isaac. Sarah's insistence that the son of the slave (παιδίσκη) "shall not share in the inheritance with my son Isaac" is confirmed by God: "whatever Sarah tells you, obey her, for it is through Isaac that your descendants shall be called by your name" (Gen 21:12 LXX). Hagar and her son are sent away: Ishmael marries an Egyptian, and establishes a new dynasty, settled close by Egypt.[26] Isaac, on the other hand, marries into the family of Abraham's brother and settles in the promised land; following God's command not to go down to Egypt (as his parents had done),[27] Isaac will have nothing to do with Egypt.[28]

Philo's Hagar

Genesis puts great emphasis on Hagar's Egyptian identity, reminding the reader that Hagar's story is one of danger averted where the descendants of Abraham and Sarah are concerned:[29] it is not Ishmael, but Isaac and his descendants who will inherit their father's estate, the promised land and the divine blessings. Other early Jewish interpreters pass over the question of Hagar's Egyptian identity in silence or make nothing of it.[30] Philo, by contrast, interprets the figure of Hagar in many different contexts and often expands on the significance of her Egyptian origins. Interpreted allegorically, the story of Hagar is central to Philo's reading of Abraham as "the man of wisdom," whose journey towards divine wisdom requires preliminary training, symbolised by his temporary relationship with Hagar, before progressing to conceive true wisdom through intercourse with Sarah, the figure of virtue. Within this allegorical framework, Hagar becomes the symbol of school learning, the essential but transient stage of education through which the student must pass before moving on to the higher

---

[25] According to the majority of Greek manuscripts, the blessings of royal posterity apply to a neuter or masculine pronoun, referring to Isaac; Philo agrees with MT and the minority Greek tradition in connecting the promise to Sarah. See further John W. Wevers, *Notes on the Greek Text of Genesis*, SBLSCS 35 (Atlanta, GA: Scholars Press, 1993), 237.

[26] Gen 21:14–21; 25:12–18.

[27] Gen 12:10–20.

[28] Gen 24:1–67; 26:1–5.

[29] This is stated four times in the traditional Hebrew text, followed for the most part in LXX: Gen 16:1, 3; 21:9; 25:12 (not LXX).

[30] See, for example, Josephus, *Ant.* 1.187, 220, who follows Genesis in referring to Hagar's Egyptian identity, but makes no comment on it: cf. Sarah J. K. Pearce, *The Land of the Body: Studies in Philo's Representation of Egypt* (Tübingen: Mohr Siebeck, 2007), 169–170.

discipline of philosophy. Reflecting the broader framework within which Philo interprets biblical Egypt as "the land of the body," the starting point for the migration of the soul, Philo interprets Hagar's Egyptian identity as a symbol of the bodily characteristics of the school learning—the education based on the bodily senses and the perception of material things. Abraham, figure of the mind undergoing formation, must mate with Hagar, but she is not his final destiny, just as school education is not the final stage of learning for the philosopher.[31]

While Philo's allegorical interpretations offer a rich and varied exploitation of the figure of Hagar, his life of Abraham (*De Abrahamo*) assigns her only a marginal role, in striking contrast to the complex development of Hagar's story in Genesis. In this context, Hagar herself is not "the story": Philo's principal concern is rather with the exposition of the virtues of Sarah by way of explaining Abraham's grief at her death (Gen 23:2). Thus, Philo argues, the clearest proof of Sarah's virtue is apparent in her action to ensure that Abraham should not remain childless, by proposing that her husband should try to conceive a child by another woman: the offspring would be legitimate (γνήσια), belonging to Abraham, but it would also be Sarah's by adoption (θέσει).[32] Philo frames Sarah's offer to Abraham in the following terms: to avoid any suspicion of jealousy on her part, he is to take

... my servant (θεραπαινίς), in bodily terms (σῶμα) a slave, but in matters of the mind (διάνοια) of free and noble birth, tried and tested by me for many years from the day when she was first brought into my household, an Egyptian by birth (γένος), but a Hebrew by her way of life (προαίρεσις Ἑβραία). (*Abr.* 251)

In this remarkable statement, the Egyptian Hagar is not, as in Philo's allegorical interpretations, the education of the schools, but the schooled; she is trained by the virtuous Sarah in the wisdom which, interpreting the Hebrew way of life in Stoic terms, is the hallmark of the truly free and noble. As Mendelson rightly observes, "this elevation of Hagar is not warranted by Scripture."[33] Philo's Sarah advocates the reproduction of legitimate children with women of non-Hebrew origin, provided that they have undergone the transformative experience of training in the life of virtue, represented by her education in Sarah's household. It is this training which renders the woman who is Egyptian by ancestry, a Hebrew by her way of life (προαίρεσις), and makes her an acceptable mating partner for

---

[31] This interpretation of Hagar is elaborated most fully in Philo's allegorical treatise *De congressu quaerendae eruditionis gratia*, interpreting Gen 16:1–6. On Philo's allegorical interpretations of Hagar see Pearce, *The Land of the Body*, 167–177.

[32] *Abr.* 250.

[33] Mendelson, *Philo's Jewish Identity*, 72.

Abraham. The meaning of "choice" associated with προαίρεσις hardly seems apt for a slave; but in this context, as elsewhere, Philo uses the term of those who have been trained to act resolutely according to the principles of Mosaic Law.³⁴ It is not clear whether Philo here envisages Hagar as a "convert" to Judaism. It seems significant that he never uses προαίρεσις of the choice made by converts to abandon their ancestral customs for the laws of Moses. Hagar's transformation is a tribute to the virtuous Sarah who, like the truly wise, shares her good things with others.

Philo's story is not about Hagar, but about Sarah's virtuous dedication to the continuity of "the household beloved of God,"³⁵ and Abraham's admiration for her virtuous "wifely affection" (φιλανδρία).³⁶ While it is true that Philo makes no reference here to Hagar's being cast out of the household, as she is in Genesis, he nevertheless assures his readers that, following the "most accurate" interpretation of the story, Abraham abstained from intercourse with the pregnant Hagar, by virtue not only of his "natural self-control" (ἐγκράτεια) but also of the honour due to Sarah as his "lawful wife" (γαμετή).³⁷ Philo is at one with the Genesis tradition in emphasizing the unequal status of Sarah and Hagar in relation to Abraham and his children. But in drawing the contrast between the Egyptian παιδίσκη and Sarah as γαμετή, Philo also goes beyond the biblical tradition, constructing the status of Sarah as the "lawful wife" in terms familiar not from the Greek Bible but from the legal traditions of the Greek world.³⁸

---

³⁴ *Praem.* 4 (of the disciples of Moses); *Contempl.* 2, 17, 29, 32, 67, 79 (of the Therapeutae, cf. Francis H. Colson, *Philo* IX (Cambridge, MA: Harvard University Press, 1941), 518; *Hypoth.* 11.2 (of the Essenes); *Legat.* 230 (of Jews in general). On Hagar's "conversion," see, for example, Maren R. Niehoff, *Philo on Jewish Identity and Culture* (Tübingen: Mohr Siebeck, 2001), 26.

³⁵ *Abr.* 247.

³⁶ *Abr.* 245–246, 253–257.

³⁷ *Abr.* 253; for Sarah as γαμετή to Abraham, *Abr.* 168, 246; cf. *Congr.* 152; *QG* 3.20–24.

³⁸ γαμετή, "married woman, wife" as opposed to "concubine" is illustrated by sources from Hesiod to Hellenistic Egypt and beyond. Philo's treatment of Hagar, insisting through Sarah on the legitimacy of her offspring by Abraham, would appear to get round the recommended ideal in sexual relations according to Plato's *Laws*: namely, that a freeborn citizen should not dare to have intercourse with any one but his "wedded wife" nor to sow "any unholy and bastard seed with concubines..." (*Leg.* 841d). In the LXX corpus, γαμετή occurs only in 4 Macc 2:11: reason/Mosaic law is superior to love for a wife, which is why the Law requires husbands to rebuke their wives if they transgress the Law. For a different perspective on Philo's Hagar, see Niehoff, *Philo on Jewish Identity*, 24–28, who argues for the influence of Roman law in defining Ishmael's status as illegitimate by virtue of matrilineal descent and Hagar's slave status; but cf. the significant criticisms of this interpretation of Philo on intermarriage in Ellen Birnbaum's review in *SPhiloA* 14 (2002): 186–193, esp. 188–190.

Moreover, in contrast to Genesis, Philo never refers in this context to Hagar as "wife" (LXX γυνή) of Abraham: that title belongs to Sarah alone.[39]

To sum up, in Philo's treatment of their relationship, the union of Hagar with Abraham does not represent a "marriage": Philo goes beyond Scripture in insisting on Hagar's inferior status in relation to Sarah as the legitimate wife; and in contrast to Genesis, he avoids designating Hagar as the "wife" of Abraham. Even within the limited scope of her temporary, functional relationship with Abraham, her Egyptian identity is set aside: the Hagar that has intercourse with Abraham is the "Hebrew by way of life" and, in this sense, the relationship hardly constitutes an example of "intermarriage" or relationship with an outsider. Any "elevation" of Hagar ultimately serves the construction of Sarah as a model of virtue in her role as the "legitimate wife," an interpretation in which Philo is fundamentally guided by Scripture.

2. Jacob, Bilhah and Zilpah

The figures of Bilhah and Zilpah, the mothers of four of the twelve patriarchs born to Jacob, enter the Genesis narrative in a role similar to that of Hagar. According to the Book of Genesis, Jacob's wives Rachel and Leah each gave their servant (LXX παιδίσκη), Zilpah and Bilhah respectively, to Jacob as a "wife" (LXX γυνή).[40] Bilhah is also described as Jacob's "concubine" (LXX παλλακή).[41]

Philo's Bilhah and Zilpah

For the most part, Philo interprets Bilhah and Zilpah allegorically, focusing on their servile origins as the handmaidens to "virtue" (Rachel and Leah), or as concubines and slaves, in contrast to Jacob's "legitimate wives." Like the figure of Hagar, Bilhah and Zilpah represent the world of the body and the mortal as necessary, but inferior foundations for the life of the soul.[42]

---

[39] Abr. 93, 98–101,108–9, 112, 132 (= Gen 18:3 LXX), 245, 248, 253, 255.

[40] Gen 30:4, 9; cf. 37:2. According to Gen 29:24, 29, each woman was originally the maidservant (LXX παιδίσκη) of Laban, father of Leah and Rachel, who gave the servants to his daughters on their marriage to Jacob. Cf. also Gen 35:26; 46:18, 25.

[41] Gen 35:22. In context, this serves to define Bilhah as Jacob's property, violated by Jacob's son Reuben when he had intercourse with Bilhah.

[42] Bilhah: as Rachel's maidservant (παιδίσκη, Leg. 2.94–96; 3.146); Bilhah and Zilpah as handmaidens (θεραπαινίδες, Congr. 30) "slaves and concubines" (δοῦλαι καὶ παλλακαί, Congr. 31, 33). Philo's figurative association of both women with the world of the body is at

Apart from the fact that they are not said to be related to him,[43] nothing in Genesis defines Bilhah and Zilpah as any more foreign to Jacob than his wives, Rachel and Leah, the daughters of Laban, defined in Greek Genesis as "the son of Bathouel the Syrian, the brother of Rebekah," mother of Jacob: all are located in Haran.[44] In his discussion of Philo's approach to intermarriage, however, Mendelson suggests that Philo's implicit reference to Bilhah and Zilpah in his treatise *On Virtues* indicates their foreign status and that their relationship with Jacob constitutes an example of intermarriage in which Philo goes beyond the Genesis narrative in elevating the status of these women.[45] Is this conclusion justified? The evidence, I suggest, is not clear.

In *Virt.* 223, Philo clearly refers to Bilhah and Zilpah when he introduces unnamed "handmaids born beyond the Euphrates, in the remote parts of Babylonia" (θεράπαιναι τῶν ὑπὲρ Εὐφράτην ἐν ἐσχατιαῖς τῆς Βαβυλῶνος), who had been given as a dowry to their mistresses (Leah and Rachel) on their marriages.[46] This example serves to illustrate the wider thesis of this treatise, that true "nobility" (εὐγένεια), is proved by the possession of virtue rather than by ancestry, illustrated by the lives of people—such as the sons of Bilhah and Zilpah—whose ancestors were "blameworthy" with regard to offences against virtue, but who themselves

---

least partly grounded in etymological interpretations of their Hebrew names, identifying them with bodily functions (Bilhah = "swallowing;" Zilpah = "a walking mouth"); cf. Lester L. Grabbe, *Etymology in Early Jewish Interpretation: the Hebrew Names in Philo* (Atlanta, GA: Scholars Press, 1988), 140, 162. Interpreting Gen 37:2, which introduces the young Joseph as helper to the sons of Jacob's "wives" (LXX γυναῖκες), Bilhah and Zilpah, Philo draws out the implications of this setting for revealing what the character of Joseph stands for here: the image of the young Joseph represents the immature mind, which keeps company with human and mortal opinions, represented by "illegitimate (νόθοι) brothers, as the sons of concubines, of low parentage (οἳ παλλακίδων ὄντες ἀπὸ τοῦ χείρονος γένους), relating to the women (γυναῖκες)" (*Deus* 121).

[43] This issue is taken up, for example, in the Greek Testament of Naphtali, in which Bilhah is said to be descended from the "family of Abraham." Cf. the fragmentary Qumran Testament of Naphtali (4QTNaph), which seems to have served as a source for the Greek work, Michael E. Stone, "The Genealogy of Bilhah," *DSD* 3 (1996): 20–36.

[44] Gen 28:5 (LXX τοῦ Σύρου = MT *'Aram*, "Aramaean"); Gen 29:1 (not MT).

[45] Mendelson, *Philo's Jewish Identity*, 73; cf. Niehoff, *Philo on Jewish Identity*, 28–29 on Philo's construction of Bilhah and Zilpah as foreign and of their sons as non-Jews and therefore illegitimate.

[46] Philo does not mention the women by name here, in line with his usual practice throughout this discussion of biblical exempla of true εὐγένεια in which, of all the biblical figures referred to in *Virt.* 211–225, only Tamar is named (*Virt.* 221). This strategy is perhaps intended to allow the exempla a more universal significance, cf. Walter T. Wilson, *Philo of Alexandria, On Virtues: Introduction, Translation, and Commentary*, PACS (Leiden: Brill, 2011), 386.

lived model lives of virtue.[47] Judged worthy to pass over to the "marriage-bed" (εὐνή) of the "wise man" (Jacob), these women, Philo argues, first passed over "from the status of concubines to the name and rank of wedded wives" (ἐκ παλλακίδων εἰς γαμετῶν ὄνομα καὶ σχῆμα). As γαμεταί, Philo allows Bilhah and Zilpah to achieve a rank that he emphatically denies to Hagar. By favoring the promotion of their servants to share the same dignity as they themselves enjoy, Rachel and Leah represent "the souls of the wise and free" in sharing "their good things" with others; the same equality of treatment is also extended to the sons of the concubines, creating a community of harmony and mutual affection, despite the "apparent inferiority" of the children by Bilhah and Zilpah.[48] In other words, Zilpah and Bilhah and their sons represent the possibility of acquiring virtue, and of being recognised as equals by the community of the virtuous, despite their ignoble origins.[49]

Their ancestral origins, however, do not seem to play a part in the argument. Philo's description of the women as "born beyond the Euphrates" defines them by their association with their owners, based in Haran in northern Mesopotamia, which was also the home of Jacob's mother, Rebekah.[50] This is ancestral territory for Jacob. While Philo goes beyond Genesis in stating that the women were born "in the remote parts of Babylonia," he is true to the Genesis narrative in associating them with that part of the world. But, as in Genesis, this makes them no more foreign than their owners, Leah and Rachel: Bilhah and Zilpah are from shared ancestral territory. On this basis, Bilhah and Zilpah are probably not in themselves relevant for illustrating intermarriage among the patriarchs. Indeed, this conclusion seems to be further supported by the broader context in which Philo introduces Bilhah and Zilpah, exemplifying the nobility of virtue attainable by those otherwise deemed ignoble on account of their low birth, contrasting with the immediately previous example of "nobility" in Tamar, who, according to Philo, "though a foreigner (ἀλλόφυλος), was, at any rate, a free woman (ἐλευθέρα)."[51]

---

[47] *Virt.* 211. *Virt.* 187–227 (Περὶ εὐγενείας, *De nobilitate*) represents the last of four subtreatises within *De Virtutibus*; Wilson, *On Virtues*, 21–23, 381–418; on Philo's lists of biblical examples in this context, Peder Borgen, *Philo of Alexandria: An Exegete for His Time* (Leiden: Brill, 1997), 48–56.

[48] *Virt.* 224–225.

[49] *Virt.* 226–227; cf. Wilson, *On Virtues*, 412–414.

[50] Gen 24. Haran was also the first place of settlement by Abraham after his departure from Ur of the Chaldees, and the starting point for his departure for Canaan (Gen 11:31; 12:4–5).

[51] *Virt.* 222. For a different view, cf. Niehoff, *Philo on Jewish Identity*, 29, who suggests that this statement indicates that Bilhah and Zilpah were also ἀλλόφυλος, while also

3. *Judah and Tamar*

In Genesis, the figure of Tamar occupies a central role in ensuring the continuity of the descendants of Jacob. According to Genesis 38, Judah, the fourth son of Jacob and eponymous ancestor of the royal house of Judah, took Tamar as a wife (LXX γυνή) for his first-born (Gen 38:6). Nothing is said of Tamar's origins. By contrast, Genesis states that Judah's wife, the mother of his sons, was the daughter of a Canaanite (Gen 38:2).[52] As the narrative progresses, it becomes clear that Judah will not have descendants through the union of Tamar with the sons born to him by the Canaanite woman. The first son dies, punished for some unnamed transgression against the Deity. Onan, the second son, also dies for displeasing the Deity, having refused to produce children for his deceased brother by performing the duties of levirate marriage with the widowed Tamar.[53] Judah refuses to give his last surviving son to Tamar, for fear that he too will die (Gen 38:6–11). It is Tamar who takes action to ensure the continuity of the line, disguising herself as a prostitute to entice her father-in-law to impregnate her. On discovery of her true identity, instead of burning the pregnant Tamar for fornication, Judah declares her "more righteous (LXX δεδικαίω-ται) than I, because I did not give her to my...son" (Gen 38:26). Their sexual union is restricted only to the conception of Judah's heirs by Tamar, the narrative clarifying that "he did not know her again" (LXX οὐ προσέθετο ἔτι τοῦ γνῶναι αὐτήν) (Gen 38:26). The tale concludes with the birth of twin boys—Perez, the ancestor of King David, and Zerah. Despite Tamar's status as daughter-in-law to the father of her sons—a sexual relationship explicitly prohibited in the Torah[54]—she receives a decidedly positive evaluation for her action in ensuring the continuity of Judah's descendants.

Philo's Tamar

When he interprets the tale allegorically, Philo treats Tamar as a figure of virtue. Her widowhood symbolizes the death of the soul's relations with the passions; her relations with Judah, the soul's transformation from a lover of the body to a lover of God; her disguise, virtue's challenge to her

---

correctly acknowledging that the point does not seem to be relevant in Philo's treatment of these women..

[52] LXX names her Sava, corresponding to Hebrew Shuah; the traditional Hebrew text assigns the name to the Canaanite woman's father, while the woman herself remains nameless.

[53] Levirate marriage: Deut 25:5–10; Ruth 4; cf. Gen 38:8 LXX γαμβρεύω.

[54] Lev 18:15; subject to the death penalty, Lev 20:12.

students to uncover her beauty; her pregnancy, the virtuous soul "impregnated" by divine inspiration.[55]

Within the *Exposition*, Tamar is also the personification of virtue in Philo's treatise *On Virtues*, where, in the sequence of exempla of the virtue of εὐγενεία, she appears between Abraham, the model proselyte, and Bilhah and Zilpah. Here, Tamar represents the "nobility" zealously pursued not just by "men beloved of God" (such as Abraham),[56] but also by

> ...women who unlearnt the unlearning (ἀπομαθοῦσαι ἀμαθίαν) with which they were brought up, concerning the honour given to objects wrought by hand, and who became educated (παιδευθεῖσαι) in the knowledge of the monarchical principle by which the universe is governed (*Virt.* 220).

Like Philo's Abraham, Tamar is a model of the nobility represented by those who abandon home and family for monotheism: moving from darkness to light, deserting to the cause of piety, dedicating herself to the service of the One God. Philo's Tamar is constructed in the terms he also uses of the proselyte who, in this treatise, exemplifies the virtue of μετάνοια, "repentance."[57] Philo gives special emphasis to Tamar's commitment to the cause of piety, underlining her outstanding courage in risking death for the sake of the life of virtue by rejecting idolatry.[58] While Philo speaks of Tamar as "married" (γημαμένη) to two wicked brothers, the first her "lawful husband" (κουρίδιος), and the second, according to the law of the rights of the next of kin (ἐπιδικασία),[59] he makes no explicit reference to Tamar as Judah's wife, nor to their relationship. In contrast to her wicked husbands (Onan's death is not reported in this context), Tamar, states Philo, had the

---

[55] *Leg.* 3.74; *Deus* 136–137; *Congr.* 124–126; *Fug.* 149–156; *Mut.* 134–136; *Somn.* 2.44; cf. J. W. Earp, in Francis H. Colson and J. W. Earp, *Philo*, 10 vols. with 2 supplements, LCL (Cambridge: Harvard University Press, 1962), 10:358–359, 427–428.

[56] *Virt.* 212–219.

[57] *Virt.* 178–186; cf. Madeleine Petit, "Exploitations non-bibliques des thèmes de Tamar et de Genèse 38: Philon d'Alexandrie—textes et traditions juives jusqu'aux Talmudim," in *Alexandrina: Hellénisme, judaïsme et christianisme à Alexandrie; mélanges offerts a P. Claude Mondésert* (Paris: Cerf, 1987), 77–115 (79–80); Ellen Birnbaum, *The Place of Judaism in Philo's Thought: Israel, Jews, and Proselytes*, SPhiloM 2 (Atlanta, Scholars Press, 1996), 201, 214; Wilson, *On Virtues*, 410. On repentance see Gregory E. Sterling, "'Turning to God': Conversion in Greek-Speaking Judaism and Early Christianity," in *Scripture and Traditions: Essays on Early Judaism and Christianity in Honor of Carl Holladay*, ed. Patrick Gray and Gail O'Day, NovTSup 129 (Leiden: E. J. Brill, 2008), 69–95.

[58] On the courage of the convert: *Spec.* 1.52; 4.178; cf. Petit, "Exploitations," 80, on the theme of martyrdom.

[59] Philo refers to the principle of levirate marriage in terms drawn from Athenian law concerning the right of next of kin to claim a propertied woman who otherwise lacked a male guardian. Cf. Colson, *Philo* 8:299, n. c; Wilson, *On Virtues*, 411.

strength to keep her own life "spotless" (ἀκήλιδωτος), as befits the model of virtue.[60] It is in this context that he refers only in the most oblique terms to her union with Judah in terms that reinforce her status as a model of virtue: her ability to "obtain the good reputation (εὐφημία) which belongs to the good,"[61] alluding presumably to Judah's vindication of her righteousness; and to "become the starting point of nobility" (εὐγενείας ἀφορμή) for those who would come after her, alluding to her conceiving by Judah.[62] If Philo's readers did not already know the tale of Judah and Tamar, they would have been hard pressed to see that this was the story of a sexual relationship, let alone a marriage.

Within the context of the argument of *On Virtues*, the power of the example of Tamar as a representative of nobility in a person of ignoble ancestry lies precisely in the fact of her origins, like Abraham, among foreign idolaters.[63] She is, according to Philo, "a woman from Palestinian Syria, brought up in a household and city of many gods," filled with all the kinds of images and idols proscribed in the Torah;[64] she is a "foreigner" (ἀλλόφυλος), and, in contrast to Bilhah and Zilpah, a "free woman, of free ancestry." Philo goes so far as to hint at Tamar's illustrious antecedents (καὶ οὐκ ἀσήμων ἴσως).[65] Tamar's status as "foreigner" is presented as a given, suggesting that this interpretation is probably not Philo's invention but an established tradition familiar to his readers. As a "woman from Palestinian Syria," this Tamar belongs, in the terms in which Philo refers elsewhere to this territory, to the people of the biblical land of Canaan.[66] Indeed, for readers of the Greek Bible, the definition of Tamar as ἀλλόφυλος would

---

[60] Cf. Wis 4:9.

[61] Cf. *Migr.* 86–93, in which Philo interprets the promise of a "great name" to Abraham (Gen 12:2) as the promise of a great reputation (y), a reputation which, he argues, is obtained by practising the laws.

[62] *Virt.* 222.

[63] Ignoble roots: *Virt.* 211; Abraham: *Virt.* 212–219.

[64] *Virt.* 221. Philo's terms for the forbidden images in his description of Tamar's city as γεμούσῃ ξοάνων καὶ ἀγαλμάτων καὶ συνόλως ἀφιδρυμάτων match those he uses regularly to define what is prohibited by the Second Commandment of the Decalogue (Exod 20:4–6; Deut 5:8–10), cf. *Decal.* 66–81.

[65] *Virt.* 222.

[66] *Abr.* 133, cf. *Mos.* 1.163 ("Palestine"); and, referring to this territory in his own time, *Prob.* 75 (the location of the Essenes). On the use of the terms "Syria Palestine" and "Palestine" in Hellenistic and early Roman-period authors, including Philo, see Menahem Stern, *Greek and Latin Authors on Jews and Judaism*. Edited with Introductions, Translations and Commentary, Volume One: *From Herodotus to Plutarch* (Jerusalem: The Israel Academy of Sciences and Humanities, 1974), 3–4, 349.

reinforce this identification, given the consistency of the LXX identification of the *palishtim* of the Hebrew Bible as ἀλλόφυλοι.[67]

Philo's emphasis on Tamar's definitively alien origins, based on her identification with Palestinian Syria and, by implication, with the biblical Canaanites, is without precedent or parallel in antiquity. Moreover, it is directly contradicted by earlier Jewish sources from the Hellenistic period. Both Jubilees and the Testament of Judah construct Tamar as an "Aramean;" in other words, as descended from the same stock as Abraham.[68] Both traditions, shaped by profound hostility towards intermarriage, elaborate the schemes of Judah's Canaanite wife and her children in trying to keep Tamar out of the family because of her non-Canaanite descent.[69] Also deeply opposed to intermarriage with non-Jews,[70] the *Biblical Antiquities* of Pseudo-Philo, probably from the first century CE, presents Tamar as a leading proponent of that opposition: unwilling to separate from the sons of Israel, she insists that it is better to die for having become pregnant by her father-in-law than to have relations with Gentiles.[71] It is not clear

---

[67] If Philo's readers were aware of LXX Exod 34:15 (Codex B), which describes the inhabitants of the land with whom there must be no "covenant" as ἀλλόφυλοι, they would also see that the definition of Tamar as ἀλλόφυλος placed her among those peoples explicitly prohibited in the Greek Torah as marriage partners. See further Pearce, "Rethinking the Other," 147–148. In Philo's works, ἀλλόφυλος occurs a further seven times in total, referring generally to what is alien in contrast to relatives or fellow nationals (*Her.* 42; *Virt.* 160; *Prob.* 93; *Legat.* 211); more specifically, to the Chaldaean language, abandoned by Abraham (*Somn.* 1.161); and to local enemies of the Israelites/Judaeans and their institutions either in the past or in the present (*Spec.* 1.56, referring to the Moabite women of Numbers 25; *Legat.* 200, referring to people from nearby countries now settled in Jamnia).

[68] Jub. 41.1, "from the daughters of Aram;" T. Judah 10.1, the "daughter of Aram," brought by her first husband Er "from Mesopotamia." On the Aramean connections of Abraham and his descendants, cf. Gen 10:22; 22:21; 25:20; 28:5; Deut 26:5.

[69] Jub. 41.2–7; T. Judah 10.2–6. On Judah's hostility towards intermarriage between Canaanites and his sons, and his condemnation of himself for transgressing God's law in intermarrying with a Canaanite, explained as the result of youthful drunkenness, cf. T. Judah 11.1–5; 13.3–8; 14.6; 16.4; 17.1.

[70] Frederick J. Murphy, *Pseudo-Philo: Rewriting the Bible* (Oxford: Oxford University Press, 1993), 57.

[71] Pseudo-Philo, LAB 9.5. On the translation, see James L. Kugel, *Traditions of the Bible: A Guide to the Bible as It Was at the Start of the Common Era* (Cambridge, MA: Harvard University Press, 1998), 420. On the elevation of Tamar in Pseudo-Philo, see Pieter van der Horst, "Portraits of Biblical Women in Pseudo-Philo's *Liber Antiquitatum Biblicarum*," *JSP* 5 (1989): 29–46. On the wider context of early Jewish interpretation of Tamar, cf. Cecilia Wassen, "The Story of Judah and Tamar in the Eyes of the Earliest Interpreters," *Literature and Theology* 8.4 (1994): 354–366; Donald C. Polaski, "On Taming Tamar: Amram's Rhetoric and Women's Roles in Pseudo-Philo's *Liber Antiquitatum Biblicarum* 9," *JSP* 7 (1995): 79–99; Esther Marie Menn, *Judith and Tamar (Genesis 38) in Ancient Jewish Exegesis: Studies in Literary Form and Hermeneutic* (Leiden: Brill, 1997).

whether this source regards Tamar as a proselyte or a born Israelite. Later rabbinic traditions likewise construct Tamar as an Israelite or a proselyte.[72] Josephus omits the tale completely in his rewriting of Genesis, perhaps, as Louis Feldman suggests, because of its "embarrassing connotations."[73] In contrast to Philo, then, no other Jewish source from antiquity or late antiquity spells out her Canaanite background, let alone brings it to the fore.

How then should we account for Philo's identification of Tamar as a Canaanite? First, it is important to note that it is only in her role as an example of "nobility," comparable to Abraham in her migration from idolatry to monotheism, that Philo mentions Tamar's foreign status; he never mentions it in any other context, clearly indicating that the wider framework of *On Virtues* shapes the decision to highlight Tamar's origins. Secondly, it is not difficult to find indications in the Genesis text itself, which might lead to the reasonable supposition that Tamar was probably a Canaanite, a position also taken by leading modern commentators on Genesis.[74] Key to the identification of Tamar as a Canaanite are the following points:

(1) the fact that she is not described like Rebekah, the wife of Isaac, or Rachel and Leah, the wives of Jacob, as a descendant of Bethuel, the brother of Abraham (Gen 25:20; 28:5), who were explicitly sought as marriage partners because they were not Canaanite women (Gen 24:3–4; 28:1);[75]

(2) the emphasis in Genesis 38 on the Canaanite environment—situating Judah in Canaanite territory, separated from his brothers, allied to an

---

[72] In most of these traditions, Tamar is understood as an Israelite, "the daughter of Shem," taken as a reference to her descent from a priest, justified on the basis of Judah's threat to burn Tamar as a harlot, conforming to the death-penalty for the daughters of priests who commit harlotry (Lev 21:9): Genesis Rabbah 85.10; cf. b. Avodah Zarah 36b. The Babylonian Talmud also reports the interpretation of Rabbi Samuel b. Nahmani that, when Judah asked Tamar whether she was a Gentile, before having intercourse with her, she replied that she was a proselyte, thus showing that, in this respect, Judah conformed to rabbinic law: b. Sotah 10a. See further, Petit, "Exploitations," 90, 101.

[73] Louis H. Feldman, *Flavius Josephus. Judean Antiquities 1–4: Introduction and Commentary* (Leiden: Brill, 2000), 142. Another possibility is that, like most modern commentators, Josephus thought the story of Judah and Tamar out of place within the Joseph story; nevertheless, he did not find another place for it in his reordering of Mosaic traditions. In Josephus's *A.J.* 2, the story of Jacob's grief for the loss of Joseph, sold into slavery, is followed immediately by the events of Joseph's life in Egypt (*A.J.* 2.38–39).

[74] John A. Emerton, "Judah and Tamar," *VT* XXIX.4 (1979): 403–415, esp. 410–412; Claus Westermann, *Genesis 37–50: A Continental Commentary* (London: SPCK, 1987), 50–51; cf. Gruen, *Rethinking*, 289–293.

[75] Colson, *Philo* 8:298a; Wilson, *On Virtues*, 410.

Adullamite,[76] and married to a Canaanite, with Tamar's family based not far away.[77]

While Genesis does not say that Tamar was a Canaanite—a point that must have helped to stimulate reflections in other sources on her non-Canaanite status—it is not difficult to see why Philo, or his tradition, might reasonably have arrived at the conclusion that she was, simply on the basis of reading the Genesis text.

In short, Philo's Tamar is constructed as a model of virtue, a female equivalent of Abraham; the parallel calls for an emphasis on Tamar's foreign origins, which may be drawn out from the details of Genesis. Philo's elevation of Tamar goes beyond Scripture, and well beyond other Second Temple period sources, but Philo's approach is fundamentally shaped by the details of Scripture regarding her "good reputation," and by her function as an exemplar of "nobility" from ignoble roots.

4. *Joseph and Aseneth*

One of the more striking aspects of Philo's celebration of Joseph's life in Egypt is his treatment of the patriarch's marriage with an Egyptian woman. The fact of the marriage is based on the statement in Genesis 41:45 that when Pharaoh promoted Joseph as his second-in-command, he also "gave him as wife Aseneth, daughter of Petephres, priest of Heliopolis" (LXX). Philo follows Genesis in presenting this trophy bride as a reward, but he goes beyond Scripture in making clear that Aseneth was not a reward for services to Pharaoh, but for Joseph's loyal service to God. Thus, Philo tells us that the Egyptian king

> ... pledged in marriage to Joseph the most distinguished of the women of Egypt, the daughter of the priest of the Sun (Ἥλιος). Such are the rewards of the pious ... (*Ios.* 121–122)[78]

True to the spirit of the Genesis narrative, this statement reveals no discomfort over the fact of this marriage between a Hebrew and an Egyptian, and indeed expands on the unrivalled social status of the bride,

---

[76] Gen 38:1, 12.

[77] On the location of Timnah, in the vicinity of Tamar's father's household (Gen 38:11–12), see John A. Emerton, "Some Problems in Genesis XXXVIII," *VT* 25 (1975): 338–361, esp. 343–346.

[78] Aseneth is not the only reward, according to Philo: others include Joseph's high office as διάδοχος of the kingdom of Egypt, symbols of royal favor, and a new name (*Ios.* 119–121).

befitting a man who had reached the very top of Egyptian society. Philo is not alone here—Josephus describes Joseph's marriage as very distinguished (ἀξιολογώτατον), while the Testament of Joseph, in a most un-self-deprecating portrait of the patriarch, has Joseph speak of his marriage as a reward for his own "humility and patient endurance."[79] Not all Jewish commentators would take such a positive view.[80] Sources of the Hellenistic period mention the marriage without comment, presumably following the lead of Genesis.[81] Perhaps also from the Hellenistic period, the Greek Jewish novel *Joseph and Aseneth* allows the marriage only after the bride's conversion to her husband's faith;[82] some later rabbinic traditions effectively deny that Joseph "married out" at all, making Aseneth a descendant of Jacob through his daughter Dinah.[83] In Philo's account, by contrast, Aseneth is clearly an Egyptian and remains an Egyptian; there is no hint here of conversion. In this respect, Philo stays close to Genesis, expanding on the qualities of this Egyptian woman only to magnify the achievements of Joseph.

5. *Moses, Zipporah and the Ethiopian woman*

Exodus 2:21 records that the priest of Midian (Reuel/Jethro), the territory in which Moses is said to have sought refuge from Pharaoh after killing an Egyptian, gave his daughter Zipporah (LXX Semphôra) to Moses as wife (γυνή).[84] When Philo treats Zipporah in the context of allegorical inter-

---

[79] Josephus, *A.J.* 2.91; T. Jos. 18.3, trans. Howard C. Kee, "Testaments of the Twelve Patriarchs," in James H. Charlesworth, *The Old Testament Pseudepigrapha*, 2 vols. (Peabody, MA: Hendrickson, 1983), 1:775–828.

[80] A more negative view appears in the Allegorical Commentary, in which Philo makes extensive use of biblical Egypt as a symbol of the body. Here Joseph's connections by marriage symbolize the acceptance of the "citizenship (πολιτεία) of the body;" his father-in-law, priest of Heliopolis, "Sun City," serves the Sun, symbol of the human mind, instead of serving the Uncreated (*Somn.* 1.78).

[81] Jub. 34.20; 44.24; Demetrius in Eusebius, *Praep. ev.* 9.21.12; Artapanus in Eusebius, *Praep. ev.* 9.23.3. The lack of comment is particularly striking in Jubilees, given the exceptional hostility of this work towards intermarriage in general. On Aseneth's burial beside Joseph's mother Rachel, see T. Jos, 20.3. On Hellenistic Jewish images of Joseph: Erich S. Gruen, *Heritage and Hellenism: The Reinvention of Jewish Tradition* (Berkeley, CA: University of California Press, 1998), 73–109.

[82] Jos. As. 1–22; cf. Gruen, *Heritage*, 89–99. John Barclay, *Jews in the Mediterranean Diaspora*, 215, sees in the story an "evident concern to discourage exogamy."

[83] Victor Aptowitzer, "Asenath, the Wife of Joseph: A Haggadic Literary-Historical Study," *HUCA* 1 (1924): 239–306.

[84] Cf. Exod 2:21; 18:2–7 (which appears to locate Zipporah and her sons by Moses in Midian during the period in which Moses returns to Egypt to lead the Hebrews out). On wider issues of the interpretation of Zipporah and intermarriage in the biblical narrative,

pretations of Scripture, he always associates her with positive values, as a symbol of virtue, and of Moses's acceptance of God-given reason.[85] Philo makes no reference to Zipporah's origins in these contexts. In his *Life of Moses*,[86] however, he situates Zipporah's family (though not mentioned by name) among the "Arabs" (*Mos.* 1.51),[87] and expands on the Exodus narrative in several ways that clearly heighten the status of Zipporah when compared to the Exodus narrative, and that are without parallel in the extant literature of ancient Judaism.[88] Thus, Philo goes out of his way to explain why Moses first found the daughters of the Midianite priest watering their father's flock (Exod 2:16), insisting that the "Arabs" employ all kinds of people for tending cattle, including "those of the highest position (τῶν ἄγαν ἐπιφανῶν)" (*Mos.* 1.51). Furthermore, while Exodus does not explain why it was that, of his seven daughters, the priest of Midian gave Zipporah to Moses, Philo explains that, because he recognized the καλοκαγαθία of Moses, the Midianite "gave him the most beautiful (καλλισ-

---

see Karen Strand Winslow, "Ethnicity, Exogamy, and Zipporah," *Women in Judaism* 4.1 (2006): 1–13.

[85] *Cher.* 41,47; *Mut.* 120; *Post.* 77–78. The allegorical interpretation of Zipporah as "bird" (ὀρνίθιον), plays on an etymological interpretation of Hebrew *tsippôr*, "bird," which Philo relates, for example, to virtue ascending to heaven to contemplate divine truths (*Cher.* 41).

[86] Philo's two-volume biography of Moses is closely connected to the Exposition, but stylistic and structural differences suggest that it is an independent composition. See further, James R. Royse, "The Works of Philo," in Adam Kamesar (ed.), *The Cambridge Companion to Philo* (Cambridge: Cambridge University Press, 2009), 32–64 (47). For a counter view see Gregory E. Sterling, "'Prolific in Expression and Broad in Thought': Internal References to Philo's Allegorical Commentary and Exposition of the Law," *Euphrosyne* 40 (2012): 55–76, esp. 72–74.

[87] Midian corresponds to an area in north-west Arabia.

[88] Of earlier Jewish sources, only Ezekiel the Tragedian refers explicitly to Zipporah's origins: in relation to Moses, she is "the wife of an alien," and, based on Num 12:1, identified with Africa ("Libya") and "the dark-skinned Ethiopian" (*Exagoge* 60–67). The statement implies a positive view of intermarriage: Gruen, *Heritage*, 129–30; John J. Collins, *Between Athens and Jerusalem: Jewish Identity in the Hellenistic Diaspora*, 2nd ed. (Grand Rapids: Eerdmans, 2000), 226; for reservations, Barclay, *Jews*, 138. The Hellenistic historian Demetrius, by contrast, conjectures that Zipporah was, through her father, a descendant of Abraham by his third wife Keturah, and thus a distant relation of Moses (in Eusebius, *Praep. ev.* 9.29.1–3), a calculation that allows Demetrius "the Chronographer" to prove that Moses and Zipporah were alive at the same time, lending credibility to the biblical story. So Collins, *Between Athens and Jerusalem*, 34. Josephus says nothing about the qualities of Zipporah, but he appears to emphasise that by this marriage, the great Moses proved himself without prejudice against barbarians: *A.J.* 2.263; cf. Feldman, *Judean Antiquities 1–4*, 208.

τεύουσα) of his daughters" as wife (γυνή) (*Mos.* 1.59).[89] This description not only serves to explain the union of Moses with a Midianite, but also perhaps to remind the reader of her symbolic connection with virtue, as the "most beautiful" member of the chorus that represents the hierarchy of the virtues.[90]

It is not clear whether Philo takes Zipporah to be the same person as the "Ethiopian woman" married to Moses. The Book of Numbers, recounting the journey of the Hebrews through the wilderness, tells us that Miriam and Aaron spoke out against Moses, "because of the Cushite [Ethiopian] woman whom he had married, for he had indeed married a Cushite woman" (Num 12:1). Since there is no other mention of this woman as Moses's wife, some interpreters took her to be one and the same as Zipporah.[91] Philo does not make an explicit connection between them, but he treats Moses's marriage with the Ethiopian woman as a symbol of the highest spiritual values associated with Moses.[92] Far from deserving the criticism of his siblings, Philo argues, Moses should be eulogized for this union. The Ethiopian's identity, apparently connected by Philo to intense blackness of complexion, is fundamental to the interpretation: "because he took the Ethiopian woman, the nature that has been tested by fire and cannot be altered; for just as the part of the eye that sees is black, so the soul's power of sight is called the Ethiopian woman" (*Leg.* 2.67).[93]

---

[89] Mendelson, *Philo's Jewish Identity*, 73, underplays the significance of this passage, in my view, when he states that Philo does not say anything about Zipporah or her foreign status; cf. Feldman, *Jew and Gentile*, 78.

[90] On piety as the "most beautiful" of the chorus in relation to the virtues, see, for example, *Abr.* 27; *Spec.* 2.259; *Praem.* 53. The beauty and virtue of Zipporah, identified with the Ethiopian woman of Num 12:1, is also emphasized in Tg. Neof. Num 12:1.

[91] Ezekiel the Tragedian, *Exagoge* 60–65; Tg. Neof. Num 12:1. According to Demetrius (in Eusebius, *Praep. ev.* 9.29.3), Zipporah was not an Ethiopian, but she was designated such in Num 12:1 because of her descent from the sons of Abraham who made their home in the "East;" cf. Kugel, *Traditions*, 512–513, 534. Josephus exploits an earlier Hellenistic source, probably originating in the Alexandrian Jewish community, which recounts the exploits of a heroic Moses in a military campaign against the Ethiopians. In this version of the story, Tharbis, daughter of the king of the Ethiopians, falls in love with Moses and proposes marriage, agreeing to his demand to surrender the city, which results in the annihilation of the Ethiopians; cf. Josephus, *A.J.* 2.252–253. On the interpretation of Josephus in relation to other sources for the legend, including Artapanus (who does not mention Moses's wife), see Tessa Rajak, "Moses in Ethiopia: Legend and Literature," *JJS* 29 (1978): 111–122.

[92] "It was God Himself who wedded (ἡρμόσατο) to Moses the Ethiopian woman," who signifies the disposition that does not change, i.e. the firm commitment of Moses to God (*Leg.* 2.67).

[93] *Leg.* 2.67; cf. PLCL 1:481.

What do Philo's commentaries on Scripture reveal about his thinking on intermarriage? In his exposition of the prohibition of intermarriage in *Special Laws* 3.29, Philo is very clear about the fundamental importance of upholding the prohibition and he devotes his efforts to explaining its purpose. His rationale for the prohibition of intermarriage takes its lead from Scripture (Deut 7; Exod 34) in treating the prohibition as a means of combatting the danger of apostasy as a result of intermarriage. In Philo's terms, it is a matter of the danger posed to the children of intermarriage through the risk that they will unlearn—or never learn—the honor due to the one God. While the scriptural prohibition envisages intermarriage as incurring divine wrath and the extermination of the community, Philo's formulation suggests that he thinks of the ultimate penalty in terms of the death of the soul, abandoned by God. Intermarriage leads to loss of knowledge of the service of the One God by the next generation and to the spiritual extirpation of the individual. As in other contexts in his work, Philo's Platonism guides him in avoiding any implication that the Deity inflicts harm; Philo does not avoid spelling out that the consequences of intermarriage can be fatal, nonetheless, and in this respect follows Scripture. We should not read Philo's alleged 'failure' to specify a physical penalty for intermarriage as a sign of his laxness on this topic. Philo extends the terms of the scriptural prohibition, which forbids unions with peoples of the land, to all foreigners. In so doing, Philo effectively updates the terms of the prohibition so that it applies in all times and all places, and is not restricted to people within the confines of the biblical land of Canaan. Philo leaves his readers in no doubt: the prohibition of intermarriage is under-pinned by reason and it serves the positive goal of sustaining the education that teaches the service of the one God. This is a law to be observed in Philo's community.

Through his interpretation of the narratives of the Torah, Philo's treatment of the lives of the ancestors presents a more complicated picture with respect to their unions with outsiders or foreigners.

(i) In the case of Abraham's union with Hagar, Genesis presents Hagar as Abraham's 'wife.' In contrast to the record of Scripture, Philo's bio-graphy of Abraham (*Abr.* 248–254) does not refer to the Egyptian Hagar as Abraham's wife and he is at pains to emphasize that Hagar was not the 'legitimate wife'; that title belongs only to Sarah. Hagar is made fit to conceive a legitimate heir (legitimized through adoption by Sarah) to Abraham through her schooling in the household of Sarah; there she becomes a Hebrew by way of life. In Philo's terms, however, this does not seem to be a matter of conversion; Hagar's transformation under Sarah's instruction serves to ennoble Sarah in the reader's eyes, as the embodiment of virtue in sharing her good gifts with others.

(ii) Philo's treatment of Bilhah and Zilpah (*Virt.* 223) suggests (contra Mendelson) that he thinks of these servants of Rachel and Leah as not foreign. Their case is probably not relevant as an example of intermarriage among the patriarchs. As with Hagar, the elevation of Bilhah and Zilpah serves primarily to illustrate the virtue of their owners and the potential of those of ignoble origin, like Bilhah, Zilpah and their children, to attain virtue.

(iii) Philo's Tamar (in *Virt.* 220–222) represents a striking case in which he, alone among ancient interpreters, spells out her Canaanite background; but he makes no explicit reference in this context to Tamar's sexual union with the patriarch Judah. In Philo's *On Virtues*, Tamar represents the 'nobility' identified with 'women who unlearnt the unlearning with which they were brought up,' i.e. the world of idolatry, and who became students of monotheism. This educational aspect of Tamar's transformation recalls the fundamental place of schooling in Philo's explanation of the purpose of the prohibition of intermarriage and the training received by Hagar in Sarah's household as preparation for Hagar's mating with Abraham. In Philo's terms, this makes Tamar a proselyte, a status he does not appear to have associated with Hagar. Tamar's education and her spiritual migration to knowledge of the honor due to the One God makes her, implicitly at least, a worthy partner for Judah. Why does Philo emphasize Tamar's foreign origins, thereby identifying her with the peoples of the land with whom relations are forbidden, according to the prohibition of inter-marriage? In the context of his works as a whole, Philo only mentions this background in connection to Tamar's role as an example of nobility from ignoble origins, comparable to Abraham's migration from ignorance to knowledge of the One God. This context shapes Philo's decision to empha-size Tamar's ancestry. Moreover, as I have argued, Philo, or the tradition on which he draws, could have inferred Tamar's Canaanite identity from the Genesis narrative. Certainly, Philo goes beyond Genesis and differs from other Second Temple sources in his elevation of Tamar; but in doing so, he is influenced by details in his scriptural text (Tamar's 'good reputation') and her role as an exemplar of nobility from ignoble roots.

(iv) It is only with Aseneth, Zipporah and the Ethiopian woman that we may properly speak of examples of intermarriage in Philo's treatment of the ancestral narratives. In each case, Philo elevates the status of the woman to magnify the virtues of their husbands. There is, by contrast with some other ancient interpreters of the same material, no sense of defensiveness about these unions, no attempt to hide the foreign origins of these women. In taking this approach, Philo is simply following the lead of Scripture, augmenting what is already there. But there is also a clear sense of pride in these connections. With Aseneth and Zipporah, in particular, Philo's insistence on their high status reminds the reader of the extraordinary qualities of Joseph and Moses, and that these marriages should be seen as an expression of the wider world's admiration for the ancestors of the Jews.

University of Southampton

The Studia Philonica Annual 27 (2015): 27–52

WASTED SEED AND SINS OF INTENT:
Sexual Ethics in *De specialibus legibus* 3.34–36
in the Case of Infertile Marriage

MICHAEL FRANCIS*

Introduction

It would be difficult to label Philo of Alexandria a latitudinarian in sexual matters. On any assessment, a contrast between Philo's position and the less inhibited perspective most characteristic of rabbinic Judaism is evident in some significant respects.[1] Chief among the differences between Philonic and rabbinic perspectives is the question of the legitimacy of nonprocreative sex. The rabbis sanction various acts of marital intercourse even when consciously nonprocreative. Philo, in contrast, apparently finds no legitimate place for nonprocreative sex.[2]

De specialibus legibus 3.34–36 is one of the more interesting passages in

---

* All translations of Philo in this study are my own.

[1] See especially Daniel Boyarin, *Carnal Israel: Reading Sex in Talmudic Culture* (Berkeley: University of California Press, 1993), who offers a maximalist assessment of the contrast, and David Winston, "Philo and the Rabbis on Sex and the Body," in *The Ancestral Philosophy: Hellenistic Philosophy in Second Temple Judaism—Essays of David Winston*, ed. Gregory E. Sterling, BJS 331, SPhiloM 4 (Providence, RI: Brown Judaic Studies, 2001), 199–219, who challenges Boyarin's dichotomous analysis at various points. On the presence of an underestimated degree of ambivalence in Palestinian rabbinic thought concerning sex, see David Biale, *Eros and the Jews: From Biblical Israel to Contemporary America* (New York: Basic Books, 1992).

[2] This assessment is widely supported in the literature on Philo. See now especially William Loader, *Philo, Josephus, and the Testaments on Sexuality: Attitudes towards Sexuality in the Writings of Philo and Josephus and in the Testaments on Sexuality* (Grand Rapids: Eerdmans, 2011), 61–65. Both the severity and, in its own way, coherence of Philo's perspective on sex has been underscored by Kathy L. Gaca's analysis of Pythagorean sexual mores in *The Making of Fornication: Eros, Ethics, and Political Reform in Greek Philosophy and Early Christianity* (Berkeley: University of California Press, 2003), and, more briefly, "Philo's Principles of Sexual Conduct and their Influence on Christian Platonist Sexual Principles," *SPhiloA* 8 (1996): 21–39. Gaca points, across a range of sources, to a strict "procreationist principle" she identifies as a Pythagorean (or Neopythagorean) teaching, and draws attention to the similarities with Philo's position.

which Philo deals, in one way or another, with sexual conduct. In this part of the Exposition of the Law, Philo considers the case of infertile marriage or, more specifically, the case of marriage to an infertile wife. The passage is of particular interest for two reasons. First, unlike the surrounding material, Philo appears to have no scriptural basis for his exposition in this section. What prompts Philo to include this passage? Second, Philo distinguishes between two particular situations, and offers a contrasting assessment of each: in the one, the wife's infertility is known before the marriage is formed; in the other, her condition is discerned only by extended experience of childlessness once the marriage has begun. In the former case, Philo is outspoken in his reproach of the male partner and condemnation of the sexual conduct that characterizes the union. In the latter, Philo offers what appears to be qualified approval of the childless marriage as a going concern, and, intriguingly, does not specify sexual abstinence for partners who, on the face of it, cannot engage in procreative intercourse. This silence is particularly pointed when viewed against the preceding section. In *Spec.* 3.32–33, Philo unambiguously prohibits sexual activity for the duration of another situation not conducive to procreation, the time of a woman's monthly period. Is Philo's position on sex in the subsequent section at odds with the more austere perspective that characterizes his thought in *Spec.* 3.32–33 and elsewhere? If Philo implicitly approves of ongoing sexual activity in some marriages long since proved to be infertile, why or on what basis might he do this?

These are the major issues we will examine in the present study. We will proceed in five steps. First, as a preliminary measure, we will consider the procreationist principle that informs Philonic thought concerned with sexual intercourse. Second, we will locate and consider *Spec.* 3.34–36 alongside several related sections of the surrounding material with which it shares a conspicuous characteristic, the rationalization of certain prohibitions in the conceptualization of illicit sexual activity as a condemnable wasting of seed. Third, we will consider the phenomenon of the inclusion of this passage in Philo's presentation of biblical law. Fourth, we will address the particular puzzle identified above. What should we make of Philo's failure to specify sexual abstinence in *Spec.* 3.35? If *Spec.* 3.35 does indeed provide implicit sanction for ongoing sexual activity in certain cases of infertile marriage, on what basis might Philo (or his interpreters on his behalf) justify the permission? Fifth, the study concludes with some reflections on the contribution of *Spec.* 3.34–36 for our understanding of Philonic sexual ethics, and the challenges involved in offering a summary assessment of Philo's perspective on marriage and sexual conduct.

Philo and the Procreationist Principle

A seemingly conventional perspective concerning sexual intercourse emerges in several texts written by Diaspora Jews in the Second Temple period.[3] Such intimacy is considered appropriate only as engaged in by a man and his wife, and that only as part of a procreative agenda. The perspective itself does not represent a thoroughgoing contrast with the outlook of the Hebrew Bible.[4] Nevertheless, insofar as the emerging Diaspora perspective reconceptualizes the blessing of procreation as reproductive duty and spells out the procreative agenda as necessary condition for intercourse, so it represents a distinct development in the Jewish ethical tradition.[5]

Repeatedly, then, Philo makes clear that there is one acceptable purpose for entering into marriage, procreation. Philo's position on marriage reflects his understanding of why created humankind was divided into two sexes. The division of created humanity into man and woman (Gen 1:27) was to serve the purpose of reproduction (*Her.* 164; cf. *Opif.* 152). Consequently, those seeking marriage must be guided by the creational goal (*Ios.* 43). Philo's insistence on the procreative purpose of marriage emerges most

---

[3] Josephus, *C. Ap.* 2.199; *B.J.* 2.161. Among the many Philonic passages that might be cited, see e.g. *Det.* 102; *Congr.* 12; *Ios.* 43; *Spec.* 3.9–10, 3.113; *Virt.* 207; *Mos.* 1.28; *QG* 4.86, 4.154. It may be that the same concern with procreation stands behind one of the maxims found in the Sentences of Pseudo-Phocylides: μηδ᾽ ὕβριζε γυναῖκα ἐπ᾽ αἰσχυντοῖς λεχέεσσιν (189); see the discussion in Pieter W. van der Horst, *The Sentences of Pseudo-Phocylides*, SVTP 4 (Leiden: Brill, 1978). Further afield (as it were), it is also just possible that a similar concern is found in the Damascus Document (4Q270 7 I, 12–13; 4Q267 9 VI, 4–5); in review of the relevant passages, however, William Loader, argues against this reading (*The Dead Sea Scrolls on Sexuality: Attitudes towards Sexuality in Sectarian and Related Literature at Qumran* [Grand Rapids: Eerdmans, 2009], 172–173). On the existence of a common ethical tradition among Diaspora Jews in the Second Temple period, see Gregory E. Sterling, "Was There a Common Ethic in Second Temple Judaism?" in *Sapiential Perspectives: Wisdom Literature in Light of the Dead Sea Scrolls. Proceedings of the Sixth International Symposium of the Orion Center for the Study of the Dead Sea Scrolls and Related Literature, 20–22 May 2001,* ed. John J. Collins, Gregory E. Sterling, and Ruth A. Clements (Leiden: Brill 2004), 171–194.

[4] Where, I take it, the general goal of procreation in marriage is presupposed throughout. On marriage in the Hebrew Bible, see the essays by Joseph Blenkinsopp ("The Family in First Temple Israel") and John J. Collins ("Marriage, Divorce, and Family in Second Temple Judaism") in *Families in Ancient Israel,* ed. Leo G. Perdue et al. (Louisville: Westminster John Knox, 1997).

[5] In speaking of the transformation of blessing into duty, I follow Michael Satlow, *Jewish Marriage in Antiquity* (Princeton: Princeton University Press, 2001), 17–18. Satlow offers an important discussion of roughly similar developments in Palestinian rabbinic sources (17–21). On the interpretive history of Gen 1:28, see Jeremy Cohen, *"Be Fertile and Increase, Fill the Earth and Master It": The Ancient and Medieval Career of a Biblical Text* (Ithaca, NY: Cornell University Press, 1989), and the discussion of Philo's reading of Gen 1:28 at 72–76.

clearly in connection with Abraham—as well it might, given the patriarch's profile in Philo's beloved Genesis and yet, embarrassingly, Abraham's experience a as married yet childless man. It is important that Sarah should clarify the situation as she explains her suggestion that Hagar should act in her stead (*Abr.* 247–249, on Gen 16). Sarah knows that Abraham would countenance sex with her maid only to fulfill the necessary law of nature— a requirement that Moses, naturally, affirms (*Praem.* 108–109, on Exod 23:26; cf. e.g. *Spec.* 3.112–113; *QG* 4.154; *Congr.* 12; *Virt.* 207).[6]

The Philonic (and Josephan) position undoubtedly reflects the influence of certain Greco-Roman ideals and perspectives. In the Roman world, the decisive transformation of moral disapproval for those single or married but childless into legal penalty occurs with the Augustan marriage laws, the *Lex Iulia de maritandis ordinibus* in 18 BCE.[7] Much earlier, however, from the time of the Persian Wars onwards, legal and ethical norms appear in Greek sources promoting the priority of marriage and a citizen's responsibility to reproduce.[8] The duty of procreation is intrinsic to the formation of the *oikos*, and thus establishes the priority of marital reproductive intercourse. Plato, concerned with the havoc wrought by uncontrolled sexual passions to individuals and their communities, insists on the duty to marry. Men single from the age of thirty-five onwards should be assessed an annual fine (*Leg.* 721b, 774a). Legislation that would limit sexual activity to the purpose of reproduction represents an attractive ideal (*Leg.* 838e). Not only would such be a natural law, it would control the sexual instinct and promote in men affection for their wives rather than desire for the wives of others (*Leg.* 839a–b).

While Plato does not, ultimately, push the ideal as a uniform prescription to regulate sexual conduct in all cases—so long as a citizen's reproductive duty is fulfilled, other avenues and thus purposes for sexual intercourse can be accommodated insofar as they are kept in their place—certain subsequent moralists do not balk in a similar way.[9] The clearest case of

---

[6] Cf. *Abr.* 253, where Abraham is said to abstain from sex with Hagar once she is pregnant. Note also Abraham's concerns on sending his servant to find a wife for Isaac (*QG* 4.86, on Gen 24:2). The oath-taking ritual Abraham demands signifies his concern to arrange a marriage that has as its goal the procreation of legitimate children.

[7] Revised shortly thereafter in 9 CE by the *Lex Papia Poppea*.

[8] On the emergence of these ideas see David Daube, "The Duty of Procreation," in *Collected Works of David Daube, Vol. 3: Biblical Law and Literature*, ed. Calum Carmichael (Berkeley: Robbins Collection, 2003), 951–970.

[9] On the importance of distinguishing between perspectives in which procreative marital intercourse is the sole sexual activity permitted, and those in which it is merely the most important kind, see Gaca, *Making of Fornication*, 97–99. In the *Laws*, Plato's primary concerns in sanctioning nonprocreative intercourse are to ensure that it (a) does not

such exacting procreationism is found in a discourse by the first-century Stoic, Musonius Rufus.

> Men who are not wantons or immoral are bound to consider sexual intercourse justified only when it occurs in marriage and is indulged in for the purpose of begetting children (ἐν γάμῳ καὶ ἐπὶ γενέσει παίδων συντελούμενα), since that is lawful, but unjust and unlawful when it is seeking bare pleasure, even in marriage (κἂν ἐν γάμῳ).[10]

For Musonius and others of a similar persuasion, marital sex for the purpose of procreation is not simply a nonnegotiable sexual duty, it is the only legitimate kind of sexual intercourse at all.[11] On the face of it, there are clear similarities between Philo's perspective and that advocated by Musonius.[12] Philo appears not to limit the reproductive duty to the marital relationship taken as a whole. Rather, there are signs that he holds that the procreative mandate should pertain to all sexual intercourse engaged in by man and wife.[13] Isaac's marriage at the age of forty confirms that sexual intimacy with Rebekah will be for the sake of begetting children rather than sensual pleasure (*QG* 4.154). The appropriate use of the reproductive organs is defined by that which lawfully begets and propagates the human race (*Det*. 102). Those who commit infanticide (*Spec*. 3.113)—who engage in sex with their wives but not for the sake of procreation—not only break the laws of nature, they are condemned as pleasure-lovers who pursue sex like

---

impinge on the fulfillment of the reproductive duty (*Leg*. 784e), and (b) remains a private matter (*Leg*. 841). In the *Republic*, Plato allows those who have passed the age for children to engage in intercourse with whomever they wish, with certain consanguineous exceptions (*Resp*. 461b–e). On higher and lower standards of conduct in Plato's vision for Magnesia, see *Leg*. 841a–842a, and the discussion in Trevor J. Saunders, "Plato on Women in the *Laws*," in *The Greek World*, ed. Anton Powell (Routledge: London, 1995), 591–609 (at 602–604). Cf. the comments on Jewish texts in n. 13 below.

[10] Musonius Rufus, fr. 12; text and translation (adjusted) from Cora E. Lutz, "Musonius Rufus: 'The Roman Socrates,' " YCS 10 (1947): 87. Though the identification of this perspective as Neopythagorean rather than Stoic is an important part of her wider thesis, Gaca accepts the identification of Musonius as a Stoic philosopher.

[11] The Pythagorean treatises under the pseudonyms Charondas and Ocellus appear to share this position. See Hölger Thesleff, *The Pythagorean Texts of the Hellenistic Period* (Åbo: Akademi, 1965), 59–67, 124–138.

[12] As noted by A. C. van Geytenbeek, *Musonius Rufus and Greek Diatribe* (Assen: Van Gorcum, 1962), 73, and followed by Gaca in "Philo's Principles," 23–26, and *Making of Fornication*, 204–206.

[13] A stringency also evident in the particular claim of Josephus in *C. Ap.* 2.199 (cited above). Justin M. Rogers suggests that the strict procreationist position was, in fact, the standard teaching of the Hellenistic synagogue ("The Philonic and the Pauline: Hagar and Sarah in the Exegesis of Didymus the Blind," *SPhiloA* 26 [2014]: 57–77, here 63).

animals.[14] Similarly, those who indulge in intercourse without appropriate limits include those who act lustfully with their own wives (*Spec.* 3.9). It would seem that neither the connubial context nor a track record of reproductive success is sufficient to establish the validity of sexual intimacy.

The Problem with Nonprocreative Sex

This procreationist perspective is evident in the Exposition of the Law as Philo addresses the Mosaic legislation concerned with sexual sin. First of all, it is reflected in Philo's treatment of adultery. Whatever else is at stake in breaking the Sixth Commandment, the forfeiture of the opportunity for producing legitimate offspring as marital ties are compromised is constitutive of the tragedy suffered by the betrayed (*Spec.* 3.11).[15] The same perspective emerges in a particular guise as Philo treats, under the heading of the Sixth Commandment, other laws dealing with sexual misconduct.[16] Philo interprets Lev 18:22 as a directive against pederasty (*Spec.* 3.37–42),[17] conduct that merits death for both partners. The wrongdoing of the dominant partner is explained with reference to the illegitimate use of his reproductive resources (*Spec.* 3.39).

> And the lover of boys ... pursues an unnatural pleasure, and, insofar as it depends on him, renders the cities desolate and empty of all inhabitants by spoiling the seed (διαφθείρων τὰς γονάς).

Not only does the lover of boys pursue an unnatural pleasure, he works against the ongoing viability of society by wasting the procreative seed.[18]

---

[14] See Adele Reinhartz, "Philo on Infanticide," *SPhiloA* 4 (1992): 42–58. Cf. Josephus, *C. Ap.* 2.202.

[15] Similarly, *Decal.* 126; *Spec.* 4.203. Cf. also Musonius Rufus, fr. 12.

[16] In order of occurrence in *Spec.* 3, the cases concern (a) sex during menstruation (*Spec.* 3.32–33); (b) the case of an infertile wife (*Spec.* 3.34–36); (c) pederasty (*Spec.* 3.37–42). We will consider (c) first, as the selection of parallel passages in which Philo addresses this subject (or, at least, same-sex intercourse) allows the greatest confidence in staking out Philo's position. For the parallel passages, see n. 23 below.

[17] Note also Lev 20:13. Homosexual behavior among Greek males primarily took the form of encounters between man and youth; so K. J. Dover, *Greek Homosexuality*, 2nd ed. (Cambridge: Harvard University Press, 1989).

[18] See e.g. Plato, *Leg.* 836c; Musonius Rufus, fr. 12; Josephus, *C. Ap.* 2.273 on the common trope of homosexual relations as contrary to nature. Most of Philo's treatments of same-sex intercourse concern pederasty. Philo's assessment of sex between adult men does not differ much, however. See Holger Szesnat, " 'Pretty Boys' in Philo's *De Vita Contemplativa*," *SPhiloA* 10 (1998): 87–107; and Loader, *Philo, Josephus, and the Testaments*, 204–216. For Philo, homosexual intercourse subverts the reproductive mandate incumbent upon

While the male seed should be sown in a place equipped to facilitate its germination, instead it is left for dead in a place where growth is impossible. Later in *Spec.* 3.39, Philo expands on the imagery.

> And finally, in the manner of a bad farmer, he lets the deep-soiled and fruitful fields lie barren, contriving to keep them fruitless, while he labors in things night and day from which no offshoot whatsoever is expected.

Such criticism is clearly shaped by the procreationist concerns considered above. Each man is an agriculturalist with an inviolable responsibility to disperse his seed wisely. Choosing boys rather than women as the objects of his sexual exploits, he fails in this duty. Philo defends the biblical prohibition by appeal to the intrinsically nonprocreative character of same-sex intercourse.[19]

The image of woman as field to be ploughed or sown is ubiquitous in classical sources.[20] Correspondingly, the conceptualization of illicit heterosexual sexual activity from a procreationist perspective as a matter of irresponsible husbandry—insofar as it does not consist of vaginal intercourse with a suitable female candidate—is not difficult to appreciate. It is already found in Plato, in the section of the *Laws* considered above in which the Athenian acknowledges the attractiveness of the ideal that would restrict all sexual activity to its natural, reproductive purpose (*Leg.* 838e).[21] Similarly, the Athenian continues (*Leg.* 841d), it would benefit every state if men refrained from sowing illegitimate seed in young girls, and sterile seed,

---

humanity in two related ways: (a) such actions compromise possession of the raw materials of reproduction, as sterility ensues for those who engage in homosexual acts (*Abr.* 135; *Contempl.* 62); (b) alternatively, the problem with same-sex intercourse is that it represents a chronic mishandling of the reproductive materials. It is hard to tell which sense of "spoiling the seed" is in view in *Spec.* 3.39.

[19] Philo's procreative concerns do not constitute the only grounds for his criticism of homosexual activity. Philo is also concerned with the sexual entailments of the hierarchy he discerns between the categories of male and female (on which see Richard A. Baer, Jr., *Philo's Use of the Categories of Male and Female*, ALGHJ 3 [Leiden: Brill, 1970]). Note, e.g., *Spec.* 3.37 on boys who are sick with νόσον θήλειαν.

[20] See Helen King, "Sowing the Field: Greek and Roman Sexology," in *Sexual Knowledge, Sexual Science: The History of Attitudes to Sexuality*, ed. Roy Porter (Cambridge: Cambridge University Press, 1994), 29–46; and Page duBois, *Sowing the Body: Psychoanalysis and Ancient Representations of Women* (Chicago: University of Chicago Press, 1998). Note the Greek betrothal formula, spoken by the father of the bride, παίδων ἐπ' ἀρότῳ γνησίων (e.g. Menander, fr. 720 [Kock], cited in Helen King, "Making a Man: Becoming Human in Early Greek Medicine," in *The Human Embryo: Aristotle and the Arabic and European Traditions*, ed. G. R. Dunstan [Exeter: University of Exeter Press, 1990], 10–19, at 17).

[21] I have not searched for earlier examples.

against nature, in men. Both parties are unqualified to act as suitable receptacles for the procreative seed.[22]

Likewise for Philo this typology of sexual misconduct is not limited to his assessment of homosexual activity.[23] He also applies it in his interpretation of Lev 18:19, the Mosaic prohibition of intercourse with a woman during the time of her monthly period (*Spec.* 3.32–33). Where the original concern of the legislation is with the treatment of menstrual impurity, Philo explains the Mosaic interdiction by way of appeal to procreationist principles. Once more, the biblical prohibition accords with the law of nature. More to the point, it directs the husband towards an appropriate use of his reproductive powers (*Spec.* 3.32).

> Whenever the monthly issue should come about, a man must not touch a woman but must during that time cease from intercourse, respecting the law of nature, and also being taught ahead of time not to bring forth ineffectual seed (ἀτελεῖς γονάς) for the sake of an ill-timed and gross pleasure.

The problem with intercourse during menstruation is that the seed deposited in the womb does not achieve its proper reproductive purpose.[24] Philo illustrates the problem with the example of a farmer who, on account of drunkenness or madness, sows grain in pools and streams rather than fertile plains. Such seed will inevitably be wasted; such profligacy is to be avoided. Similarly, a man should refrain from intercourse with a woman when her womb is inundated each month with the menstrual fluids. When the uterine field has drained, however, he may resume intercourse and sow his seed confidently, no longer fearing that what he lays will perish (*Spec.* 3.33). Once more, the biblical prohibition is justified by appeal to the singular purpose of the raw material of reproduction at stake in the act of intercourse. As in the case of homosexual behavior, the agricultural typology of sexual misconduct provides a rationalization for the Mosaic legislation.[25]

---

[22] The supply of children—a supply of optimum size and quality—for Magnesia motivates the regulations concerning marriage and divorce. See Saunders, "Plato on Women," 599–600.

[23] Among other Philonic texts, see especially *Contempl.* 62; *Anim.* 49.

[24] On the optimal timing for procreative intercourse in ancient Greek medical texts, see, e.g., Soranus, *Gynecology*, 1.35–38 (again, the conceptualization of woman as land to be sown is to the fore).

[25] I note that my analysis of Philonic texts concerned with wasted seed coheres with the wider history of the idea in Jewish texts sketched by Michael Satlow in " 'Wasted Seed,' The History of a Rabbinic Idea," *HUCA* 65 (1994): 137–175 (with brief treatment of Philo on 163–164). Satlow shows that the idea that the nonprocreative emission of semen is by definition condemnable is found no earlier than the redactional strata of the Bavli; in

The Case of the Infertile Wife

A similar logic informs Philo's explanation of the Mosaic legislation concerned with sexual misconduct in one more case treated in *Spec.* 3.12–82. In *Spec.* 3.34–36, Philo addresses the case of men who marry and thus have sexual relations with infertile women. To introduce this passage in this way is misleading, however. While, self-evidently, *Spec.* 3.34–36 is presented as part of Philo's exposition of scripture, Philo neither cites nor alludes to any biblical law or precedent as warrant for this section. Nevertheless, Philo pronounces that such men should be reproached, and for a reason similar to that offered in the preceding case. If sex with a menstruating woman constitutes a blameworthy wasting of seed on flooded ground where it is inevitably swept away, sex with a barren woman is a matter of spoiling the seed by ploughing hard and stony land. In addressing this kind of irresponsible husbandry, Philo has a particular situation in view: the case of intercourse with women known to be barren at the point of entry into marriage.

θήρα γὰρ αὐτὸ μόνον ἡδονῆς ἀκράτορος ὡς οἱ λαγνίστατοι τὰς γονὰς ἑκουσίῳ γνώμῃ διαφθείρουσιν· ἐπεὶ τίνος ἄλλου χάριν ἐγγυῶνται τὰς τοιαύτας; οὐ μὴν δι᾽ ἐλπίδα τέκνων, ἣν ἴσασιν ἐξ ἀνάγκης ἀτελῆ γενησομένην, ἀλλὰ δι᾽ ὑπερβάλλοντα οἶστρον καὶ ἀκρασίαν ἀνίατον... ὅσοι δὲ προδεδοκιμασμένας ἑτέροις ἀνδράσιν ὡς εἰσὶν ἄγονοι μνῶνται συῶν τρόπον ἢ τράγων ὀχεύοντες αὐτὸ μόνον, ἐν ἀσεβῶν στήλαις ἐγγραφέσθωσαν ὡς ἀντίπαλοι θεοῦ· τῷ μὲν γὰρ ἄτε φιλοζῴῳ καὶ φιλανθρώπῳ δι᾽ ἐπιμελείας τῆς πάσης ἐστὶ σωτηρίαν καὶ μονὴν τοῖς γένεσιν ἅπασιν ἐργάζεσθαι, οἱ δ᾽ ἅμα τῇ καταβολῇ σβέσιν τοῖς σπέρμασι τεχνάζοντες ἐχθροὶ τῆς φύσεως ὁμολογουμένως εἰσίν. (*Spec.* 3.34, 36)

For in the quest for only immoderate pleasure, like the most lustful of men, they spoil the seed by voluntary inclination. For on account of what other factor would they pledge themselves to such women? It cannot be on account of the hope of children, which they know will fail, of necessity, to be accomplished; but it is on account of a surpassing madness, and incurable lack of self-control... But those who copulate in only this way, with those proved beforehand with other husbands to be childless, they call to mind the manner of pigs or goats, and they should be inscribed in the records of the ungodly as enemies of God. For while he (God), in his love of animals and humankind, through his care of all that is, works for the preservation and continuance of everything that comes into being, those who contrive towards the extinction of the seed at the time of its sowing are, by common consent, enemies of nature.

---

earlier texts, the actual concern of the authors is not with the waste of the reproductive material itself. I have tried to capture this in my analysis by referring to the idea of wasted seed, as it appears at various points in Philo, as a typology of sexual misconduct.

Such women are known to be infertile on account of a previous childless marital union. And, so the logic goes, if they could not conceive before, their infertility is set in stone.[26] Those who desire marriage with such women cannot do so on account of the singular appropriate reason for seeking marital union, procreation. Rather, there is another rationale for their designs. Their pursuit of marriage is none other than a quest for immoderate pleasure, the scheme of those afflicted with madness and a chronic lack of self-control. The core of Philo's concern is with the agenda of the male partner who enters into marriage with a woman experientially certified as infertile. These are men who spoil the seed voluntarily,[27] whose conduct confirms them as enemies of God and nature. While the philanthropic deity works to sustain the life of everything that comes into being, these men contrive towards the extinction of the seed of life at the point of its sowing.

The concern with the dishonorable purpose of the male suitor furnishes a point of contrast for Philo as he turns to address a second scenario. In an additional section, Philo contrasts the case of one who elects to marry an evidently infertile woman with the case of another who enters marriage ignorant of his partner's compromised fecundity.[28]

ὅσοι μὲν οὖν ἄγονται κόρας ἀγνοίᾳ τοῦ πῶς ἔχουσιν εὐθὺς εὐτοκίας ἢ τοὐναντίον, ὁπόταν χρόνῳ μακρῷ ὕστερον ἐκ τῆς ἀγονίας αἰσθανόμενοι στείρας αὐτὰς μὴ ἀποπέμπωνται, συγγνώμης εἰσὶν ἐπάξιοι συνηθείας, βιαστικωτάτου πράγματος, ἡττώμενοι καὶ φίλτρα ἀρχαῖα συμβιώσει μακρᾷ ταῖς ψυχαῖς ἐνεσφραγισμένα λύειν ἀδυνατοῦντες. (*Spec.* 3.35)

Those who take young wives in ignorance of whether at that time they are fertile or not, and when following a long time of childlessness they should perceive that they are sterile and do not send them away, they are worthy of pardon as they yield to intimacy, a most forceful thing, and they are unable to loosen the long-held affection impressed on their souls by long companionship.

As with the previous scenario, the situation Philo addresses is specific. This is not just the case of one who deduces that his spouse is infertile after entering the union in good procreative faith. It is the case of one who on finding himself in this situation following a long period of childlessness

---

[26] Philo's discussion in *Spec.* 1.10–11 shows he is aware of the phenomenon of male infertility, but it does not figure as a factor in *Spec.* 3.34–36. For this reference I am indebted to Adele Reinhartz, "Parents and Children: A Philonic Perspective," in *The Jewish Family in Antiquity*, ed. Shaye J. D. Cohen, BJS 289 (Atlanta: Scholars Press, 1993), 61–88 (at 70).

[27] Note Plato, *Leg.* 838e, on participants in homosexual sex as murderers ἐκ προνοίας.

[28] I take it that the use of κόρη indicates the bride's virginity. This contrasts with the women considered in the first situation, whose infertility has been proved beforehand. Cf. n. 58 below.

does not send his partner away in divorce. Again, Philo diagnoses the internal forces that drive the external behavior. These men are constrained by the force of intimacy,[29] captivated by the affection impressed on their souls by long companionship.[30] For such there is pardon.[31]

Situating De specialibus legibus 3.34–36

What should we make of *Spec.* 3.34–36? First, let us consider the inclusion of this material here in Philo's presentation of the law. Most obviously, *Spec.* 3.34–36 is an example of an exegetical move observable at various points in Philo's interpretation of the pentateuchal legislation in this commentary series, the expansion of biblical law to cover cases unaddressed by the scriptural legislation itself.[32] Closest to hand, the rape of a widow or woman separated from her husband is addressed by Philo in his treatment of the laws concerned with sexual assault (*Spec.* 3.64; cf. Exod 22:16–17; Deut 22:22–29). The treatment of infanticide in *Spec.* 3.110–119 is similar. The exposure of children is not addressed specifically in the biblical material, but Philo deals with the subject immediately following his treatment of feticide (*Spec.* 3.108–109, on Exod 21:22) as part of his treatment of the Seventh Commandment. Whether or not the Exposition is usefully identified as an example of "rewritten scripture," the kind of revision of the biblical material by way of legal expansion observable in *Spec.* 3.34–36 is a common enough feature in Philo's paraphrastic handling of the Mosaic code. Further, we can see readily why Philo introduces the additional material exactly here. Following immediately on the treatment of the scriptural prohibition of sex with a menstruating woman, it deals with another kind of nonreproductive heterosexual (in fact, marital) sex.[33]

---

[29] I assume συνήθεια has a nonsexual meaning here (LSJ: "habitual intercourse, acquaintance"). Note Philo's similar usages in *Spec.* 4.161; *Praem.* 18.

[30] Cf. Musonius Rufus, fr. 13a, cited below, on the necessity of συμβίωσις in marriage.

[31] On the meaning of συγγνώμη, see n. 48 below.

[32] Similarly, Adele Reinhartz, "Philo's *Exposition of the Law* and Social History: Methodological Considerations," *Society of Biblical Literature 1993 Seminar Papers*, SBLSP 32 (Atlanta: Scholars Press, 1993), 6–21; reprinted in *Reading Philo: A Handbook to Philo of Alexandria*, ed. Torrey Seland (Grand Rapids: Eerdmans, 2014), 180–199.

[33] Thus *Spec.* 3.34–36 serves in its own way as evidence of the importance of thematic connections for Philo as he interprets and moves between biblical texts. Philo quite frequently exploits thematic connections as he selects and transitions between secondary (or tertiary) lemmata in the Allegorical Commentary; see David T. Runia, "The Structure of Philo's Allegorical Treatises: A Review of Two Recent Studies and Some Additional Comments," *VC* 38 (1984): 209–256 (and the summary observations at 240–241, 245 in particu-

Of course, the formal analysis begs a follow-up question. Why does Philo expand the legislation in this particular way? The parallels identified above between *Spec.* 3.32–33, 3.34–36, and 3.37–42 point in an obvious direction. The same procreationist discourse and value judgments inform Philo's treatment of sexual misconduct in each case. For one who repeatedly interprets the relevant biblical legislation through a procreationist lens, we might suppose that the case of infertile marriage might also be a point of particular—and, thus, scriptural—interest. To put it another way, Philo's procreationist focus is not merely a rationalization that buttresses his presentation of biblical law; rather, it is a sufficiently consequential concern that it induces expansion of the Mosaic legislation in this particular way.[34]

We can press this point much further, however. There is solid evidence that a woman's fertility and its matrimonial significance, ethically or politically considered, was a matter of some concern in the Greco-Roman context in which Philo interpreted scripture. Within the Philonic corpus, there is evidence elsewhere that the question of marriage to a woman ill-equipped to bear children was a live one for Philo—and, perhaps, was live within the Alexandrian tradition of biblical interpretation of which Philo was part. In *QG* 1.27 (on Gen 2:21), Philo scolds those who take wives who have passed their prime as those who destroy the laws of nature. The scenario and assessment Philo proposes closely resemble his concern in *Spec.* 3.34, 36: the decision to wed a woman who cannot (*Spec.* 3.34, 36) or can no longer (*QG* 1.27) conceive is made by those who oppose nature (*Spec.* 3.36) and its laws (*QG* 1.27).

Beyond Philo's works, in the wider context sketched above and within which Philo's own sexual ethics emerge, we observe a concern with the issue of spousal fertility in a variety of settings. In the program of Plato's *Laws*, the cardinal principle for one seeking a wife is to select a partner suitable for the procreation of children (*Leg.* 778d). In the case of Musonius (fr. 13a), while the value attached to companionship and love within marriage is striking, it would appear not to dilute the reproductive imperative incumbent on those considering marital union. If the chief end of marriage

---

lar). In *Spec.* 3.34–36, we might say that Philo's expansion of biblical law serves, in effect, to create an additional scriptural lemma with tight thematic connections to the immediately surrounding material, *Spec.* 3.32–33 (on Lev 18:19) and *Spec.* 3.37–42 (on Lev 18:22). I am grateful to Greg Sterling for pushing me to clarify my thinking on this point.

[34] This coheres with the observation that Philo's procreationist concerns sometimes emerge in relation to texts that do not, on the face of it, address issues pertaining to marriage or sex at all.

is community of life, it is so with a view to the procreation of children.[35] The reproductive purpose of marriage shapes the advice Musonius offers on the selection of a partner.

> But as for the body it is enough for marriage that it be healthy, of normal appearance, and capable of hard work, such as would be less exposed to the snares of tempters, better adapted to perform physical labor, and not wanting in strength to beget or bear children. (Lutz)[36]

The more specific issue of the ongoing validity of a childless marriage, and the question of what the constituent husband should do about it, was a matter of particular interest in this wider Greco-Roman context—and unsurprisingly so for those concerned with the procreative duty, given the opportunity for divorce.[37] Indeed, the conciliatory position Philo adopts in *Spec.* 3.35 towards those who do not send their barren wives away most likely betrays Philo's familiarity with—and in some sense, recognition of the legitimacy of—an alternative course of action on the part of men who find themselves in this situation. If there are those who learn by experience that their wives are infertile who choose to remain in marriage, there are others who proceed to terminate the union. In the society envisaged in Plato's *Laws*, a couple childless throughout the ten-year period designated for procreation is obligated to separate so that the reproductive duty might be fulfilled with a more suitable partner (*Leg.* 784b, 930a).[38] In Roman law, by tradition following precedent in the case of the senator Carvilius Ruga, from the late third century BCE onwards a husband enjoys the right to divorce his infertile wife (e.g. Plutarch, *Comp. Thes. Rom.* 6.3; *Comp. Lyc. Num.* 3.6).[39] In some sources, the assessment of her condition is established

---

[35] Gretchen Reydams-Schils observes that for Musonius procreation is not a sufficient condition for marriage (*The Roman Stoics: Self, Responsibility, and Affection* [Chicago: University of Chicago Press, 2006], 151). I note that it remains a necessary condition, however.

[36] On fertility as qualification for marriage, see Susan Treggiari, *Roman Marriage: Iusti Coniuges from the Time of Cicero to the Time of Ulpian* (Oxford: Clarendon Press, 1991), 100–103. In relation to *QG* 1.27, note Treggiari's observation that it was considered discreditable for a man to marry a woman much older than himself (103).

[37] On the provision for divorce in ancient Greece, see Douglas M. MacDowell, *The Law in Classical Athens* (Ithaca, NY: Cornell University Press, 1978), 86–89. On divorce under Roman law, see Suzanne Dixon, *The Roman Family* (Baltimore: Johns Hopkins University Press, 1992), 71–83; and Treggiari, *Roman Marriage*, 435–482. There is clear evidence of divorce in a Roman context as early as the fifth century BCE.

[38] Plato does not address remarriage in *Leg.* 784b. The procreational condition for remarriage is found in 930a in connection with those previously divorced on account of temperamental incompatibility.

[39] For additional references see Daube, "Duty of Procreation," 959–960; also Alan Watson, "The Divorce of Carvilius Ruga," *TvR* 33 (1965): 38–50.

over the course of a five-year failure to conceive.[40] With the addition of the Augustan incentives for reproductively fruitful marriages, it is not difficult to see why men whose marriages have proved childless might look to cut ties with their existing wives and start over. Perhaps most interesting for comparison with Philo are two Roman examples in which the integrity and motivation of a husband who would elect *not* to divorce his wife in such circumstances is evident, the appeal of the alternative course of action notwithstanding. A first-century BCE funerary inscription (by convention, *Laudatio Turiae*) records the memory of an infertile woman who had herself proposed divorce out of respect for the procreative needs of her husband— an offer nevertheless declined by a partner who could not contemplate the severing of the marital bond.[41] Elsewhere, it is alleged that certain contemporaries of Carvilius Ruga himself disapproved of his divorce precisely because they saw marital loyalty as something not to be compromised even by the desire for children.[42]

In treating the case of infertile marriage in his exposition of biblical law, then, Philo offers a kind of contemporizing exegesis. The Mosaic legislation expands to encompass an issue addressed in both Greek and Roman sources, and on which, in some important respects, there is disagreement concerning the most appropriate course of action. Can we specify the impetus for Philo's inclusion of *Spec.* 3.34–36 within the Exposition more precisely? This is a complex question, and turns to some degree on several larger issues in the study of Philo.

First, any answer depends in part on the audience and aims proposed for the Exposition of the Law. On the assumption of a Jewish audience, and Philo's corresponding concern with the realia of Jewish family life, Adele Reinhartz suggests that the tone and scale of the discussion in *Spec.* 3.34–36 convey Philo's disapproval of a situation known to him from the Alexandrian Jewish community.[43] Alternatively, if Philo's audience in the

---

[40] Seneca the Elder, *Contr.* 2.5; Quintilian, *Decl. min.* 251. Treggiari, *Roman Marriage*, 462, considers the five-year requirement a legal fiction.

[41] Column 2, lines 31–44; for the Latin text, see Hermann Dessau, *Inscriptiones Latinae Selectae*, vol. 2 pt. 2 (Berlin, 1906), 924–928. For translation, see Mary R. Lefkowitz and Maureen B. Fant, *Women's Life in Greece and Rome*, 3rd ed. (Baltimore: Johns Hopkins University Press, 2005), 135–139. I note the similarities between certain aspects of the course of action formerly proposed by the wife in this case (she would identify a suitable new partner for her husband, and would regard the ensuing offspring as her own), and Philo's laudatory account of Sarah's actions in the initial episode with Hagar in *Abr.* 248– 252 (she was eager to find a new bride for Abraham, and would consider the ensuing offspring her own by adoption).

[42] Valerius Maximus 2.1.4; see Dixon, *Roman Family*, 68–69.

[43] "*Exposition of the Law* and Social History," 17.

Exposition is, at least materially, composed of non-Jews, the inclusion of *Spec.* 3.34–36 represents a particular gambit in Philo's overall concern either to explain and promote the law to the uninitiated, or defend it against external attack—a stratagem that proceeds by bringing an issue of wider contemporary concern within the purview of biblical law.[44]

Second, the answer also turns on the relationship presupposed between Philo and other roughly contemporaneous interpreters of scripture. There is no direct evidence in either Josephus or the Sentences of Pseudo-Phocylides of a shared exegetical tradition concerning infertile marriage among Diaspora Jews. This does not prove that no such tradition existed, and does not eliminate the possibility that the issue was addressed by other Alexandrian interpreters known to Philo in their treatment of biblical law. It does, however, at least allow that this particular exegetical move—the application of a scriptural-procreationist ethic to the case of infertile marriage—is undertaken by Philo without recourse to other Jewish exegetes or traditions within his most immediate interpretive milieu. This suggestion requires immediate qualification, however, on account of a factor notoriously difficult to weigh in the study of Philo: evidence of the presence of similar concerns in early rabbinic texts, in other words, among other Jews also, in their own way, concerned with the explanation of biblical law. In a ruling contained in the Mishnah, strikingly similar to the position proposed by Plato in the *Laws*, it is stipulated that a couple childless for ten years should divorce unless the husband has already, by other means, fulfilled what is taken to be the scriptural reproductive mandate (m. Yebam. 6:6).[45] Correspondingly, the general permission afforded in tannaitic sources towards marriage to an infertile partner appears always to be qualified by the

[44] Ellen Birnbaum, *The Place of Judaism in Philo's Thought: Israel, Jews, and Proselytes*, BJS 290, SPhiloM 2 (Atlanta: Scholars Press, 1996), 20, argues that the Exposition is addressed to both Jews and non-Jews. In *Philo on Jewish Identity and Culture*, TSAJ 86 (Tübingen: Mohr Siebeck, 2001), Maren Niehoff builds a strong case for the significance of the Roman context for Philo's exegesis. In her subsequent *Jewish Exegesis and Homeric Scholarship in Alexandria* (Cambridge: Cambridge University Press, 2011), Niehoff suggests that the Exposition may have been written specifically for Roman readers (170). Note also Mary Rose D'Angelo's sophisticated discussion, "Gender and Geopolitics in the Work of Philo of Alexandria: Jewish Piety and Imperial Family Values," in *Mapping Gender in Ancient Religious Discourses*, ed. Todd Penner and Caroline Vander Stichele (Leiden: Brill, 2007), 63–88. D'Angelo argues persuasively for the footprint of imperial family values in Philo's works, "recast in the interest of the claims he makes for Judaism" (87).

[45] נשא אשה ושהא עימה עשר שנים ולא ילדה אינו רשיי ליבטל ("if he married a woman and lived with her for ten years and she bore no child, he may not abstain [i.e. from the duty of procreation]"). Cf. also e.g. b. Yebam. 64a.

condition that the procreative duty is not thereby compromised.[46] Now, it is immediately evident that in *Spec.* 3.34–36 Philo does not offer the same ruling as the rabbinic texts; in some cases, Philo allows precisely what the tannaitic rabbis do not, or at least he fails to spell out the condition on which the Mishnaic ruling turns. Both the Philonic and rabbinic texts, nevertheless, address the subject of infertile marriage and the participants' standing with reference to their procreative duty. It is at least possible that Philo is familiar with a pre-Mishnaic halakhic tradition that provides precedent for subjecting the case of infertile marriage to the authority of Moses in some way.[47]

These larger questions notwithstanding, I suggest that the details of the two cases Philo addresses, considered against the wider background sketched above, present the best clues concerning the motivation for and dimensions of Philo's discussion in *Spec.* 3.34–36. Once again, it is vital to observe that Philo does not treat the subject of infertile marriage in either a comprehensive or a generic way. Rather, his treatment of the subject consists of two very specific cases, the first concerned with the inception of certain marriages, the second with the failure of other marriages to be brought to an end. In the first case, Philo adopts a position on which we observe a significant degree of agreement among ancient moralists and legislators: the identification of those who choose to marry without due regard for their reproductive duty as those worthy of censure. In the second case, Philo takes what amounts to a mediating position in regard to an issue on which we find greater evidence of disagreement among other ancient authors and sources. In the circumstance of marriage that unexpectedly proves to be childless, while some insist on divorce, and others urge the parties to stay together, Philo presents a sympathetic perspective towards childless couples who married in good procreative faith. It goes beyond the evidence of *Spec.* 3.35 itself to conclude that it reveals Philo's conviction either that such a marriage really ought to be ongoing or, alternatively,

---

[46] Following Michael Satlow, *Tasting the Dish: Rabbinic Rhetorics of Sexuality*, BJS 303 (Atlanta: Scholars Press, 1995), 224–231, 262–264. On the tension between monogamous and polygynous ideals and concessions in Palestinian rabbinic law, see Satlow, *Jewish Marriage*, 189–192. We encounter the prioritization of loyalty over procreative duty in a famous later story (Song Rab. 1.31; on which see Boyarin, *Carnal Israel*, 53–56).

[47] Jewish and non-Jewish influences on Philo's position in *Spec.* 3.34–36 are not mutually exclusive. Note, correspondingly, the similarity of assumptions concerning marriage and sexual ethics in Palestinian rabbinic sources with relevant Greek and Roman ideas; so Michael Satlow, "Rabbinic Views on Marriage, Sexuality, and the Family," in *The Cambridge History of Judaism*, vol. 4, *The Late Roman–Rabbinic Period*, ed. Steven T. Katz (Cambridge: Cambridge University Press, 2006), 612–626.

brought to an end.[48] Rather, Philo offers what amounts to a hakakhic permission for the marriage as a going concern.[49] If non-Jewish readers constitute at least a significant part of Philo's target audience in the Exposition—and I believe they do—I suggest that it is most likely that in *Spec.* 3.34–36 we find Philo, perhaps independently of his nearest interpretive cousins, crafting a legislative hook to capture the interest and sympathies of his non-Jewish readers. Not only does the pentateuchal law speak to an area of contemporary concern, it does so in a specific, principled, and yet balanced way. The stringency of the law of Moses cannot be doubted, at least where such strictness is appropriate, as in the case of the shameful behavior of those who marry for discreditable reasons. Yet, concurrently, the law is suitably magnanimous towards those who find themselves in a double bind, as in the case of those who wed rightly but then find themselves constrained by both procreative duty and the force of their relational ties.[50]

---

[48] On the one side, Niehoff, *Jewish Identity*, 101, maintains that Philo actually encourages the couple considered in *Spec.* 3.35 to stay together. On the other, David Daube, "Duty of Procreation," 966, and Samuel Belkin, *Philo and the Oral Law: The Philonic Interpretation of Biblical Law in Relation to the Palestinian Halakah* (Cambridge: Harvard University Press, 1940), 221, conclude that Philo holds that the husband of a barren woman ought to divorce her. I suggest that the recognition of συγγνώμη in this case, presumably for failure to comply with the reproductive mandate of nature, in and of itself allows that Philo considers the failure to divorce in this situation either no material wrongdoing at all or a more serious wrongdoing for which, yet, there is pardon. The range of situations in which συγγνώμη might be sought or enjoyed is illustrated in Philo's use of the terminology in relation to the distinction between voluntary and involuntary sin, an issue of particular interest to Philo. Most frequently, συγγνώμη is the lot of those who sin involuntarily or in ignorance (*QG* 1.68; *Deus* 134; *Flacc.* 7). It is also sought, however, by one who has sinned voluntarily (*Spec.* 1.235), and is the value or principle God privileges ahead of punishment (κόλασις) on the Day of Atonement, the feast on which supplicants seek remission (παραίτησις) of sins voluntary and involuntary both (*Spec.* 2.196; cf. *Praem.* 166). On Philo's concern with the distinction between voluntary and involuntary sin, see Michael Francis, "Borderline Bad: Philo of Alexandria on the Distinction Between Voluntary and Involuntary Sin" (PhD diss., The University of Notre Dame, 2015).

[49] I concur with Niehoff's assessment elsewhere: "Philo determined that it is halakhically acceptable for a married couple to stay together even though a problem of infertility has arisen" ("Mother and Maiden, Sister and Spouse: Sarah in Philonic Midrash," *HTR* 97 [2004]: 413–444, at 422).

[50] The presentation (or defense) of Jewish law as both appropriately strict and yet characteristically magnanimous is an important concern of Philo's elsewhere (e.g. *Hypoth.* 8.7.1, 8.7.9) and among other Diaspora authors of the time (note also the presentation of God in *Spec.* 3.36 as φιλόζωος and φιλάνθρωπος). See the summary by John M. G. Barclay, *Flavius Josephus: Translation and Commentary*, vol. 10, *Against Apion* (Leiden: Brill, 2007), 358. In addition, I note that the discussion of texts above might be taken to support Maren Niehoff's suggestion that Philo wrote the Exposition of the Law with Roman readers in

De specialibus legibus 3.35 and the Focus of Philo's Sexual Ethics

Might Philo's failure to specify abstinence in *Spec.* 3.35 suggest that he approves of ongoing sexual activity in such cases? First of all, we should be clear, Philo does not explicitly authorize or prohibit further sexual intercourse in *Spec.* 3.35.[51] To answer this question, then, requires some speculation. Nevertheless, the degree of consistency usually attributed to Philo's perspective on sex—confirmed at various points so far in this study—encourages further speculation, suitably qualified, in the case of *Spec.* 3.35, and points towards the principle factor that such conjecture ought to address. If Philo offers tacit approval for sexual activity in the case of certain infertile marriages, we might assume that the procreative character of such activity is preserved in some way, the challenging circumstances notwithstanding.

Maren Niehoff suggests that the couple in view in *Spec.* 3.35 is free to continue to engage in sexual intercourse. Such activity is not out of step with Philo's position on sex elsewhere because the marriage itself provides the procreative context that furnishes the partners' sexual activities with reproductive legitimacy.[52] Thus, while Philo condemns sexual intercourse with a wife previously known to be infertile because such relations cannot lead to procreation (*Spec.* 3.34, 36), in the situation addressed in *Spec.* 3.35 ongoing sexual activity is sanctioned as Philo encourages the partners to stay together as the procreative purpose of the relationship remains in a "theoretical" way.[53] Niehoff's interpretation of *Spec.* 3.34–36 is part of her discussion of Philo's sexual ethics in general. Niehoff contends that the locus of Philo's procreationist concern has been misidentified in discussions of Philo's ethics.[54] For Niehoff, Philo's focus is never on the sexual act itself. Rather, Philo's concern—the axis on which his procreationist perspective

---

mind (*Jewish Exegesis*, 170). Arguably, the sources most salient for comparison with Philo's position, at least in the case of *Spec.* 3.35, are Roman.

[51] The combined force of συνήθεια, φίλτρα and συμβίωσις resulting from married life is not presented as warrant for sexual activity (cf. above on Musonius, fr. 13a). What these attributes prompt Philo to recognize, rather, is that entering and exiting marriage are not symmetrical concerns.

[52] *Jewish Identity*, 100–101. Strictly speaking, Niehoff does not spell out her conclusion that ongoing sexual relations are permitted in this case, but I cannot see any other way to interpret her comments given her emphases and arguments in the surrounding material.

[53] *Jewish Identity*, 101.

[54] Niehoff criticizes van Geytenbeek (*Musonius Rufus*) for overplaying the similarities between Musonius and Philo. I would add that this criticism might apply equally if not more so to Gaca, for whom the parallels between Philo and Musonius are even more tightly drawn.

turns—is with the wider context or general framework within which sex occurs.[55] In his important recent study, Loader endorses Niehoff's assessment of *Spec.* 3.34–36.[56]

I suggest, however, that there is a problem with Niehoff's reading of *Spec.* 3.34–36—that is to say, as it stands, it is not sufficient to explain the details of the passage.[57] It is very difficult to distinguish between the two cases addressed by Philo simply by way of appeal to a difference in the procreational context in each situation. As is implicit in the discussion above, Philo gives no indication of a difference in the native reproductive capacities of the woman concerned in each case.[58] To use Niehoff's terms, I do not see how the procreative purpose of the relationship might be maintained theoretically in one case of infertile marriage but not the other, at least merely by appeal to the wider context in which sex occurs. To the extent that the cases can be differentiated concerning the legitimacy of sexual activity, it is not at the level of a general framework for sexuality established by circumstance. Any difference between the cases in terms of procreative agenda, considered theoretically or otherwise, exists at a level or in relation to a factor not yet specified. If Philo simply prohibits sexual activity wherever and whenever pregnancy is impossible—with a male, with a menstruating woman, or with a woman previously known to be infertile—he likely prohibits it also if a woman's infertility has more recently come to light.[59]

Can we posit an alternative or additional factor that might allow Philo to sanction ongoing sexual activity in one kind of infertile marriage but not the other? Kathy Gaca observes in passing that Philo might allow a childless couple to remain sexually active if such activity represents their

---

[55] Note Niehoff's comments in relation to *Spec.* 3.32–33: "It would thus appear that the married couple was left in peace by Philo during all the days of the month that the woman was not directly bleeding" (*Jewish Identity*, 100–101).

[56] *Philo, Josephus, and the Testaments*, 203–204, 254.

[57] In the concluding section of this study I discuss briefly my agreement with certain aspects of Niehoff's important discussion in this section of *Jewish Identity*.

[58] I note above (n. 28) that a difference in age is presupposed for the brides in each of the two cases Philo considers in *Spec.* 3.34–36. In the first case, the women are old enough to have been married and proved infertile before; in the second case, the women are young virgins. Crucially, however, this difference pertains to the point of marriage only. The scenario Philo addresses in *Spec.* 3.35 occurs after a period of childlessness. In other words, there are no grounds to conclude that the women in the one case are younger, that is, closer to their fertile prime, than the other.

[59] I suggest that *Spec.* 3.9 also poses a challenge to Niehoff's assessment of the locus of Philo's procreationist concerns. Surely, the wider procreative context remains in the case of those who are, yet, condemned for their approach to sex with their very own wives.

perseverance in attempting to reproduce.[60] In other words, the legitimacy of sexual activity would be grounded in the couple's ongoing procreative intent. Gaca notes that Philo might appeal to an impeccable biblical precedent for the legitimacy of further sexual activity in this situation, the example of Abraham and the birth of Isaac to Sarah after decades of infertility.[61] Gaca's brief suggestion has much to commend it; in the following paragraphs I will attempt to strengthen it.

First of all, the appeal to the partners' intentions in the act of sex itself as the differentiating factor in the two cases of infertile marriage considered by Philo cuts with the grain of *Spec.* 3.34–36. As we have seen, the formal contrast Philo establishes is between two different approaches to the pursuit and maintenance of the marital union. In the first instance, Philo addresses the situation of one who enters marriage for an illegitimate reason. In the second, Philo deals with the case of another who refuses to terminate a marriage for a reason with which Philo has sympathy. The pivotal factor in the comparison is the intention or motivating concern of the male partner. Both cases deal with a reproductively deficient marriage. What is at stake in the difference between the two is the relationship between this deficiency and the aims of the husband. In the one case, Philo insists, one who knows what he is getting into in marrying an infertile woman only does so on account of his insatiable hunger for pleasure. In the other, two motivating concerns are evident. First, we can assume that the marriage was originally pursued out of a proper respect for the procreational duty. Second, the union continues once the wife's infertility has come to light on account of the bonds of friendship that knit the partners together.[62] Thus while in the one case, the pursuit of pleasure is the lodestar of the relationship, in the other, it is at no point the defining concern. The fundamental contrast between the two husbands pertains to their intentions towards their partners. The priority of this factor is reflected in the language Philo employs in describing the actions of the husband in the first case: such men spoil the seed by voluntary inclination (ἑκουσίῳ γνώμῃ), and contrive (τεχνάζω) towards its extinction.

---

[60] "Philo's Principles," 23. Niehoff does not interact with Gaca's suggestion.

[61] Alas, Philo is silent concerning the act of intercourse responsible for Isaac's conception (an assessment that needs to be qualified with the recognition that there is no treatment of Gen 21–22 in the extant text of the *Quaestiones*). On the conception of Isaac, see the further comments at n. 72 below.

[62] The varying scenarios Philo describes thus feature a contrast between powerful and different forces: overwhelming desire for pleasure, on the one hand, and the force of relational ties, on the other.

Second, this reading of *Spec.* 3.34–36 is illustrative of an important feature of Philo's treatment of marriage and sexual activity more widely. Time and again, the focus of Philo's procreationist concern is with the goal of sexual activity, or the motivation of the parties to sex. This focus emerges most clearly in Philo's comments concerning pleasure as it relates to intercourse.[63] The centrality of the issue of pleasure to the discussion in *Spec.* 3.34–36 typifies Philo's position elsewhere. Repeatedly across the Philonic passages considered briefly earlier in this study, we observe Philo distinguish between two kinds of approach to marriage or sexual activity: on the one hand, for the sake of procreation, on the other, for the sake of pleasure (e.g. *Ios.* 43; *Virt.* 207; *QG* 4.86, 4.154). The latter would appear to be the sole and blameworthy alternative to properly reproductive sex. Philo does have a place for the legitimate expression of sexual desire, and, perhaps, even, the experience of pleasure as it accompanies sexual activity.[64] What Philo will not allow as legitimate is the striving for pleasure as the goal of sex, which is inevitably the case when sex is undertaken on account of desire rather than for an appropriate, rational reason. The single motivation Philo acknowledges as legitimate for engaging in sexual intercourse is the propagation of the human race.[65] Insofar as sexual activity is guided by this rational control, it qualifies as acceptable conduct; where this is not the case, it stands condemned as an uncontrolled expression of irrational desire (e.g. *Abr.* 249).[66] Accordingly, the appeal to the husband's procreative intent as the factor legitimizing further sexual activity in the case addressed in *Spec.* 3.35 might be supported by recognition of Philo's attention to the problem of pleasure as motivating concern in *Spec.* 3.34–36 and in his treatment of sexual ethics elsewhere.

[63] Philo's comments on pleasure are almost invariably negative; for the bodily, earthbound human, the lure of pleasure is a persistent and serious danger. The Epicurean *oikeiosis*, with pleasure as the goal of life, is resolutely opposed by Philo; the pleasure-seeker (ἡδονικός) or pleasure-lover (φιλήδονος) is among his favorite targets.

[64] On the legitimate expression of desire for sex, see especially *Opif.* 151–152 and the discussion by Winston in "Philo and the Rabbis." Philo grants the legitimacy of desire for sexual intercourse as it serves the reproductive goal. In this text, however, Philo's assessment of bodily pleasure as it pertains to sex is thoroughly negative: it is the starting point of wicked and law-breaking deeds. In general, Philo concedes that certain pleasures are, in and of themselves (not as goals), necessary and useful. On occasion, at least, he allows that sexual pleasure might also be assessed in this way (e.g. *Leg.* 3.157).

[65] On *Virt.* 112, where Philo allows that a female captive might marry her captor either on account of love or for the sake of the birth of children, see the comments below.

[66] Here I follow Hans Svebakken's analysis of Philo's theory of desire and the self-control that ought to attend it, in *Philo of Alexandria's Exposition of the Tenth Commandment*, SPhiloM 6 (Atlanta: SBL Press, 2012). Svebakken applies his general analysis to the issue of sex briefly on 94.

Third, we might note that the appeal to the husband's procreative intention in engaging in sex with his infertile wife as providing legitimation for ongoing sexual activity within the marriage can be taken as a specific example of a general principle Philo assumes or defends quite frequently elsewhere. It is a human agent's intention or motivation by which the character of the agent's actions is to be judged. The difference between virtue and vice is not, primarily, a matter of what is undertaken, but, rather, the way it is done.[67] Just as it is possible for formally correct actions to be undermined by the motive of the doer, so it is possible for apparently condemnable actions to be undertaken for laudable reasons and to be assessed positively as a result—as in the case of a doctor who deceives or causes pain to the benefit of the patient (*Cher.* 14–17; *Deus* 64–68). On the one hand, then, Balaam is an evil diviner of evil things, his benedictory words notwithstanding, on account of his motivation for speaking (*Migr.* 113–114). On the other, in several passages Philo commends the Levites whose slaughter of their kinsmen at Sinai was praiseworthy rather than blameworthy since it occurred for the very best of reasons (e.g. *Ebr.* 65–68). Judged against these other passages, Philo certainly has theoretical grounds by which he might consider further sexual activity legitimate in the case of childless partners who nevertheless persist in their attempts to procreate.

I suggest, then, that if indeed Philo's failure to specify abstinence in *Spec.* 3.35 amounts to implicit permission for ongoing sexual activity in some cases of infertile marriage, the outstanding candidate for satisfaction of the procreative requirement is the procreative intention or goal of the husband (and to extend Philo's focus, wife). No similar permission in the other case of infertile marriage is possible due to the husband's fixation on pleasure. This suggestion is able to account for the other cases of sexual misconduct in the surrounding material in which Philo employs the typology of wasted seed. In the case of pederasty, no procreative motivation for intercourse is ever possible. In the case of sex during menstruation, we might suppose that the close proximity of the fertile portion of the monthly

---

[67] The interiorization of ethical concern is characteristic of post-Aristotelian philosophy, and is especially prominent in Stoic ideas. On the concern with the internal in Hellenistic ethics, see the discussion in A. A. Long, "Hellenistic Ethics and Philosophical Power," in *From Epicurus to Epictetus: Studies in Hellenistic and Roman Philosophy* (Oxford: Clarendon Press, 2006), 3–22. By Albrecht Dihle's assessment, Greek moral thought came increasingly to stress the primacy of intention from the sixth century onwards (*The Theory of the Will in Classical Antiquity* [Berkeley: University of California Press, 1982], 33). For a survey of the various ways in which Philo manifests a concern with intention, see Aurelian Botica, *The Concept of Intention in the Old Testament, Philo of Alexandria, and the Early Rabbinic Literature: A Study in Human Intentionality in the Area of Criminal, Cultic and Religious and Ethical Law*, PHSC 9 (Piscataway, NJ: Gorgias), 169–317.

cycle to the term of menstruation suggests that one seeking sex during the brief period of infertility cannot be motivated by the procreative goal.[68] Correspondingly, if permission for continued sexual activity is implicit in *Spec.* 3.35, I suggest that we do not find in *Spec.* 3.34–36 consistent support for Niehoff's reappraisal of the register of Philo's procreationist concern. I agree with Niehoff that Philo does not attend to the mechanics of the sexual act in conveying his procreative perspective. From this observation Niehoff deduces that Philo's concern is with the context in which such activity occurs—that is, we might say, it is external to the act itself. The evidence of *Spec.* 3.34–36 points, I suggest, in another direction. Philo's greatest concern in this passage is internal to the action itself, with the intention of the agent(s) concerned. To the degree that Philo reasons consistently in his twofold treatment of infertile marriage, I do not see how he might permit sexual activity in one case but not the other without recourse to a relevant subjective or internal distinction between the parties involved.

De specialibus legibus 3.34–36 and Philo's Procreationist Perspective

The discussion in the preceding section offers only a hypothesis to account for one explanation of Philo's silence in *Spec.* 3.35 regarding the legitimacy of ongoing sexual activity in certain cases of infertile marriage. It is certainly possible that Philo's failure to authorize further sexual activity in *Spec.* 3.35 might imply that he does in fact expect couples in this situation to refrain from sex.[69] Which is the likelier interpretation of *Spec.* 3.35? It is impossible to be sure. With greater confidence, however, I suggest that the preceding discussion directs attention towards the challenge of framing Philo's overall perspective on marriage and sexual conduct as accurately as possible. There is nothing in the present study that fatally compromises the accuracy of the consensus assessment of Philo's perspective on sex. Philo brings a stringent procreationist perspective to the interpretation of scripture, and this perspective is presupposed in the expansion of scripture in

---

[68] I suggest that it is able to account for Philo's perspective in *Spec.* 3:9 too (on which see the comments at n. 59 above).

[69] Similarly, Gaca, "Philo's Principles," 23. Note also the discussion in *Sacr.* 112–117, in which Philo contrasts the pursuit of virtue, which is always of value in and of itself, with toil in intermediate arts and other necessities (in Stoic terms, things indifferent), engaged in for the benefit of the body and the acquisition of externals, which is without profit unless progress results (so e.g., athletes would do well to call a halt to their failures, while travelers prone to repeated disasters should find a new way to spend their time).

Spec. 3.34–36. We do not find in this passage clear Philonic approval for sexual activity that does not satisfy the procreative requirement.

I suggest, nevertheless, that the interpreter of Philo does face a secondary but important challenge in accounting for what Philo does *not* say on certain related issues and, correspondingly, what he appears *almost* to allow here and there. In *Spec.* 3.35, Philo's failure to specify the requirement of celibacy and the approving attention he gives to the marital phenomena of affection and companionship make for a tantalizing combination. Elsewhere, Philo nowhere specifies a requirement of celibacy for older couples formerly fertile but rendered infertile by age.[70] Neither does Philo unambiguously prohibit intercourse during pregnancy, an omission all the more surprising given the presence of legislation to this effect in contemporary Jewish sources (*C. Ap.* 2.202; Ps.-Phoc. 186).[71] In one additional passage, Philo creeps even closer towards expressing approval for sexual intimacy on nonprocreative grounds. In *Virt.* 112, dealing with the Mosaic legislation concerning the appropriate treatment of female captives taken in war (Deut 21:10–14), Philo allows two grounds according to which a captive might marry her captor: either on account of love of her partner or for the sake of the birth of children (ἢ δι' ἔρωτα τοῦ συνιόντος ἢ διὰ τέκνων γένεσιν). Yet Philo does not follow through and confirm that the woman's love for her husband will constitute legitimate grounds for ongoing spousal intercourse.

What is the best way to account for these silences or, we might say, loose ends within Philo's perspective on marriage and sexual conduct as a whole? As discussed above, Niehoff (followed by Loader) takes them as evidence that the severity of Philo's sexual ethic has been exaggerated, and concludes that in heterosexual marriage the procreative requirement for sexual activity is largely satisfied by the formal arrangement itself. This proposal makes good sense of some of the data (especially, silences), and is both important and successful in drawing attention to the observation that Philo does not, in fact, say everything that we might expect one possessed of particularly strict procreationist convictions to say. Certainly, he does not spell out the particulars of what in practice counts as legitimate procreative activity. I have argued, however, that Niehoff's assessment, short of adjustment or supplementation, does not account for the details of *Spec.* 3.34–36 (or *Spec.* 3.9). My own reading of *Spec.* 3.34–36 leaves me suspicious of the

---

[70] Recall *QG* 1.27, however, discussed above, on those who choose wives who are past their prime.

[71] Note *Abr.* 253, and Loader's comments in *Philo, Josephus, and the Testaments*, 203–204.

deduction that Philo's silence concerning certain sexual specifics bespeaks his approval of marital intercourse per se.

My consideration of *Spec.* 3.34–36 in the present study prompts me to ask whether the issue should not be explored in an alternative way. Rather than being indicative of a measure of moderation in principle in Philo's core commitments, it may be that Philo's silence on some issues, his failure to spell out certain implications that would appear to follow inevitably from other statements he makes, is attributable to the negotiation between procreationist convictions, scripture, and literary goal undertaken by Philo at various points in his exegetical works. All intercourse, marital, of course, ought to be procreative, that is, pursued only for the purpose of reproduction and that in a context in which there is at least some kind of defensible warrant for the aspiration of reproductive success. However, Philo does not always find it expedient to spell this out, and is not prompted uniformly by the biblical text to do so. In the case of *Spec.* 3.35, Philo's failure either to spell out the requirement of celibacy or specify the procreative goal that must be maintained if sexual intercourse is to continue might be taken as a strategic silence. In the Exposition of the Law at this point, it does Philo no good to press home the strict procreationist position willy-nilly if, as suggested above, in *Spec.* 3.34–36 we find Philo reshaping biblical law to capture the interest and approval of his non-Jewish readers. In the preceding case of sex during menstruation, there is a biblical prohibition to defend. In the case of infertile marriage, however, Philo is not similarly constrained.[72] It may be that in *Spec.* 3.35, Philo quite intentionally frames a legal provision such that it glosses over the implications of his procreationist convictions in regard to a situation sure to evoke the sympathies of his readers. I note with interest that in the passage identified above in which Philo does appear to sanction intercourse on nonprocreative grounds in the consummation of certain marriages (*Virt.* 112), his primary concern is with the demonstration of the φιλανθρωπία of the law of Moses. More specifically, in the particular case of the treatment of women conquered in wartime—a common source of moral apprehension in antiquity—Philo's immediate exegetical aim is to insist that the legislation of Deuteronomy 20 makes proper provision for female captives, and even prescribes measures

---

[72] An observation that would also apply in the case of Philo's silence concerning the act of intercourse responsible for the conception of Isaac. In Gen 21:1, it is God (true to his word) rather than Abraham who interacts with Sarah such that she conceives. Accordingly, Philo's primary interest in this turn in the patriarchal narrative is allegorical, interpreting it as an account of the divine begetting of virtue (*Cher.* 43–45; note also e.g. *Leg.* 3.218; *Cher.* 106; *Det.* 60; *Mut.* 137). On the "ménage à trois" Philo discerns in Gen 21:1–2, see the discussion in Niehoff, "Mother and Maiden," 435–436.

that accord with their own wishes.[73] In both *Spec.* 3.34–36 and *Virt.* 112, we might say, there is a kind of humanitarian and apologetic agenda that prompts Philo to skate over certain aspects or entailments of his procreationist convictions. Do these passages mark a degree of moderation in these convictions? I am not persuaded that they do, at least in principle. They give clearer evidence, I suggest, of the way these procreationist commitments are regulated by the exegetical and rhetorical situation at hand.

University of Notre Dame

---

[73] See the discussion of *Virt.* 109–115 provided by Walter T. Wilson in *Philo of Alexandria, On the Virtues*, PACS 3 (Leiden: Brill, 2011), 265–266. Wilson discusses the treatment of captive women as a source of moral concern in a variety of sources on 266. In this case, Philo shares a common interpretive tradition with Josephus (*Ant.* 4.257–259). A comparison between the Philonic and Josephan passages is instructive, however. While both interpreters identify the birth of children as a (the) purpose of the marital union, only Philo attributes this goal to the woman herself. Similarly, while Josephus insists that the conquering male must respect the woman's wishes (θεραπεύειν αὐτῆς τὸ βουλητόν), only Philo specifies the woman's love of her partner (ἔρωτα τοῦ συνιόντος) as a condition on the basis of which the union might proceed. In Josephus's account, then, the marriage is without the woman's explicit consent (in agreement with Louis H. Feldman, *Flavius Josephus: Translation and Commentary*, vol. 3, *Judean Antiquities 1–4* [Leiden: Brill, 2000], 430). In Philo's account, implicitly, her consent is required.

The Studia Philonica Annual 27 (2015): 53–70

COSMIC MOTHERS IN PHILO OF ALEXANDRIA AND IN NEOPYTHAGOREANISM

ARCO DEN HEIJER

In a number of passages, Philo of Alexandria calls wisdom "mother" with respect to the cosmos. The background of this expression has been sought in Plato's description of the Receptacle as "mother," in the Hellenistic cult of Isis or in the Pythagorean Dyad as the primary mother-goddess in Xenocrates's theological fragment. In this article, I will argue that these parallels do not explain Philo's depiction of wisdom as mother adequately. Instead, I will turn to the use of the expression "mother of all things" or "mother of the universe" in Neopythagorean descriptions of Justice and of the Tetractys or Decad and examine the value of these parallels for understanding Philo's description of wisdom.

1. *Wisdom as Mother of All Things in Philo of Alexandria*

Philo has inherited from the biblical and early Jewish wisdom literature the personification of wisdom, who was with God when he created the world.[1]

---

* This article presents parts of the findings of my master thesis, written in the context of the HLCS research master literary studies at the Radboud University in Nijmegen, under supervision of dr. ir. F.A. Bakker and available online at https://radboud.academia. edu/ArcoDenHeijer/. All translations from Greek and Latin in this article were made by me.
    [1] The principal biblical text for Philo is Prov 8:22–31, he does not mention Job 28. Cf., *inter alia*, Hans Friedrich Weiss, *Untersuchungen zur Kosmologie des hellenistischen und palästinischen Judentums*, TU 97 (Berlin: Akademie, 1966); Burton L. Mack, *Logos und Sophia: Untersuchungen zur Weisheitstheologie im hellenistischen Judentum*, SUNT 10 (Göttingen: Vandenhoeck & Ruprecht, 1973); Karl-Gustav Sandelin, *Wisdom as Nourisher: A Study of an Old Testament Theme, Its Development within Early Judaism and its Impact on Early Christianity*, Acta Academiae Aboensis, Ser. A. Humaniora, 64,3 (Åbo: Åbo Akademie, 1986); Jacques Cazeaux, "Sagesse II: La sagesse selon Philon d'Alexandrie," *DSpir* 14:81–91; Martin Neher, *Wesen und Wirken der Weisheit in der Sapientia Salomonis*, BZAW 333 (Berlin: De Gruyter, 2004); Martin Leuenberger, "Die personifizierte Weisheit vorweltlichen Ursprungs von Hi 28 bis Joh 1," *ZAW* 120 (2008): 366–386.

In five passages, Philo explicitly calls "wisdom" (σοφία) or the equivalents "virtue" (ἀρετή), or "knowledge," (ἐπιστήμη), "mother" in a cosmological sense.[2] I will briefly review these passages in their context.

1.1. *QG* 4,97

In *QG* 4,97, Philo explains the name of Bethuel, the father of Rebecca. According to Philo, his name means "daughter of God," and he wonders: "And who is to be considered the daughter of God but wisdom, who is the first-born mother of all things and most of all of those who are greatly purified in soul?"[3] The remarkable fact that this "daughter of God" is also the *father* of Rebecca is explained by Philo as indicating that wisdom is female (receptive, subordinate) with respect to God but male (actively sowing virtues) with respect to the human soul. That wisdom is "the first-born mother of all things and most of all of those who are greatly purified in soul" is mentioned parenthetically and is not central to the argument. In the comment on the meaning of Bethuel in the *Allegorical Commentary*, the motherhood of wisdom is not mentioned.[4]

1.2. *Leg.* 2, 49

Several pairs of parents mentioned in the Bible are interpreted with reference to God and wisdom as the universal parents. The first pair is that of Gen 2:24, where the creation of the woman out of man is seen as the basis for the union of husband and wife in marriage. The biblical text states that man shall leave behind his father and mother, and shall cleave to his wife, and Philo interprets this with respect to the human soul:

> Due to sense-perception, the mind, whenever it is enslaved to it, leaves behind both the father of the universe, God, and the mother of all things, the virtue and wisdom of God, and cleaves to and unites itself with sense-perception, and is unloosened into sense-perception, so that the two become one flesh and one passion.[5]

---

[2] In this article, I do not discuss passages in which wisdom is presented as mother of the sage, like *Conf.* 49; *Her.* 53; *Det.* 115–116.

[3] *QG* 4.97, trans. Marcus (PLCL suppl. 1.381).

[4] *Fug.* 51.

[5] *Leg.* 2, 49: ἕνεκα τῆς αἰσθήσεως ὁ νοῦς, ὅταν αὐτῇ δουλωθῇ, καταλείπει καὶ τὸν πατέρα τῶν ὅλων θεὸν καὶ τὴν μητέρα τῶν συμπάντων, τὴν ἀρετὴν καὶ σοφίαν τοῦ θεοῦ, καὶ προσκολλᾶται καὶ ἑνοῦται τῇ αἰσθήσει καὶ ἀναλύεται εἰς αἴσθησιν, ἵνα γένωνται μία σὰρξ καὶ ἓν πάθος οἱ δύο.

In a similar passage, *Cher.* 40–52, Philo contrasts Adam's corporeal intercourse with Eve, as sense-perception, to the spiritual marriage of the patriarchs with the virgin virtues. In that passage, the virtues are presented as the offspring of God and virtue, which God does not produce for himself, but as a gift for humans. The knowledge of the universal Cause (God), virtue, and the virtues as their offspring,[6] is presented as the secret contents of a mystery: both the mystery terminology and the contrast between corporeal offspring and the virtues as spiritual offspring allude to Diotima's "initiation" of Socrates in the *Symposium*.[7] In *Cher.* 40–52, wisdom is not called "mother," but is has the same central place in the ontological structure as in *Leg.* 2.49.

1.3. *Det. 54*

In *Det.* 54, it is the "father and mother" mentioned in the fifth commandment of the Decalogue ("Honor your father and your mother") that are interpreted as God and wisdom:

> If you deem worthy of honor him who conceived the cosmos as father, and the wisdom through which the All was completed as mother, you will be well off yourself.[8]

Because God and wisdom are not in need of anything, the honor paid to them benefits not them, but the person who pays it.

1.4. *Ebr. 30-33*

A similar explanation is advanced in *Ebr.* 30–33, one of the most extensive passages on the cosmological function of wisdom. Here, the exegetical context is the interpretation of a law stipulating what parents should do when they have a disobedient son (Deut 21:18–21). Philo first interprets this pair of parents as the Craftsman (δημιουργός) and the knowledge of the Maker. After elaborating on this interpretation, Philo discards it as not

---

[6] *Cher.* 48: ἡ περὶ τοῦ αἰτίου καὶ ἀρετῆς καὶ τρίτου τοῦ γεννήματος ἀμφοῖν ἐπιστήμη.

[7] Cf. Christoph Riedweg, *Mysterienterminologie bei Platon, Philon und Klemens von Alexandrien*, Untersuchungen zur antiken Literatur und Geschichte 26 (Berlin: De Gruyter, 1987), 71–92. Note that Philo could have read the account of the *Symposium* in such a way that the vision of "some single knowledge of such a kind, which is that of such a beauty" (τινὰ ἐπιστήμην μίαν τοιαύτην, ἥ ἐστι καλοῦ τοιοῦδε.) was the final stage before the vision of the Beautiful itself (Plato, *Symp.* 210d-e).

[8] *Det.* 54: πατέρα μὲν τὸν γεννήσαντα <τὸν> κόσμον, μητέρα δὲ τὴν σοφίαν, δι᾽ ἧς ἀπετελέσθη τὸ πᾶν, τιμῆς ἀξιώσῃς, αὐτὸς εὖ πείσῃ·

applicable to the present passage and suggests another meaning, the father being right reason and the mother the encyclical education. It is the former interpretation that interests us, however, and because the passage is of central importance to this article, I will quote it completely:

> Father and mother have different meanings, though the words are the same. For we shall rightly say that the Craftsman who made this universe is also the father of that which had thus come into being, and that the Maker's knowledge is the mother. When God had intercourse with her, not in the manner of a human, he sowed coming-to-be. And she, having received the seeds of God, with productive birth pangs gave birth to her only and beloved visible son, this cosmos. Now, by one member of the divine choir, wisdom is presented as speaking about herself in this way, "God acquired me as the first of his works, and before the ages he founded me" [Prov 8:22]. For it was necessary that all that which came into being should be younger than the mother and nurse of the whole. Well, who would be able to resist an accusation from these parents? Indeed, not even a moderate threat or most gentle blaming. For even of their gifts, nobody can contain their bounteous multitude, not even the cosmos, but as a cistern that is too small, it will quickly be filled up from the great overflowing spring of God's gifts, so as to boil over and overflow. But if we are unable to receive their benefits, how shall we think to endure their punitive powers? However, the parents of the universe are to be left out of the present discussion. Now, let us examine their disciples and relatives, who have received as their lot the care for and leadership of souls which are not ill-bred or without taste.[9]

1.5. *Fug.* 109

Finally, the parents of the high priest are interpreted along the same lines, when Philo comments on Lev 21:11. The high priest cannot be defiled by his parents "because, I suppose, he has received imperishable and most

---

[9] *Ebr.* 30–33, πατρὸς δὲ καὶ μητρὸς κοιναὶ μὲν αἱ κλήσεις, διάφοροι δ' αἱ δυνάμεις. τὸν γοῦν τόδε τὸ πᾶν ἐργασάμενον δημιουργὸν ὁμοῦ καὶ πατέρα εἶναι τοῦ γεγονότος εὐθὺς ἐν δίκῃ φήσομεν, μητέρα δὲ τὴν τοῦ πεποιηκότος ἐπιστήμην, ᾗ συνὼν ὁ θεὸς οὐχ ὡς ἄνθρωπος ἔσπειρε γένεσιν. ἡ δὲ παραδεξαμένη τὰ τοῦ θεοῦ σπέρματα τελεσφόροις ὠδῖσι τὸν μόνον καὶ ἀγαπητὸν αἰσθητὸν υἱὸν ἀπεκύησε, τόνδε τὸν κόσμον. εἰσάγεται γοῦν παρά τινι τῶν ἐκ τοῦ θείου χοροῦ ἡ σοφία περὶ αὑτῆς λέγουσα τὸν τρόπον τοῦτον· ὁ θεὸς ἐκτήσατό με πρωτίστην τῶν ἑαυτοῦ ἔργων, καὶ πρὸ τοῦ αἰῶνος ἐθεμελίωσέ με· ἦν γὰρ ἀναγκαῖον τῆς μητρὸς καὶ τιθήνης τῶν ὅλων πάνθ' ὅσα εἰς γένεσιν ἦλθεν εἶναι νεώτερα. τούτων οὖν τῶν γονέων τίς ἱκανὸς ὑποστῆναι κατηγορίαν; ἀλλ' οὐδὲ μετρίαν ἀπειλὴν ἢ ἐλαφροτάτην κατάμεμψιν. οὐδὲ γὰρ τῶν δωρεῶν ἱκανὸς οὐδεὶς χωρῆσαι τὸ ἄφθονον πλῆθος, ἴσως δὲ οὐδ' ὁ κόσμος, ἀλλ' οἷα βραχεῖα δεξαμενὴ μεγάλης ἐπιρρεούσης τῶν τοῦ θεοῦ χαρίτων πηγῆς τάχιστα ἀποπληρωθήσεται, ὡς ἀναβλύσαι τε καὶ ὑπερεκχεῖσθαι. εἰ δὲ τὰς εὐεργεσίας ἀδυνατοῦμεν δέχεσθαι, τὰς κολαστηρίους δυνάμεις πῶς ἐπιφερομένας οἰσόμεν; τοὺς μὲν δὴ τοῦ παντὸς γονεῖς ὑπεξαιρετέον τοῦ παρόντος λόγου, τοὺς δὲ φοιτητὰς καὶ γνωρίμους αὐτῶν τὴν ἐπιμέλειαν καὶ προστασίαν εἰληχότας ψυχῶν, ὅσαι μὴ ἀνάγωγοι καὶ ἄμουσοι, νῦν ἐπισκεψώμεθα.

pure parents, as father God, who is also the father of all things, and as mother wisdom, through which the universe came into being."[10]

2. *"Wisdom" as Allegorical Interpretation*

The texts reviewed show that wisdom comes to Philo's mind quite naturally as an allegorical interpretation of mothers which he encounters in the biblical text. God and his wisdom occupy a central place in Philo's universe, and in that of his Jewish audience as well: in most instances, he mentions the cosmological function of wisdom parenthetically, without any need for explanation. In *Ebr.* 30, he introduces his interpretation with "we shall rightly say" (ἐν δίκῃ φήσομεν): he does not seem to expect to surprise his readers. In the *Exposition of the Law,* which is not written for an audience thoroughly acquainted with the Jewish scriptures and their allegorical interpretation, personified wisdom is hardly mentioned.[11] Her cosmological role is completely taken over by the *logos.* So, if wisdom as mother is part of Philo's Jewish background, how should we understand this mother-figure?

3. *A Syncretistic Mother Goddess?*

According to Weiss, the involvement of wisdom in the creation of the world, and her depiction as "mother" is evidence "daß hinter allen diesen

---

[10] *Fug.* 109: διότι, οἶμαι, γονέων ἀφθάρτων καὶ καθαρωτάτων ἔλαχεν, πατρὸς μὲν θεοῦ, ὃς καὶ τῶν συμπάντων ἐστὶ πατήρ, μητρὸς δὲ σοφίας, δι᾽ ἧς τὰ ὅλα ἦλθεν εἰς γένεσιν·

[11] A search on the lemma σοφία in the treatises belonging to the *Exposition of the Law* (*Opif., Abr., Ios., Mos.* 1 and 2, *Dec., Spec.* 1–4, *Virt., Praem.*) yields 44 passages. Only in 7 of these, is wisdom personified, and still in a rather loose sense (*Opif.* 158; *Abr.* 100; 220; 258; *Spec.* 1.50; 1. 269). A representative example is *Opif.* 158, which speaks about instruction as the "food, which wisdom gives by discourses and doctrines to those who love contemplation" (τροφήν, ἣν ὀρέγει τοῖς φιλοθεάμοσι διὰ λόγων καὶ δογμάτων σοφία). On the different audiences of the various treatises of Philo, cf. recently Charles A. Anderson, *Philo of Alexandria's Views of the Physical World,* WUNT 2.309 (Tübingen: Mohr Siebeck, 2011), 18–22; Christian Noack, *Gottesbewußtsein: exegetische Studien zur Soteriologie und Mystik bei Philo von Alexandria,* WUNT 2.216 (Tübingen: Mohr Siebeck, 2000), 18–31; Martina Böhm, *Rezeption und Funktion der Vätererzählungen bei Philo von Alexandria: zum Zusammenhang von Kontext, Hermeneutik und Exegese im frühen Judentum,* BZNW 128 (Berlin: De Gruyter, 2005); Maren Niehoff, *Jewish Exegesis and Homeric Scholarship in Alexandria* (Cambridge: Cambridge University Press, 2011).

Spekulationen über die Weisheit ursprünglich mythologische Vorstellungen von einer Mutter-Gottheit standen."[12] He sees this mother goddess in the background of the entire tradition of personified wisdom in the Jewish wisdom literature. In Palestine, the mythological nature of wisdom was suppressed to the point of being almost indiscernible, but in the syncretistic Hellenistic world of Alexandria, it is allowed to reappear to a certain degree. This is a highly speculative reconstruction. Even though there are evident links between the Egyptian personification of righteousness and truth, Ma'at, and the Hebrew personification of wisdom,[13] there was no need to "suppress" anything. As Müller emphasizes, it must have been clear from the outset that the personification of wisdom was a literary phenomenon used to describe aspects of YHWH's nature to emphasize the authority of the wisdom as taught by the sages.[14] She is part of a richly metaphorical theological discourse, which is fundamentally different from the polytheistic constellations of the gods of cultic religion. Jan Assmann described this distinction with respect to Egyptian religion as a distinction between implicit theology, which operates with constellations of gods who derive their identity from their relation to other gods (such as the triad father-mother-son, which is central in Egyptian mythology) and explicit theology, which uses mythological terms to describe aspects of the relation between the divine (conceived as a unity) and the world.[15] This distinction can help to conceptualize the fundamental difference between a depiction of wisdom as God's wife, and, for example, Asherah as the wife of YHWH. Against the latter, the biblical authors polemicized vigorously, whereas there are no indications whatsoever that the former ever presented a problem to Jews.

Another problem with the hypothesis of a mythological depiction of a "mother goddess" as the background of specifically Philo's depiction of

---

[12] Weiss, *Untersuchungen zur Kosmologie*, 205. Cf. also Ursula Früchtel, *Die kosmologischen Vorstellungen bei Philo von Alexandrien: Ein Beitrag zur Geschichte der Genesisexegese*, ALGHJ 2 (Leiden: Brill, 1968), 174: "Die Vermutung liegt nahe, daß Philo eine mythologische Vorstellung von der Zeugung des Kosmos aus einer männlichen und weiblichen Gottheit gekannt hat, welche er besonders in Prov. 8,30 wiederzufinden glaubte. Gleichzeitig hat Philo diese mythologische Vorstellung entmythologisiert, indem er betont daß diese kosmische Zeugung keine Analogie im menschlichen Zeugungsvorgang hat."

[13] Cf. Christa Kayatz, *Studien zu Proverbien 1–9: Eine form- und motivgeschichtliche Untersuchung unter Einbeziehung ägyptischen Vergleichsmaterials*, WUNT 22 (Tübingen: Mohr Siebeck, 1966), 93–119; Leuenberger, "personifizierte Weisheit," 376.

[14] Achim Müller, *Proverbien 1–9: Der Weisheit neue Kleider*, BZAW 291 (Berlin: De Gruyter, 2000), 212.

[15] Jan Assmann, *Ägypten: Theologie und Frömmigkeit einer frühen Hochkultur* (Stuttgart: Kohlhammer, 1984), 198–282.

wisdom, is that wisdom stimulates spiritual procreation and even outright asceticism. The Therapeutae are virgins and abstain from food out of their love for wisdom.[16] As such, wisdom is the exact antithesis of the various mother goddesses of the ancient world, who are worshipped to ensure the fertility of the earth and of human sexuality. Indeed, "mother of all things" (μήτηρ πάντων) is an expression which Philo's wisdom shares with Mother Earth in the Homeric Hymns, but the difference between these mothers could hardly be greater.[17]

4. *Plutarch's* Isis *and Plato's* Timaeus

Various authors have seen a parallel between Plutarch's depiction of Isis and Philo's depiction of wisdom.[18] These parallels are especially intriguing because Plutarch and Philo share a Platonist worldview. In his treatise *On Isis and Osiris,* Plutarch addresses a priestess of the Isis-cult in order to teach her to interpret the myth of Isis and Osiris in a philosophically sound way. His final interpretation consists in identifying Isis with matter, which longs for Osiris, the Good as the supreme God, to order her by his *logos*.[19] The resulting cosmos is represented by their son, Horus. Thus, Plutarch interprets Osiris, Isis and Horus by relating them to Plato's *Timaeus,* which likens the intelligible world to a father, the receptacle to a mother, and the cosmos to their son.[20] Osiris is said to sow "emanations and resemblances" (ἀπορροὰς καὶ ὁμοιότητας) into Isis, who becomes pregnant with "generations" (γενέσεων).[21] This seems quite similar to Philo's statement that "when God had intercourse with her, not in the manner of a human, he sowed coming-to-be (γένεσις). And she, having received the seeds of God, with productive birth pangs bore her only and beloved visible son, this cosmos."[22] Philo's use of the title "mother and nurse" for wisdom sounds

---

[16] *Contempl.* 35, 68.

[17] *Hom. Hymn.* 30, entitled Εἰς Γῆν μητέρα πάντων. Philippe Borgeaud, "Mother Goddesses," *Brill's New Pauly,* 12 August 2015, http://referenceworks.brillonline.com/entries/brill-s-new-pauly/mother-goddesses-e813510.

[18] E.g., John M. Dillon, *The Middle Platonists: A study of Platonism 80 B.C. to A.D. 220,* (London: Duckworth, 1996), 164; Mack, *Logos und Sophia,* 108–184, especially 155–158 on Wisdom and Isis as mother.

[19] An illuminating analysis from a feminist perspective is provided in Ann Chapman, *The Female Principle in Plutarch's Moralia* (Dublin: University College Dublin, 2011), 6–10.

[20] Plato, *Tim.* 50d-51a; 52d.

[21] Plutarch, *Is. Os.* 53, 372F.

[22] *Ebr.* 30, Greek text in note 9.

like a direct allusion to the *Timaeus*.[23] However, Weiss already noted the fundamental difference between Philo's wisdom and both Plato's receptacle and Plutarch's Isis: wisdom is actively involved in creating the world and is not a passive principle like matter. Moreover, Philo actually refers to the material receptacle as "mother and feeder and nurse of the created things"[24] later in the same treatise *On Drunkenness*, and makes it quite clear that this mother has a negative connotation: Sarah (who represents wisdom and virtue) is not born from this material mother, but is motherless, born directly from God.[25] Apparently, Philo does not reserve the term "mother and nurse" exclusively for the mother and nurse mentioned in the *Timaeus*.[26]

5. Wisdom as "Dyad in disguise"

John Dillon, observing the similarities between Philo's Wisdom and Plutarch's Isis as well, has given a more refined interpretation of them: he sees the Neopythagorean Dyad at the background of Philo's depiction of Wisdom. The (indefinite) Dyad is the principle of matter in the generation of the cosmos (thus linking it to the Receptacle in Plato's *Timaeus* and Isis in Plutarch) but it is also a material principle in the generation of the Form Numbers from the Monad.[27] Commenting on the passage from *On Drunkenness* quoted above, Dillon states,

> God, as the Monad, requires some sort of "female" principle in order to generate anything further, whether the form-numbers, or, ultimately, the physical universe, and the least threatening form that this other principle can take for Philo is God's Wisdom, as emanating from himself. Philo has absorbed

[23] *Ebr.* 31; *Conf.* 49. Cf. Plato, *Tim.* 49a; 50d; 51a; 52d; 88d.

[24] *Ebr.* 61, μητέρα καὶ τροφὸν καὶ τιθήνην τῶν ποιητῶν.

[25] *Ebr.* 61.

[26] Cf. David T. Runia, *Philo of Alexandria and the* Timaeus *of Plato*, PhilAnt 44 (Leiden: Brill, 1986), 285, who follows Nikiprowetsky in the conclusion that "Philo's use of the same image for matter and for its virtual opposite, σοφία in the guise of the κόσμος νοητός, is not problematic: he uses symbols and images plastically."

[27] Cf. the *Pythagorean Notebooks* (second century BCE) in Diogenes Laertius 8.25: "the Monad is principle of all things; from the Monad, the indefinite Dyad exists as matter to the Monad, which is cause; and from the Monad and the Dyad are the Numbers" (ἀρχὴν μὲν τῶν ἁπάντων μονάδα· ἐκ δὲ τῆς μονάδος ἀόριστον δυάδα ὡς ἂν ὕλην τῇ μονάδι αἰτίῳ ὄντι ὑποστῆναι· ἐκ δὲ τῆς μονάδος καὶ τῆς ἀορίστου δυάδος τοὺς ἀριθμούς·). The origin of this conception is the early Academy. Cf. John M. Dillon, *The Heirs of Plato: A Study of the Old Academy (347–274 BC)* (Oxford: Oxford University Press, 2003), 18–22, which is based mostly on Aristotle's criticism of Plato's theory of (Form) Numbers and their principles in *Metaph.* M and N.

the Neopythagorean Indefinite Dyad into his monistic system, with the help of the Jewish concept of God's Wisdom.[28]

Thus, wisdom would represent the Dyad in its transcendent function. According to Dillon, the *logos*, as the offspring of God and wisdom (in *Fug.* 109), performs the function of the world-soul, in the guise of Dikē; a system that Dillon believes to derive from Xenocrates.[29] However, the identification of the Dyad with wisdom is never made explicit by Philo. Moreover, the relation between wisdom and the *logos* is not as systematic as Dillon presents it; rather, it appears to me that they are more or less interchangeable metaphysical entities which Philo can choose according to the gender of the biblical figure of which he needs an allegorical interpretation.[30] Finally, wisdom as "the Maker's knowledge" is much more comprehensive than the indefinite Dyad as the formless principle of multiplicity. What the Maker knows, are the Forms. Hence, wisdom represents the entirety of the formal paradigm, as it is made by God to apply itself to the world (wisdom receives "coming-to-be" [γένεσις] from God in order to give birth to the visible cosmos).[31] Only as such (and not as indefinite Dyad) can it perform its function as heavenly home of the wise and as supreme virtue,[32] reflecting the double function of the Forms in Plato as both ethical paradigm for humanity and physical paradigm for the ordering of the cosmos by the gods.[33]

---

[28] John M. Dillon, "Pythagoreanism in the Academic Tradition: The Early Academy to Numenius," in *A History of Pythagoreanism*, ed. Carl A. Huffman (Cambridge: Cambridge University Press, 2014), 265.

[29] Dillon, *Heirs of Plato*, 102–107. Dillon's argument depends on his reconstruction of a supposed lacuna in the doxographical testimony of Aëtius on Xenocrates' theology (Aëtius, *Placit.* 1.7.30 = Xenocrates fr. 213 Isnardi Parente). It is only by assuming a lacuna in the Aëtius passage that it can be made to speak about Dikē. In the form in which Aëtius is transmitted to us, the Dyad is simply said to be "in the manner of the mother of the Gods" (μητρὸς θεῶν δίκην, with δίκην as adverb), which is parallel to the description of the Monad as "holding the rank of father" (πατρὸς ἔχουσαν τάξιν). I think the passage makes sense without the hypothesis of a lacuna. Cf. Margherita Isnardi Parente, *Senocrate— Ermodoro. Frammenti*, La scuola di Platone 3 (Naples: Bibliopolis, 1982), 405.

[30] Cf. Runia's criticism of Dillon's interpretation of the *logos* in David T. Runia, "The Beginnings of the End: Philo of Alexandria and Hellenistic Theology," in *Traditions of Theology: Studies in Hellenistic Theology, its Background and Aftermath*, ed. Dorothea Frede and André Laks, PhilAnt 89 (Leiden; Boston; Köln: Brill, 2002), 295–296. On p. 296, he remarks, "Philo may well have been not discontented with the variability of his various theological schemes, which often depend on the exegetical context."

[31] *Ebr.* 31.

[32] E.g. *Agr.* 65; *Migr.* 28.

[33] On Plato's theology, cf. Gerd Van Riel, *Plato's Gods*, Ashgate Studies in the History of Philosophical Theology (Farnham: Ashgate, 2013).

6. *"Mother of all things" in Neopythagoreanism*

Still, I think Dillon is right in emphasizing the close affinity of Philo to the Pythagoreanism of both Eudorus of Alexandria and the corpus of pseudo-Pythagorean writings in Doric dialect.[34] Centrone has argued that these pseudo-Pythagorean writings are to be situated in first-century BCE Alexandria, in the same milieu in which Eudorus and Philo operated.[35] In the remainder of this article, I will examine this Pythagorean milieu as a possible background for the depiction of wisdom as "mother" of the universe. I will discuss three texts: a fragment from a Pythagorean pseudepi-graph attributed to Ocellus which praises justice (δικαιοσύνη) as "mother and nurse of all things," the *Hymn to Number* preserved in Neoplatonist authors, which praises the Decad as "mother of all things," and, finally, Irenaeus's depiction of the role of the Tetrad or Tetractys as "mother of the universe" in the system of various teachers from the school of the Christian teacher Valentinus. Regrettably, what is preserved of Neopythagorean texts is only the tip of the iceberg of what circulated in antiquity. For this reason, I think it is justified to use such late antique sources as the *Hymn to Number* to explain an expression in Philo, if proper caution is taken in the evaluation of the parallels.

6.1. *Ps.-Ocellus about Justice as Mother and Nurse of All Things*

Justice, with the properties of reciprocity and equivalence, was a central virtue of Pythagoreanism already in the time of Aristotle, associated with the number four or nine, as the squares of respectively the first even or the first odd number.[36] The *Pythagorean Notebooks* (3rd-2nd century BCE)[37] report:

---

[34] Dillon, "Pythagoreanism," 263–266. Cf. also Ekaterina Matusova, "Allegorical Interpretation of the Pentateuch in Alexandria: Inscribing Aristobulus and Philo in a Wider Literary Context," *SPhiloA* 22 (2010): 1–51, on the Pythagorean background of the allegorical method employed by Aristobulus and Philo.

[35] Bruno Centrone, "The Pseudo-Pythagorean Writings," in *A History of Pythagoreanism*, ed. Carl A. Huffman (Cambridge: Cambridge University Press, 2014), 315–340, which gives a good overview in English of what he argued for in his Italian commentary on four ethical treatises from the pseudo-Pythagorean corpus (Bruno Centrone, *Pseudopythagorica ethica: i trattati morali di Archita, Metopo, Teage, Eurifamo*, Elenchos 17 [Naples: Bibliopolis, 1990]).

[36] Aristotle *Eth.Nic.*, 1132b21; Alexander of Aphrodisias, *Comm. Metaph.* 38.10. Cf. Oliver Primavesi, "Aristotle on the 'So-Called' Pythagoreans'," in *A History of Pythagoreanism*, ed. Carl A. Huffman (Cambridge: Cambridge University Press, 2014), 237–238; M. Laura Gemelli Marciano, "The Pythagorean Way of Life and Pythagorean Ethics," in *A*

Righteousness (τὸ δίκαιον) is sworn by (ὅρκιον), and therefore Zeus is called Zeus-Invoked-by-Oath. And harmony is virtue, health, the whole good and god; therefore, also, the universe is established according to harmony. And friendship is harmonious equality.[38]

In this triad (righteousness, harmony and friendship) we recognize the core of Pythagorean ethics. A fragment of a treatise attributed to Ocellus elaborates on the concept of justice as harmony, appearing in various forms in the different strata of the universe.[39] In the cosmos it is "the providence and harmony that conducts [as a general] the principle of the universe,"[40] in the city it is peace and lawfulness, in the household the harmonious living together of husband and wife. In the body it is health, and in the soul it is wisdom (σοφία).[41] In view of all this, the author introduces his praise of justice with the words:

> It seems right to me to call men's righteousness the mother and nurse of the other virtues.[42]

History of Pythagoreanism, ed. Carl A. Huffman (Cambridge: Cambridge University Press, 2014), 143.

[37] Diogenes Laërtius quotes the *Pythagorean Notebooks* from Alexander Polyhistor (ca. 110–40 BCE) in 8.25–33. Cf. Charles H. Kahn, *Pythagoras and the Pythagoreans: A Brief History* (Indianapolis: Hackett, 2001), 79–83. Anthony A. Long, "The Eclectic Pythagoreanism of Alexander Polyhistor," in *Aristotle, Plato and Pythagoreanism in the First Century BC. New Directions for Philosophy,* ed. Malcolm Schofield (Cambridge: Cambridge University Press, 2013), 139–159 argues that Alexander Polyhistor actually forged the work to look like a doxography of Pythagorean philosophy, but according to André Laks, "Diogenes Laertius' *Life of Pythagoras,*" in *A History of Pythagoreanism,* ed. Carl A. Huffman (Cambridge: Cambridge University Press, 2014), 377 the issue "cannot be decided on the basis of the available information."

[38] In Diogenes Laertius 8.33: Ὅρκιόν τ' εἶναι τὸ δίκαιον καὶ διὰ τοῦτο Δία ὅρκιον λέγεσθαι. τήν τ' ἀρετὴν ἁρμονίαν εἶναι καὶ τὴν ὑγίειαν καὶ τὸ ἀγαθὸν ἅπαν καὶ τὸν θεόν· διὸ καὶ καθ' ἁρμονίαν συνεστάναι τὰ ὅλα. φιλίαν τ' εἶναι ἐναρμόνιον ἰσότητα.

[39] Ps.-Ocellus fr. 2 ed. Harder. Stobaeus 3.9.51 introduces the fragment as Ἐκ Πώλου Πυθαγορείου Λευκανοῦ Περὶ δικαιοσύνης. Holger Thesleff, *The Pythagorean Texts of the Hellenistic Period* (Åbo: Åbo Akademie, 1965), 77 emends the text to Ἐκκέλου Πυθαγορείου Λευκανοῦ Περὶ δικαιοσύνης. However, no Eccelus Lucanus is known from the ancient world, so Richard Harder, *Ocellus Lucanus: De universi orbis natura,* Neue phil. Untersuchungen 1 (Berlin: Weidmann, 1926), 26 is right in including the fragment among those of Ocellus Lucanus.

[40] Ps.-Ocellus fr. 2.6–7 ed. Harder: τὰν ὅλων ἀρχὰν διαστραταγοῦσα πρόνοιά τε καὶ ἁρμονία.

[41] Ps.-Ocellus fr. 2.13 ed. Harder. An English translation is available in Kenneth S. Guthrie, *The Pythagorean Sourcebook and Library: An Anthology of Ancient Writings Which Relate to Pythagoras and Pythagorean Philosophy* (Grand Rapids: Phanes, 1987), 253. Guthrie follows Stobaeus in attributing the fragment to Polus.

[42] Ps.-Ocellus fr. 2.1–2 ed. Harder: Δοκεῖ μοι τῶν ἀνδρῶν τὰν δικαιοσύναν ματέρα τε καὶ τιθηνὰν τᾶν ἀλλᾶν ἀρετᾶν προσειπέν·

And, even more boldly, the fragment ends with the conclusion:

> If it thus rears and saves the universe and its parts, making it united and mutually agreeing with each other, how could it not be called with all votes mother and nurse of all things?[43]

Just like in Philo, the expression "mother and nurse" does not refer to Plato's *Timaeus*. In fact, another aspect of motherhood is in view in the use of the metaphor. Whereas in the *Timaeus*, the materiality of the contribution of the mother to the child is emphasized, as well as her receptiveness towards the formative seed of the father, here motherhood denotes primarily a supreme origin, on which other virtues, and indeed, all things, depend. It is in this sense, that Philo uses the expression for wisdom as well.

6.2. *The Decad as "Mother of All Things" in the Hymn to Number*

In a similar way, the expression "mother of all things" is used in the context of Pythagorean arithmology. Again, it is used as a laudatory term, in a hymn in praise of number that is preserved in several Neoplatonist authors. In its fullest extent, it is preserved as follows in Syrian's commentary on the *Metaphysics* of Aristotle:

> For the divine number 'proceeds
> from the hiding-place of the pure Monad, until one comes
> to the sacred Tetrad; she, then, bore the mother of all things,
> all-containing, old, setting a boundary around all things,
> unchangeable, inexhaustible; they call her pure Decad,
> the immortal gods and earthborn men.'[44]

The hymn is quoted twice by Proclus as well; their shared source may have been a lost work of Iamblichus (ca. 240–325 CE).[45] In this hymn, the Decad

---

[43] Ps.-Ocellus fr. 2 ed. Harder, 14–16: εἰ δ᾽ αὐτὰ τὸ ὅλον καὶ τὰ μέρεα οὕτω παιδαγωγεῖ τε καὶ σῴζει ὁμόφρονα καὶ ποτάγορα ἀλλάλοις ἀπεργαζομένα, πῶς οὐ <κα> μάτηρ καὶ τιθηνὰ πασᾶν †τε καὶ πάντων† παμψαφεὶ λέγοιτο;

[44] Syrian, *in Metaph.* M 4, 1078b12, 106.17 ed. Kroll (cf. also Syrian. *in Metaph.* M 8, 1083a12, 147.29 ed. Kroll):
"πρόεισι" γὰρ ὁ θεῖος ἀριθμὸς
"μουνάδος ἐκ κευθμῶνος ἀκηράτου, ἔστ᾽ ἂν ἵκηται
τετράδα ἐπὶ ζαθέην· ἣ δὴ τέκε μητέρα πάντων,
πανδοχέα, πρέσβειραν, ὅρον περὶ πᾶσι τιθεῖσαν,
ἄτροπον, ἀκαμάτην· δεκάδα κλείουσί μιν ἀγνήν.
ἀθάνατοί τε θεοὶ καὶ γηγενέες ἄνθρωποι."

[45] Proclus, *In R.* II 169.25; *In Tim.* I 316.18; II 233.23; III 53.3; 107.14. Cf. also the other arithmological hymns assigned to the *Hymn to Number* by Otto Kern, *Orphicorum Fragmenta* (Berlin: Weidmann, 1922), 320–325 (Orph. fr. 309–317).

is called the "mother of all things," born itself from the Tetrad. Whereas the Monad is praised for its purity, the Decad is praised for its fullness: it is "all-containing," "inexhaustible." We may compare this to what Theon of Smyrna (second century CE) writes about the Decad: "The Decad brings all number to an end, encompassing all nature within it, even and odd, moving and unmoved, good and bad."[46] The all-containing nature of the Decad may have inspired the metaphor of the mother, but it is quite different from the mother-receptacle of the *Timaeus*. This mother is actively limiting, and, moreover, unchangeable and pure, characteristics that are the exact opposite of what Platonists and Pythagoreans would say about matter.

In the hymn, the Decad is called "old" (πρέσβειραν): as mother of all things, it is prior to the universe which it generates. In this respect, it recalls the Platonic world-soul, which the *Timaeus* describes as "prior to and older than the [cosmic] body in origin and virtue."[47] In fact, however, the Decad was equated from the early Academy onwards not with the world-soul, but with the paradigm of the Forms: the Decad contains all numbers, just like the paradigm contains the Forms, so that in the arithmeticized version of the theory of Forms in the early Academy, the Decad could be considered as the paradigm of the Form Numbers.[48] Before Syrian quotes the hymn, he asserts that the Forms exist "mentally and tetradically in the soul, and intellectually and decadically in the demiurgic intellect."[49] This is rather cryptic Neoplatonist terminology, but the idea that number exists as paradigm in the intellect of the Demiurge can be traced back to older Neopythagorean texts, such as the Neopythagorean tradition about Hippasus: "The acousmatics around Hippasus said that Number is the first paradigm of the making of the world, and also that it is the instrument by which the cosmos-making God is able to discern."[50] Likewise, Nicomachus claims in his *Introduction to Arithmetic* (a second century CE school manual that reflects traditional material): "we say that [arithmetic] preexists in the mind of the artificer God before all other things, as a kind of cosmic and paradigmatic *logos*, at which the Craftsman of the universe fixes his eyes, as at a

---

[46] Theon Sm. 106: ἡ μέντοι δεκὰς πάντα περαίνει τὸν ἀριθμόν, ἐμπεριέχουσα πᾶσαν φύσιν ἐντὸς αὑτῆς, ἀρτίου τε καὶ περιττοῦ κινουμένου τε καὶ ἀκινήτου ἀγαθοῦ τε καὶ κακοῦ.

[47] Plato, *Tim.* 34c: καὶ γενέσει καὶ ἀρετῇ προτέραν καὶ πρεσβυτέραν ψυχὴν σώματος.

[48] Cf. Dillon, *Heirs of Plato*, 19–22.

[49] Syrian, *In metaph.* M 4, 1078b12, 106.17 ed. Kroll: νοητῶς μὲν καὶ τετραδικῶς ἐν τῷ αὐτοζῴῳ, νοερῶς δὲ καὶ δεκαδικῶς ἐν <τῷ> δημιουργικῷ νῷ.

[50] Iamblichus, *In. Nic.* 10, 20 (= Hippasus DK 18.11) οἱ δὲ περὶ Ἵππασον ἀκουσματικοὶ ἀριθμὸν εἶπον παράδειγμα πρῶτον κοσμοποιίας καὶ πάλιν κριτικὸν κοσμουργοῦ θεοῦ ὄργανον. Cf. also Iamblichus, *In. Nic.* 10, 12–15.

design and archetypical paradigm, in order to arrange the products made out of matter, and to make them achieve their proper end."[51]

Indeed, if this paradigmatic *logos* in the mind of the Demiurge was described simultaneously as a "mother of all things" that proceeds from the One and actively sets boundaries to everything itself, it would provide an excellent parallel to Philo's description of the demiurgic function of wisdom. The only problem is that the *Hymn to Number* cannot be dated with any certainty before its hypothetical quotation in Iamblichus somewhere around the turn of the third to the fourth century CE. Nevertheless, the use of the expression "mother of the universe" for the Tetractys—the sum of the first four numbers, hence equal to the Decad—can be traced back to the middle of the second century, as I will argue in the next section.

6.3. *Valentinian Teachers on the Tetractys as "Mother of the Universe"*

Irenaeus's *Against the Heresies* furnishes us with a second century attestation for the Pythagorean Tetractys as "mother of the universe." A prominent object of Irenaeus's polemics is Marcus, a Christian teacher who taught a basically Valentinian doctrine with special emphasis on arithmology and speculations about the numerical value of the alphabet.[52] Marcus claimed to have received revelations from the supreme Tetrad or Tetractys, who appeared to him in the form of a woman and explained to him the generation of the *plērōma* of the Aeons from the letters of the divine name, spoken to the Pre-Father (προπάτωρ) by his *logos*.[53] When Irenaeus reports about the genesis of Jesus according to Marcus, he designates this first Tetrad as the "mother of the universe" (μήτηρ τῶν ὅλων).[54]

---

[51] Nicomachus *Ar.* 1.4.2: ἔφαμεν αὐτὴν ἐν τῇ τοῦ τεχνίτου θεοῦ διανοίᾳ προυποστῆναι τῶν ἄλλων ὡσανεὶ λόγον τινὰ κοσμικὸν καὶ παραδειγματικόν, πρὸς ὃν ἀπερειδόμενος ὁ τῶν ὅλων δημιουργὸς ὡς πρὸς προκέντημά τι καὶ ἀρχέτυπον παράδειγμα τὰ ἐκ τῆς ὕλης ἀποτελέσματα κοσμεῖ καὶ τοῦ οἰκείου τέλους τυγχάνειν ποιεῖ. Cf. also section 1.6.1 from the same work. Cf. Kahn, *Pythagoras*, 113.

[52] On Marcus and his community, cf. Niclas Förster, *Marcus Magus: Kult, Lehre und Gemeindeleben einer valentinianischen Gnostikergruppe. Sammlung der Quellen und Kommentar*, WUNT 114 (Tübingen: Mohr Siebeck, 1999).

[53] Irenaeus, *Haer.* 1.14.1–3. In 1.14.1 (p. 206 Rousseau & Doutreleau), Irenaeus states that Marcus claimed that "the supreme Tetrad herself descended to him from the invisible and nameless places in the form of a woman" (Αὐτὴν τὴν πανυπερτάτην ἀπὸ τῶν ἀοράτων καὶ ἀκατονομάστων τόπων Τετράδα κατεληλυθέναι σχήματι γυναικείῳ πρὸς αὐτόν), in 1.14.3 (p. 215 Rousseau and Doutreleau) the same female figure is referred to as the Tetractys (Τετρακτύς).

[54] Irenaeus, *Haer.* 1.15.2 (p. 236 Rousseau and Doutreleau).

Other Valentinian teachers used the expression "mother of all things" for the Tetrad or Tetractys as well, although we do not read that they claimed to have seen the Tetrad in the form of a woman.[55] Irenaeus reports the following interpretation of Gen 1:1:

> For Moses, they say, when he begins his treatise on the creation, points out the mother of the universe right at the start, when he says: "In the beginning, God made heaven and earth." Now, by naming these four: God and beginning, heaven and earth, he represented their Tetractys, as they say.[56]

The expression found its way into liturgical formulas of Valentinian communities as well. Irenaeus reports the following baptismal formula: "Into the name of the unknowable Father of the universe, into Truth, the mother of all things, into Him who descended into Jesus, into union, redemption, and communion with the powers."[57] Here, it is Truth, which counts as "mother of all things," which demonstrates the associative flexibility of these quasi-philosophical Christian systems.[58] Marcus, too, claimed revelations not only of the Tetrad, but also of Truth and of Silence, and the distinctions between these personifications are not always clear.[59] According to Ptolemy, another Valentinian teacher, whose doctrinal system is expounded at length by Irenaeus at the beginning of his work *Against Heresies*, the pre-existent arch-aeon Pre-Beginning, Pre-Father or Abyss emanated Beginning (ἀρχή) as a seed in the womb of Silence, who gave birth to Intellect, and, together with Intellect, Truth. These four (Abyss and Silence, Intellect and Truth) are then identified as "the first and original Pythagorean Tetractys, which they also call root of all things."[60]

---

[55] Cf. Förster, *Marcus Magus*, 10–13, who argues that Irenaeus's account in *Haer.* 1.18–21 concerns Valentinians in general, and not specifically followers of Marcus.

[56] Irenaeus, *Haer.* 1.18.1 (p. 272 Rousseau and Doutreleau): Ὁ γὰρ Μωϋσῆς, φασί, ἀρχόμενος τῆς κατὰ τὴν κτίσιν πραγματείας, εὐθὺς ἐν ἀρχῇ τὴν μητέρα τῶν ὅλων ἐπέδειξεν, εἰπών· Ἐν ἀρχῇ ἐποίησεν ὁ Θεὸς τὸν οὐρανὸν καὶ τὴν γῆν. Τέσσαρα οὖν ταῦτα ὀνομάσας, Θεόν, καὶ ἀρχήν, οὐρανόν, καὶ γῆν, τὴν τετρακτὺν αὐτῶν, ὡς αὐτοὶ λέγουσι, διετύπωσε.

[57] Irenaeus, *Haer.* 1.21.3 (p. 299 Rousseau and Doutreleau): Εἰς ὄνομα ἀγνώστου Πατρὸς τῶν ὅλων, εἰς Ἀλήθειαν μητέρα πάντων, εἰς τὸν κατελθόντα εἰς Ἰησοῦν, εἰς ἔνωσιν καὶ ἀπολύτρωσιν καὶ κοινωνίαν τῶν δυνάμεων.

[58] Cf. Förster, *Marcus Magus*, 406–409.

[59] In Irenaeus, *Haer.* 1.14.3 (p. 215–217 Rousseau and Doutreleau), the Tetractys shows Truth to Marcus, which appears to him as a body of which the body parts are equated with the letters of the alphabet. Moreover, this body is identified as the "mouth of unspoken Silence" (τῆς σιωπωμένης Σιγῆς στόμα, p. 217 Rousseau and Doutreleau) and in 1.15.1 (p. 233 Rousseau and Doutreleau) it is all-wise Silence who relates to Marcus the genesis of the twenty-four letters.

[60] Irenaeus, *Haer.* 1.1.1 (p. 28–30 Rousseau and Doutreleau), quote on p. 30 Rousseau & Doutreleau: πρώτην καὶ ἀρχέγονον Πυθαγορικὴν Τετρακτύς, ἣν καὶ ῥίζαν τῶν πάντων καλοῦσιν·

Thus, although the appearance of the Tetractys as a woman seems to have been an invention of Marcus, its central place in the generation of the *plērōma* was shared by other Valentinians. The background of this concept is clearly Pythagorean,[61] and Irenaeus attacks Marcus for not admitting this, "when he spoke about the Pythagorean Tetractys as origin and mother of all things."[62]

Hence, if the Valentinian Christians inherited the notion of the Tetractys as "mother of the universe" or "mother of all things" from Pythagoreanism, it must have been current around the middle of the second century at the latest, and it is not too farfetched to presume that the expression was in use a century earlier, in Philo's time, as well.

7. Conclusion: the value of the Neopythagorean parallels for understanding Philo

Now that we have established the use of the expression "mother of all things" both for justice (in a Pythagorean pseudepigraph, first-century BCE or CE) and for the Tetractys or Decad (middle of the second century CE), what is the value of these parallels for the interpretation of Philo's depiction of wisdom as mother? I think that three conclusions can be drawn from the parallels, with the third conclusion being the most tentative one.

Firstly, the parallel demonstrates the importance of the Pythagorean literature for understanding Philo's highly metaphorical language. Ps.-Ocellus praises justice as mother of all things not because he regards Justice as a cosmic mother goddess, but as a metaphor for the crucial role of this virtue in all the levels of the universe. Philo exploits this metaphorical language to an unprecedented extent because of the great source of imagery which he has at his disposal in the narratives of the Pentateuch.

Secondly, the parallel with the description of the Tetractys or Decad suggests that Philo applied epithets from Pythagorean arithmology to the personification of wisdom which he inherited from the Jewish wisdom literature. We have better evidence of this process with regard to the epithet "motherless" (ἀμήτωρ), which is used by Philo a couple of times to designate Wisdom or Virtue (allegorically represented by Sarah, of whom Abraham said that she was "the daughter of my father, but not the daughter of my mother" [Gen 20:12], which Philo takes to indicate that Sarah was

---

[61] On the Tetractys in Neopythagoreanism, cf. Theon Sm. 93–99.

[62] Irenaeus, *Haer.* 2.14.6 (p. 140 Rousseau and Doutreleau): *Pythagorae quaternationem uelut genesim et matrem omnium enarrans.*

motherless).[63] In all other occurrences, however, Philo uses "motherless" to describe the number seven, drawing on a Pythagorean arithmological source which likened the generation of the seven from the one (without any "mother" number within the Decad) to Athena's birth from Zeus.[64] Moreover, wisdom is related to the number seven in several ways: already in Prov 8:30–31 LXX, personified wisdom is associated with God's rest on the seventh day. Aristobulus interprets the seventh day allegorically as the first day, as the origin of light, which he connects with the Wisdom from Prov 8:22–31.[65] Finally, Philo, in his treatise *On the Creation of the World*, regards the intellectual light created on the first day as the *seventh* creation,[66] which, as the image of the *logos*, is "again incorporeal and intelligible paradigm of the sun and of all the light-bearing stars which [God] would set up together in the heaven."[67] In *On the Migration of Abraham*, however, it is wisdom which is "the archetypical sunlight, of which the sun is a copy and image."[68] Thus, analogously to the application of the Hebdomad's epithet "motherless" to wisdom, one could speculate that Philo applied the Decad's epithet "mother of all things / of the universe" to wisdom.

Finally, and most tentatively, I would suggest not only that the use of the metaphor "mother of all things" was taken from the Decad or Tetractys, but also that the underlying concept of the Decad as paradigm in the mind of the Demiurge, which actively applies itself to reality, influenced Philo's depiction of the demiurgic function of wisdom. When *Ebr.* 30–33 describes Wisdom as the "Maker's knowledge" which receives from God the seed of γένεσις in order to give birth to the visible cosmos, this is most naturally understood as the generation of the visible cosmos from the intelligible cosmos as it existed in God's intellect. The use of the biological metaphor gives Philo's depiction in *Ebr.* 30–33 an emanative touch that is different from the craft metaphors used by Plato in his depiction of the Demiurge in

---

[63] *QG* 4.145; *Ebr.* 61; *Her.* 62.

[64] *Mos.* 2.210; *Decal.* 102; *QG* 2.12; *Her.* 170; 216; *Opif.* 100 (where the Pythagorean association of the 7 with Athena is mentioned); *Spec.* 2.56. On the arithmological source, cf. Frank E. Robbins, "The Tradition of Greek Arithmology," *CP* 16,2 (1921): 97–123.

[65] Eusebius, *Praep. ev.* 13.11.9–13 (=Holladay fr. 5). The association of wisdom with the light created on the first day may actually be suggested in Prov 8 LXX as well, as David-Marc d'Hamonville and Épiphane Dumouchet, *Les Proverbes*, La Bible d'Alexandrie 17 (Paris: Cerf, 2000), 90–91 argue.

[66] After the heaven, the earth, the darkness (i.e., air), the abyss (i.e., the void), water and spirit (πνεῦμα), *Opif.* 29.

[67] *Opif.* 29, ὃ πάλιν ἀσώματον ἦν καὶ νοητὸν ἡλίου παράδειγμα καὶ πάντων ὅσα φωσφόρα ἄστρα κατὰ τὸν οὐρανὸν ἔμελλε συνίστασθαι.

[68] *Migr.* 40, αὕτη θεοῦ τὸ ἀρχέτυπον [ἡλίου] φέγγος, οὗ μίμημα καὶ εἰκὼν ἥλιος.

the *Timaeus* and other late dialogues.[69] It is precisely this emanative aspect that comes to the fore in the description of the generation of the Tetractys from the One, and of the cosmos from the Tetractys as "mother of the universe," in the Neopythagorean texts which we have examined. It is hard to imagine that Philo would not be attracted by such a depiction, especially since his use of the concept of wisdom allows him to describe the coming-to-be of the world without the need for a world-soul.[70] At least, Philo's depiction of wisdom shows more resemblance to the Pythagorean Tetractys than to the Pythagorean Dyad, which John Dillon proposed as standing behind Philo's wisdom figure. Nonetheless, we lack the evidence necessary to prove definitively that Philo indeed used the Pythagorean Tetractys to enhance his understanding of the metaphysical function of wisdom.

Radboud University, Nijmegen
The Netherlands

---

[69] Outside the *Timaeus*, god is presented as cosmic craftsman in Plato, *Soph.* 265c, *Pol.* 273b and *Phileb.* 27d.

[70] Cf. Runia, *The End of Hellenistic Theology*, (2002), 295: "Philo tries to develop a basically Platonist view of creation without allowing any room for a world-soul." Cf. also Runia, *Philo and Plato's* Timaeus (1986), 204–208.

The Studia Philonica Annual 27 (2015): 71–85

THE THEFT OF PHILOSOPHY:
PHILO OF ALEXANDRIA AND NUMENIUS
OF APAMEA

GREGORY E. STERLING

Eusebius of Caesarea devoted the eleventh and twelfth books of his *Praeparatio evangelica* to the demonstration of the harmony between Platonic philosophy and Christian thought. In a famous comment following a citation of Numenius, the Bishop of Caesarea said: "Numenius wrote these things, clearly interpreting the statements of Plato and the much earlier statements of Moses. It is fitting that that saying is attributed to him in which he is remembered to have said, 'What is Plato but Moses speaking in Attic?'"[1] The saying became a commonplace in early Christian writers and is attested in Clement of Alexandria,[2] twice in Eusebius,[3] and in Theodoretus.[4] The tenth century Suda, like Eusebius, attributed it to Numenius.[5]

The relation between Moses and Plato was unsurprisingly important for early Christians who were anxious to demonstrate the antiquity of their new religion. It is surprising to find that it was important to the first attested witness and putative source of the aphorism, Numenius of Apamea.[6] How did a pagan philosopher come to have such a positive view of Moses and Judaism?

---

[1] For the *Praeparatio evangelica* see Karl Mras, *Die Praeparatio evangelica*, GCS 43.1–2 (Berlin: Akademie Verlag, 1954). The statement is frg. 8 in Édouard des Places, *Numénius Fragments*, 2ⁿᵈ ed. (Paris: Les Belles Lettres, 2003).

[2] Clement, *Strom.* 1.22.150.4 (=Menahem Stern, *Greek and Latin Authors on Jews and Judaism,* 2 vols. [Jerusalem: The Israel Academy of Sciences and Humanities, 1974], §363a [2:209]). Hereafter abbreviated *GLAJJ*.

[3] Eusebius, *Praep. ev.* 9.6.9 (*GLAJJ* §363b [2:209–210]) and *Praep. ev.* 11.10.14 (*GLAJJ* §363c [2:210]).

[4] Theodoretus of Cyrrhus, *Graecorum affectionum curatio* 2.114 (*GLAJJ* §363d [2:210]).

[5] Suda, Νουμήνιος (*GLAJJ* §363e [2:210–211]).

[6] John G. Gager, *Moses in Greco-Roman Paganism*, SBLMS 16 (Nashville: Abingdon, 1972), 66–68, defended the authenticity of the saying.

Unfortunately we know very little about Numenius.[7] We know that, like Poseidonius, he came from the rather large city of Apamea.[8] Johannes Lydus referred to him as "Numenius the Roman," perhaps a hint that he spent some time teaching in the capital of the empire.[9] This might help to explain the role of his works in the school of Plotinus.[10] His dates are not known specifically, although it is safe to put his *floruit* in the mid-second century CE, prior to Clement of Alexandria.[11]

We have fragments of four works:[12] *Concerning the Good* (frags. 1–22), *Concerning the Secrets of Plato* (frags. 23), *Concerning the Dissension of the Academicians with Plato* (frags. 24–28), and *Concerning the Incorruptibility of the Soul* (frag. 29). Thanks to Origen, we know that he wrote at least three other works: *The Hoopoe, Concerning Numbers,* and *Concerning Place* (frag. 8). In addition to the twenty-nine fragments that we can attribute to the first four works, we have another thirty-two fragments that cannot be placed, including one doubtful fragment (frags. 29–60; frag. 60 is dubious).

What led Numenius to form such a positive impression of Judaism? More particularly, did the works of Philo of Alexandria play any role in the formation of his judgment? Like many others, I have noted some of the similarities between the two in earlier works but always in connection with larger concerns.[13] I have long thought that it would be worthwhile to do

---

[7] The most helpful recent discussions include Philip Merlan, "Greek Philosophy from Plato to Plotinus," in *The Cambridge History of Later Greek and Early Medieval Philosophy,* ed. A. H. Armstrong (Cambridge: Cambridge University Press, 1970), 96–106; John Dillon, *The Middle Platonists (80 B.C. to A. D. 220)* (Ithaca, NY: Cornell University Press, 1977), 361–379; Michael Frede, "Numenius," *ANRW* II.36.3:1034–1075; and idem, "Numenius," *Brill's New Pauly* 9:896–898.

[8] On Apamea see Henri-Charles Puech, "Numénius d'Apamée et les theologies orientales au second siècle," *Melanges Bildez* 2 (1934): 745–778, esp. 749–754. *CIL* no. 6687, reports a population of 117,000 at the time of Quirinius's census in the first century CE.

[9] Frg. 57.

[10] Porphyry, *Vit. Plot.* 14, Numenius was read in Plotinus's school; 17, Plotinus was accused of plagiarizing Numenius. See also *Vit. Plot.* 3, where Amelius who wrote out the works of Numenius was part of Plotinus's school.

[11] The *terminus ante quem* is the reference in Clement, *Strom.* 1.22.150.4. Some place him in the first half of the second century (e.g., Jan H. Waszink) and some in the second half (e.g., Édouard des Places).

[12] I have used the edition of des Places, *Numénius Fragments.* There is an older edition with an English translation: Kenneth Guthrie, *Numenius of Apamea, the Father of Neo-Platonism: Works, Biography, Message, Sources, and Influence* (London: G. Bell & Sons, 1917; repr., *The Neoplatonic Writings of Numenius,* Great Works of Philosophy Series 4 [Lawrence, KS: Selene Books, 1987]).

[13] Gregory E. Sterling, "Platonizing Moses: Philo and Middle Platonism," *SPhiloA* 5 (1993): 96–111, esp. 108–110, and idem, "Recherché or Representative? What Is the

more than to give a passing nod to this issue. Two reasons have motivated my thinking. First, in spite of the fragmentary nature of Numenius's evidence, there is more to work with here than there is with any other philosopher. Second, Numenius had a significant impact on Plotinus who also shares some striking conceptual parallels with Philo of Alexandria.[14] Clarification of the relationship between Philo and Numenius might help us understand possible ties with Plotinus as well.

The Transmission of Numenius's Works

We need to begin by noting the line of transmission of Numenius's works. Numenius's *Concerning the Good*, an exposition of the understanding of the divine in Plato and in oriental traditions, was preserved primarily by Origen and Eusebius: twenty of the twenty-two fragments that have come down to us appear in either Origen's *Contra Celsum*[15] or Eusebius's *Praeparatio evangelica*.[16] There are also two parallel fragments preserved by Nemesius, the fourth century bishop of Emesa,[17] and Calcidius, another fourth century Christian,[18] and two additional fragments preserved by Proclus.[19] The same route of transmission is also true for *Concerning the Secrets of*

Relationship between Philo's Treatises and Greek-Speaking Judaism?" *SPhiloA* 11 (1999): 1–30, esp. 18–19.

[14] On the relationship between Numenius and Plotinus see Fredrich Theodinga, "Plotin oder Numenios?" *Hermes* 52 (1917): 592–612; 54 (1919): 249–278; 57 (1922): 189–218; and A. H. Armstrong, *The Architecture of the Intelligible Universe in the Philosophy of Plotinus*, Cambridge Classical Studies (Cambridge: Cambridge University Press, 1940), 7–9. On the debate whether Plotinus knew the works of Philo see David T. Runia, *Philo in Early Christian Literature: A Survey*, CRINT III.3 (Assen: Van Gorcum; Philadelphia: Fortress, 1993) 9–11 and Sterling, "Recherché or Representative?" 29.

[15] Frag. 1b (=Origen, *Cels.* 1.15), 1c (=Origen, *Cels.* 4.51), 10a (=Origen, *Cels.* 4.51).

[16] Frag. 1a (=Eusebius, *Praep. ev.* 9.7.1), 2 (=Eusebius, *Praep. ev.* 11.21.7–22), 3 (=Eusebius, *Praep. ev.* 15.17.1–2), 4a (=Eusebius, *Praep. ev.* 15.17.3–8), 5 (=Eusebius, *Praep. ev.* 11.9.8–10), 6 (=Eusebius, *Praep. ev.* 11.10.6–8), 7 (=Eusebius, *Praep. ev.* 11.10.9–11), 8 (=Eusebius, *Praep. ev.* 11.10.12–14), 9 (=Eusebius, *Praep. ev.* 9.8.1–2), 11 (=Eusebius, *Praep. ev.* 11.17.11–18), 12 (=Eusebius, *Praep. ev.* 11.18.6–10), 13 (=Eusebius, *Praep. ev.* 11.18.13–14), 14 (=Eusebius, *Praep. ev.* 11.18.15–19), 15 (=Eusebius, *Praep. ev.* 11.18.20-21), 16 (=Eusebius, *Praep. ev.* 11.22.3–5), 17 (=Eusebius, *Praep. ev.* 11.18.22–23), 18 (=Eusebius, *Praep. ev.* 11.18.24), 19 (=Eusebius, *Praep. ev.* 11.22.6–8), 20 (=Eusebius, *Praep. ev.* 11.22.9–10).

[17] Frag. 4b (=Nemesius, *Concerning the Nature of Man*, 2.8–14) which parallels Frag 4a (=Eusebius, *Praep. ev.* 15.17.3–8).

[18] Frag. 10b (=Calcidius, *In Timaeum* 295–299) which is a much fuller version of the material in 10a (=Origen, *Cels.* 4.51).

[19] Frags. 21 (=Proclus, *In Timaeum* 1.303.27–34), 22 (=Proclus, *In Timaeum* 3.103.28–32).

Plato,[20] *Concerning the Dissension of the Academicians with Plato*,[21] and *Concerning the Incorruptibility of the Soul*:[22] Eusebius preserved the fragments for the first two of these and Origen for the last. Twelve different authors preserved the fragments that cannot be attributed to a specific work: Porphyry has nine,[23] Proclus six,[24] Iamblichus[25] and Lydus[26] four each, Macrobius three,[27] Olympiodorus two,[28] and five authors one fragment each.[29]

The data suggest that Origen had a copy of some of Numenius's works in the library that he brought from Alexandria to Caesarea where he used them when he wrote *Contra Celsum*[30] and the later bishop used them when he wrote the *Praeparatio evangelica*. There is an alternative view that Eusebius encountered the works of Numenius in Apamea where Amelius may have taken them.[31] While this is possible, Origen's use of Numenius when he wrote *Contra Celsum* late in his life when he resided in Caesarea, suggests that the Alexandrian brought Numenius's works with him to Caesarea where they became a part of the Episcopal library that Eusebius knew and used.[32] It is well known that this is also the primary line of transmission for the writings of Philo of Alexandria.[33]

The common route of the transmission of the works of two authors leads us to ask whether there is any connection between the two corpuses during their transmission. Henri Dominique Saffey pointed out that there are three sections in Eusebius's eleventh book of the *Praeparatio evangelica*

---

[20] Frag. 23 (=Eusebius, *Praep. ev.* 13.4.4–5.2).

[21] Frags. 24 (=Eusebius, *Praep. ev.* 14.4.16–59), 25 (=Eusebius, *Praep. ev.* 14.5.10–16), 26 (=Eusebius, *Praep. ev.* 14.7.1–15), 27 (=Eusebius, *Praep. ev.* 14.8.1–15), 28 (=Eusebius, *Praep. ev.* 14.9.1–4).

[22] Frag. 29 (=Origen, *Cels.* 4.57).

[23] Frags. 30, 31, 32, 33, 36, 44, 45, 46c, 60.

[24] Frags. 35, 37, 39, 40, 50, 51.

[25] Frags. 41, 42, 43, 48.

[26] Frags. 56, 57, 58 59.

[27] Frags. 34, 54, 55.

[28] Frags. 38, 46a.

[29] Aeneas Gazaeus frag. 49; Calcidius frag. 52; Ioannes Philoponus frag. 47; Origen frag. 53; and Syrianus frag. 46b.

[30] Eusebius, *Hist. eccl.* 6.36.2. For a discussion, see Henry Chadwick, *Origen:* Contra Celsum: *Translated with an Introduction and Notes* (Cambridge: Cambridge University Press, 1953), xiv-xv.

[31] Luc Brisson, "Amelius," *ANRW* II.36.2: 809.

[32] So also Andrew James Carriker, *The Library of Eusebius of Caesarea*, VCSup 67 (Leiden: Brill, 2003), 94–95. On the contents of Origen's library see ibid, 8–9 and Arthur J. Droge, *Homer or Moses? Early Christian Interpretations of the History of Culture*, HUT 26 (Tübingen: Mohr Siebeck, 1989), 191–192.

[33] The most important treatment of this is Runia, *Philo in Early Christian Literature*, 16–31.

where the bishop provided alternating citations between the biblical text on the one hand and Plato and Numenius's *Concerning the Good* as a commentary on Plato on the other hand. He called these "dossiers." Saffey argued that Eusebius took these juxtapositions over directly from Numenius or through the intermediate agency of Clement or Origen.[34] Andrew Carriker argued that Eusebius was himself responsible for the juxtapositions.[35]

This source critical debate forces us to ask whether there are any indications that Eusebius or Origen before him linked a Philonic text with a Numenian text. The best way to answer this question is to look for places in the *Praeparatio evangelica* where Philo's texts were juxtaposed with Numenius's fragments. There is only one place where this occurs. Eusebius opened his discussion of the Second Cause by setting out the biblical texts followed by Philonic commentary. He then turned to the Platonic tradition and used the same pattern: he cited the Pseudo-Platonic *Epinomis* and then quotations from Plotinus and Numenius that served as commentaries. Eusebius's use of Plotinian texts suggests that the juxtaposition of the biblical and Platonic tradition was his own—although it is possible that he inserted the texts from Plotinus into an earlier pattern that he had found.

Since Eusebius had found Philo's discussion of the Logos as a compatible witness to Numenius's presentation of the Second Cause, we should ask whether Numenius had already made the connection. The only way to answer this is to ask whether any of the biblical texts that Eusebius cited as a warrant for the Second Cause or the citations of *Epinomis* 986C and 322C were found in Philo. The biblical texts that Eusebius cited can be grouped into three clusters: texts that use a double reference to the Lord showing that there is another Lord besides God,[36] texts that refer to the Word of God as God's agent,[37] and texts that, in Eusebius's reading, refer to Wisdom as a hypostasis.[38] Only one of these is from the Pentateuch, the first text in Eusebius's list and the only one also to appear in Philo. Genesis 19:24 reads: "the Lord rained upon Sodom and Gomorrah brimstone and fire from the Lord out of heaven." Eusebius drew a distinction between "the Lord" and "from the Lord." While Philo used the text to describe the Logos based on

---

[34] Henri D. Saffey, "Les extraits du Περὶ τἀγαθοῦ de Numénius dans le livre XI de la Préparation évangelique d'Eusèbe de Césarée," *StPatr* 13 (1975): 46–51 and idem, "Un lecteur antique des oeuvres de Numénius: Eusèbe de Césarée," *Forma futuri: Studi in onore del Cardinale Michele Pellegrino* (Torino: Bottega d'Erasmo, 1975), 145–153.

[35] Carriker, *The Library of Eusebius of Caesarea*, 92–95.

[36] Gen 19:24; Ps 110:1.

[37] Ps 33:6; 107:20.

[38] Prov 8:12, 22; 3:19; Wis 7:21; 6:22; 7:22; 8:1.

the reference to the sun in the previous verse,[39] he did not draw the distinction between the two references to the Lord.[40] Similarly, there is no evidence that he cited the Pseudo-Platonic *Epinomis*.[41] In short, I could not find any evidence that Philo and Numenius were directly linked prior to Eusebius, only that early Christians found them important sources for the harmonization of biblical and Platonic thought.

Numenius and the Jews

We are now ready to turn to the fragments of Numenius. Before we explore the fragments that may have overlap with Philo, we need to address the larger question of Numenius's treatment of the Jews. Numenius knew and used Jewish material and used it often. Eusebius reported that he referred to "the Brahmans, Jews, Magi, and Egyptians" as oriental peoples who grasped and taught ancient wisdom.[42] Origen said that Numenius included the Jews among the nations who considered God incorporeal "and did not hesitate to make use of the prophetic oracles and to interpret them allegorically in his writings."[43] The Christian scholar repeated this when he wrote that Numenius "frequently sets out the teachings of Moses in his writings and interprets them allegorically in a credible way."[44] Numenius's esteem for Moses was striking and is most famously captured by the aphorism with which we opened: "What is Plato but Moses speaking in Attic?"[45] Numenius knew stories about Moses and referred to the legendary Jannes and Jambres, the Egyptian scribes,[46] who successfully competed with Moses as Moses tried to free the Hebrew people.[47] Numenius referred to Moses both as "Moses" (Μωσῆς)[48] and as "Musaios" (Μουσαῖος),[49] making

---

[39] Philo, *Somn.* 1.85–86.

[40] For other Philonic allusions to Gen 19:24 see *Deus* 60; *Ebr.* 223; *Abr.* 138, 142; *Mos.* 2.53, 55, 263; *QG* 4.51.

[41] See David Lincicum, "A Preliminary Index to Philo's Non-Biblical Citations and Allusions," *SPhiloA* 25 (2013): 139–167, esp. 156–159, for the references to Plato's works.

[42] Frag. 1a (=Eusebius, *Praep. ev.* 9.7.1).

[43] Frag. 1b (=Orign, *Cels.* 1.15)

[44] Frag. 1c (=Origen, *Cels.* 4.51).

[45] Frag. 8 (=Eusebius, *Praep. ev.* 9.6.9).

[46] Frags. 9 (=Eusebius, *Praep. ev.* 9.8.1–2) and 10a (=Origen, *Cels.* 4.51). Numenius is not the only pagan to know this tradition. See also Pliny, *Nat.* 30.11 (*GLAJJ* §221 [1:498–499]) and Apuleius, *Apol.* 90 (*GLAJJ* § 361 [2:203–204]).

[47] Frag. 9 (=Eusebius, *Praep. ev.* 9.8.2). See also 2 Tim 3:8.

[48] Frag. 8 (=Eusebius, *Praep. ev.* 9.6.9).

[49] Frag. 9 (*bis*) (=Eusebius, *Praep. ev.* 9.8.1–2).

the same move that the earlier Jewish author Artapanus made when he connected Moses to the Orphic tradition.[50] Origen's claim that Numenius used the Jewish Scriptures appears to be confirmed by two of the fragments: one has an allusion to Exodus 3:14 (see below)[51] and the other cited Genesis 1:2 : "They (i.e., the Jews) hold that souls settle on the God-inspired water, as Numenius says that it was for this reason that the prophet said that God's spirit hovered over the water."[52] Finally, Numenius knew something about the Jerusalem temple and the exclusive nature of the Jewish cult.[53]

Why did Numenius use Jewish material? Scholars have—unsurprisingly—been divided. Some have thought that Numenius was syncretistic and combined sources eclectically, drawing from sources based on their appeal to his wider but unsystematic perspective.[54] Others have argued that he gave an *interpretatio Graeca* to oriental material, but his allegiances were clearly to the Greek philosophical tradition.[55] Still others have argued that Numenius was not syncretistic, but grasped an underlying unity in Eastern traditions and Western philosophy.[56]

We will begin by looking at Numenius's own statement: "With respect to this it will be necessary, after having stated and interpreted the testimonies of Plato, to return to and unite them with the views of Pythagoras." He continued, "then to summon the highly regarded nations, adducing their rites, teachings, and basic tenets as far as they concur with Plato—whatever

---

[50] Artapanus frag. 3 (=Eusebius, *Praep. ev.* 9.27.3). Jacob Freudenthal, *Alexander Polyhistor und die von ihm erhaltenen Reste jüdischer und samaritanischer Geschichtswerke*, Hellenistische Studien (Beslau: H. Skutsch, 1875), 173, thought that Numenius knew Artapanus. Albert Pietersma, *The Apocryphon of Jannes & Jambres the Magicians: Edited with Introduction and Commentary*, RGRW 119 (Leiden: Brill, 1994), 3–4, is appropriately much more skeptical.

[51] Frag. 13 (=Eusebius, *Praep. ev.* 9.18.14).

[52] Frag. 30 (=Porphyry, *Antr. nymph.* 10).

[53] Frag. 56 (Lydus, *De mensibus* 4.53).

[54] Some of the most important representatives are Puech, "Numénius d'Apamée," 747 and E. R. Dodds, "Numenius and Ammonius," *Entretiens sur l'Antiquité Classique, Vol. 5: Les Sources des Plotin* (Genève: Fondation Hardt, 1957), 4–11, esp. 11: "The main fabric of Numenius' thought is no doubt derived from Neopythagorean tradition (I should rather call him a Neopythagorean rather than a Middle Platonist). But because he was as Macrobius says *occultorum curiosior*, he welcomed all the superstitions of his time, whatever their origin, and thereby contributed to the eventual degradation of Greek philosophical thought."

[55] The most important representative of this position is André J. Festugière, *La Révélation d'Hermès Trismégiste*, 4 vols., 1st–3rd ed. (Paris: J. Gabalda, 1949–1954), 4:130–132. Festugière called the appeal of Eastern traditions "le mirage oriental" (1:20).

[56] I have argued this in "Platonizing Moses," 110.

the Brahmans, Jews, Magi, and Egyptians have to say."[57] Numenius's agenda appears to have involved three steps. First, he wanted to clarify Plato's teachings. His work, *Concerning the Dissension of the Academicians with Plato* (frags. 24–28), rejected not only the skepticism of the New Academy that began with Arcesilaus and Carneades, but also appears to have broken ranks with Antiochus of Ascalon by rejecting his claim that he had returned to the Old Academy.[58] Numenius's call *ad fontes* was essentially a call to return to Plato without the benefit of the Stoa as Antiochus had done. The second step was to demonstrate the connection between Plato and Pythagoras.[59] It is for this reason that it is possible to debate whether Numenius was a Middle Platonist or a Neopythagorean. He claimed allegiance to both and argued for the unity of thought. The third and final step in his system was to work back to the ancient peoples of the East, a move that included but was not restricted to the Jews. He thought that, just as it was possible to understand Platonic and Pythagorean thought as unified, so it was possible to perceive some forms of Eastern and Western thought as unified.

This is a different perspective than what some have claimed for Numenius. For example, the Suda's entry on Numenius reads: "He is the one who accused the mind of Plato of having stolen the concept of God and the origins of the cosmos from Moses. For this reason he said, 'What is Plato but Moses speaking in Attic?'"[60] The implication of this view is that Plato read Moses and plagiarized him. As bizarre as this is to us, this was not an impossible view to hold in the ancient world. Aristobulus argued that there was a Greek translation prior to the LXX in Egypt.[61] A significant number of authors mentioned Plato's visit to Egypt. It was possible for some to put these pieces together and to conclude that Numenius believed that Plato

---

[57] Frag. 1a (=Eusbeius, *Praep. ev.* 9.7.1).

[58] Frag. 24 (=Eusebius, *Praep. ev.* 14.4.16–59). Dillon, *the Middle Platonists*, 365, has an apt summary: "Last, but not least, we have, preserved by Eusebius, lengthy passages from a racy and entertaining polemic entitled *On the Divergence of the Academics from Plato*, a survey of the skeptical new Academy from Arcesilaus to Philo of Larisa (with, it must be added, a final broadside directed against Antiochus for going over to Stoicism), alleging personal motives of an unphilosophical nature for Arcesilaus' desertion of true Platonism."

[59] See also frags. 7 (=Eusebius, *Praep. ev.* 11.10.9–11), 24 (=Eusebius, *Praep. ev.* 14.4.16–59), 52 (=Calcidius, *In Timaeum* 295–299).

[60] Suda, Νουμήνιος (*GLAJJ* §363e [2:210–211]).

[61] So Aristobulus frag. 3 (=Eusebius, *Praep. ev.* 13.12.1) and 3a (=Clement, *Strom.* 1.22.150.1–3).

had read a Greek version of Moses's writings on his visit to Egypt.[62] This is, however, far from necessary and becomes unduly complicated. It would also require—at least if the argument is to be consistent—that Pythagoras made a visit to Egypt and read Moses in Greek translation as well! It is more credible to think that while Numenius recognized the antiquity of the Brahmans, Jews, Magi, and Egyptians, he thought of a common wisdom about the ultimate realities.[63] Subsequent authors turned his view into the "theft of philosophy" argument for apologetic purposes.

What place did the Jews have among these ancients? The amount of material that we have about the Jews in Numenius is more extensive than the amount that we have about the Brahmans, Magi, or Egyptians. This has led some to conclude that Numenius considered the Jews to be the most ancient people and therefore the most significant.[64] This may be over-reading the evidence that we have. We should remember that the fragments that we have considered came down to us largely through Origen and Eusebius who had a natural bias towards the inclusion of Jewish material. Numenius could have just as easily included Babylonian and Egyptian material that Origen and Eusebius elected not to include.

Where did Numenius acquire his knowledge of Jewish traditions? Some have argued that Numenius was a Jew.[65] This, however, does not seem likely to me. While there are other examples of Jewish authors who are open to different traditions, for example, Artapanus claimed that Moses established the Egyptian cults,[66] openness to Jewish views does not require ethnic identity. There are some differences between Jews who were open to the views of others and pagans who were open to the views of Jews. The fundamental difference between Artapanus and Numenius is that there is no evidence that Numenius traced everything back to the Jewish tradition. If, our argument above is correct, Judaism was only one of several traditions that he found acceptable and these were measured by their agreement with the Platonic-Pythagorean tradition that he reconstructed.

---

[62] For an example of a modern author who holds this position see Droge, *Homer or Moses?* 62–65.

[63] So also Stern, *GLAJJ*, 2:209.

[64] Droge, *Homer or Moses?* 146–149 and Peter Pilhofer, *Presbyteron Kreitton: Der Alterbeweis der jüdischen und christlichen Apologeten und seine Vorgeschichte*, WUNT 2.39 (Tübingen: Mohr Siebeck, 1990), 218–220, esp. 219.

[65] Charles Bigg, *The Christian Platonists of Alexandria* (Oxford: Clarendon Press; New York: Macmillan, 1886; repr., New York: AMS, 1970), 300 n. 1, and Puech, "Numénius d'Apamée," 754, 774, who thinks that he may have been Jewish but was certainly a Semite.

[66] Artapanus frag. 3 (=Eusebius, *Praep. Ev.* 9.27.4).

A second possibility is that he learned these traditions from the Jewish community in Apamea. Josephus claimed that it was one of three cities in Syria where the local populace did not react against the local Jewish community at the outbreak of the First Jewish War. The historian wrote: "Only Antioch, Sidon, and Apamea spared those residing there and did not allow any Jews to be killed or imprisoned; perhaps because of their own populace they disdained Jewish uprisings, but more likely in my opinion because they took pity on people in whom they saw no evidence of revolution."[67] Numenius could have learned about Jewish traditions from his local community as well as other communities that he might have visited or dwelled.

The question that we must now address is whether we can identify specific literary sources for Numenius. It appears that he knew a Greek translation of the Pentateuch—whether directly or indirectly is debatable. He may have known the *Apocryphon of Jannes and Jambres*.[68] The question that we need to ask is whether he knew the works of Philo of Alexandria.

Philo and Numenius

The two shared a common outlook. Both were part of a larger tradition that brought sacred Eastern texts into alignment with Greek philosophical thought through allegorical exegesis. They were not alone: Chaeremon, the Egyptian priest and Stoic philosopher, interpreted Egyptian mythology via Stoicism. Westerners also participated: Plutarch's essay *On Isis and Osiris* is a good example.[69] Philo expressed the basic perspective as succinctly as anyone: "For what comes to the adherents of the most esteemed philosophy, comes to the Jews through their laws and customs, namely the knowledge of the highest and most ancient Cause of all and the rejection of the deception of created gods."[70] For Philo and for Numenius, the place where the greatest intersection occurred was in the understanding of the divine. It is to this understanding that we turn.

Numenius wrote: "Again, just as there is rapport between the cultivator (γεωργός) and the planter (ὁ φυτεύων), the first God has the same rapport with the Demiurge." He explained: "The Self-Existent (ὁ μέν γε ὤν) sows the seed of every soul into everything that participates in him. The Lawgiver

---

[67] Josephus, *B.J.* 2.479. This is the view of Pilhofer, *Presbyteron kreitton*, 220.

[68] Pietersma, *The Apocryphon of Jannes and Jambres the Magicians*, 24–25.

[69] For details see Sterling, "Platonizing Moses," 103–107.

[70] Philo, *Virt.* 65. See also *Spec.* 2.164–167.

plants, distributes, and transplants into each of us what has already been set down by the former."[71] There are several fascinating hints in this fragment. First, Numenius juxtaposed the cultivator and the planter. It is hard not to think of the two-treatise work that Philo composed *Concerning Agriculture* (Περὶ γεωργίας) that today we know as *De agricultura* and *De plantatione*.[72] The juxtaposition was probably common, but it is worth noting that the concept of planting in both Philo and Numenius is common: God plants in the human soul.[73]

Second, Numenius referred to the first God as the Self-Existent (ὁ μέν γε ὤν). E. R. Dodds thought that the Greek was problematic and proposed an emendation to ὁ μέν γε α′ ὤν (= πρῶτος θεός). The problem is that it is difficult to relate the actions of the First God and the Demiurge consistently to Plato's descriptions of them in *Timaeus* 41C-D: the functions of Plato's Demiurge are here transferred to the First God. Further, Dodd thought that the line ὁ μέν γε ὤν σπέρμα πάσης ψυχῆς σπείρει required a predicate for ὁ ὤν.[74] John Whittaker correctly recognized that this was not necessary if the phrase ὁ ὤν is recognized as a Septuagintalism based on Exod 3:14.[75] The Jewish translators of the famous אהיה אשר אהיה by ἐγώ εἰμι ὁ ὤν made the construction a substantive that does not require a predicate. Whittaker is undoubtedly correct. The masculine reference to the First Cause is striking: this is the only time that Numenius used it. His standard way to refer to the First Cause is by the neuter τὸ ὄν that appears 22 times in the extant fragments.[76] The neuter is drawn from Plato's *Timaeus* and is expected in a second century Platonist.[77] The singular use of ὁ ὤν is an aberration from Numenius's normal speech and requires some explanation. The most likely explanation is that it reflects dependence on the biblical text.

---

[71] Frag. 13 (=Eusebius, *Praep. ev.* 11.18.13–14).

[72] On the relationship between the two see Albert Geljon and David T. Runia, *Philo of Alexandria, On Cultivation: Introduction, Translation, and Commentary*, PACS 4 (Leiden: Brill, 2013), 3.

[73] Francesca Calabi, "The Agriculture of God in Philo and Numenius" (paper presented at the Readers of Philo Conference, Yale University, March 2014), developed this at length in a fine paper.

[74] Dodds, "Numenius and Ammonius," 15–16.

[75] John Whittaker, "Moses Atticizing," *Phoenix* 21 (1967): 196–201. The allusion to Exod 3:14 has been recognized by many, e.g., Festugière, *La Révélation d'Hermès Trismégiste*, 3:44 n. 2

[76] Frags. 2.19, 23; 3.1, 8, 9; 4.7, 9, 12; 5.5, 6, 13–14, 18 (*bis*), 19, 25; 6.7, 8, 15; 7.2, 13, 14; 8.2.

[77] Plato, *Tim.* 27D.

The question is why would Numenius alter his standard language and use a biblical expression? The most straightforward answer is that he was following a source that equated the neuter of the Platonic tradition and the masculine of the biblical text. The most likely candidate—although not the only candidate—for this is Philo of Alexandria who routinely equated the two.[78] So, for example, in his discussion of God's name in *De mutatione nominum*, he said: "Therefore it follows that it is not possible to assign a proper name to the truly Self-Existent (τῷ ὄντι πρὸς ἀλήθειαν)." He then asked: "Don't you see that to the prophet who wanted to know how to respond to those who would ask him about his name, he said: 'I am the Self-Existent' (ἐγώ εἰμι ὁ ὤν), which means I am by nature Self-Existent, not to be named."[79] He went on to say: "It is so impossible to name the Self-Existent (τὸ ὄν) that not even the powers that serve him tell us a proper name."[80] This is the reverse of the same process that appears in Numenius: Philo moved from the biblical text to the Platonic language;[81] Numenius moved from Platonic language to the language of the biblical text.

But what prompted Numenius to make this move? There are two passages in Philo that may help. The phrase in Numenius, "The Self-Existent (ὁ μέν γε ὤν) sows the seed of every soul (σπέρμα πάσης ψυχῆς σπείρει) into everything that participates in him" is very close to Philo's description of God's sowing in *De posteritate Caini*: "But God sows in souls nothing unproductive" (σπείρει δ' ὁ θεὸς ἐν ψυχαῖς ἀτελὲς οὐδέν where ἀτελὲς οὐδέν refers to σπέρμα).[82] Numenius's statement is not a quote from Philo, but the language is very close. There is another possibility: Philo's treatise *De plantatione* repeatedly refers to God as the planter.[83] For example, the Alexandrian wrote: "It is necessary to understand that the beneficent God plants (ἐμφυτεύειν) in the soul as it were a garden of virtues and the deeds that accompany them, a garden that leads the soul to complete well

---

[78] Philo was not the only author to do so, e.g., Pseudo-Justin, *Ad Graecos de vera religione*, 22.

[79] Philo, *Mut.* 11.

[80] Philo, *Mut.* 14.

[81] John Whittaker, "Ammonius on the Delphic E," *CQ* 19 (1969): 185–192, esp. 189, aptly captured the essence of Philo's move: "Philo is a good case in point. On the basis of the LXX version of Exodus 3:14 he refers to God as ὁ ὤν. But because of his desire to identify his God with the absolute reality conceived in impersonal Platonic terms he frequently and tendentiously substitutes for the masculine form of the participle the neuter τὸ ὄν or τὸ ὄντως ὄν." Compare Plutarch, *Is. Os.* 352A and *E Delph.* 393A.–B, who makes a similar move.

[82] Philo, *Post.* 171.

[83] Philo, *Plant.* 2–3, 28–37, 84

being."[84] Philo also discussed the role of the Logos, just as Numenius described the role of the Demiurge. While there is no text in Philo that is a verbal echo of the final sentence in frag. 13 of Numenius ("The Lawgiver plants, distributes, and transplants into each of us what has already been set down by the former"), the basic roles of the Logos in both authors are equivalent.[85]

While I do not consider it provable, I wonder whether Numenius's statement was inspired by a reading of Philo's works, especially the two volume work *Concerning Agriculture.* All of the relevant pieces are present: the distinction between the cultivator and the planter, the identification of the absolute reality with the Self-Existent,[86] the sowing or planting of the seed by the First Cause, and the cultivation of the soul by the Logos.

This is not the only text where intriguing similarities exist between the two writers. Shortly after Eusebius cited the fragment above, he quoted another statement of Numenius: "These are the lives, the one of the First, the other of the Second God. This is to say that the First God will be stable (ἑστώς), but the Second God, on the contrary, is in motion (κινούμενος). The First deals with the intelligibles, the Second with the intelligibles and the sense-perceptibles."[87] There are a couple of striking statements in this fragment. Like Numenius, Philo called the Logos or the Second Cause "the Second God."[88] More strikingly, both Philo and Numenius used ἑστώς to refer to God's immutability. So, for example, in *De posteritate Caini*, Philo wrote: "that which is unswervingly stable is God; that which is motionable is creation."[89] Philo routinely commented on verbs of "standing." The trope became even more famous in Plotinus.[90] David Runia explored the use of this trope in Philo, Numenius, and Plotinus. He pointed out that while Philo employed it at least 15 times, it is unknown in other Middle Platonic texts.[91] Numenius's distinction between the First and Second God and their

---

[84] Philo, *Plant.* 37.

[85] Philo, *Plant.* 9–10, 18–22.

[86] E.g., Philo, *Agr.* 52, 171.

[87] Frag. 15 (=Eusebius, *Praep. ev.* 11.18.20-21). See also frag. 4.

[88] Philo, *QG* 2.62, "for nothing mortal can be cast in the image of the highest and Father of All, but with the Second God (πρὸς τὸν δεύτερον θεόν), which is his Logos." There is a Greek fragment for this. See Francoise Petit, *Quaestiones in Genesim et in Exodum: Fragmenta graeca*, PAPM 33 (Paris: du Cerf, 1978).

[89] Philo, *Post.* 23. See also § 27. On this see Marguerite Harl, *Quis rerum divinarum heres sit*, PAPM 15 (Paris: Du Cerf, 1986), 101–102 n. 4.

[90] Plotinus, *Enn.* 6.9.

[91] David T. Runia, "Witness or Participant? Philo and the Neoplatonic Tradition," in *The Neoplatonic Tradition: Jewish, Christian and Islamic Themes*, ed. Arjo Vanderjagt and Detlev Pätzold, Dialectica Minora 3 (Köln: Dinter, 1991), 36–56, esp. 47–51.

different relationship to the created world reminds us of Philo's argument that God created the intelligible world in the Logos and through the Logos the sense-perceptible world.[92] The basic concepts are close.

Conclusions

We could expand on the similarities between Philo and Numenius, but the evidence would not be different in character than what we have examined —except to say that it might be more tenuous.[93] What may we conclude? It is clear that the works of Philo and Numenius were both part of the library that Origen took from Alexandria to Caesarea. Both Origen and Eusebius thought that the two were significant witnesses to the unity of thought between the biblical text and Platonism. Numenius knew Jewish material. He had access to a Greek translation of some parts of the Pentateuch, although it is not clear whether his knowledge was direct or indirect. He may well have known other works such as the *Apocryphon of Jannes and Jambres*. He certainly knew the legend, although once again it is not clear whether he knew it via oral stories or a written document.

What about the works of Philo, did he know any of them? The evidence is not so clear that a definitive answer is possible. I have often used a sliding scale in thinking about ancient history. It moves from what is certain to what is probable to what is possible, down to what is improbable, and finally to what is impossible. If we applied this scale to the evidence that we have examined, I would judge that minimally it is possible that Numenius knew some of Philo's works and maximally it is probable that he did.

The significance of this conclusion is that we should not dismiss out of hand the possibility that Philo influenced Hellenistic philosophical thought. At minimum he was a witness to the possibility that biblical thought was compatible with Platonism. At maximum, his works convinced Numenius of the compatibility of Judaism and Platonism. The level of influence between Philo and Numenius would not have been profound: it was certainly not that of teacher to student. Rather, it would have been the incorporation of Philo's thought into the framework of Numenius's general project. What

---

[92] Philo, *Opif.* 18–25. See the commentary of David T. Runia, *Philo of Alexandria, On the Creation of the Cosmos according to Moses* PACS 1 (Leiden: Brill, 2001), 132–155. Cf. also Philo, *Fug.* 12.

[93] E.g., Philo, *Fug.* 56–57 and Numenius frag. 17 on the immortality of the soul. See Esther Starobinski-Safran, *De fuga et invention*, PAPM 17 (Paris: Du Cerf, 1970), 141 n. 4.

would have made Philo's works attractive to Numenius was that they had made the case for Judaism that most interested Numenius who looked for ways to bridge the East and the West via his reconstruction of Platonism. In this way they would have been different from the works of the Egyptian priest Chaeremon whose Stoicism would not have appealed to Numenius. In other words, at minimum Philo was a precedent and at maximum he was a helpful witness to one tradition within Numenius's larger project.

Yale Divinity School

PHILO'S PREPOSITIONAL METAPHYSICS WITHIN EARLY CHRISTIAN DEBATES ABOUT THE RELATION OF DIVINE NATURE AND AGENCY

ORREY MCFARLAND

1. *Introduction*

In the fourth century, Didymus the Blind, Basil of Caesarea, and John Chrysostom all employed a concatenation of Gen 4:1 and 40:8, with a specific focus on the role of prepositions in defining and describing the activity of God. Often these verses were used to demonstrate that the biblical authors were not constrained in their use of specific prepositions with regard to the members of the Godhead. For example, prepositions of causation were not restricted solely for God the Father, nor were prepositions of instrumentality used exclusively for Jesus or the Spirit. Rather, the same prepositions could be used for God, Jesus, and the Spirit alike, and applying different prepositions for each person's agency did not point to a distinction in nature. If a preposition did signify such a distinction, and thus a distinction between the nature of the divine persons, it needed to be redefined. This article will argue that the source of this linked use of Gen 4:1 and 40:8, particularly in relation to divine agency, is Philo of Alexandria (cf. *Cher.* 124–30). As a mixture of Platonic and Aristotelian thought and traditions, Philo's prepositional metaphysics—"the use of specific prepositions to denote metaphysical causes"[1]—restricted prepositions of causation properly to God, making prepositions of instrumentality unequivocally inappropriate as a way of thinking about God's activity.

In Gen 4:1, the speaker claims, "I have obtained a man *through* God" (Ἐκτησάμην ἄνθρωπον διὰ τοῦ θεοῦ); likewise, in Gen 40:8, the speaker explains, "The interpretation of the dreams will be found *through* God" (οὐχὶ

---

[1] Gregory E. Sterling, "'Day One': Platonizing Exegetical Traditions of Genesis 1:1–5 in John and Jewish Authors," *SPhiloA* 17 (2005): 127. Cf. also idem, "Prepositional Metaphysics in Jewish Wisdom Speculation and Early Christological Liturgical Texts," *SPhiloA* 9 (1997): 219–38.

διὰ τοῦ θεοῦ ἡ διασάφησις αὐτῶν ἐστιν).[2] Philo's interpretation of these verses, in which the speakers use a preposition of instrumentality (διά) in relation to God, is a form of *Sachkritik*: the speakers are misguided, because we know that "God is cause, not instrument." It appears that Philo's distinct interpretations of these verses were known to early Christians of various theological persuasions. Philo's afterlife in early Christianity is a complex subject which often reveals that Philo was held in high regard.[3] Didymus and Chrysostom elaborate on Gen 4:1 through 40:8, making the same basic point Philo does. But for Basil, Philo's interpretation has to be revised, nuanced, or modified, because the subject matter has changed from describing God's actions to describing how the actions of the persons of the Trinity relate. We might see the "seeds of unrest" with Philo's interpretation in Didymus if the treatise *De Trinitate* is authentic, but otherwise he provides a positive starting point for the reception of this tradition from Philo. Thus, we will be able to trace the sort of malleable use that Philo—his biblical interpretation and theology—could be put to for early Christian authors, even if they were not wholly aware they were using Philo. (Though, as we will see, there are good reasons to think they did know.) While these early Christian theologians could depend on Philo favorably in many cases, their interpretations of Gen 4:1 and 40:8 show that, ultimately, they could, and at times necessarily did, distance themselves somewhat from Philo hermeneutically and theologically in their understanding of the agency of God. Accordingly, by establishing a significant link between Philo and these important early Christian authors, this article will seek to bring further nuance to the question of Philo's reception in early Christianity.[4]

The argument will proceed in two main steps. First, I will set out Philo's prepositional metaphysics as it is expounded in his treatise *De Cherubim* in relation to his interpretation of Gen 4:1 and 40:8. Second, I will explore how these two verses were employed by Didymus, Basil, and John Chrysostom, in order to see what can be deduced about their relationship to Philo or Philonic tradition. David Runia states, "It is a well-known fact that the

---

[2] This translation of Gen 40:8—as a statement rather than a question—aligns more closely with Philo's explanation of the verse in *Cher*. 128.

[3] On this topic, see especially the impressive work of D.T. Runia, *Philo in Early Christian Literature: A Survey* CRINT 3.3 (Assen: Van Gorcum; Minneapolis: Fortress, 1993).

[4] According to my own searching, both through reading, scouring concordances, and through TLG searches, I was unable to find either a use of this concatenation prior to Philo (which would give evidence that Philo himself could have been dependent on an already existing tradition) or in any other places in early Christian literature. Of course, other places where these verses are used could be discovered.

massive corpus of writings of Philo of Alexandria only survived because he was taken up in the Christian tradition as a church father *honoris causa.*"[5] As we will see, for these authors (with the possible exception of Chrysostom), there is unambiguous evidence that Philo was often viewed favorably—for a plethora of reasons—and it is this fact that makes their use of these two verses, in ways that are variously related to Philo's use, interesting for a test-case in thinking about what kind of afterlife Philo had in early Christianity.[6]

2. Genesis 4:1 and 40:8 in Philo's De Cherubim

For Philo, human piety is defined by one's belief in God's causation: it is absolutely crucial that God alone created all things. This belief is the confirmation of one's piety (εὐσεβείας βεβαίωσις).[7] Conversely, rejecting belief in God's causation is an unequivocal marker of impiety.[8] One can misunderstand causation by locating it in either humanity, polytheism, or the created world.[9] As Philo vividly puts it, all who do not view God as cause so are like archers who, "aiming at many things and not aiming skillfully at any mark, put forward innumerable sources and causes of the creation of the universe, all of which are false, and are ignorant of the one Creator and Father of the universe."[10] But for Philo it is also crucial that God's causation be understood *well*: there are particular ways to

---

[5] David T. Runia, "Why Does Clement of Alexandria Call Philo 'The Pythagorean'?" *VC* 49 (1995): 1. For the story of Philo's "adoption" by early Christians and eventual rejection, see Runia, *Early Christian Literature*, 3–33. As Runia puts it, "The pendant to Philo's loss of his status of Church Father *honoris causa* is the rediscovery of his status as a Jewish author" (32).

[6] As Runia, *Early Christian Literature*, 6 explains, there were two main ways Philo was viewed by early Christians: Philo was either (1) "seen as a Jew who, on account of the content and method of his exegesis, stands rather close to the Christian tradition and can be usefully adduced in its support"; or (2) "portrayed as a Jew who fails to recognize the distinctive message of the Christian faith, and for that reason should be criticized, or even condemned."

[7] *Mut.* 155. On the relation of piety and divine causation, see further, among many possible texts, *Abr.* 78; *Conf.* 124; *Deus* 87; *Ebr.* 105–07; *Her.* 113–24; *Leg.* 1.82; *Spec.* 2.171–80, 204. On knowing God as cause, see *Post.* 167–69.

[8] *Sacr.* 54–57 is a key text for explaining the various erroneous views one can have that result in either denying God's causation or not viewing it properly; cf. also *Agr.* 173; *Conf.* 123; *Ebr.* 108–10; *Legat.* 118; *Migr.* 179–81; *Mut.* 221; *Spec.* 1.10, 13. Sarah Pearce, *The Land of the Body: Studies in Philo's Representation of Egypt* (Tübingen: Mohr Siebeck, 2007), 144, 155.

[9] Cf. *Spec.* 2.198.

[10] *Conf.* 144. Cf. *Leg.* 3.29–31; *Somn.* 2.75–77.

understand and speak of God as Cause. *De Cherubim* 124–130 is a key text for understanding how God is to be conceived of as the Cause of all things.

De Cherubim is one of the treatises that comprise Philo's great set of allegorical commentaries on the Pentateuch. The treatise divides into main two sections: the first (1–39) covers the expulsion of Adam and Eve from Eden, with an allegory of the Cherubim; and the second (40–130), the latter half of which will be the primary concern here, interprets the birth of Cain. In sections 40–83, Philo interprets Gen 4:1 allegorically as the problem of the Mind (Adam) mating with Sense Perception (Eve), which produces Cain, who represents the impious Mind's belief that all sense perceptions are one's own rather than the result of God's creation.[11] Sections 84–130 then assert God's claim to sole ownership of all things. Here Philo extrapolates from Numbers 28:2 not only the divine gift-nature of all reality, but also the perfection of God's nature. Leviticus 25:23 corroborates God's sovereignty and ownership of all things with the claim from God that "all the land is mine."[12]

Only after proving from Scripture God's exclusive possession of all created reality (πάντων οὖν ἀνωμολογημένων θεοῦ κτημάτων [124]) does Philo return specifically to Gen 4:1 at the end of the treatise to point out the poverty of thought in *Adam's* declaration, "I have obtained a man through God" (Ἐκτησάμην ἄνθρωπον διὰ τοῦ θεοῦ). A proper understanding of God as owner of all things necessitates also a proper understanding of the way in which things come from God to humanity. Somewhat implausibly, Philo takes Adam to be the one who makes this statement (in Genesis Eve is clearly the speaker), but more interesting is that, in a form of *Sachkritik*, Philo asserts that Adam has gone wrong in this simple utterance (κατὰ τοῦτο διαμαρτών). According to Philo, this is "because God is cause, not instrument" (ὁ θεὸς αἴτιον, οὐκ ὄργανον [124]). For Philo, ὑπό, παρά, and sometimes ἐκ can describe God's agency, but rarely διά.[13] Whatever comes into existence is "through an instrument, but by a cause" (τὸ δὲ γινόμενον δι'

---

[11] Cf. *Cher.* 65. For Philo, Cain is the true archetype of renouncing God's causation; cf. *Post.* 33–39; Hindy Najman, "Cain and Abel as Character Traits: A Study in the Allegorical Typology of Philo of Alexandria," in *Eve's Children*, ed. G.P. Luttikhuizen (Leiden: Brill, 2003), 107–18; Albert C. Geljon, "Philonic Elements in Didymus the Blind's Exegesis of the Story of Cain and Abel," *VC* 61 (2007): 282–312. As Jutta Leonhardt, *Jewish Worship in Philo of Alexandria* (Tübingen: Mohr Siebeck, 2001), 198 notes, Cain's essential "offence is not to give God His due, which…is equivalent to the skeptic's denial of God's creative power." See also Jean LaPorte, *Eucharistia in Philo* (New York: Edwin Mellen, 1983), 133.

[12] *Cher.* 108.

[13] However, in *Leg.* 1.41 Philo states that some things come into existence both by (ὑπό) and through (διά) God.

ὀργάνου μὲν ὑπὸ δὲ αἰτίου πάντως γίνεται). By misidentifying the Cause for the instrument, Adam makes himself the cause.[14]

Philo's interpretation of this text is guided by his commitment to an Aristotelian understanding of the four causes used in relation to specific prepositions, and thus a form of prepositional metaphysics,[15] which he explains with the example of the creation of the universe. As Philo states, "in the creation of anything, many things must come together."[16] Accordingly, Philo lists his four causes: God is the first or efficient cause, the "by whom" (τὸ ὑφ' οὗ);[17] the four elements are the material cause (τὸ ἐξ οὗ); the instrument is God's Logos, through which all things are created (τὸ δι' οὗ); and the final cause (τὸ δι' ὅ) is the "goodness of the Demiurge"—the "for the sake of which" or purpose of God's causation.[18] Without question, God

---

[14] Philo does place a strong emphasis on the role of parents in childbirth in relation to God's causation. For example, in *Her.* 171–72, parents are instruments of creation (ὄργανα γενέσεως). Likewise, mortal parents imitate the divine creative power: God is the "beginning of creation" (ἀρχὴ γενέσεως) and human parents are the end (τέλος). See also *Cher.* 43–46; *Decal.* 51; *Ebr.* 73; *Spec.* 2.2; Cf. Maren Niehoff, *Philo on Jewish Identity and Culture* (Tübingen: Mohr Siebeck, 2001), 170.

[15] The origin of prepositional metaphysics is difficult to locate with precision, though many philosophical streams made use of varying configurations of the basic idea. As Sterling, "Platonizing Exegetical Traditions," 127, broadly summarizes, the "Hellenistic philosophical traditions took up Aristotle's causes and assigned prepositions to them." On this theme, see David T. Runia, *Philo of Alexandria and the Timaeus of Plato* (Leiden: Brill 1986), 104, 133, 171–74; Ronald R. Cox, *By the Same Word: Creation and Salvation in Hellenistic Judaism and Early Christianity* (Berlin: de Gruyter, 2007), 43–51; Thomas H. Tobin, *The Creation of Man: Philo and the History of Interpretation* (Washington, D.C.: CBAA, 1983), 67–72. The term was popularized by John Dillon, *The Middle Platonists: A Study of Platonism, 80 B.C. to A.D. 220* (Ithaca: Cornell University Press, 1977), 138, following Willy Theiler, *Die Vorbereitung des Neuplatonismus* (Berlin: Weidmann, 1964); see also Heinrich Dörrie, "Präpositionen und Metaphysik," *Museum Helveticum* 26 (1969): 217–28. For an overview of the development of prepositional metaphysics, see Sterling, "Prepositional Metaphysics," 219–38. Sterling points out that Philo's varied use of prepositions in his corpus "suggests that Philo knows more than one analysis" (227–28).

[16] *Cher.* 125.

[17] Cf. *Fug.* 12: γέγονέ τε γὰρ ὁ κόσμος καὶ πάντως ὑπ' αἰτίου τινὸς γέγονεν. R. J. Hankinson, *Cause and Explanation in Ancient Greek Thought* (Oxford: Oxford University Press, 2001), 342, notes that understanding the efficient cause as the true cause is Stoic. For example, in *Opif.* 7–9 Philo calls God the δραστήριον αἴτιον and the world τὸ παθητόν. For commentary on this text, see David T. Runia, *Philo of Alexandria: On the Creation of the Cosmos According to Moses: Introduction, Translation and Commentary* (Leiden: Brill, 2001), 115–17; see also Gretchen Reydams-Schils, "Stoicized Readings of Plato's Timaeus in Philo of Alexandria," *SPhiloA* 7 (1995): 85–102.

[18] *Cher.* 127. Cf. Sterling, "Prepositional Metaphysics," 227: "Like Seneca, [Philo] identifies each of these in the Platonic cosmos."

is cause: God is τὸ αἴτιον and his goodness is ἡ αἰτία.[19] This is the knowledge of those who love the truth (φιλαλήθης).

But those who claim to have obtained something *through God* make the Demiurge an instrument (τὸ μὲν αἴτιον ὄργανον τὸν δημιουργόν), thus supposing that the human mind is truly the cause (τὸ δ᾽ ὄργανον αἴτιον τὸν ἀνθρώπινον νοῦν). This is gross impiety. At this point, Philo employs Gen 40:8 for reinforcement, a second biblical example of a character—Joseph— who does not rightly understand God's causation.[20] Thus, as Philo states, right reason itself would find fault with Joseph for saying, "The inter-pretation of the dreams will be found through God" (οὐχὶ διὰ τοῦ θεοῦ ἡ διασάφησις αὐτῶν ἐστιν).[21] Joseph should rather have said that the "unfolding and precise meaning of the unseen" would occur "by him as cause" (ὑπ᾽ αὐτοῦ ὡς αἰτίου). "For we are the instruments through whom the particular energies" are at work, but the "craftsman" (ὁ τεχνίτης) is the one by whom all things move (ὑφ᾽ οὗ πάντα κινεῖται).[22]

A consolidation of various strands of Aristotelian and Platonic thought is therefore here the standard of orthodoxy for Philo: the use of their doctrines specifies God's precise role in causation. These philosophical tools for reading the text are not introduced without warrant. Philo reads this text knowing the negative story of Cain to come soon afterwards, and that Adam in Gen 4:1 is the Mind that has been justifiably kicked out of the Garden of Eden by God—and thus, Philo's philosophical constraints rein-force a negative interpretation of a character, or two characters that the text itself colors negatively at times. Hermeneutically, Philo contracts the whole of Cain's story into Adam's statement, as well as Adam's prior folly in the Garden, and consequently Philo's prepositional metaphysics is a key to Philo's negative reading of Adam's statement, that Adam caused nothing because God alone is Cause. The same should be said of Joseph, who also misinterpreted reality by not attributing sole causation to God.

Thus, for Philo different prepositions have different metaphysical referents. To apply a preposition incorrectly, as Adam and Joseph did, is a

[19] Philo's view of God's goodness as the final cause brings to mind Plato's argument in the *Timaeus* that the cause of God's creation was that "he was good" (ἀγαθὸς ἦν). Sterling, "Prepositional Metaphysics," 228: "both Philo and Seneca allude to or cite Plato, *Tim.* 29d-e in connection with the final cause. The best explanation of this common allusion is that it had become part of the tradition."

[20] Philo's portrayal of Joseph is inconsistent: throughout the allegorical treatises he is a rather negative character, but in the treatise on Joseph he is presented in a positive man-ner. Numerous explanations for this discrepancy exist, but the key here is that in Philo's allegorical mode of thought here Joseph is not to be emulated.

[21] *Cher.* 128.

[22] *Cher.* 128.

woeful indication of a soul in dire straits. God is Cause and God's actions should be defined and described by using appropriate prepositions. To use an incorrect preposition would be either to point to something other than God as the cause, or to make God something other than what God truly is. As Philo explains, those who cannot make these distinctions in causation are unlearned, ignorant (ἀμαθεῖς), and those who purposefully pervert the true understanding of causation should be avoided as quarrelsome (ἐριστι-κοί).[23] Only those who make an accurate examination of the things revealed and attach the proper values to each thing follow a "true philosophy" and can be considered praiseworthy. Philo thus closes with a saying from Moses (Exod 14:13): "Stand and see the salvation that comes from the Lord (παρὰ τοῦ κυρίου), which he will do for you." Moses thus teaches that salvation comes not *through God* but *from him as Cause* (παρ' αὐτοῦ ὡς αἰτίου).[24] Like ὑπό, παρά is an appropriate preposition for the Cause.

Thus, Philo uses Gen 4:1 and 40:8 together to point to the impiety of attributing *divine* causation to something other than God. As we will now see, some early Christian authors marshaled these verses as part of related arguments, but sometimes to different ends. For these authors, it could not always be the case that using different prepositions necessarily contributed to a claim about distinctions in ontology.

3. *Philo and Divine Agency in Three Early Christian Authors*

In this section, I will briefly set out the evidence about whether our three early Christian authors knew and used Philo; and then I will demonstrate that they made use of his textual connection between Gen 4:1 and 40:8 from *De Cherubim* for similar purposes—or at least in the context of similar discussions.[25] Runia's work on Philo's relation to each author provides a convenient starting point for our examination, both in considering how each author viewed and used Philo and how to get from Philo to each

---

[23] *Cher.* 129.

[24] *Cher.* 130.

[25] Naturally, many authors interpreted these two verses in Genesis separately—especially as part of commentaries—and found aspects in them interesting (sometimes even making comments that are like what we will see here). There is always the chance that Philo could have possibly affected the interpretation of any of the verses taken alone, but that is (relatively) less likely and beyond the scope of this article. We are interested here solely in the connection of the verses which, as we will see, points unambiguously to Philo.

author, though here a lack of evidence regularly frustrates attempts to settle specifics. This will not be a main feature of the discussion here.[26]

3.1. *Didymus the Blind (313–398 CE)*

As one of the leading Alexandrian theologians, following after Clement and Origen,[27] it is unsurprising that Didymus the Blind would be well acquainted with Philo.[28] As Runia notes, Didymus refers to Philo by name at least seven times and once by periphrasis ("one of the sages engaged in Mosaic learning").[29] Didymus's use of Philo shows that he was favorably viewed; for example, Didymus could name Philo and use his interpretation of Hagar to support his own interpretation of Prov 5:18 in his commentary on Ecclesiastes.[30] Runia thus summarizes the evidence: "It is striking how warmly [Didymus] commends [Philo]. Philo is clearly a repository of knowledge that the exegete can draw on freely."[31] Furthermore: "In Didymus we see most clearly how completely and unreservedly Philo had been absorbed into the Alexandrian Christian tradition."

[26] But see esp. the schematic depiction of the transmission of Philo's writings in Runia, *Early Christian Literature*, 18 and the narrative reconstruction in 22–24.

[27] The connection between Philo, Clement, and Origen is also well established. For Clement, see esp. Annewies W. van den Hoek, *Clement of Alexandria and His Use of Philo in the Stromateis: An Early Christian Reshaping of a Jewish Model* (Leiden: Brill, 1988) and Runia, "Why Does Clement of Alexandria Call Philo 'The Pythagorean'?," 1–22. For Origen, see Annewies W. van den Hoek, "Philo and Origen: A Descriptive Catalogue of Their Relationship," *SPhiloA* 12 (2000): 44–121. A survey of both figures in their relationship to Philo, as well as scholarship on the topic, can be found in Runia, *Early Christian Literature*, 132–83. For Philo's place in Alexandrian theology more broadly, and particularly in possible connection to Arius, see Rowan Williams, *Arius: Heresy and Tradition* (Grand Rapids: Eerdmans, 2001), 117–24 and all of section II.B.

[28] For relevant background on Didymus, see Richard A. Layton, *Didymus the Blind and His Circle in Late-Antique Alexandria: Virtue and Narrative in Biblical Scholarship* (Urbana: University of Illinois Press, 2004). On Didymus's Genesis commentary, see chap. 6. On Didymus's biblical interpretation, see also B. Stefaniw, *Mind, Text, and Commentary: Noetic Exegesis in Origen of Alexandria, Didymus the Blind, and Evagrius Ponticus* (New York: Peter Lang, 2010).

[29] Runia, *Early Christian Literature*, 198. For discussion of the passages, see 198–202. For the periphrastic reference to Philo, see the relevant portion of text in *Comm. Zach.* 320.9–10. On this text, see *Didymus the Blind: Commentary on Zechariah*, Robert C. Hill, trans. and ed., The Fathers of the Church, vol. 111; (Washington, DC: Catholic University of America Press, 2006).

[30] *Comm. Eccl.* 275–276. Didymus could also set in parallel Philo's and Paul's allegories, giving them equal weight and authority (see *In Gen.* 235.25–236.11); the text for the Genesis commentary is Louis Doutreleau and Pierre Nautin, *Didyme l'Aveugle. Sur la Genèse*, vols. 1–2, SC 233, 244 (Paris: Éditions du Cerf, 1976–1978).

[31] Runia, *Early Christian Literature*, 204.

The concatenation of Philo's Genesis texts can be seen in two places in Didymus's corpus: *In Genesim*, one of the finds in the Tura discovery of 1941, and *De Trinitate*, a writing whose authenticity been questioned. We shall look at these two sources in turn.

It is not surprising that Philo would make an appearance in Didymus's commentary on Genesis, given how much of Philo's oeuvre is dedicated to interpreting Genesis.[32] Philo is mentioned here in four separate passages. Two helpful studies have addressed Philo's influence on the commentary. The first, by Émilien Lamirande, argues that "Didyme prolonge surtout l'enseignement de Philon et d'Origène."[33] Lamirande's study focuses primarily on the relation between male and female in Philo and Didymus; while insightful, it does not touch on the possible Philonic influence to be examined here. The work of Runia and Lamirande shows that we can assume both Didymus's deep acquaintance with Philo's thought and that Philo was used positively in the Genesis commentary; yet neither of them note the connection to be set forth here.[34] A more recent study by Albert C. Geljon, however, has drawn out the significance of the Philonic background for the passage of interest here.[35]

The relevant passage is where Didymus is interpreting Gen 4:2 (118.24–29; 119.3–4): "And she gave birth (again) to the brother of Cain, Abel."[36] Here Didymus states that Philo desires (Ὁ Φίλων...βούλεται) for the two brothers to be born from one conception. The reader must decide whether Philo is correct or not (ὑγιῶς ἔχει ἢ οὔ). Interestingly, Didymus asserts that the "lover of learning" will know Philo's allegorical interpretation (ὅσα μὲν οὖν Φίλων εἰς τοῦτο ἀλληγορῶν εἶπεν, ὁ φιλόκαλος εἴσεται), and he then goes

---

[32] On the place of Genesis in Philo, see Gregory E. Sterling, "When the Beginning Is the End: The Place of Genesis in the Commentaries of Philo of Alexandria," in *The Book of Genesis: Composition, Reception, and Interpretation,* ed. Craig A. Evans, Joel N. Lohr, and David L. Petersen, Formation and Interpretation of Old Testament Literature (Leiden: Brill, 2012), 427–446.

[33] Émilien Lamirande, "Le masculin et le féminin dans la tradition alexandrine: le commentaire de Didyme l'Aveugle sur la 'Genèse,'" *Science et Esprit* 41 (1989): 137–65, citation from 138. Further: "Philon apparaît comme un grand ancêtre, à la frontière de deux mondes. Il est un intermédiaire important dans la transmission du platonisme aux chrétiens. Ceux-ci ont beaucoup appris de lui. Plusieurs lui ont emprunté ses méthodes d'exégèse, mais également se sont inspirés de son genre de vie" (153).

[34] Lamirande briefly discusses Didymus's interpretation of Gen 4:1, but not with reference to Philo; cf. 'commentaire de Didyme,' 150.

[35] Albert C. Geljon, "Philonic Elements in Didymus the Blind's Exegesis of the Story of Cain and Abel," *VC* 61 (2007): 282–312, esp. 286–87.

[36] This translation is meant to reflect the awkwardness of the Greek προσέθηκεν τεκεῖν, which clearly means something different in the original Hebrew than it did for Philo.

on to explain the reading.[37] The specific Philonic text Didymus is referring to is unknown, but the ideas are common enough for Philo's thought.[38] This highly positive reference to Philo is interesting enough, and it lends authority to Philo's work. But what has been overlooked by most interpreters—excluding Geljon—is what Didymus says right before this text in his interpretation of Gen 4:1. I will reproduce the Greek text here:

ἀκολούθως δέ, ἅτε μὴ πάντῃ ἐ[ξῃρ]ημένη τὸν περὶ προνοίας λόγον, εἶπεν· Ἐκτησάμην ἄνθρωπ[ον] διὰ το[ῦ Θεοῦ] (Gen 4:1)· εἰ γὰρ ὑπηρέτησαν ὡς γονεῖς τῇ ἀποτέξ[ει], ἀλλ᾽ ἀγω[γῇ] Θεοῦ τὸ πᾶν ἤρτυται. Τὸ δὲ διὰ τοῦ Θεοῦ ἁπλούστ[ερο]ν ἐκλαβεῖν δεῖ ἀντὶ τοῦ παρὰ τοῦ Θεοῦ· οὕτως γὰρ καὶ ὁ Ἰωσ[ὴφ] εἶπεν· Οὐχὶ διὰ τοῦ Θεοῦ ἡ διασάφησις αὐτῶν ἐστιν; (Gen 40:8) ἀντ[ὶ το]ῦ παρὰ Θεοῦ. (118.18–23)

In his comments on Gen 4:1, Didymus says that Adam and Eve "served as parents in the birth," but all things have been brought about by God's leading. Eve did not reject providence (τὸν περὶ προνοίας λόγον), God's role in the birth of the child, but said, "I have acquired a man through God." For Didymus, it is thus necessary (δεῖ) to understand the phrase (ἐκλαβεῖν) διὰ τοῦ Θεοῦ as παρὰ τοῦ Θεοῦ. The preposition ἀντί with the genitive could mean either "instead of" or "as an equivalent to."[39] Here, the latter meaning is strongly implied; there would be no other reason to introduce the phrase ἀντὶ τοῦ παρὰ τοῦ Θεοῦ twice if διά were meant to be understand simply as διά. Didymus's use of παρά, which could come from Philo's citation at the end of *Cher.*, as the proper alternative for διά might be significant, as none of the other authors do this. For Didymus here, as for Philo, the prepositional phrase plays a significant part in signifying the roles played by the parents in childbirth vis-à-vis God's "flavoring" of τὸ πᾶν. Accordingly, then, Didymus uses Gen 40:8 for support: "for in this way Joseph said, 'Does the interpretation of dreams not come through God?' which means 'from God.'" Using Gen 40:8 to support 4:1 would seem curious without having Philo's use of the verses as background. But even stranger would be Didymus's clarification of the prepositions. As Geljon states, "Didymus does not make explicit why the words 'through God' have to be rejected,"

---

[37] For the explanation, see Geljon, "Philonic Elements," 287–90.

[38] James R. Royse, "Cain's Expulsion from Paradise: The Text of Philo's *Congr* 171," *JQR* 79 (1988–89): 224 suggests that Didymus could be referring to a lost work by Philo. For the general ideas alluded to in this text, Runia, *Early Christian Literature*, 201 n. 93 points to *QG*. 1.78 and *Sacr.* 4, 17. It is possible that Didymus came into contact with Philo's reading of Genesis through Origen, but (1) we do not have Origen's commentary on Genesis, and (2) it is clear from Didymus's manner of engagement that he knew Philo.

[39] Cf. Herbert W. Smyth, *Greek Grammar* (Cambridge: Harvard University Press, 1920), 373.

but "Didymus's exegesis is only comprehensible against the Philonic background."[40]

Consequently, in this passage we have the use of the same verses as in *Cher.* 124–30, a focus on the meaning of the prepositions is present, and the discussion directly precedes an explicit (positive) naming of Philo and his interpretation of Cain and Abel. Didymus uses these verses in the same way as Philo does: Gen 4:1 plays the major role, as with Philo, and for Didymus too we should not simply take the speaker's words at face value (ἁπλούστ[ερο]ν) rather than clarifying the use of the preposition, because παρά rightly signifies God's providential activity in creation and childbirth. Then, like Philo, Didymus uses Gen 40:8 to confirm that διά can and should be interpreted in the sense of παρά when used in reference to God's agency. One change is that Didymus does not color the biblical speakers negatively; where, for Philo, Gen 40:8 provided another instance of a negative character applying prepositions to God improperly, Didymus simply notes how the διά is *actually* being used.[41] It is noteworthy that Didymus does not name Philo in this section; rather, Philo's interpretation is silently affirmed, though Philo's unique *Sachkritik* is muted. Furthermore, in this text Didymus does not draw out the significance of prepositions for describing who God is. For Philo, one should not use διά because that would mutate God into something not-God; Didymus does not comment on that aspect of Philo's argument. Rather, he simply notes that we should accept the biblical witness in a modified form. Therefore, this text provides our first point of contact for understanding how Philo's Genesis concatenation could be used, and, in this case, used positively. The story becomes more interesting from here.

In a second text, the concatenation appears in a context where Philo's interpretation must be rejected. The work *De Trinitate* has long been considered to be spurious, but some scholars remain open to the possibility of its authenticity.[42] Given Didymus's knowledge of Philo, as well as his

---

[40] Geljon, "Philonic Elements," 286–287.

[41] Interestingly, none of the early Christian authors *critique* the biblical authors, but rather they say what the preposition *really means*. This is a noteworthy difference, as it reveals different hermeneutical approaches to Scripture.

[42] See the discussion in and literature cited in Claudio Moreschini and Enrico Norelli, *Early Christian Greek and Latin Literature: A Literary History*, Volume Two: *From the Council of Nicea to the Beginning of the Medieval Period*, trans. Martin J. O'Connell (Peabody, MA: Hendrickson, 2005), 77–78 and Francis M. Young, *From Nicaea to Chalcedon: A Guide to the Literature and Its Background*, second ed (London: SCM, 2010), 95. I have consulted the text in PG 773–992. As A. Heron, "Some sources used in the De Trinitate ascribed to Didymus the Blind," in *The Making of Orthodoxy: Essays in Honour of Henry Chadwick*, ed. Rowan Williams (Cambridge: Cambridge University Press, 1989), 173 notes, "the De Trinitate has

use of Gen 4:1 and 40:8 in *In Genesim*, it seems that the present argument could possibly play a small role in arguing for the authenticity of this text, though that, of course, is not the purpose here. If Didymus is not the author, this text still presents evidence for using Gen 4:1 and 40:8 together —here in a manner opposed to Philo's use of the verses, though while discussing a similar subject matter.

In context, the relevant section of the work is mostly a parading of different biblical texts to show how numerous prepositions are all used equally of Father, Son, and Spirit. I will present some of the context of the quotations here:

> περὶ τοῦ Πατρός, Ἡσαΐας ἀπὸ τοῦ Πατρὸς πρὸς τὸν Υἱόν· Ἰδοὺ προσήλυτοι προσελεύσονταί σοι δι᾽ ἐμοῦ. Ἐπιτήρησον, ὡς διὰ τὸ ἰσότιμον καὶ ὁμοούσιον, προσάγει τὰ ἔθνη τῷ Υἱῷ ὁ Πατήρ· καὶ πάλιν· Οὐαὶ οἱ βαθέως βουλὴν ποιοῦντες, καὶ οὐ διὰ Κυρίου. Καὶ ἐν τῇ Γενέσει Ἀδὰμ λέγει· *Ἐκτησάμην ἄνθρωπον διὰ τοῦ Θεοῦ* (Gen 4:1)· καὶ πάλιν· Ὅσα ἐνετείλατο Μωϋσῆς τῷ Ἰσραὴλ διὰ τοῦ προστάγματος Κυρίου (Num 36:5). Καὶ Ἰωσὴφ πρὸς τοὺς εὐνούχους φησίν· *Οὐχὶ διὰ τοῦ Θεοῦ ἡ διασάφησις αὐτῶν ἔσται* (Gen 40:8)· Ἀλλὰ καὶ Παῦλος Ἑβραίοις· Ἔπρεπεν γάρ, φησίν, αὐτῷ, δι᾽ ὃν τὰ πάντα, καὶ δι᾽ οὗ τὰ πάντα, πολλοὺς υἱοὺς εἰς δόξαν ἀναγαγόντα, τὸν ἀρχηγὸν τῆς σωτηρίας αὐτῶν διὰ παθημάτων τελειῶσαι. Σημειωτέον, πῶς παραπλήσιον τοῦτο μάλιστα τῷ ἐκκειμένῳ κεφαλαίῳ τῷ, Εἷς Κύριος Ἰησοῦς Χριστός, δι᾽ οὗ τὰ πάντα. (39.932.13–29)[43]

The purpose of this passage is different, of course, than in *In Genesim*; there Didymus used Philo to support the idea that the action of God alone, described by the text with διά, should actually be understood by παρά. Here Didymus is arguing precisely that different prepositions do not imply a contradiction of τὸ ἰσότιμον καὶ ὁμοούσιον between the Father and Son (the Spirit is also in view in the wider context). The difference between the two contexts is whether Didymus is discussing God's action in itself, or the relation of action between different persons of the Trinity. The latter context necessitates a different argument. Accordingly, Didymus enlists a great amount of biblical evidence to show that each divine person has the same prepositions used to define their action; here, διά applies to both Father and Son. Rather than being a key part of the argument, Gen 4:1 and 40:8 are simply a plank in the greater argument, they do not strictly interpret each

---

received relatively scant attention, though it is arguably more theologically substantial and significant than [Didymus's] commentaries, whether or not Didymus is the author." Further, "the *De Trinitate* seems beyond all reasonable doubt to date from late fourth-century Alexandria. If Didymus is not the author, it is hard to imagine who else could have been. There is, quite simply, no other known Alexandrian theologian of that period who would have been able to produce a work of this caliber" (178).

[43] Genesis 4:1 is also cited in 39.824.25.

other, and, significantly, there is one verse intervening (Num 36:5).[44] Furthermore, here Didymus does not introduce the possibility of reading διὰ τοῦ Θεοῦ differently than its plain sense. It is assumed that διά means διά and rightly so, for the biblical witness is consistent on the score that διά can stand before each person of the Trinity.

Again, the presence of these two texts used together, for this purpose, is significant. If this text is by Didymus, he could have used the texts in this connection from memory without thinking of Philo, or his use of Philo in *In Genesim* could have brought these two texts together in his mind (and therefore also Philo's interpretation). If not by Didymus, using these two texts together could have been part of a tradition, or perhaps the anonymous author knew Philo as well. Either way, what is significant is that Philo started a distinctive use of these two verses together for a particular purpose, and in both of these Didymian texts, the verses are used in a manner that relates to Philo's use of them. Again, the use of the verses in this way in *De Trinitate* could either show how Philo's concatenation could be used variously—Philo could be supported or left behind—depending on the context of use and theological exigency, or it could point to the inauthenticity of the work (because Didymus in *In Genesim* clearly follows Philo).

Didymus's use of Philo's Genesis concatenation in these two texts displays the kind of wrinkle that can be present in one's use of a figure to whom one needs to show no ultimate loyalty. Runia is on key with his summary: "Philo is clearly a repository of knowledge that the exegete can draw on freely. Naturally this should be done with tact. The repeated warning that one should avoid 'pedantry' no doubt is meant to encourage a selective and creative use of the material that Philo furnishes in abundance."[45] As we have seen, Didymus's use of Philo is almost uniformly positive, and the possible use in *De Trinitate* could point in its own way to Didymus's "selective and creative" use of Philo's interpretation of Genesis when needed.[46]

---

[44] Heron, "Sources," 174, explains that the work is "a vast compendium of exegetical and theological arguments dating from around the end of the Arian controversy and therefore very likely to have drawn on a whole host of sources."

[45] Runia, *Early Christian Literature,* 204.

[46] The combination of verses for similar purposes also appears in the spurious work attributed to Athanasius of Alexandria, *Testimonia e scriptura* (text: PG 29–80).

3.2. *Basil of Caesarea (320–379 CE)*

As with Didymus, Basil's connection to Philo is not questioned.[47] With Basil it is possible that he got this tradition from Origen,[48] though we have no evidence that Origen used this concatenation; or it is possible (and likely) that there was a more direct link from Basil's own reading of Philo, because we know he knew Philo, and it seems like his discussion of the text may be more detailed than would suggest an indirect connection.

The hub of the discussion of Basil's relationship to Philo has been Basil's possible references to Philo in his *Homilies on the Hexaemeron*, the most influential early Christian writing on the creation of the world. Given the importance of this work historically, it has received much scholarly attention; and given that it is primarily dedicated to interpreting the six days of creation, speculation about its relation to Philo's work *De Opificio Mundi* has been substantial.[49] For example, Emmanuel Amand de Mendieta considered Philo's treatise to be one of the four main works Basil used in researching and writing the *Hexaemeron*.[50] Similarly, the French translator Stanislas Giet listed a number of passages where he believed Philo had strongly influence Basil.[51] The most significant passage is Basil's interpretation of Gen 1:26, where Basil critiques an explicitly Jewish opponent who "fight[s] against the truth, asserting that God was conversing with himself" even though the second person of the Trinity was being "disclosed in a

---

[47] For example, Basil mentions Philo's interpretation of the manna in *Ep.* 190.3—though the discussion of Philo's interpretation corresponds to no known text of Philo.

[48] For background on Basil, see esp. Philip Rousseau, *Basil of Caesarea* (Berkeley: University of California Press, 1998). Runia, *Early Christian Literature*, 235, explains how Basil was deeply interested in Origen's theology and the Alexandrian tradition (e.g., he went to Alexandria and made a study of Origen); see also R. Lim, "The Politics of Interpretation in Basil of Caesarea's 'Hexaemeron,'" *VC* 44 (1990): 351–52. It is noteworthy that Origen brought the works of Philo to Caesarea. It is also possible, though unlikely, that Basil could have received the use of these verses via Didymus.

[49] See the literature cited in Runia, *Early Christian Literature*, 237. I am indebted to Runia for directing me to the relevant portions by Amand de Mendieta and Giet on the question of Philo's influence on Basil. For a thorough discussion of Philo's creation account in relation to patristic authors, Paul M. Blowers, *Drama of the Divine Economy: Creator and Creation in Early Christian Theology and Piety* (Oxford: Oxford University Press, 2012), 39–66 on Philo and and 101–38 on interpretations of the *Hexaemeron*.

[50] Emmanuel Amand de Mendieta, "La préparation et la composition des neuf Homélies sur l'Hexaémeron de Basile de Césarée: Le problème des sources littéraires immédiates," StPatr 16 (1985): 349–67.

[51] Stanislas Giet, *Basile de Césarée. Homélies sur l'hexaéméron*, second ed., SC 26 (Paris: Éditions du Cerf, 1968), 236. Cf. also Lim, "The Politics of Interpretation," 352. Again, the loss of Origen's commentary makes it difficult to ascertain how direct Philo's influence was on the *Hexaemeron*.

secret fashion."[52] This opponent is later called a "fighter against Christ," as Basil argues that God was clearly conversing with his "companion in the work of creation."[53] The diatribe follows on the same track for awhile, with Basil fuming about Jewish impiety caused by their un-Christological reading of Gen 1:26. Scholars have believed that Philo was the intended target of this attack (cf. *Opif.* 23, 72–75).[54]

However, Runia has offered a convincing counterargument that Philo is not in view here, and therefore one cannot argue that Basil had a negative view of Philo based on this text.[55] Runia notes that Basil's critique shifts between singular and plural, indicating that "the single Jew must be read as a *collective figure*," who stands for Jewish exegesis of the creation account.[56] Likewise, as Runia displays, Basil is not interested in Jewish exegesis in itself, but in relation to the Heteroousian heresy (propounded most forcefully by Aetius and Eunomius), which argued for dissimilarity (ἀνόμοιος) between Father and Son; this, for Basil, meant they essentially advocated Judaism. The argument continues in the same vein; the full lines of argument need not detain us here.[57] What is important is that Runia shows why Philo is unlikely to be the denounced individual, the χριστομάχος, because the grounds for identifying Philo with Basil's foe are flawed, and therefore there is little justification for viewing Basil's picture of Philo through a negatively colored lens. As Runia summarizes: "It would be more correct to conclude that Basil's attitude is rather neutral. We may presume that he sees Philo as part of the Alexandrian tradition of biblical exegesis, and so

---

[52] *Hex.* 9.6 87.B; translation from Runia, *Early Christian Literature*, 238.

[53] *Hex.* 9.6 87.D-E.

[54] Cf., e.g., Giet, *Basile de Césarée*, 514; Jean Daniélou, "Philon et Grégoire de Nysse," in *Philon d'Alexandrie: Lyon 11–15 Septembre 1966: Colloques nationaux du Centre National de la Recherche Scientifique* (Paris: Éditions du Centre national de la recherche scientifique, 1967), 333–45, citation from 336.

[55] As, e.g., Daniélou, "Philon et Grégoire," 337 does.

[56] Runia, *Early Christian Literature*, 239.

[57] See further David T. Runia, "'Where, Tell Me, Is the Jew…?': Basil, Philo and Isidore of Pelusium," *VC* 46 (1992): 175–80. For example, while Basil's argument presumes that the Jewish figure believed God created alone, with no other being present—like a carpenter talking by himself, to his tools—Philo clearly does believe that other beings were present and active in the creation of *humans* (cf. *Opif.* 72–75). Indeed, on these grounds, as Runia points out, Isidore of Pelusium could say that Philo came so close to belief in the Trinity that he came "into conflict with his own religion" (181). According to Runia, Isidore's statements about Philo might be a defense of Philo vis-à-vis Basil's negative statements about the Jews in the *Hexaemeron*. Of course, finding a form of trinitarian belief in Philo was not restricted only to early Christians; see, for example, the wonderfully titled work of Caesar Morgan, *An Investigation of the Trinity of Plato and of Philo Judaeus and of the Effects which an Attachment to their Writings had upon the Principles and Reasonings of the Fathers of the Christian Church*, rev. ed. (Cambridge: Cambridge University Press, 1853).

feels free to draw on the material he offers, but sees no compelling reason to draw attention to his particular contribution."[58]

Now we might be able to add another data point for relating Basil to Philo, from Basil's work *De Spiritu Sancto*.[59]

The work begins with Basil's commendation of a certain Amphilochios, particularly for his deep understanding of the truth that "none of the words used to describe God should be passed over without exact examination, no matter what their context" (1.1).[60] Amphilochios is thus set in contrast to those who "spew forth elaborately constructed inquiries" but do "not really hop[e] to learn anything useful from them." They who do not seek righteousness fervently also "count theological terminology as secondary" in importance (1.2). But, as Basil states, setting up the argument, "to scrutinize syllables is not a superfluous task." Accordingly, "I am aware that little words express a great controversy (μέγιστον...ἐν μικροῖς ῥήμασι τὸ ἀγώνισμα), and in hope of winning the prize I will not hesitate to work."[61] The problem is that some have critiqued Basil and his like-minded associates for their use of prepositions in their doxologies. These critics believed Basil et al. were using prepositions in a contradictory way, applying multiple prepositions to different members of the Trinity (1.3).[62] But for Basil, these opponents are not being pious in their observation of syllables; rather, they represent a "deep and hidden plot against true religion" (2.4). I will quote Basil's explanation of the problem:

[58] Runia, *Early Christian Literature*, 241.

[59] Sterling, "Prepositional Metaphysics," 219–20 opens his study by noting Basil's contention with Aetius over the use of prepositions in 1 Cor 8:6, but he does not note the use of Gen 4:1 and 40:8 in Basil's *De Spiritu Sancto*.

[60] I quote the translation by David Anderson, *St. Basil the Great: On the Holy Spirit* (Crestwood, NY: St. Vladimir's Seminary Press, 1980). References are to chapter and section. The critical text used is Benoit Pruche, *Basile de Césarée. Sur le Saint-Esprit,* 2nd ed., SC 17 (Paris: Éditions du Cerf, 1968), 250–530.

[61] Thus, as David G. Robertson, "Basil of Caesarea on the Meaning of Prepositions and Conjunctions," *CQ* 53 (2003): 167 summarizes, Basil "devoted himself to explaining the meaning of prepositions and conjunctions in order to support his theological programme against his opponents in the church."

[62] It is easy to oversimplify the relation of Basil to his opponents as well as the theology of his opponents (as if they were a homogeneous entity), so I will not try to enter into that conversation in the limited space here. For discussions of Aetius, Eunomius, and Basil, and the many issues relating to their theologies, see esp. Andrew Radde-Gallwitz, *Basil of Caesarea, Gregory of Nyssa, and the Transformation of Divine Simplicity* (Oxford: Oxford University Press, 2009), 87–174; Rousseau, *Basil of Caesarea,* 93–132; Mark DelCogliano, *Basil of Caesarea's Anti-Eunomian Theory of Names: Christian Theology and Late-Antique Philosophy in the Fourth Century Trinitarian* Controvers, VCSup 103 (Leiden: Brill, 2010); and R.P.C. Hanson, *The Search for the Christian Doctrine of God: The Arian Controversy 318–381* (repr., Edinburgh: T&T Clark, 2005), 598–637.

They have an old trick invented by Aetius, the champion of their heresy, who writes in one of his letters that things whose natures are dissimilar are expressed in dissimilar terms (τὰ ἀνόμοια κατὰ τὴν φύσιν ἀνομοίως προφέρεσθαι), and, vice-versa, dissimilar terms are used to describe things whose natures are dissimilar. In his attempts to prove this he even drags in the Apostle's words: "one God and Father, *from* Whom (ἐξ οὗ) are all things...and one Lord Jesus Christ, *through* Whom (δι᾽ οὗ) are all things" (1 Cor 8:6). He then goes on to say that the relationship between these prepositions (*from* and *through*) indicates the relationship between the *natures* they describe (αἱ δι᾽ αὐτῶν σημαινόμεναι φύσεις), and, since the expression "from whom" differs from "through whom," the Father is therefore different from the Son. This pestilence of a heresy depends entirely upon the subtleties of these men concerning the above prepositions... [where] one prepositional phrase is always made to indicate a corresponding nature. (2.4)

Basil explains in the next chapter that these men have been led astray through reading "pagan writers" who make distinctions in nature based on prepositional phrases (3.5). Basil provides a précis of a kind of prepositional metaphysics (here, with six causes),[63] the "vain and empty distinctions" that these men have introduced to the "simple and uncluttered doctrine of the Spirit, using them to belittle God the Word and to deny the divine Spirit." Chapter four begins the counter-argument that "the freedom of the Spirit" in Holy Scripture is not "controlled by pagan pettiness" (4.6).[64] Rather, different prepositions are used in various contexts, as needed. Scripture is *most likely* to use ἐκ for God, "the supreme cause" (ἐπὶ τῆς ἀνωτάτω αἰτίας), but it can also be used of, e.g., different created elements. Chapter five, then, the most important section for our purposes, explains how διά can be used of God the Father and ἐκ of the Son and Spirit.[65]

---

[63] On which, see Sterling, "Prepositional Metaphysics," 219, 229.

[64] As Stephen M. Hildebrand, *The Trinitarian Theology of Basil of Caesarea: A Synthesis of Greek Thought and Biblical Truth* (Washington, DC: Catholic Uuniversity of America Press, 2007), 179 summarizes, for Basil there "are no laws governing the use of prepositions in the Bible whereby one preposition may be said to be used of the Father alone, another of the Son alone, and still another of the Spirit alone." Even if one thinks the New Testament authors knew and were potentially influenced by various streams of prepositional metaphysics—as, e.g., Sterling, "Prepositional Metaphysics," 232–38 does—Basil would still be on solid ground here, at least in terms of a unified rule for prepositions that governs the whole canon. For a helpful study on prepositions in the New Testament, see Murray J. Harris, *Prepositions and Theology in the Greek New Testament: An Essential Reference Resource for Exegesis* (Grand Rapids, MI: Zondervan, 2012).

[65] For discussion of Basil's understanding of prepositions within the development of his trinitarian theology, see Volker H. Drecoll, *Die Entwicklung der Trinitätslehre des Basilius von Cäsarea. Sein Weg vom Homöusianer zum Neonizäner* (Göttingen: Vandenhoeck & Ruprecht, 1996), esp. 212–18; see also Hildebrand, *Trinitarian Theology of Basil*. More broadly, see Lewis Ayres, *Nicaea and its Legacy: An Approach to Fourth-Century Trinitarian Theology* (Oxford: Oxford University Press, 2004), 187–221.

Basil begins with 1 Cor 8:6, which uses ἐκ for the God the Father and διά for Jesus. For Basil, this distinction is not meant to "introduce any division of natures," but "to prove that the union of Father and Son is without confusion" (5.7). Basil then uses Rom 11:36 to show that his opponents' argument will not stand: the three prepositions found therein (ἐξ αὐτοῦ καὶ δι' αὐτοῦ καὶ εἰς αὐτὸν) refer *either* to the Son *or* to the Father, and in either case (Basil thinks the Son is the referent), an improper preposition is used (5.7–8). Numerous passages are then cited to show that "from" (ἐκ) can be used for Jesus and the Spirit (cf., e.g., John 1:16; Luke 8:46; Gal 6:8; 1 John 3:24). Finally, Basil begins to show how διά is used equally of all three persons.

There are too many scriptural references using διά for the Son, so Basil does not even bother; his opponents, of course, know this (5.10). But Basil employs 1 Cor 1:9; 2 Cor 1:1; Gal 4:7; Rom 6:4; and Isa 29:15 as examples of διά used to denote God's activity; and 2 Tim 1:14 and 1 Cor 12:8 suffice to confirm the use of διά for the Spirit. Similarly, a number of texts display the use of ἐν for the Father; the evidence for the Son and Spirit, again, are too abundant, and therefore unnecessary, to list (5.11). Basil closes this section of the argument with the following: "I cannot easily refrain from remarking that the 'wise hearer' may easily discover that if terminological differences indicate differences in nature, then our opponents must shamefully agree that identical terminology is used for identical natures. Thus ample proof of our proposition has been provided."[66]

One would have expected Philo's Genesis concatenation to show up in the examples of the use of διά for God; but instead, curiously, it appears in a section whose argument is that "the meanings of prepositions themselves are often interchangeable and are transferred from one subject to the other" (5.12). Immediately after this statement, the Genesis concatenation is used; and the passage is worth quoting in full:

Οἶον· Ἐκτησάμην ἄνθρωπον διὰ τοῦ Θεοῦ (Gen 4:1), φησὶν ὁ Ἀδάμ,[67] ἴσον λέγων τῷ ἐκ τοῦ Θεοῦ.

---

[66] On the relation of Basil's Greek education and his reading of scripture, see Hildebrand, *Trinitarian Theology of Basil*, 150–72. Cf. also the introductory material by Mark DelCogliano and Andrew Radde-Gallwitz to *St. Basil of Caesarea: Against Eunomius* (Washington, D.C.: Catholic University of America Press, 2011), 55–60.

[67] Note the attribution of the words to Adam, as also in *Eun.* 2.20; this attribution is likely dependent on Eusebius in *Eccl. theol.* 3.2.21–23, though, as already noted, Philo also attributes the saying to Adam. As Sterling, "Prepositional Metaphysics," 238 n.93 notes, it is clear from Eusebius' *Praeparatio evangelica* 11.14–19 that early Christians knew about different views of causation, and specifically knew Philo's view on the second cause. The heading of book 11 chapter 15 is: ΦΙΛΩΝΟΣ ΠΕΡΙ ΤΟΥ ΔΕΥΤΕΡΟΥ ΑΙΤΙΟΥ. The brief

Καὶ ἑτέρωθι· Ὅσα ἐνετείλατο Μωϋσῆς τῷ Ἰσραὴλ διὰ τοῦ προστάγματος Κυρίου (Num 36:5). Καὶ πάλιν· Οὐχὶ διὰ τοῦ Θεοῦ ἡ διασάφησις αὐτῶν ἐστιν; (Gen 40:8) ὁ Ἰωσὴφ περὶ τῶν ἐνυπνίων τοῖς ἐν τῷ δεσμωτηρίῳ διαλεγόμενος, σαφῶς καὶ αὐτὸς <u>ἀντὶ τοῦ ἐκ Θεοῦ εἰπεῖν διὰ τοῦ Θεοῦ</u> εἴρηκε. (5.12)

A few things can be noted about Basil's use of the concatenation here. First, the verses are presented in the same order as in Didymus's *De Trinitate*: Gen 4:1, with Num 36:5 interrupting, and then Gen 40:8.[68] Second, however, the use of these verses in the argument is more like Didymus's use in *In Genesim*; that is, the issue is showing an equivalence in meaning for a preposition, thus moving the attention away from the discrete preposition itself.[69] But there is also a difference. For Didymus, διά should be understood as παρά in order to make a *proper interpretation* of what the Genesis texts are saying about God's agency. For Basil, διά is *equivalent* to ἐκ (ἴσον λέγων τῷ ἐκ τοῦ Θεοῦ)[70] because, as he shows in the rest of the argument, Paul can sometimes use ἐκ where διά is more accurate (e.g. 1 Cor 11:12). Altogether, the argument thus shows that *from whom* and *through whom* are used interchangeably for the same subjects, depending on the context of the passage. Basil concludes with a question: "so how can anyone say that the phrases can be invariably distinguished from each other, falsely attempting to find fault with true religion?" Third, then, the point is not simply about matching the right preposition to the divine nature and agency, but rather that because multiple prepositions can be used of God, διά and ἐκ overlap semantically.[71] As with Didymus, Basil believes the biblical authors were

---

section contains a few quotations of passages about the Logos from Philo's *Det.* It is purely speculation, but again, it is possible that the attribution of the words of Genesis 4:1 to Adam, not Eve, could have entered through Philo (possibly by way of Eusebius).

[68] It would be rather hazardous to venture that 1) Didymus wrote *De Trinitate*, and then also that 2) Basil was dependent on Didymus for the use of this concatenation; consequently, I will just imply here that it is a possibility. Mark DelCogliano, "Basil of Caesarea, Didymus the Blind, and the Anti-Pneumatochian Exegesis of Amos 4:13 and John 1:3," *JTS* 61 (2010): 644–58 has recently argued that Basil in his *Against Eunomius* was dependent on Didymus's work *On the Holy Spirit* for aspects of his "Pro-Nicene Pneumatology." The overlap between the structure and wording of the verses in *De Trinitate* and *De Spiritu Sancto* is noteworthy, if nothing else.

[69] Cf. Robertson, "Meaning of Prepositions," 169, who argues that Basil's method depends on "first taking the preposition or conjunction and forming a unit from the nominals taken together with the preposition or conjunction, then taking the predicate along with the subject, and then looking at the joint contribution of these elements to the meaning of the sentence." The preposition in itself is not king.

[70] The distinction between ἐκ and παρά here is trivial.

[71] Cf. Drecoll, *Entwicklung der Trinitätslehre*, 218: "Eine theologische Argumentation ergibt sich dann erst anhand dieser Übersicht, wo Basilius das Ziel seiner konkordanzartigen Zusammenstellung zusammenfaßt: Wenn nämlich der Unterschied der Bezeich-

safe in using διά for the Father, because διά is not locked into a relationship with instrumentality.[72]

Again, the question is: why use *these verses* for *this argument* if not because of the original Philonic usage? Like Didymus, Basil does not critique the biblical speakers (Philo alone does that), nor does he say διά was inappropriate to use (like Philo). Rather, he clarifies how διά is used. Because of the argumentative context, something like a Philonic anxiety about prepositions is present—even though Philo's argument fits more readily with Basil's opponents![73]—but Basil's argument is different from Philo's. Since now the issue is about the relation of each person of the Trinity vis-à-vis the one divine nature, prepositions cannot make a distinction in nature, even though it is still the case that διά is not simply διά. With Basil, then, we again find an interesting use of Philo's Genesis concatenation, used to a similar effect as Didymus, with the same sorts of worries as seen in Philo; but Basil would necessarily have to leave Philo's interpretation of the verses behind as a theologically anemic understanding of the divine nature in its relation to the grammar of Scripture. This conclusion, then, adds a somewhat negatively tinted data point to Runia's conclusion that Basil's view of Philo would be largely neutral. Grammar was not trivial for either Philo or Basil, and they disagreed here fundamentally about how to apply it to speech about the one true God who stands behind all reality.

3.3. *John Chrysostom (349–407 CE)*

John Chrysostom is our final author to discuss, though we can be much briefer here.[74] John's use of the Genesis concatenation is interesting especially because there is little to no evidence that he knew Philo.[75] So we

---

nung einen Unterschied in der φύσις aufzeigen soll, dann bedeutet die Gleichheit der Wörter doch die Unterschiedlosigkeit in der οὐσία."

[72] Cf. Robertson, "Meaning of Prepositions," 167: "there is no rigid, one-to-one link between particular prepositions and conjunctions used in Scripture…and particular theological claims regarding unity and equality of the persons of the Trinity." See also the discussion of prepositions in chapter 25 of *De Spiritu Sancto*; Drecoll, *Entwicklung der Trinitätslehre*, 254–63.

[73] It would be easy simply to identify Philo as a potential source of the "pagan pettiness" Basil is attacking; discerning whether Philo actually stood behind Basil's opponents as a resource is beyond the scope of this article and the ability of its author.

[74] On Chrysostom, see, e.g., Wendy Mayer and Pauline Allen, *John Chrysostom* (London: Routledge, 2000); J.N.D. Kelly, *Golden Mouth: The Story of John Chyrsostom. Ascetic, Preacher, Bishop* (Ithaca, NY: Cornell University Press, 1995).

[75] Cf. the judgment of Runia, *Early Christian Literature*, 270–71: "One will look in vain for a reference to Philo in the vast body of works written by or associated with John Chrysostom." But as Runia adds, "We should not exclude the possibility…that…Philonic

finally have something like a fully "traditional" use of Philo's Genesis concatenation in relation to discussions about prepositions and the divine nature, with—apparently—the same concerns of our other authors.

Chrysostom's use of the two Genesis texts occurs in his work *In Matthaeum.*[76] I will reproduce the relevant section below:

Εἰ δὲ, Δι᾽ οὗ, λέγει, μὴ θαυμάσῃς. Οὐ γὰρ ὡς ἑτέρου δι᾽ αὐτοῦ εἰσάγοντος τοῦτό φησιν, ἀλλ᾽ ὡς αὐτοῦ τὸ πᾶν κατασκευάζοντος. Οἶδε γὰρ τὸ δι᾽ οὗ, τὸ ὑφ᾽ οὗ λέγειν ἡ Γραφή· ὡς ὅταν λέγῃ· Ἐκτησάμην ἄνθρωπον διὰ τοῦ Θεοῦ (Gen 4:1)· οὐ τὸ δεύτερον αἴτιον, ἀλλὰ τὸ πρῶτον τιθεῖσα. Καὶ πάλιν· Οὐχὶ διὰ τοῦ Θεοῦ ἡ διασάφησις αὐτῶν ἐστι; (Gen 40:8) καὶ, Πιστὸς ὁ Θεὸς, δι᾽ οὗ ἐκλήθητε εἰς κοινωνίαν τοῦ Υἱοῦ αὐτοῦ.

This portion of text comes after a citation of Matt 18:7 (οὐαὶ τῷ ἀνθρώπῳ δι᾽ οὗ τὸ σκάνδαλον ἔρχεται). There is no mention of Philo, but Gen 4:1 and 40:8 are used to support Chrysostom's reassurance that his readers should not be amazed (μὴ θαυμάσῃς) if διά is used for God. This use does not mean the author is referring to any other than the one who created all things. Rather, Scripture knows that διά refers to the first cause, just like ὑπό. The Genesis concatenation provides an example of this: "As when it says..." Accordingly, Gen 4:1 speaks not of the second cause but the first (οὐ τὸ δεύτερον αἴτιον, ἀλλὰ τὸ πρῶτον τιθεῖσα). "And again" (Καὶ πάλιν), Gen 40:8 shows that διά refers to God who τὸ πᾶν κατασκευάζων. Lastly, in this portion of the text, Chrysostom uses 1 Cor 1:9 to seal the argument. Because Scripture knows that the "through whom" means the "by whom," it is not constrained in its use of prepositions: God remains the first cause whether God's action is governed by διά or ὑπό.

As with Didymus and Basil, Chrysostom does not critique either Scripture or the characters speaking in the text; rather, he clarifies what is actually meant. Chrysostom's use of the concatenation follows Didymus's use in *In Genesim*, rather than *De Trinitate* or Basil's use in *De Spiritu Sancto*, both of which placed a verse between the two Genesis texts. We could only speculate how or why Chrysostom came to use these two texts together, but we are on fairly solid ground to say that by this time Philo's Genesis concatenation had become a set pair of texts that could handily be used in discussions of divine causation, prepositions and the divine nature, and the action of God in general. However, simply because Philo's verses were

---

material is present" in writings of authors like Chrysostom and authors who do not explicitly mention Philo. Such a presence is "awaiting identification by observant scholars."

76 The text of *In Matthaeum* I have consulted is in J.-P. Migne, PG 57–58. Cf. Kelly, *Golden Mouth*, 92: "...the sprawling Matthew commentary... [is] full of moral and ascetical exhortation shot through... with Stoic presuppositions."

used does not mean that his interpretation—or intent—was followed. Here, Chrysostom makes a fairly Philonic move in explaining how exactly διά could be used of God, but he does not 'correct' the usage in the same way Philo does. Nevertheless, this text in *In Matthaeum* represents something like a positive presence of Philonic material in Chrysostom's corpus.

4. Conclusion

The purpose of this article has been to provide a new data point for the use and influence of Philo of Alexandria's writings on early Christian authors. As we have seen, in the writings of Didymus the Blind, Basil of Caesarea, and John Chrysostom, Philo's concatenation of Gen 4:1 and 40:8—used for the purpose of describing how prepositions relate to the activity of God— had an interesting, and permanent, afterlife.[77] While it is possible that these verses could have been used separately for the topic of God's nature/ agency and there would be no reason to point to dependence on Philo, starting with Didymus's *In Genesim* we see a very particular use of these verses together, with a specific focus on using prepositions rightly to describe God's actions; and this use branches out in Basil, developing into the more serious concern of rightly not making a distinction in nature between the persons of the Trinity. There is little reason to think the concatenation of these two Genesis verses would have been used in this way without Philo's influence. And it is interesting to trace how it could be used, vis-à-vis Philo, positively, negatively, or neutrally.

As already noted, the use of the intervening verse in Didymus's *De Trinitate* and Basil's *De Spiritu Sancto*—as well as the presence of the concatenation in Chrysostom's *In Matthaeum*, which shows no evidence of knowing Philo—might mean that the use of these two verses had become a kind of common tradition, stock verses to use in this discussion. This use would have come from Philo; and yet the eventual meaning of the concatenation could be used to make points Philo would never have made. The issue, then, is not simply the author's direct relation to Philo; the issue here is how the author is using Philonic material or a Philonic exegetical move. If it is directly dependent, as in the case of Didymus, then we get

---

[77] The use of these two verses for the topic of divine activity did not stop with these early Christian authors; indeed, it also shows up in a number of medieval authors, includeing Joannes XI Beccus (thirteenth century, *De Unione Ecclesiarum* and *Ad Theodorum Sugdeae episcopum*), Georgius Metochites (thirteenth century, *Historiae dogmaticae liber I*), Gennadius Scholarius (fifteenth century, *Tractatus de Processu spiritus sancti II*), and Marcus Eugenicus (15th century, *Capita syllogistica adversus Latinos de spiritus sancti ex patre processione*).

another clear data point for construing their relationship; if it is not directly dependent, but stemming from a now-commonplace use of Philo, as in perhaps John Chrysostom, then that too provides a data point—not in terms of direct dependence, but still in terms of how one could use Philo, or of how Philo had influenced the exegetical-theological tradition. Basil, of course, provides the most striking example. As we have seen, the central contextual question that determines the use of Philo was, "Are we describing how a preposition defines God's action, or are we describing how the use of prepositions defines the relations of the members of the Trinity?" In relation to either question, Philo lurked; but the context produces variegated use or rejection of Philo's own interpretation.

This article has limited itself to the rather circumscribed project of examining particularly how a Philonic concatenation of Gen 4:1 and 40:8 was used by early Christian authors. There are a number of related avenues of inquiry one could take, and there are doubtlessly more connections between Philo and early Christian authors like the one provided here that will be discovered eventually. As Runia puts it, "…far more research can be done on the history of the transmission and exploitation of Philo's writings. The story…needs to be told in far greater detail, and a fascinating tale it will be."[78]

Knox Theological Seminary

---

[78] Runia, *Early Christian Literature*, 31.

The Studia Philonica Annual 27 (2015): 111–127

PHILOSOPHY'S INQUISITOR:

Franz Rosenzweig's Philo between Judaism,
Paganism, and Christianity

BENJAMIN POLLOCK

The German-Jewish thinker Franz Rosenzweig (1886–1929) was the author of *The Star of Redemption* (1921), one of the most important books of Jewish philosophy written in the modern period. He was also a reader of Philo. The diaries Rosenzweig wrote while serving on the German Balkan front in the First World War, housed today at the Leo Baeck Institute in New York City, include seven pages of notes, in Greek and German, which Rosenzweig jotted down while reading Philo.[1] It would be an exaggeration to say that Philo greatly influenced Rosenzweig's thinking. But there is no question that Rosenzweig read and thought seriously about Philo during a crucial period for the development of his own philosophical position. In what follows, I want to make two claims about Rosenzweig's engagement with Philo. The first claim is that reading Philo helped Rosenzweig clarify

---

[1] Rosenzweig's wartime notes from 1916–1917 were collected under the title Rosenzweig himself gave them: "Paralipomena." Rosenzweig sent these notes back to his parents from the warfront, where they were later transcribed, possibly under Rosenzweig's own guidance. We can accurately date those notes sent between the end of January and the middle of September, 1916, because of post stamps. Unfortunately, Rosenzweig's notes on Philo are part of the collection that appears to have been written after mid-September, 1916, but which isn't accompanied by post stamps. On a few of these notes, Rosenzweig writes "September," but it isn't clear if this is 1916 or 1917. It appears someone—from Rosenzweig himself down to the archivists—added years in the margins, but these don't make sense of the content. So, for example, if we are to believe this dating attempt, Rosenzweig read the very end of *De opificio mundi* and the very beginning of *Legum allegoriae 1* in September 1916, but read the rest of *De opificio mundi* and the rest of the *Legum allegoriae* after September 1917. This obviously won't do! I think it likely the comments on Philo all stem from the fall of 1916, but this is guesswork. The material is collected as "Paralipomena," Franz Rosenzweig Collection, AR 3001 (Manuscript in Series II, Subseries III:D, Box 2, Folder 40), Leo Baeck Institute, Center for Jewish History, New York. A selection of these wartime notes were published in the third volume of Rosenzweig's *Gesammelte Schriften* as "Paralipomena," *Zweistromland. Kleinere Schriften zu Glauben und Denken. Franz Rosenzweig. Der Mensch und sein Werk Gesammelte Schriften III*, ed. Reinhold and Annemarie Mayer (Dordrecht: Martinus Nijhoff, 1984) [henceforth: *Zweistromland*], 61–124.

what would become a central concept in his mature thought: the concept of *creation*. The second claim is that Philo's thought resisted in illuminating ways the manner in which Rosenzweig classified religious and cultural traditions of thought. Rosenzweig was prone to essentializing religious and cultural traditions such as "paganism," "Judaism," and "Christianity," and to making claims about the philosophical and historical positions these traditions represent. Rosenzweig's account of Philo is interesting precisely because Philo doesn't fit neatly for Rosenzweig into these categories. As a result, throughout these diary notes, as well as in Rosenzweig's letters, we find Rosenzweig trying to determine precisely how much Moses and how much Plato one finds in Philo's conception of creation, how much revelation and how much paganism infuse Philo's thought, and how much Judaism and how much Christianity are anticipated in his thought. In this regard, I want to clarify, in particular, the extent to which Rosenzweig sees Philo as representative of *Jewish thinking*, and of a certain role he understands Judaism to play in the course of the world's redemption. But I then want to examine how Rosenzweig sees Philo as deviating from that Jewish role and pointing "back" to paganism, or towards Christianity.

Although, as a post-Hegelian thinker, Rosenzweig was committed to a historical view of the unfolding of Being in a way that distinguishes him sharply from Philo, I want to note that the ancient philosophical and religious positions Rosenzweig worked through in the years before he wrote his magnum opus were living options for him, with all the romanticism that would have accompanied this attitude. The holistic metaphysical position Rosenzweig would arrive at in his *Star of Redemption* allowed him to overcome a dualism that had plagued him personally for a number of years and which he identified directly with Marcionism.[2] Thinking through Philo's account of creation is part of the process through which Rosenzweig overcame that Marcionist dualism and came to see the divine's relation to the *world* as essential to redemption.

Before addressing Rosenzweig's reading of Philo, let me begin with a brief survey of Rosenzweig's philosophical project, so that we might better appreciate how his own thinking dovetails with, or was influenced by, or was in conflict with Philo's thought. *The Star of Redemption* sets out to articulate the systematic unity of all beings—"the All," as Rosenzweig calls it—and the book presents this "All" as a unity formed out of the relations between three fundamental kinds of beings: God, world, and selves. For reasons that Rosenzweig spells out in the *Star*, individual beings cannot

---

[2] See Benjamin Pollock, *Franz Rosenzweig's Conversions: World Denial and World Redemption* (Bloomington, IN: Indiana University Press, 2014).

fully actualize themselves without entering into relations with others. Over the course of all time, these relations unify all beings into a redemptive whole. Rosenzweig designates the first of these relations, between God and world, as *creation*; he designates the second, between God and individual selves, as *revelation*; and he designates the third and culminating relation between selves in the world as *redemption*. As the culminating relation between beings, redemption marks for Rosenzweig that ultimate future moment in which all beings will have united through relations to form "the All." There is a structured movement to the course of relations that allows this course to be thought, a logic of *reversal* or *conversions* (*Umkehr, Umkehrungen*), which beings undergo when they enter into relations. Rosenzweig's premise is that by entering into relations with others, we are changed, "converted," but that through such conversions we in fact actualize who we are. Individuals and communities play specific roles in the advance through relations to redemption. In revelation, the individual is awakened to selfhood, and is called on to devote herself to the realization of redemptive unity through relations with others. At the communal level, Judaism and Christianity are said to play distinct but complementary roles in the economy of redemption. Christianity is tasked with advancing the charge of interpersonal relations in the world through love. Judaism's task is to anticipate the redeemed world within its liturgical life, modeling that future redemptive goal for Christians. In any given present moment, Rosenzweig suggests, the Jewish people's anticipation of redemption serves to remind Christians that redemption has not yet arrived, and thus that they must work to actualize redemption in the world. It is meant to remind Christians that the world demands redemption no less than individual souls within it, that God is the God of creation, and not just the God of revelation and redemption.[3]

Such, in broad strokes, are the claims of Rosenzweig's *Star of Redemption*. On May 10–11, 1918, a few months before he began to write his book, Rosenzweig wrote a letter to his cousin, Hans Ehrenberg, to explain his view of Judaism's role in the redemptive process, and how that role demands Judaism engage with philosophy, on the one hand, and with Christianity, on the other. According to this letter, Judaism's role in the history of philosophy, as well as generally in the world's historical advance towards redemption, is to advocate for *truth*—for that ultimate form of the

---

[3] I develop this account of the claims and purpose of *The Star of Redemption* in detail in my *Franz Rosenzweig and the Systematic Task of Philosophy* (Cambridge: Cambridge University Press, 2009), 120–311.

unity of "the All" to be realized in redemption[4]—so that Christianity will engage in acts of interpersonal *love* that will bring about this redemptive unity.[5] Rosenzweig's letter suggests that philosophy stands in the way of this advance towards redemption, perhaps because philosophy—as Rosenzweig often argues—asserts something to be true in the *present* and does not recognize that truth will only be realized in the redemptive future,[6] or perhaps because he holds that a specifically Greek philosophy understands Being in *static* rather than in *dynamic* and *relational* terms, and thus again would resist those acts of relation which Rosenzweig sees as required in order to actualize redemptive truth. Rosenzweig proceeds to depict the relations between Judaism, Christianity, and philosophy in the form of an obscure courtroom scene, in which Judaism's advocacy for truth is described as a Jewish interrogation of philosophy before a Christian court audience. It is in the context of this courtroom scene, that Rosenzweig gives us a first clue as to the role he assigns to Philo in Judaism's struggle with philosophy for the sake of truth:

> You see the relationship of Judaism and philosophy somewhat too simply. Surely, it [i.e., Judaism] cannot overcome Greekdom. But only because it *must* not overcome it. Or, from your perspective, because God is not love (and only love overcomes), but rather is Truth. Truth doesn't overcome, but rather it shines, it is its index of true and falsehood. Therein the role that Judaism has played in the history of philosophy comes together. Greekdom is the defendant. Twice, in Philo and Maimonides, Judaism leads the preliminary-investigation. The whole orderly trial occurs then before the courtroom of Christianity, to which naturally the investigating magistrate does not belong. But you can scarcely get started with these general claims. For me too they are only provisional.... Perhaps [Hermann] Cohen belongs as the third in this series, and it is ordered according to the three epochs of Church-history

---

[4] See *Star of Redemption* (Madison, WI: University of Wisconsin Press, 2004), 403–440, e.g., p. 408: "God is the truth.... Truth is the scepter of his reign. In the All and One [of redemption, BP], life is complete; it is entirely living. Insofar as truth is one with the absolutely living reality, it is its essence; but insofar as it can nevertheless separate from it—without breaking the bond in the least—it is the essence of God." On Rosenzweig's account of truth, see also Kenneth Hart Green, "The Notion of Truth in Franz Rosenzweig's *The Star of Redemption*: A Philosophical Enquiry," *Modern Judaism* 7 (1987): 297–323, and Pollock, *Franz Rosenzweig's Conversions*, 191–209.

[5] On the manner in which the Jewish people's anticipation of redemption directs Christians to act towards it, compare *Star of Redemption*, 436–440.

[6] Compare *Star of Redemption*, 256: "The All of philosophers that we had reduced to dust with full knowledge of the facts, here in the dazzling light of the midnight where Redemption is fulfilled, has finally, truly finally, come together to become the One."

because, for example, the trial at which Maimonides leads the investigation extends to the discovery of the dialectical method by Hegel.[7]

In this depiction of Judaism's courtroom interrogation of philosophical Greekdom, Rosenzweig identifies Philo as a representative of a specifically *Jewish* response to philosophy. Indeed, he presents Philo as playing a role in the history of the Jewish engagement with philosophy that is equivalent in importance to the role that Maimonides played. The problem is that Rosenzweig doesn't tell us what it is about the *thought* of Philo, Maimonides, or Hermann Cohen, for that matter, that challenges philosophy and thereby advocates for truth. We aren't told what Philo does or says to advance the cause of truth.

So we have some detective work to do. For reasons I will spell out, Rosenzweig's situating of Philo at the start of a trajectory that passes through Maimonides on its way to the "dialectical method of Hegel" gives us some basis for speculation. I will try to show that when Rosenzweig links Philo and the historical trajectory from Maimonides to Hegel (and Cohen), he is thinking of the development of the concept of *creation* as a divine activity that links God with the world, and that points to God's revelatory engagement with human beings which, on Rosenzweig's own account, directs human beings to act towards the future redemption. Even years later, at the beginning of a 1921 lecture series on "Jewish Thought," Rosenzweig would identify creation as the centerpiece of the struggle Jewish thinking has waged since Philo against Greek thought.[8] In identifying Philo as the first Jewish inquisitor in his letter to Ehrenberg, I wish to claim, Rosenzweig identifies Philo's philosophical account of creation as setting in motion the development of a kind of dialectical thinking that will ultimately allow Rosenzweig himself to grasp the unity of God, world, and selves, through the course of relations.

Let's build a case for this interpretation by examining some of Rosenzweig's wartime notes on Philo from 1916–1917. In the citations and musings he writes while reading Philo's *De opificio mundi* and *Legum allegoriae* I and II, we see Rosenzweig's protracted interest in Philo's account of God as creator. When reading *Legum allegoriae* I, Rosenzweig jots down, without

---

[7] Franz Rosenzweig, *Briefe und Tagebücher. Band 1: 1900–1918. Der Mensch und sein Werk. Gesammelte Schriften* 1, ed. Rachel Rosenzweig and Edith Rosenzweig-Scheinmann (Haag: Martinus Nijhoff, 1979), 563. Hereafter *BT*.

[8] See Franz Rosenzweig, "Guide to Jewish Thinking," *Zweistromland*, 598: "'In the beginning God created the heavens and the earth.' Is this Jewish thinking? Yes. And its opposite? Greek thinking, thinking about the real (*das Eigentlich*). And the Jewish thinkers? In them Jewish thinking has conducted a (mostly unhappy) struggle against the trained Greek. From Philo and Saadia to Cohen."

comment, Philo's description of God the creator as eternally engaged in the act of creation: "God never leaves off making, but even as it is the property of fire to burn and of snow to chill, so it is the property of God to make."[9] Moreover, reading Philo's account of God's creation of the world in *De opificio mundi* leads Rosenzweig to a series of reflections on what he sees as a crucial shift in Philo from the Platonic-Aristotelian tradition of thought to a Mosaic tradition:

> One must really assume that outside revelation, the thought "I know that without me…" cannot be thought by any mystic. Plato in any case only has the way from the soul to God … —Indeed, at ground the opposition of the creator and the unmoved mover is through the *eros*—not Its, but rather that of the things. The Philonic Logos is indeed at least as much a Mosaicizing of Plato as a Platonizing of Moses. The *Agathon* is only absolute object. Only as *Logos* does it become absolute subject.[10]

Rosenzweig offers here an account of the difference between revelatory thinking and pagan thinking about God. Although pagan thought—Plato's included—may conceive of the possibility of an individual's union with the divine, Rosenzweig claims, the movement into that relation only goes in one direction: from the individual soul of the mystic to the divine. As a result, Rosenzweig suggests, the pagan account of the human relationship to the divine does not grant human activity in the world the *significance* which revelation does. For only the view that God *acts* to reveal Godself to the individual grants that individual the sense that "without me…" something vital to the world would be missing.[11]

Moreover, Rosenzweig here suggests the shift that makes it possible to think revelation happens in Philo. In Philo, the *eros* which activates the beings of the world is rooted first and foremost in God—as Creator rather

---

[9] Rosenzweig, "Paralipomena," 2a, citing Philo, *Leg.* 1.5.

[10] Rosenzweig, "Paralipomena," p. 30a, and in *Zweistromland*, 105.

[11] The "Paralipomena" are filled with Rosenzweig's attempts to formulate the distinction between revelation and Platonism, and include claims parallel to the above that stress God's activity, as well as the unique importance of the individual and of the individual moment in the context of revelation. See, for example, the "Paralipomena" published in *Zweistromland*, 81: "The mystic outside revelation doesn't know the 'humility of God,' only the divinization of *Man*"; pp. 81–2: "freedom, where revelation was already God's essence in creation, is primordially the meaning of the world. The world was created for the sake of the *decision*"; p. 82: "The ground-paradox of revelation is that the human being is summoned to abandon his nature, and summoned thereto by the God who is Himself the creator of this nature. … This … generates the characteristic quality of revelation: the *pathos of the moment*"; and p. 100: "The Creator, for Moses, is the One of whom he says *before all*: 'וירד הי'. For Plato, the *agathon* nowhere descends, and that's why creation for him too is only 'probable.' All paganism comes only to the divinization of man and knows not that the revelation *of God* must precede it."

than as Unmoved Mover—not merely in beings seeking to imitate God. Rosenzweig claims it is in Philo's *Logos* that the Platonic "Good" is transformed from absolute object to absolute subject, and thus divinity is grasped as *actively seeking relation with the world it creates*. This transformation of divinity from object to subject, Rosenzweig suggests, should be grasped as Philo's *Mosaicizing of Plato*.[12]

Rosenzweig's account of Philo here as marking a crucial shift in the philosophical conception of divinity gives us an important clue in our attempt to understand what Rosenzweig might have meant in his 1918 letter to Ehrenberg, when he designated Philo as the first of three world-historical Jewish interventions into philosophy for the sake of truth. That Rosenzweig would attribute to Philo, and to Mosaic thought in general, this shift from thinking the highest being as absolute object to thinking it as absolute subject is significant because Rosenzweig regularly describes Hegel as completing this very same shift from thinking being as object to thinking being as subject. Further, Rosenzweig sees in Hegel's dialectical method that movement of thought through which Hegel was able to think of Spirit as both Substance and Subject.[13] Thus, in identifying Philo with a Mosaic thinking that asserts God the Creator and thereby transforms the Platonic *agathon* from absolute object to absolute subject, he does indeed set Philo at the beginning of a trajectory that leads through Maimonides down to Hegel's dialectical method.[14] It is in this sense that Philo begins the Jewish advocacy for truth over against philosophy.

[12] Cf., Rosenzweig's diary note, from June 23, 1914: "In Philo one sees how a World-Church emerging immediately out of Judaism would have had to look at that time: Platonism and religion-of-the-Book at once; revelation without carrier of revelation; enlightenment and dogmatism in one," *BT* 1:161.

[13] Franz Rosenzweig, "Das Älteste Systemprogramm des Deutschen Idealismus," *Zweistromland*, 44.

[14] Exploring how Rosenzweig understands Maimonides's role in the development of the history of philosophy towards Hegel's dialectic would take us too far afield; I hope to work out Rosenzweig's claim about a Maimonidean anticipation of Hegel in another context. But the gist of Rosenzweig's view appears to be the following. Rosenzweig appears to be taking Maimonides's conception of negative attributes, i.e., that we can only approach articulating divine attributes accurately when we attribute to God *negations of privations*, and using it as a model for thinking about creation. Putting together the movement of negating privatives with the notion of creation appears to lead Rosenzweig to conceive of Hegel's dialectical negation of negation as a dynamic version of a Leibnizian picture of creation of world through divine self-limitation (a position Rosenzweig identifies with Salomon Maimon). See Rosenzweig's diary entries on July 11, 1914 in *BT* 1:70: "'Plato' and 'Aristotle' maintain the (negated or affirmed) *concept of God* through the assumption of the world, thus always of *the world*. Maimonides and later Hegel, on the other hand, through the (negating) assumption of the *negated* world, thus through the assumption of *God*. Only in Hegel would thus Maimonides really become fruitful, entering into the history of

Rosenzweig refines further what he takes to be the significance of Philo's move to grasp the divine as active creator in the following note, in which he offers what I gather scholars of Greek will find to be a rather creative interpretation of the difference between *nous* and *logos*:

> The *noesis noeseos* is a receptive analytic self-consciousness, not a productive one. *Nous* listens, *Logos* speaks. Plato, when he wanted to explain the world, had involved a *Demiourgos*, i.e., a God who is only there for the creating (thus a mere abstraction of the mythical world-view), and for whom the absolute *Agathon* itself is already *Law*, i.e., who is not *Itself* the *Agathon*. Philo makes the creator into the true God.[15]

Rosenzweig again highlights here Philo's identification of God with the Creator. If in the last passage that we examined, Rosenzweig noted Philo's transformation of the Platonic Good into the absolute subject, here he describes Philo as elevating the Platonic *Demiurgos* to the "True God," itself the *Agathon*.[16] But Rosenzweig explains this elevation of the Creator to God on the basis of what he claims is a shift in emphasis in Philo in the designator for the divine intellect, or perhaps even is a transition from one form of divine intellect to another. *Nous* listens, *Logos* speaks. God's self-knowledge as *Nous*, Rosenzweig claims, is a receptive, passive identity in which God contemplates Godself, whereas God as *Logos* is—again—active, productive: absolute subject.

Although Rosenzweig's reading here may seem like a hard sell when we consider Aristotle's insistence that God is eternally *active* in knowing Godself, I gather that Rosenzweig is thinking here of Philo's own critique, in *De opificio mundi* 7, of those who, "having more admiration for the cosmos than for its maker, declared the former both ungenerated and eternal, while falsely and impurely attributing to God much idleness."[17] Rosenzweig appears to understand Philo's critique as directed towards the

---

philosophy"; on July 18, 1914, in *BT* 1:171–72: "This task [rationalization of the actual] remained nevertheless unsolvable, so long as the rationality of God was grasped as the simple *negation* of the actuality of the world. Only through the schema of the double negation would it be possible. Here perhaps again Maimonides would have joined in, not however, with his last metaphysical synthesis, but with the concept in which he thought the creator-ness of God as (not his *essence*—that would be the *last* synthesis) but as attribute of his essence"; and, on February 3, 1918, in *BT* 1:510: "If Maimonides' concept of creation really leads through Maimon to the concept of absolute negativity, so this would be a proof for the Judaization of the Church of John."

[15] "Paralipomena," 30a, and in *Zweistromland*, 106.

[16] Compare Rosenzweig, "Paralipomena," in *Zweistromland*, 71: "It is essential to Plato's *Timaeus* that the demiurge only 'orders,' doesn't 'create.'"

[17] Citing the translation of David T. Runia, *On the Creation of the Cosmos according to Moses*, PACS 1 (Atlanta: Society of Biblical Literature, 2005), 48.

Peripatetics here.[18] He would thereby have Philo argue that a self-knowing deity who does not act directly upon the world is ultimately passive, receptive. If so, if Rosenzweig understands Philo as implying that God is only truly *active* if God is *creative*, i.e., *productive of activity* in others, then we might suggest that Rosenzweig projects back into Philo a view he himself takes up in the *Star of Redemption*: in order for God's power to be actualized, God must assert Godself in the creation of a world that is *outside* God; in order for divine being to be realized, God must be recognized by those who are *other* than God.[19] Rosenzweig appears to project this view into Philo, for whom, on Rosenzweig's reading, a truly active God must step out of Godself and create. A God who is truly good must bestow that goodness on the world; *nous* must become *logos*; the Good must become subject— precisely in order to be in truth what It is.

It is crucial finally that Rosenzweig distinguishes divine activity from divine passivity in terms of *hearing* and *speaking*. Although Rosenzweig is fond of quoting from the *Logos-Evangelium* from the opening of John, this is the only place I've found in Rosenzweig's writings where he considers Philo's *Logos* as speech rather than as active reason. For Rosenzweig this precedent is of enormous importance. In the *Star of Redemption*, Rosenzweig identifies speech—and not reason!—as that activating force which mediates the relations between God, world, and selves.[20]

---

[18] Compare David T. Runia, *Philo of Alexandria and the* Timaeus *of Plato* (Leiden: Brill, 1986), 100–101, as well as the "Excursus on Recent Interpretations of Philo's Argument," in Runia's commentary on *Opif., On the Creation of the Cosmos according to Moses*, 121–22.

[19] See Pollock, *Franz Rosenzweig and the Systematic Task of Philosophy*, 188–236.

[20] In the first part of the *Star of Redemption*, "logos" designates the world's universally valid order, a ramified but unified intelligible network *into* which the existent individual entities of the world are seen as settling. Language, on the other hand, is the medium of relation among God, world, and selves in the *Star of Redemption*, and thereby language serves as the key that allows us to grasp the course of relations between God, world, and selves that advances towards redemption. See, for example, *Star of Redemption*, 120: "Language is truly the morning gift of the Creator to humanity, and yet at once the common good of human beings, in which each has his particular share; and finally, it is the seal of humanity in human beings. It is wholly from the beginning: the human being became human being when he spoke. And yet, even today there is no language of humanity, but rather such will be only at the end. Actual language between beginning and end, however, is common to all and yet particular to each. It connects and separates at once," [translation altered slightly, BP]; and *Star of Redemption*, 162: "Language is no content of its own here, which would have to develop itself according to an inner systematic. Rather, it is the description of the course-of-the-world-day of our constellation (*Gestirn*) on the arch of the heavens of world-time, thus the description of that course whose elements came into being for us in algebraic symbolism. We describe the course in which we believe with the words that we trust."

When Rosenzweig identified Philo as the first of three Jewish inquisitors of philosophy who advocate for truth, I've suggested, he means to point to the Philonic conception of creation in which God is grasped as active in such a way that will ultimately lay the groundwork for a dialectical thinking of being, and for Rosenzweig's own account of the unifying course of relations leading to redemption. I'd like now to speculate further and ask whether Rosenzweig may have found in the *structure* and in the details of *the movement of creation* in Philo's account, a precedent for the view of creation he himself was developing at the time. Recall that Rosenzweig understands beings to actualize themselves through a process that demands *conversion* or *reversal* (*Umkehr*) and *relation*: individual beings undergo a transformation when they enter into relations with other beings, but in so doing they realize themselves. Rosenzweig understands creation to be one of the forms of relation through which the parties to it—God and world—transform and thereby realize themselves.

Might Rosenzweig have read Philo's account of creation as hinting at this very view? There are reasons to think so. Recall that Rosenzweig appears to see the notion of divinity shift in Philo's account of creation from the *agathon* as absolute object to absolute subject, from *nous* to *logos*, from passivity to activity and productivity. We might likewise note that by the time the Divine *Logos* is "engaged in the act of creation," Rosenzweig sees Philo as describing a form of divinity that is no longer pure unity, but to the contrary, has within itself the perfect ideational unity of diversity which the material world will imitate.[21] That is, there is room to say that in Rosenzweig's reading, God realizes Godself through a reversal of sorts, and even—as I suggested earlier—that God *needs* to have the world out there to create, in order to actualize God's self.[22] On the other side of the relation of creation, it is noteworthy how Philo describes the material substance out of

---

[21] See Rosenzweig's notes on *Opif.* 15–20: "He does not even call it 'first' lest it should be reckoned with the others, but names it 'one.' (*yom ehad*). (compare Rashi) The 'one' day (compare 35) contains the creation of the intelligible archetype (*Vorbild*) of the world in (20) '*Deos Logos*'," "Paralipomena," 41a-42a; and on *Opif.* 24f., "Said baldly: 'the world discerned only by the intellect is nothing other than the *Deos Logos* when He was already engaged in the act of creation.' → Gen. 1.27! (i.e., image of God)," "Paralipomena," 42a. Hegel clearly understands the relation between Philo's divine *nous* and divine *logos* as one of identity and opposition at once. See G. W. F. Hegel, *Werke 19. Vorlesungen über die Geschichte der Philosophie II*, ed. E. Moldenhauer and K.M. Michel (Frankfurt: Suhrkamp, 1971), 421.

[22] Rosenzweig toys with a kabbalistic account of God's self-negation in creation, in the "Paralipomena," *Zweistromland*, 63. I explore Rosenzweig's account, in the *Star of Redemption*, of God's need for others in the act of creation, in *Franz Rosenzweig and the Systematic Task of Philosophy*, 188–91, 198–201.

which God creates the world. It has the potential to become a perfect world, but that potential is entrenched in a mess of negativity, described with adjectives "mostly containing alpha-privatives,"[23] as Runia has noted. Notice how creation is described, in the following passage from *Opif.* 21–22, in relation to these particular negative qualities of original matter:

> If anyone should wish to examine the reason why this universe was constructed, I think he would not miss the mark if he affirmed, what one of the ancients also said, that the Father and Maker was good. For this reason he did not begrudge a share of his own excellent nature to a material which did not possess any beauty of its own but was able to become all things. Of itself it was unordered, devoid of quality, lacking life, dissimilar, full of inconsistency and maladjustment and disharmony; but it received a turning and change to the opposite and most excellent state, order, quality, ensoulment, similarity, homogeneity, sound adjustment, harmony, indeed all the characteristics possessed by the superior idea (*Opif.* 21–22).[24]

From the side of the world, we see, creation for Philo is a transformation or conversion of material substance defined by negativity—unordered, full of disharmony—*into* a world that is good, positive, harmonious. Thus the world too, Rosenzweig would have noted, undergoes a conversion in being created.[25] Creation is an act through which God enters into relation with that nothingness that has the potential to become world, and negates its negativity. Matter is transformed from a mess of negativity into the world through God's creative activity upon it—"a turning and change to the opposite and most excellent state." Through this transformation it undergoes in its creative relation with God, the world realizes what it "was able to become."[26]

---

[23] Runia, *On the Creation of the Cosmos according to Moses*, 145.

[24] Cited from Runia, *On the Creation of the Cosmos according to Moses*, 51.

[25] See Runia's commentary in *On the Creation of the Cosmos according to Moses*, 133–34: "The activity of God's creative power results from God's essential goodness, as already affirmed by 'one of the ancients,' i.e., Plato. The antithesis between the active cause and the passive object (§ 8) is now bridged. The divine creative and beneficent activity enables the unformed material to participate in divine excellence and be converted from disorder and disharmony into an ordered and harmonious whole, in conformity with the model"; and p. 145: "The description of the material that is to receive divine beneficence emphasizes its *negativity* (Platonic, note the many alpha-privatives), and also its *potentiality* (able to become all things; this is more Aristotelian and Stoic)." Runia views the emphasis on negativity as one way in which Philo deviates slightly from the Platonic picture in the *Timaeus* which he inherits. See *Philo of Alexandria and the* Timaeus *of Plato*, 141–42.

[26] See also Rosenzweig's notes when reading *Opif.* 21: "Why has God created? Because he, as also 'men of old' said, is '*Agathos* (*midat rachamim*),' indeed the world is not good according to the measure of God's goodness, but rather according to its receptivity," in "Paralipomena," 42a.

If Rosenzweig did indeed view not only the notions of the *activity* and *subjectivity* of God to have their origins in Philo's account of creation, but likewise read into the Philonic creation this notion of self-realization through conversion into relation with an other, then we can say Philo's account had a profound impact on Rosenzweig's own notion of creation in the *Star of Redemption*. For creation in the *Star of Redemption* is not the divine production of the world out of absolute nothing, but rather a relation between an elemental God and an elemental world, through which each undergoes a kind of conversion which is at once a step towards its actualization. God's power remains stuck in an elemental divine nothingness until it converts itself into the creative ground of the world. The world's order likewise is described as stuck in elemental worldly nothingness until God's creation draws that order out of potentiality into existence. For Rosenzweig, both God and world thus realize themselves through this process of conversion brought about in the relation of creation between them.[27]

Let me sum up the claim I've been making. When Rosenzweig identified Philo as the first of the Jewish inquisitors who advocate for truth against philosophy, he is pointing to Philo's conception of creation. Philo's account of creation first articulates a conception of God as *active*, as absolute subject. Insofar as this account depicts the divine as active in relation to the world, it offers the grounds for thinking of *revelation* as an act of relation through which God awakens individuals to personal selfhood. It likewise offers the grounds for thinking of being as unfolding *developmentally*, dialectically, rather than in static form. And it even may hint at the possibility of thinking of development as involving relations between individual beings which require the respective self-conversions of the parties to such relations. Rosenzweig implies that such a conception of creation amounts to a *Jewish* contribution to the course of redemption in which Jews are called on to anticipate redemption. Only if we conceive of reality as in flux, as developing in response to divine action, are we in a position to accept that truth is unfolding towards the future, rather than statically actual already in the present. And only thusly may we come to view our own actions as critical to the attainment of that future redemptive goal.

Before I turn to examine the ways in which Rosenzweig presents Philo no longer as representative of but rather as deviating from Jewish thinking, I want to offer one last bit of speculation about the role Philo may have played in laying the ground for Rosenzweig's view of the relation between creation and revelation. As we have seen, Rosenzweig views creation as a

---

[27] Compare Pollock, *Franz Rosenzweig and the Systematic Task of Philosophy*, 194–204.

divine act of entering into relation with the world, a relation that allows the world to actualize its potential through a process of self-negation or self-conversion. We've seen, moreover, that Rosenzweig believes that it is only on the basis of such a view of God as active creator that *revelation* can be thought as a divine act of calling on the individual to recognize herself and to enter into redemptive relations with others in the world. It is noteworthy that for Rosenzweig, the process the individual self undergoes in revelation is likewise a reversal, an actualization through conversion. In this sense, revelation has the same structure as creation and is rooted in it.[28] Rosenzweig's notes show that he had great interest in Philo's account of *metanoia*, of the conversion that an individual person undergoes when she conquers her matter-bound passions through self-mastery and attains to well-being. He cites passages from *Legum allegoriae* II, in which the soul under the rule of the body's passions is described as in a condition of negativity akin to death. What is required is repentance—i.e., *metanoia*—through which that condition of spiritual death is negated and overcome. Reading *Legum allegoriae* 2.77, Rosenzweig quotes and comments in his notes, "'That which dies is not the ruling part in us, but the part that is under rule, the part that is like the vulgar herd. And so long will it incur death, as it fails to <u>repent</u> [*metanoia*] and acknowledge its fall.' The equation *metanoia* = *teshuva* is thus already—LXX?"[29] Rosenzweig is clearly struck here by the way in which the penitent's path to self-mastery is depicted by Philo, through the term *metanoia*, as a path of self-conversion that requires a moment of acknowledgement of one's fallen state of negativity. Acknowledging one's deathly condition is part of the transformative process of negating that very condition and transcending it.[30]

So, when Rosenzweig designates Philo as the first Jewish inquisitor interrogating philosophy in the court of Christianity, he presents Philo as originating a line of thinking that combats the static, non-relational thought of Greece with a view that God acts in creation and thereby sets in motion a series of relations between beings that engage each other in a course

[28] See Pollock, *Franz Rosenzweig and the Systematic Task of Philosophy*, 204–15.

[29] "Paralipomena," 46a-47a

[30] Rosenzweig's curiosity over the possibility that the Hebrew term *teshuva* was already translated as *metanoia* in the Septuagint is consistent with his earlier view, dating back to his personal decision not to convert to Christianity, that such translation in fact expresses the unbridgeable difference between Judaism and Christianity. See his letter to Rudolf Ehrenberg, November 4, 1913, in *BT* 1:142: "For us [Jews] our 'stubbornness' counts as loyalty, and our 'defection from God' ... is healed only through return, not through conversion. That the concept of repentance, which is repeated in Hebrew through 'return,' 'reversal,' 'turn again,' that thus this Hebrew word *teshuva* is designated as *metanoia* in the New Testament, this is one of the points where world history stands in the dictionary."

towards redemption. Philo *originates* this line of thinking. But, Rosenzweig suggests, Philo does not complete it; he does not follow this line of thinking through to its end. According to Rosenzweig, Philo breaks off from it in two important ways. Philo doesn't grasp that the redemptive process begun in creation requires *time*. And Philo blurs the difference between *relation* and *mediation*.

Let's begin with the second of these limitations. I have suggested that Rosenzweig may have seen Philo's depiction of the activity of God conceived as *Logos* in creation as entailing an engagement with the world as other. On Rosenzweig's reading, both God and world might be seen as undergoing a transformation into relation with the other in creation, through which each realizes itself. But in later writings, perhaps influenced by Hermann Cohen,[31] Rosenzweig comes to see Philo's divine *Logos* not as an indication of the *relation* between God and world, but rather as the objectified *mediation* of God and world, an independent hypostasized being that *unites* aspects of God and world and thereby removes the conditions for actual relation between the two. As such, Philo comes to mark for Rosenzweig a break from Judaism, and the root of an inner struggle within Christianity between excessive spiritualization, on the one hand, and redemptive engagement in the world, on the other.[32]

---

[31] See Rosenzweig's own account of Cohen's critique of Philo, in his Introduction to Cohen's *Jewish Writings:* "But as he [Cohen] thought now about the notion of the correlation of man and God, another philosopher's form from the Jewish past stood ever again before him, the earliest of all, Philo. Not as a guide, but as one who went astray. It was just at the crossroads of correlation that he, so his successor now saw, went astray and opened up the world-historical error, in that he did not assume in the two members of the correlation themselves the reciprocal pointing-one-to-the other. This was religiously-bold enough, but he went further in believing he had to assert a particular force of mediation. 'Had Philo not conceived of the Logos, so no Jew would have doubted,' so he expressed, in the Winter-lecture 1913/14, at once the demonic-gigantic magnitude, that the firstborn of all Jewish philosophy now assumed in his eyes, and the deep Un-Jewishness of his world-historical thought. ... 'The *Greek* spirit, and it is the archetype of the scientific world-sense, seeks the *mediation*, as they call it, between God and Man. To this Greek magic the *Jew Philo* fell victim with his *Logos*,'" *Zweistromland*, 213–14.

[32] Late in life, Rosenzweig asserted that the rabbinic expressions of divine anthropomorphism made it possible to resist these twin phenomena of the spiritualization of God, on the one hand, and the hypostatization of the mediation between God and human being, on the other. See his "Note on Anthropomorphism," *Zweistromland*, 740: "The first epoch of an inner-Jewish struggle against Biblical anthropomorphism has its documents in the ancient translations, from the Septuagint to the Targums. That just in this epoch Christianity came into being, is thus according to what was said, no accident. Philo's Logos was the necessary counterpart of his spiritualized God. In the Logos-gospel, there stands the sentence, which has become a danger for Christianity through the temptation to turn it around: God is Spirit. And in that Paul, as the first Jew—inconceivable to us to today!—

The second way in which Philo breaks short the trajectory of the conception of creation Rosenzweig holds him to have introduced to philosophy is wrapped up in his attitude towards temporality. According to Rosenzweig, it is essential that the course to redemption which creation activates is a *temporal course*. Creation, for Rosenzweig, is the start of a process that extends through time and will reach an end in redemption. It is not an *eternal act* of transforming matter into world. My *metanoia*, if it comes, comes at a particular moment and draws me into a web of relations unifying beings towards redemption at that very moment. My personal decision for or against redemption *matters* for Rosenzweig, revelation allows me to say "without me…" the world would be essentially different, only because time matters. The moment in which I live and act hangs in the balance and my actions impact the process that has the potential to lead to redemption.

Rosenzweig identifies and remarks on what he sees as a lack of temporality in Philo's thought.[33] He notes Philo's view of creation as eternal act. He notes that Philo advocates the immortality of the soul, rather than asserting the possibility of individual resurrection.[34] This absence of temporality suggests to Rosenzweig that Philo has not thought through the consequences of the notion of God as creator, of absolute subjectivity, to their end. He thereby views Philo as marking only the *beginning* of the contribution Jewish thought has to make to the world's redemptive course.

Rosenzweig's view that Philo deviates from Judaism by failing to grasp redemption as a temporal process comes out distinctly in his claim that Philo does not have a conception of the Messiah:

---

who saw the God of the Bible as the God of strict, compassionless justice, he also had to come to attribute the compassionate, undeniably divine love to the mediator. Judaism then had saved itself out of the two extremes of the Jewish-Greek spirit-God and the Jewish-Christian God-man in the bold anthropomorphisms of the Talmudic *aggada*, i.e., in the adamant certainty that everything we experience from God, comes from him himself. We owe our continued existence as Jews to this certainty, right along with the law and the learning."

[33] Compare Rosenzweig's later diary comment from June 30, 1922: "The idealism of antiquity in Philo denied time in order to be able to allow substances to be metaphysically real," in *Briefe und Tagebücher. Band 1I: 1918–1929. Der Mensch und sein Werk. Gesammelte Schriften* 2, ed. Rachel Rosenzweig and Edith Rosenzweig-Scheinmann (Haag: Martinus Nijhoff, 1979), 800.

[34] See Rosenzweig's note on *Opif.* 135: "'man … was created at once mortal and immortal, mortal in respect of the body, but in respect to mind immortal,' thus *no* resurrection," "Paralipomena," 43a. Elsewhere in the "Paralipomena," *Zweistromland*, Rosenzweig likewise writes: "That in the concept of 'resurrection' the fact of Platonic immortality is translated into the *Active*, thus tied with Messianism, is the important thing. Thereby the fate of the individual is chained to the fate of humanity."

One indeed sees actually out of Philo, how much Plato was a *pedagogos towards Christ*. Yet, Philo at the same time "assimilated" revelation to Plato, in that he sacrificed the Messianic idea. For this reason Jewish Alexandrianism had to disappear. In that it gave way together with the Greek to Christianity, it was really hit by just that Jewish idea which it had betrayed for purposes of assimilation.[35]

On the one hand, Rosenzweig claims here, Philo makes explicit the extent to which Plato points to the Christian account of revelation. Perhaps this is because he sees the "turning around" that is the key to ascending out of the cave in Plato as anticipating Christian conversion; perhaps it is because in Philo's *Logos* Rosenzweig still sees a transition from Platonic creation to an account of creation that would ground revelation. But Rosenzweig now accuses Philo of "assimilating" revelation back to Plato, rather than finding in him the beginning of a process of the Mosaicization of Plato. Philo assimilates revelation to Plato, according to Rosenzweig, by abandoning the Messianic idea.

What Rosenzweig suggests is the following. Without an account of redemption as the *future completion of a temporal course begun in creation*, Philo's account of creation itself remains incomplete.[36] Philo's creation amounts to a false start of sorts, and thus remains ineffective. Moreover, Rosenzweig suggests Philo's failure to grasp the Messianic is a failure to articulate a Jewish position. For Rosenzweig, recall, Jews have the task of anticipating the future redemption, so as to remind Christians to act towards that goal in the world. Rosenzweig even suggests that Philo's failure here had practical consequences. Alexandrian Jewry disappeared. Rosenzweig implies that its disappearance is directly linked to the absence of Messianism in the thought of its most important philosophical representative. Without taking seriously the Jewish task of anticipating redemption, without committing to the advocacy for that redemptive truth, Rosenzweig suggests, Alexandrian Jewry could not sustain its difference from the surrounding peoples, and thus assimilated. Without taking time seriously, Philonic thinking remained rooted in a static—and thus, for Rosenzweig, quintessentially *pagan*—view of truth. It remained torn between the activity

---

[35] "Paralipomena," 47a.

[36] Compare Franz Rosenzweig to Gertrud Oppenheim, May 30, 1917, in *BT* 1:412: "With the knowledge of the mere *createdness* of things, nothing is really known; there is also no paganism, from the Babylonian priests to the Jena Monists, that doesn't have its creation myths. But rather only that the 'created' … things are 'created' for the sake of the *End* and He, who is the first, is also the Last (as *Yeshayahu* 44:6, 48:12) or the Alpha *and* the Omega (as John says)—only this gives knowledge."

of creation and passivity with regard to the task of redemption—torn, we might say, between Judaism and paganism.[37]

So Philo does not fit neatly into any of the religious or cultural categories—paganism, Judaism, Christianity—into which Rosenzweig might have set him. His account of creation initiates a line of Jewish thought, according to Rosenzweig, that grounds the possibility of thinking the course of the interactions between beings in a temporal unfolding towards redemption. But in his failure to think creation *together with redemption*, in his failure to take creation as the *temporal* beginning of the course towards redemption, Philo remained pagan, leaving his form of Judaism and his *Logos* to be absorbed into Christianity. But in not fitting into the categories of paganism, Judaism, and Christianity, I would submit, Philo sets a precedent for another Jewish thinker who does not fit neatly into any one of these categories: Franz Rosenzweig himself.[38]

[37] Compare Franz Rosenzweig to Benno Jacob, May 17, 1927: "Philo? Certainly, so we too basically write it today, in particular if we write 'In Flaccum.' But what remained of the whole Alexandrian grandeur of the Jews? Was not Philo's nephew already a Roman pogrom general? And in any case we—you and I—owe that we are and that Jews are not to these satisfied state-citizens of the diaspora, but rather to the contemporary and later *Tana'im* of Palestine," *BT* 2:1145. See also Rosenzweig's "Spirit and Epochs of Jewish History," *Zweistromland*, 535: "In Alexandria, the struggle of eternal life with eternal spirit was taken up and—defeated. Philo, the in-between-form: he makes the father of the philosophers out of the father of the prophets, and volatilized the fact of eternal life into the confession of an 'Ism.' What does it help that he called time and future into the timeless and futureless Greek life. It remains a call, a word."

[38] I wish to express my thanks to Christopher Frilingos, my colleague at Michigan State University, who devoted hours to helping me read through and identify Rosenzweig's handwritten Greek citations of Philo.

SPECIAL SECTION

DE DECALOGO: PHILO OF ALEXANDRIA AS INTERPRETER OF THE TEN COMMANDMENTS

INTRODUCTION

SARAH PEARCE

In the history of Jewish thought, Philo's treatise *On the Decalogue* (*De Decalogo*) has a very special place as the earliest sustained commentary on the Ten Commandments. Indeed, in the words of Yehoshua Amir, this work deserves "a place of honor..." for its status as the first attempt to produce such a study. As an "innovator," Philo often presents in this treatise what Amir called "the seminal formulation of questions about the revelation at Sinai and the contents of the Ten Commandments that have challenged the exegetes of every generation since his day."[1] In addition to "a place of honor," Philo's *De Decalogo* also deserves a much bigger place in scholarship than it has occupied till now. Though well served by Leopold Cohn's critical edition of 1902, and some fine translations into modern languages, this treatise remains a very neglected work.[2] Among the most significant studies to date, Amir contributed a key article on "The Deca-

---

[1] Yehoshua Amir, "The Decalogue according to Philo," in *The Ten Commandments in History and Tradition* ed. Ben Tziyon Segal; ET translated by Gershon Levi (Jerusalem: Magnes Press, 1990), 121–160.

[2] The standard critical edition of the Greek text of *De Decalogo* remains that of Leopold Cohn, *Philonis Alexandrini Opera Quae Supersunt*, vol. 4 (Berlin: George Reiner, 1902), 269–307. The important German and English translations produced in the first half of the twentieth century include relatively little introduction or commentary: Leopold Treitel, Philo, *On the Decalogue. On the Special Laws, Books 1–3*, trans. Francis H. Colson, LCL (Cambridge: Harvard University Press, 1937). Other fine editions of the treatise, building on Nikiprowetzky's work, include: Suzanne Daniel-Nataf, ed., *Philo of Alexandria: Writings, Volume Two: Exposition of the Law, Part I* (Jerusalem: Bialik Institute and Israel Academy of Sciences and Humanities, 1991) [Hebrew]; Francesca Calabi, *De Decalogo: Filone di Alessandria* (Pisa: Edizioni ETS, 2005).

logue according to Philo," focusing primarily on the series of questions with which Philo grapples as a prelude to his discussion of the Commandments themselves, and on the relation of Philo's interpretations to rabbinic traditions.[3] The most valuable resource for the study of Philo's *De Decalogo* as a whole remains Valentin Nikiprowetzky's 1965 translation and commentary of the treatise.[4] Based on Nikiprowetzky's doctoral thesis, this remarkably accomplished work underlines the fundamental importance of approaching Philo's *De Decalogo* as a commentary on the Greek Pentateuch and prepares the ground for Nikiprowetzky's path-breaking work in *Le Commentaire de l'Écriture chez Philon d'Alexandrie* (1977), a study that decisively influenced future scholarship in emphasizing that Philo's starting point as a commentator is always in the words of Moses, embodied in the Septuagint translation.[5]

The three essays published in this section are based on invited papers given to the Philo Seminar at the Annual Meeting of the Society of Biblical Literature in San Diego (November 2014) in a session devoted to work on the forthcoming commentary on *On the Decalogue* for the Philo of Alexandria Commentary Series. We are proud to offer them here as key contributions to our knowledge on fundamental questions about the treatise. Focusing on the Greek manuscript tradition, which represents a substantial body of evidence for the treatise, Jim Royse explores the remarkable evidence of the "Vatican Palimpsest" (Vaticanus gr. 316), the oldest Greek manuscript witness to the text of *De Decalogo*; based on meticulous analysis of the text surviving within the palimpsest, Royse demonstrates the significant value of this witness in supplying a substantial body of readings not incorporated into Cohn's critical edition and which, in some cases, appear to represent a 'superior text' which should be preferred over Cohn. Abraham Terian's treatment of the ancient Armenian textual tradition of Philo's *De Decalogo* examines the use of Armenian variants included by Cohn in the critical apparatus to his edition of the treatise. Of those examined, around 25 percent of Cohn's variants prove to be of questionable value. Moreover, it emerges that Cohn's methodology effectively restricted the number of potential Armenian variants that could have been included in the critical edition of *De Decalogo*. Terian identifies two important areas in which the Armenian material not included in Cohn may help with textual questions: where an Armenian reading may prove decisive on its

---

[3] See above, n. 1.

[4] Valentin Nikiprowetzky, *Philon d'Alexandrie: De Decalogo* (Paris: Cerf, 1965).

[5] Valentin Nikiprowetzky, *Le Commentaire de l'Écriture chez Philon d'Alexandrie: son Caractère et sa Portée; Observations Philologiques* (Leiden: Brill, 1977).

own or in conjunction with other Greek witnesses; and where the Armenian supports the received Greek text and can help to supply a better sense of the meaning of the Greek when the latter appears ambiguous. The work of Royse and Terian underlines the need for careful attention to material not included in Cohn and ultimately for a new critical edition of the treatise. Finally, following the lead of Nikiprowetzky's view of *De Decalogo* as an exegetical commentary and his high evaluation of its rhetorical style, Manuel Alexandre Jr. offers the first detailed examination of Philo's use of rhetorical devices within this treatise. Alexandre's analysis of a range of material within *De Decalogo*, including Philo's substantial introduction to questions about the revelation of the Commandments at Sinai and his extensive treatment of individual Commandments, reveals how rhetorical form and content determine meaning in the treatise and the extent to which these patterns of argument and rationalization reflect the rhetorical codes found elsewhere in Hellenistic culture. In Alexandre's judgment, Philo is not to be considered an "innovator" in this respect, but "an effective user of the features he found most adequate to each unit of the commentary."

The Studia Philonica Annual 27 (2015): 133–142

THE TEXT OF PHILO'S *DE DECALOGO* IN VATICANUS GR. 316[1]

JAMES R. ROYSE

The treatise *De Decalogo* is very well attested, being contained in at least twenty-one Greek manuscripts as well as in the Armenian version. In the fourth volume of the Cohn-Wendland edition, Cohn presents most of this evidence with, as it seems, his customary thoroughness and reliability. But there are two important exceptions. First, the representation of the Armenian is not always satisfactory, and Abraham Terian discusses this issue with his usual acumen.[2] Second, the evidence of the oldest Greek witness to the text of *De Decalogo* was entirely unknown at the time of that fourth volume. My own discussion, instead of attempting an overview of these textual witnesses or the various textual problems, will concentrate on that oldest witness.

Vaticanus gr. 316, designated R in the fifth volume of PCW, is a palimpsest from around 900, which was dismembered in the thirteenth century and re-used for various comments on Aristotle's works. As a mansucript of Aristotle it was discussed in 1831 by Brandis, who notes the presence at fol. 62ᵛ of the subscription to *Decal.* and then the title of *Spec.* 1, and at fol. 42ᵛ of the subscription to *Mos.* and then the title of *Decal.*[3] Subsequently, in 1853, there was a brief mention of this palimpsest by Mai in a long footnote to his publication of Leo Allatius's "De Philonibus."[4] Mai mentions some of the titles, including that of *De Decalogo*, which occurs ("more prisco" as Mai states) both before and after the treatise, but does not give the number of the ms. This vagueness led to a lengthy and perplexed comment by Pitra in the course of his investigation of the Philonic material in Vatican mss.:

---

[1] Presented to the Philo of Alexandria Section at the annual meeting of the Society of Biblical Literature in San Diego, November 25, 2014.

[2] His paper was also delivered in San Diego, and is published here at pp. 155–165.

[3] Christian August Brandis, "Die Aristotelischen Handschriften der Vaticanischen Bibliothek," *Abhandlungen der Königlich Preussischen Akademie der Wissenschaften* (1831), 47–86; Brandis discusses the philonic lower text at 60–61.

[4] *Nova Patrum Bibliotheca* 6 (Rome: Typis Sacri Consilii Propagando Christiano Nomini, 1853), part 2, 40–71 (see 67 n. 1 [–68]).

> Exstat denique, uti opinor, etiam in Vaticana ignotus Philonis codex, omnium
> sane qui ubi vis exstant, longe antiquissimus, immo et palimpsestus, quem vidit
> et introspexit acutissimus Maius, ut fert ejus testimonium ... Sed ubinam
> tandem et quisnam est codex ille palimspestus? Hactenus in tumulo Maii latet
> arcanum.[5]

Pitra was, of course, intimately familiar with the holdings of the Vatican Library, and one can thus judge from his perplexity the difficulty in tracking mss.

As will be discussed below, the official catalogue for Vaticanus gr. 316 was published by Mercati in 1923.

Originally Vaticanus gr. 316 was an extensive collection of Philonic works, written on large folios in two columns. Substantial portions of the original ms. have been lost, but the surviving folios contain the complete text of *Decal.*, as well as *Spec.* 1, and portions of *Spec.* 2, *Migr.*, *Ios.*, and *Mos.* 1.[6] However, despite the earlier notices of the presence of Philonic works during the nineteenth century (of which only Brandis actually identifies the ms.), R escaped the notice of Cohn and Wendland until shortly after their work on PCW 4. As a result it is not cited in PCW 4, where Cohn edits *Decal.* So the still-standard critical edition of Philo's works that have been preserved in Greek presents to the reader a text of *Decal.* with an apparatus in which R is absent.

Now, once Cohn found R, he did try to correct for this absence. In the first place, he devoted a long article to it, which was published in 1905.[7] And in the second place, the reader is informed about the existence of R in the preface to PCW 5, although the notice is very brief, and as far as the text of *Decal.* is concerned does not do much more than refer to Cohn's article on R. But even that article, devoted to this very valuable manuscript, gives less than a page to the readings of R in *Decal.* A detailed look at the readings that Cohn presents there will be given below, but we will see that what Cohn cites is in fact a very limited selection. This selection nevertheless shows that R contains some very interesting readings, including (as it seems) some correct readings not found elsewhere. But Cohn does not give any further attention to R in *Decal.*

---

[5] Jean-Baptiste Pitra, *Analecta sacra spicilegio solesmensi* 2 (Typis Tusculanis, 1884), 315: "Morever, there exists, I believe, also in the Vatican an unknown codex of Philo, by far the most ancient of all that are extant anywhere, a palimpsest, which the most acute Mai saw and inspected, as his testimony states.... But where and which one is this palimpsest codex? So far the secret lies hidden in Mai's tomb."

[6] See PCW 5:v–vi.

[7] "Ein Philo-Palimpsest (Vat. gr. 316)," *Sitzungsberichte der königlich preussischen Akademie der Wissenschaften* (Berlin), 1905, 36–52.

Readings from R cited by Cohn[8]

a) shared errors:

§62   τὸ ἴσον ἀποδιδόντες M (PCW) : τῶν ἴσων μεταδιδόντες R
ceteri

§112   ἔχοντες Arm (PCW) : μέλλοντες R ceteri

§171   παρακαταθηκῶν Arm (PCW) : παρακαταθήκαις R ceteri

b) unique errors:

§128   μοιχίδιοι ceteri (PCW) : μοιχιμαῖοι R

§156   ἀγάλματα ceteri (PCW) : ἃ ἦν ἀγάλματα R

§177   αἱρῆται ceteri (PCW) : ὁρᾷ R

c) good or noteworthy readings:

§5   ἀνισότητος R (PCW, coni. Mangey) : ἀνοσιότητος ceteri
Arm[9]

§8   φύσει ceteri Arm (PCW) : φύσει πατρός R

§13   πόλιν ceteri : πόλεις R Arm (Mangey)

§31   κατακεκλιμένος ceteri : κατακλινόμενος R Arm[10]

§36   ἀπορῆσαι GH² (PCW) : ἀπορῆσαι MFH¹ : ἀπορήσοι AP
(Mangey) : διαπορήσαι R

§64   καθό ceteri (PCW) : πρὸς ὅ M : παρόσον R

§88   ἐγὼ μέν γε Cohn (PCW) : ἐγὼ μὲν γάρ M : ἐγὼ μέν ceteri :
ἐγὼ μὲν οὖν R[11]

§89   ἐπεί R (PCW, = Arm) : ἐπί M : om. ceteri

---

[8] Ibid., 41.

[9] PCW does not cite Arm here. In fact, the Armenian reads *anaržanut'iwn*. According to Gabriel Awetik'ean, Xač'atowr Siwrmelean, and Mkrtič' Awgerean [Aucher], *Nor bargirk' haykazean lezowi* (2 vols.; Venice, Press of St. Lazarus, 1836–37), abbreviated henceforth as *NBHL*, 1:116A, this corresponds to ἀνάξιον, ἀπαξία, indignitas. The term corresponding to ἀνισότης is *anzugut'iwn* (*NBHL* 1:146B), as seen at *Spec.* 1.121; *Contempl.* 70; *QG* 2:14; *QE* 1:6 (see Petit's note), 2:64. On the other hand, ἀνοσιότης does not occur in Philo. However, ὁσιότης does, and it is rendered by *aržanut'iwn* (see *NBHL* 1: 357C, where no Greek is given, but a reference to *aržanaworut'iwn*) at *Decal.* 110, 119; and by *aržanawor* at *Spec.* 1.304; but by *aržanaworut'iwn* (*NBHL* 1:357A gives ἀξιότης) at *Spec.* 1.154; *Abr.* 198, 208; by *aržanaworut'iwn ew srbut'iwn* at *Abr.* 172. Given these equivalents, we can see that *anaržanut'iwn* (in Armenian the prefix *an-* functions like the α -privative in Greek) at *Decal.* 5 must represent ἀνοσιότητος. (It is curious that none of these Armenian words is cited by Marcus in his index.)

[10] PCW does not cite Arm here, but the form *ənkołmanelov* seems to reflect a present participle.

[11] In PCW Cohn places "(Arm?)" after the reading of M. Indeed, it seems that the Armenian *vasn zi* would most likely reflect the Greek γάρ, as at *Prov.* 2.30.

§96   τῆς κατὰ θεὸν νουμηνίας ceteri Arm (PCW) : τῆς κατὰ σελήνην νεομηνίας R (= Cohn's earlier conjecture[12])

§138   ἱερώτερον R v (PCW) : ἱερώτατον ceteri D Arm (*srbagoyn terunean.*)

§147–48   ἀσθενήσαντες

Cohn does not mention this, but in fact almost all of these readings are to be found within very limited areas of R. To understand this, we need to visualize how the original manuscript of Philonic works was re-used for the Aristotelian works. An original large folio was turned at a right angle and folded in half in order to form a double folio (i.e., four pages). Four of these double folios were then gathered into a quaternion, and the scribe wrote on each of the resulting sixteen pages. Since the original folios had been turned sideways, the upper writing was perpendicular to the lower writing. Thus, when we look at the resulting manuscript, the upper writing on a page covers the lower writing on either the top half or the bottom half of one of the original pages (each written in two columns, recall). Now, in between the two pages that were formed from one side of an original page is a small area where the new double folio was folded in half. Let me call this area the "fold" of the original page. This area was not written over. And thus the writing in these folds is often quite clearly readable. Unfortunately, on occasion even here the writing has faded badly and is difficult to read,[13] and sometimes a line (in each column) that was exactly at the line of the fold has been obscured. But in general the text here, which consists of perhaps four or five lines in each of the two columns, is more or less completely legible.

Now, almost all of Cohn's readings are from these folds. He has thus selected his examples from the most legible portions of R. Given that his focus was on the portions of *Spec.* preserved in R, this was no doubt a reasonable procedure. But we should keep this in mind when thinking about the significance of his examples. He finds these readings by looking at perhaps 15% or so of the text. We could plausibly estimate that many

---

[12] "Beiträge zur Textgeschichte und Kritik der philonischen Schriften," *Hermes* 38 (1903): 543–44. In his 1905 article Cohn reports R as reading νουμηνίας with the rest of the mss. That is indeed most likely what Philo wrote, but in fact R has νεομηνίας. Note that PCW prints the form νεομηνία at *Somn.* 2.257, 257. Elsewhere (fourteen occurrences in *Spec.* 1–2) PCW prints the form νουμηνία, but Cohn notes at *Spec.* 1.181 that R has νεομηνία, and at *Spec.* 2.41 that F has νεομηνία.

[13] I note, e.g., that at fol. 17ʳ/24ᵛ B, the letters in the fold are extremely faint (to non-existent).

further readings in his three categories are to be found in the entire text of R—if, that is, we could read them.

Let me also note here that the ms. is currently arranged in an unusual state. In 1904 the later binding of the ms. was removed, so that the original large folios can be seen in their entirety.[14] These folios are not bound together, but rather each one is separately attached at a narrow end (i.e., the original top end or bottom end) to a binding. However, these folios are not arranged according to the order of the Philonic works, but according to the later writing. Now, making specific references to these original folios is a bit complicated. The foliation was made on the "new" folios,[15] which contain the upper writing, and each of the "old" folios, which contain the lower writing, consists of two of those folios. And, of course, a page is one side of a folio. For example, the original first page of *Decal.* is now found across the "new" pages that are numbered 42ᵛ and 47ʳ; thus that original first page is designated 42ᵛ/47ʳ. And there are two columns on that page. Unfortunately, as a result of the dismemberment of the original ms. and the re-ordering of the folios, nothing remains of the original order. The second page of *Decal.* is 37ʳ/36ᵛ. Fortunately, Mercati (in the Vatican catalogue, discussed below) provides a thorough listing of which Philonic texts are at which locations.

Before turning to my own work on R, let me return to the literature. The diligent student of Philo will, of course, follow the leads provided in the prefaces to the various volumes of PCW, and thus will learn of Cohn's article. The diligent student will also, of course, follow the leads found in the various bibliographies. Now, as it turns out, Goodhart and Goodenough refer at the end of their listing of Vaticanus gr. 316 (their item 107) to Cohn's article, which is more fully cited as their item 858. Of course, they could have easily followed their practice elsewhere and also referred to the discussion in PCW 5, although (again) the diligent student will have found that anyway. But they do not refer to another item of interest, namely their item 864, which is an article by Mercati devoted to R.[16] It would have been helpful if Goodhart and Goodenough had provided the information that the "Vatican palimpsest" discussed by Mercati is indeed Vaticanus gr. 316, although perhaps anyone actually pursuing these leads would have already figured that out. In fact, Mercati's article is a very valuable contribution to our knowledge of R in two respects. First, he devotes attention to a

[14] See Mercati, "Appunti dal palinsesto Vaticano di Filone," *RB* n.s. 12 (1915), 544 n. 2.

[15] Due to an error in the foliation, between f. 91 and f. 92 there are two further folios, numbered 91A and 91B.

[16] Mercati, "Appunti dal palinsesto Vaticano di Filone," *RB* n.s. 12 (1915), 540–55.

reconstruction of the contents of the various Philonic works that are found in the lower writing of R. And second, he discusses several dozen readings in R from *Spec.* 1, where Mercati's reading of R differs from that found in PCW 5. These remarks are of considerable importance, but at no point does Mercati give information about R's witness to *Decal.* Thus I will not give further attention to it on this occasion.

However, not to be found in Goodhart and Goodenough (or elsewhere in the literature on Philo, I believe) is another important work by Mercati, which is properly speaking a codicological study, but which provides some important textual information. This is the catalogue of the Vatican Greek mss. 1–329, published in 1923 by Mercati and Pio Franchi de' Cavalieri.[17] The entry on Vaticanus gr. 316 was written by Mercati, and is unusually extensive and thorough.[18] Now, I do not suppose that very many of even the most diligent students of Philo consider the manuscript catalogues of the world to be relevant reading. And in fact usually one will find nothing of textual interest beyond what Cohn and Wendland have already furnished, namely the date and contents of the manuscript. But Mercati's entry on R is a vivid exception to this general principle. Mercati not only describes very thoroughly both the upper and lower texts, but presents a very detailed listing of which Philonic texts occur on which pages. And he identifies these texts by reference to the Cohn-Wendland edition by giving for each original page three texts for orientation: the first word or two or three of column A (i.e., the first words of the page), the first word or two or three of column B, and the last word or two or three of column B (i.e., the last words of the page). Now, this is a fairly minimal amount of text, amounting to a half dozen or so words on each page. And most of the time the words are simply what one finds in Cohn-Wendland, and so serve to confirm, let us say, the wisdom of Cohn's editorial choices (since they are supported by R), as well as also the reliability of the textual tradition found in R. However, here and there Mercati presents among these little bits of text a word or two where R differs from the Cohn-Wendland text. And of course these are of very great interest.

A complete listing of these places is given below, but let me first note how much attention Mercati evidently gave to this manuscript in order to list these identifications. Some of the words are more or less easily readable, but in general considerable study is required to provide these words.

---

[17] Giovanni Mercati and Pio Franchi de' Cavalieri, eds., *Codices Vaticani Graeci* 1: *Codices* 1–329 (Rome: Vatican, 1923). In his article Mercati says at the beginning that that study arose from his work on the then forthcoming catalogue.

[18] Ibid., 467–74.

Sometimes indeed it takes a while even to find the last line of a column. Of course, the first line is usually readily found. But finding the line is only the beginning. And remember that these texts at the beginnings and ends of columns are almost always obscured (more or less) by the upper writing. (The only exception here is that sometimes the upper writing will be slightly lower on the page than the top lines of the lower writing.)

The results of this patient research are as follows, where I list only the places that disagree with the text of PCW:

§14   εὐτρεπίζονται : εὐτρεπίζοντες R H
§27   καί : om. R*, corr. al. man.
§32   εἰς ἐκκλησίαν : ἐν ἐκκλησία R APFG : om. H
     Mercati notes only ἐκκλησία, but in fact ἐν is fairly clear also.
§32   πατήρ : πρῶτος R
     This must be considered another unique error.
§34   καί : γάρ R
§76   χειροκμήτων : χειροτμήτων R M
     I am unable to confirm this; the entire page (17ᵛ/24ʳ) is very faint.
§90   εἶτα πρὸς ἅ : εἶτα ἃ πρός R
     I was unable to see the ἅ here; obviously this would be another unique error.
§100   πράξεων ἓν ἐξαήμερον PCW (Christophorson [Mangey]) :
     πράξεων ἓν ἐξάμετρον ceteri : πράξεων <ἐξ>ὰς μέτρον R Arm
     This is surely the most interesting of these readings. Note that the μετρον of R is found also in the other mss. Note further that, as Mercati states, the first two letters of εξας are not visible, but the space fits perfectly. Since the Armenian corresponds precisely, this is likely to be what Philo wrote. Note that the Armenian reads *vec'ereakn č'ap'*. This is literally "the six measure," where we have *vec'ereak* = ἐξάς + the suffixed article *n* + *č'ap'* = μέτρον. A synonym of the first word, *vec'eak*, translates ἐξάς twice in *QE* 2.46, as Marcus notes, and also at *Leg.* 1.4. But *vec'ereak* is used at *Leg.* 1.16, as well as twice at *Decal.* 159. Marcus cites occurrences of *č'ap'* for μέτρον at *Contempl.* 80 and 84, and the equivalence occurs also at *Abr.* 108; *Spec.* 1.342, 343; *Contempl.* 29; *Prov.* 2.50, 51,

100;[19] *QG* 2.64; 4.8, 4.8. In contrast, apart from *Decal.* 100 (possibly), ἑξαήμερος occurs only at *Leg.* 2.12, where ἐν τῇ ἑξαημέρῳ is translated as *i vec'erordum awur*, which is literally "on the sixth day."

§140　προσεξεργάζονται MG : προσεπεξεργάζονται R ceteri : προσεπεξάργονται N

§157　τίνα : τινας R

§169　δέ : δ' AP : om. R

Although not cited in PCW, the Armenian also lacks a connective here.

§178　χρῆσθαι : χρήσασθαι R

§178　τῷ δὲ μεγάλῳ : . . . . . μοις. τῷ δὲ μεγάλῳ R

This is according to Mercati. It's uncertain what this word ending in μοις might be, and I am unable to confirm this reading.

Finally, let me report briefly on some further readings that I noticed during my study of R, which was far from complete or systematic. Again, I ignore the many readings where R supports the text of PCW or agrees with other mss. cited in the apparatus.

title　λόγων R Cohn : λογίων FGH (R confirms Cohn's conjecture.)

§2　τί δή ποτε : τί δήποτ' ουν R : διὰ τί H

§10　τοῦ μέλλοντος ceteri : τοὺς μέλλοντας R[vid] Arm

R clearly has τους. But the ending on the participle is not clear.

§20　ἀρτίων καὶ περιττῶν καὶ ἀρτιοπερίττων ἀρτίων : ἀρτίων R*, corr. scribe

The omission by a scribal leap was corrected by the scribe by adding the omitted words at the end of the line.

§24　εἰκότως ἄν τις θαυμάσειε MAP : εἰκότως ἄν τις θαυμάσαι FGH : ἄν τις θαυμάσαι εἰκότως R

§28　καὶ μὲν δὴ τὸν κύβον, τὸν ὀκτώ, ὅς ἐστιν ἰσάκις ἴσος ἰσάκις : om. R

---

[19] *The Philo Index* cites only the first and second of these (with Colson's idiosyncratic numbering). The occurrence at 2.100 is omitted since Colson prints an alternative reading (see PLCL 9:490 n. 2, but the further discussion at PLCL 9:545–46). But the Armenian at least confirms the presence of μέτρα. See further Maurizio Olivieri, "Il secondo libro del *De Providentia* di Filone alessandrino: i frammenti greci e la traduzione armena" (diss., University of Bologna, 2000), 234–35.

§30   πρός τι, ποιεῖν, πάσχειν, ἔχειν, κεῖσθαι : πρός τι, ποῦ, πότε, ποιεῖν, πάσχειν, ἔχειν, κεῖσθαι M : πρός τι, ποιεῖν, πάσχειν, ἔχειν, κεῖσθαι, ποῦ, πότε R

§30   τὰ ὦν ceteri Arm : τὰ δ' ὦν R

§30   χρόνον καὶ τόπον : χρόνος καὶ τόπος R

§36   ἀπορήσαι GH² : ἀπορῆσαι MFH¹ : ἀπορήσοι AP : διαπορήσαι R

§41   ἐπιγραψάμενοι : ἐπιγραφόμενοι R

§41   ἁπάντων ἀνθρώπων : ἀνθρώπων ἁπάντων R : ἁπάντων M

§43   τινα ἑαυτοῦ : τινας τῶν ἑαυτοῦ R

§49   ἐν ψυχῇ : ἐν τῇ ψυχῇ R

§51   τοὺς ἐπὶ μέρους : τοὺς ἐφημέρους R

§91   εἰ καὶ μὴ : εἰ μὴ καὶ R

§95   ὡς αἰεὶ : ὡς Dᴿ : om. R

§98   προφυλακήν ceteri Fᶜᵒʳʳ : προσφυλακήν R F* : φυλακήν AP

§101   ἃ χρή : om. R

§106   προστάττεται PCW (Cohn coni.) Rᵛⁱᵈ (- Ι ται at least) Arm : πρὸς τὰ πέντε MAFHN : πρὸς τὰ ἕτερα πέντε G : πρὸς (τὰ πέντε . . . περιεχούσῃ om.) P

After his conjecture Cohn writes: "(sic Arm ut vid.)" I think there can be little doubt that the Armenian translator saw προστάττεται or something very similar. (Certainly it is not rendering anything like πρὸς τὰ πέντε.) The Armenian has *hramayeal linin*, and the *linin* indicates a passive form. Marcus does not list the verb *hramayem*, but *NBHL* (2:132A) cites κελεύω, προστάττω, and συντάττω for it. And in its aorist form it occurs twice in *Prov.*: at 2.26 for ἐκέλευσε, and at 2.27 for προσέταξεν.

§121   ἀναγραψάμενος : ἀναγράψας R

§139   μὲν et δὲ : om. et μὲν R

§140   γράφειν H : ἀναγράφειν R ceteri D Nicet.

Cohn cites the Armenian as supporting the reading of H. It is true that the Armenian has the simple verb *grel* here. But that verb can perfectly well render compounds of γράφω. For example, looking just at *Decal.* we find *grem* for ἀναγράφω at *Decal.* 1, 121, 131, 165, 169.

§143   ὀφθαλμοὺς φῶς : φῶς ὀφθαλμοὺς R

§152   ἀλλοτριοῦνται : ἀπαλλοτριοῦνται R

The Armenian has *awtaranam*, for which *NBHL* (2:1029B) cites ἀλλοτριόομαι, ἀπαλλοτριόομαι, etc. Now, ἀπαλλοτριόομαι does not occur in Philo, while the simple form occurs at 32 other places.[20] (And at none of those places is the compound form cited as a variant reading.) It thus seems likely that the scribe of R has inadvertently added the prefix.

§155   εἷς ὁ : ὁ R : ὡς Arm

R has here omitted εἷς at a line break: βασιλευς | ο.

§160   δράγμα : τὰ δράγματα R

It would be fairly easy for the plural to have been altered from:[21]

ΠΡΟϹΦΕΡΕΤΑΙΤΑΔΡΑΓΜΑΤΑΧΑΡΙϹΤΗΡΙΟΝ to
ΠΡΟϹΦΕΡΕΤΑΙΔΡΑΓΜΑΧΑΡΙϹΤΗΡΙΟΝ

§161   ἑπτά : ἕξ R

Although some of R's readings are certainly mistaken, other readings seem to preserve a superior text. The age and quality of R's text make it all the more regrettable that its witness was not included in the apparatus to PCW 4, and that much of its text is to be recovered only with great difficulty, while some portions seem to be beyond recovery at all. Nevertheless, it is a source of valuable readings, and deserves to be studied more comprehensively than it has been so far.

---

[20] According to the *Philo Index*. Günter Mayer, *Index Philoneus* (Berlin: de Gruyter, 1974), has only 31 places (including *Decal.* 152), having missed *Conf.* 150 (the occurrence of ἠλλοτριώμενου there appears to be taken as a form of ἀλλότριος) and *Virt.* 40.

[21] Thanks to Professor David T. Runia for pointing out a typo in the earlier version.

The Studia Philonica Annual 27 (2015): 143–153

THE ARMENIAN TEXTUAL TRADITION
OF PHILO'S *DE DECALOGO* [1]

ABRAHAM TERIAN

De decalogo has an odd place in the Armenian manuscript tradition of the Philonic corpus. Throughout, the treatise is imbedded in Book 3 of *De specialibus legibus*, between §§7 and 8, preceded not only by *Spec.* 3.1–7 (the significant autobiographical passage, well known to Philonists) but also— and more immediately—by a page-long fragment on the decad. The latter, conceivably a loose folio and possibly a remnant of Philo's lost treatise *Peri arithmōn (De numeris)*,[2] was placed immediately before *De decalogo*— obviously on the basis of the decadal association. As with the placement of the folio on the decad, the placement of *De decalogo* in Book 3 of *De specialibus legibus* is not altogether arbitrary. After all, the "special laws" in four books are structured around the Ten Commandments. Both of these placements clearly suggest that the archetype of the Armenian manuscripts (if not the Greek codex of the translator(s)—as we shall see) had a folio beginning with *De decalogo*. By the same token, also Book 3 of *De specialibus legibus* must have begun with a new folio which ended with §7, further suggesting that this folio was also loose at one time. Moreover, the Armenian text of *Spec.* 3.8 begins with the words of the sixth commandment, the first of the second table or set of five: «Οὐ μοιχεύσεις» ("You shall not commit adultery"; Arm. «Ոչ շնայցես» [*oč' šnayc'es*]), and omits the preceding sentence (ἐν δὲ τῇ δευτέρᾳ δέλτῳ πρῶτον γράμμα τοῦτ᾽ ἐστίν, "The first commandment in the second table, that is to say..."). It is plausible to suppose that the omission of the Greek line is due to its being the bottom line of the folio (*verso*) which began with Book 3 of *De specialibus legibus*

---

[1] Paper presented at the annual meeting of SBL, San Diego, 25 November 2014. I want to thank the organizers of the Philo Seminar, Ellen Birnbaum, Roland Cox, and Sarah J. Pearce, for their invitation to participate in the discussion about the text of this treatise.

[2] See my article, "A Philonic Fragment on the Decad," in *Nourished with Peace: Studies in Hellenistic Judaism in Memory of Samuel Sandmel,* ed. Frederick E. Greenspahn, Earle Hilgert, and Burton L. Mack, Scholars Press Homage Series 9 (Chico, CA: Scholars Press, 1984), 173–182.

(*recto*), and thus suffered an inevitable consequence of the detachment. I thus think that the Greek codex in the hands of the Armenian translator(s) (or perhaps its exemplar) had a number of loose and misplaced folia right where *De decalogo* was imbedded. Obviously, the disheveled Greek codex also had a number of missing folia, but this fact does not provide a plausible explanation for all the missing parts of the Armenian version of *De specialibus legibus* which is comprised of nearly intact units.[3]

The Armenian manuscript tradition of Philo's works shows—and that quite early in its development—a repeated attempt at rectifying the discernible problem at this juncture. At one time the title of *De decalogo* (Յաղագս տասն բանիցն / Περὶ τῶν δέκα λόγων)[4] came to replace the title of *De specialibus legibus* (at *Spec.* 3.1). At another time, *De decalogo* became the title of *Spec.* 3.8–64. The latter is explicable by the fact that treatises were concluded with the commonplace scribal (or authorial) marking of a work's end by repeating its title. In this case, "Here ends *De decalogo*." The words "here ends" (if used) were dropped and the title was stuck to what followed.[5] It will therefore be somewhat wrong to say that the Armenian version of *De decalogo* bears no title; its title has drifted both ways to where it does not belong—albeit not far removed in either direction. I cannot help but make a pun on the way *Spec.* 3.8 begins with its acquired title in Armenian: "You shall not commit adultery"—as though it expresses disapproval of the "adulterated" (re)arrangement within the Armenian corpus at this juncture, where *De decalogo* has become part of the textual flow of *Spec.* 3.

To be sure, in a comparative textual study of Philo's works (here assessing the Greek variants of *De decalogo* vis-à-vis readings of its sixth-century Armenian translation) the authorial Greek necessarily commands

---

[3] The Armenian version has the following parts: *Spec.* 1.79–161 the complete section on laws pertaining to priests; 285–345 the complete section on the maintenance of the altar and the spiritual lessons thereof—through the end; 3.1–64 nearly all the laws pertaining to the sixth commandment, on adultery, which end with *Spec.* 3.82. The missing part of this last unit (§§65–82) is—by the same count of folia length—the exact equivalent to two folia (each side of a folio corresponding to a full page in PLCL). Here I wish to correct an inadvertent mistake in the introduction to my translation of *De animalibus,* where I had *Spec.* 3.1–63 (p. 6).

[4] The emendation λόγων (from the Greek witnesses' reading of λογίων) is supported not only by the Armenian text but also by R (the palimpsest Vaticanus gr. 316).

[5] Both of these replacements of the title appear in [Garegin] Zarbhanalian's edition of Philo's works the Greek of which is extant: *P'iloni Hebrayec'woy čaŕk' t'argmanealk' i nakhneac' meroc' oroc' Hellen bnagirk' hasin aŕ mez* (*Works of Philo Judaeus, translated by our ancestors, the Greek originals of which have come down to us*) (Venice: Mekhitarist Press, 1892), 220 and 268.

the benefit of the doubt—but not always. After all, the Armenian version has its own textual merits by virtue of its antiquity, its Greek *Vorlage* being older than the extant Greek manuscripts and in many ways comparable to the text once possessed by Eusebius of Caesarea.[6] Moreover, the syntactical peculiarity of the Armenian translation—that as a rule it follows the Greek syntax, an anomaly in Armenian—allows it to serve as a valuable control when ascertaining some questionable readings in the Greek text of Philo.[7]

Thanks to Zarbhanalian's edition of the Armenian text of Philo's works the Greek of which is extant,[8] Cohn was able to note several of its variants and to incorporate a few of its readings in his critical edition of the Greek text (PCW). A brief statement is necessary here on the *codex optimus* used by Zarbhanalian for the Armenian edition: Venetian Mekhitarist ms 1040, copied in 1296 for the Cilician King Het'um II (reigned 1289–1293, 1295–1297). This is the same manuscript used earlier in the nineteenth century by Aucher for the edition of Philo's works extant in Armenian only.[9] A royal

---

[6] The textual histories of the respective versions have been discussed previously. See David T. Runia, *Philo in Early Christian Literature: A Survey*, CRINT III.3 (Assen: Van Gorcum; Minneapolis: Fortress Presss, 1993), 16–31; Abraham Terian, "Notes on the Transmission of the Philonic Corpus," *SPhiloA* 6 (1994): 91–95. Both conclude that the line of transmission of which Eusebius is a witness may not have been exclusive. Maurizio Olivieri points to a common ancestor: "Philo's *De Providentia*: A Work between Two Traditions," in *Studies on the Ancient Armenian Version of Philo's Works*, ed. Sara Mancini Lombardi and Paola Pontani, SPhA 6 (Leiden: Brill, 2011), 87–124.

[7] For a discussion of this feature see Abraham Terian, *Philonis Alexandrini De Animalibus*, Studies in Hellenistic Judaism, Supplements to Studia Philonica 1 (Chico, CA: Scholars Press, 1981), 9–14, 58–59; repeated in idem, *Alexander*, PAPM 36, pp. 23–29, 78–79). Cf. idem, "The Hellenizing School: Its Time, Place, and Scope of Activities Reconsidered," in *East of Byzantium: Syria and Armenia in the Formative Period (Dumbarton Oaks Symposium, 1980)*, ed. Nina G. Garsoïan, Thomas F. Mathews, and Robert W. Thomson (Washington, D.C.: Dumbarton Oaks, 1982), 175–186.

[8] *P'iloni Hebrayec'woy čaṙk'*, 223–267 for *De decalogo*. The volume was prepared upon Frederick C. Conybeare's request, for use in his edition of *Philo about the Contemplative Life, or the Fourth Book of the Treatise Concerning Virtues* (Oxford: Clarendon Press, 1895; repr. New York: Garland, 1987). Conybeare used three other manuscripts: Erevan, Matenadaran no. 2100 (formerly Ejjmiacin no. 2049.5), dated 1325, his B; no. 2057 (formerly Ejmiacin no. 2046.2), dated 1328, his C; and the Venetian Mekhitarists' no. 1334, from early 14th century, his D.

[9] Johannes B. Aucher (Mkrtič' Awgerian), *Philonis Judaei sermones tres hactenus inediti, I. et II. De Providentia et III. De Animalibus* (Venetiis: Typis coenobi p. Armenorum in insula s. Lazari, 1822; idem, *Philonis Judaei paralipomena armena: Libri videlicet quatuor in Genesin [sic], libri duo in Exodum, sermo unus de Sampsone, alter de Jona, tertius de tribus angelis Abraamo apparentibus* (Venetiis: Typis coenobixx p. Armenorum in insula s. Lazari, 1826). Aucher's work was done upon C. E. Richter's urging, whose 1828–1830 *Philonis Iudaei opera omnia* in 8 vols. (Leipzig: E. B. Schwickert) incorporated Aucher's Latin translation, the first as vol. 8 and the second as vol. 7.

manuscript in every sense of the word, its text —though not altogether free of inner-Armenian errors—surpasses that of all other known Armenian manuscripts of Philo except for those known to have been copied most likely from the same exemplar but not with the same exactitude. The Armenian-Venetian editors respectively used one other codex at their monastery on the Isle of San Lazzaro: ms 1334, from early 14th century,[10] to which they simply referred as "the other" when citing its rare variants. There is no critical text of the Armenian *corpus Philoneum*. More often than not, known attempts to critically emend the text of the *codex optimus* have only compounded the perceived errors.[11]

I turn now to the way Cohn treated the Armenian variants he observed in *De decalogo*—alongside the Greek variants in the *apparatus criticus* of his edition.[12] For my assignment, I checked the some 170 references made there to the variant readings in the Armenian version. The least significant and highly questionable variants observed by him are those of particles, both adverbial and conjunctional. The extraordinary number of Greek particles and the almost countless nuances created by their combinations are difficult to trace in the Armenian version where they are variously rendered with fewer particles and at times with added conjunctions. (An addition to this difficulty is the imaginable early Greek text of Philo, in uncial letters with no spacing between words and few—if any—accents, breathings, punctuation marks, etc.). Nearly a fourth of the indicated variants fall into this category.[13] Here the Armenian is of little or no help since a given Armenian particle stands for a number of Greek equivalents, and vice versa—albeit to a lesser extent. Furthermore, it is with such use that the translator(s) took most liberties in their otherwise rigidly interlinear translation, and ever so

---

[10] For a description of these and other Armenian manuscripts containing certain works of Philo, see my introduction to *De Animalibus*, pp. 14–21; *Alexander*, PAPM 36, pp. 30–35.

[11] See, e.g., Maurizio Olivieri, *Il secondo libro del* De Providentia *di Philone Alessandrino: I frammenti greci e la traduzione armena* (diss., Universita degli Studi di Bologna, 1999–2000, 102–227—besides earlier textual studies by Conybeare (*Contempl.*) and Lewy (the pseudo-Philonic *De Jona*).

[12] PCW 4.269–307.

[13] See the following: 272.22 (§20); 273.5² (§21); 277.7 (§38); 277.13 (§39); 279.10 (§46); 280.19 (§50); 281.20 (§57); 282.8 (§58); 284.19 (§69); 284.25 (§71); 286.10 (§77); 288.8 (§86); 289.1 (§87); 290.15 (§94); 292.17 (§102); 293.1 (§104); 293.14 (107); 297.21 (§127); 298.19 (§132); 300.8 (§140); 301.14 (§144); 303.12² (§155); 303.24 (§158). See also those in the following note.

often omitted particles.[14] I think Cohn was ill advised by those who helped him in this area of Armenian equivalents.[15]

There is no absolute way to determine from the Armenian whether the Greek had γάρ or οὖν, whether ὅτι or ὅτε, whether ὡς, ὥστε, or ὥσπερ; or whether the translator was looking at ἤ (disjunctive) or ἦ (asseverative). In one case, e.g., where the Greek has κἂν μέν and the Armenian qh ptwtun *(zi t'ēpēt)*, the Armenian variant in Cohn's *apparatus* is arbitrarily indicated as ἂν μὲν γάρ (289.1 [§87]). There can hardly be any doubt that the translator read κἂν μέν and rendered it accurately. However, had there been no Greek text here, there would have been no way of arriving at κἂν μέν from the Arm. qh ptwtun *(zi t'ēpēt)*. Elsewhere in the Philonic corpus κἂν is rendered as qh tpt *(zi et'ē*, as in *Abr.* 197), which is also the equivalent to εἰ, εἰ μὲν γάρ, and εἴπερ. As for Arm. qh *(zi)* in the Philonic corpus, as elsewhere, it is equivalent to ἵνα, ὡς, ὅτι, etc. Another related and equally ubiquitous particle, pwŭqh *(k'anzi)*, is the equivalent to γάρ, ἀλλὰ γάρ, διότι, ὅτι, μέν, οὖν, μὲν οὖν, etc. (and to many more when combined with tι *[ew]*, Gk. καί). At 292.17 (§102), pwŭqh *(k'anzi)* is arbitrarily given the equivalency of ἐπὶ δέ and cited as a variant of ἐπεὶ καί, and at 297.21 (§127) given the equivalency of κἂν γάρ and cited as a variant of κἂν. One will have to take "with a pinch of salt" most of Cohn's Greek equivalents to Armenian particles. As for the contribution of the Armenian particles to such text-critical comparison, it is miniscule at best.

As for the remaining variants, some substantive, I have divided them into six categories, as follows—in descending order of priority:

1. Where the Armenian reading alone is preferred.
2. Where the Armenian agrees with ms M against the rest of the witnesses.
3. Where the Armenian is decisive in determining a favored reading.
4. Where the Armenian is cited simply as another witness among those rejected.
5. Where the Armenian stands alone at times as an odd or corrupt reading.
6. Where the Armenian reading is wrongly indicated.

---

[14] The Armenian text omits δ᾽, 270.7 (§5); 280.18 (§50); 286.5 (§76); δή, 287.1 (§80); γάρ, 271.7 (§12); καί, 272.20 (§19); 282.22 (§62); 290.15[1] (§94); οὖν, 285.14 (§74); 288.4 (§85); τε, 284.10 (§67); τι, 286.9 (§76).

[15] In his reading of the Armenian text Cohn probably had the help of the Mekhitarist philologists at either of their monasteries, in Venice or Vienna.

1. *Where the Armenian Reading Alone is Preferred*

Cohn's fascination with the Armenian text stems from its textual proximity to Monacensis gr. 459, his preferred manuscript (A).[16] Were it not for this textual affinity, we would have seen many more citations of Armenian variants in his *apparatus*. Only once he rejects a variant reading common only to A and Armenian (275.8 [§30]). Some of his few adoptions of readings peculiar to the Armenian text seem to have been conditioned in part by Mangey's earlier use of the Armenian version (as noted in the *apparatus*).

271.10 (§13 πόλεις); 276.19 (§35 προϋπαντῶσα); 289.8 (§89 ἐπεί); 294.17 (§112 ἔχοντες); 297.7 (§123 τοῦ); 297.20 (§126 τόν¹); 298.21 (§133 ἁγιώτερον); 299.15 (§136 τἀληθὲς ἔργον); 300.11 (§140 τούτοις); 301.3 (§142 ἐπιθυμεῖν); 306.11 (§171 παρακαταθηκῶν); 306.22 (§174 ἐνδεχομένων); 307.9 (§177 φόβῳ).

2. *Where the Armenian Agrees with Ms M against the Rest of the Witnesses*

Most of the adopted readings based on the witness of the Armenian text are in instances where it agrees with Laurentianus X 20 (M),[17] a text constituting its own family, yet having much in common with "Family A" headed by Cohn's lead ms A. On the affinities between M and the Armenian version Cohn has this to say: "Among the better codices mention must be made of Codex M which, although infected with many errors, is quite often closely related to the Armenian version or alone supplies the authentic text."[18] Based on this single Greek witness and the *versio Armenia* there are twenty-six adopted readings. In two instances the adopted reading is based on the witness of G (Vaticano-Palatinus gr. 248) and Armenian; once each on the witness of F (Laurentianus LXXXV 10), H (Venetus gr. 40), and N (Neopolitanus II C 32 [excerpta]) with Armenian; four times on Armenian and the *Sacra Parallela* (D); and once on Armenian and v (lectio vulgata).

---

[16] For a description of this ms see PCW 1. Iv–vii; G-G p. 139 (no. 35). For Cohn's assessment of the *versio Armenia* see PCW 1. Lii–lvi.

[17] For a description of this ms see PCW 1. xxxi; G-G p. 149 (no. 100).

[18] "*Meliorem quam ceteri codices memoriam codex M prae se fert, qui, quamvis multis vitiis infectus sit, sepissime tamen vel cum versione Armenia coniunctus vel solus genuinam scripturam suppeditavit*" (PCW 4. Xxxi–ii).

With M 275.17 (§31); 275.20 (32); 276.3 (§33); 276.15 (§35); 277.1 (§37); 279.8 (§46); 279.16 (§47); 281.20 (§57); 282.2 (§58); 282.8 (§59); 283.4, 8 (§63); 283.13 (§64); 285.5 (§71); 286.9 (§76); 286.15 (§77); 286.22 (§79); 287.2–3, 3 (§80); 288.13 (§87); 289.11 (§89); 289.14 (§90); 290.2 (§91); 293.9 (§106); 293.14 (§107); 294.9 (§111).
With F 298.8 (§129).
With G 303.24 (§158); 304.1 (§158).
With H 300.14 (§140).
With N 301.7 (§142).
With D^R 290.18–19 (§94); 300.13–14 (§140); 300.14 (§140); 300.18 (§141).
With v 300.2 (§138).

3. *Where the Armenian is Decisive in Determining a Favored Reading*

Where there are conflicting readings among the witnesses, the *versio Armenia* ever so often helps tip the balance in favor of the reading adopted into the text. Sometimes the mere proximity of an Armenian reading has been enough to help emend the Greek text, as at 287.17 (§82), where the plural dative uḣnunıng (*snotwoc'*; cf. singular dative uḣnunıni, *snotwoy*) along with the plural dative ματαίοις of a single Greek witness (H=Venetus gr. 40) enables Cohn to emend the reading to the singular dative ματαίῳ.

273.9–10 (§21); 275.17 (§31); 275.20 (§32); 276.3 (§33); 276.15 (§35); 277.1 (§37); 279.8, 11^2 (§46); 281.14 (§56); 281.20 (§57); 282.2 (§58); 282.8 (§59); 282.14 (§60); 282.23 (§62); 283.1 (§62); 283.4, 8 (§63); 283.13 (§64); 285.5 (§71); 286.15 (§76); 286.22 (§79); 287.2–3 (§80); 287.3 (§80); 287.17 (§82); 304.14 (§160).

4. *Where the Armenian is Cited Simply as Another Witness among Those Rejected*

These include instances where the Armenian is rejected with all other witnesses in favor of an emendation (usually by Mangey, followed by Cohn). At times, however, the rejected reading (including the Armenian variant) is equally suited to the context as, e.g., the singular τὸ ἀποκυόμενον at 298.1–2 (§128).

275.14 (§31); 280.6 (§50); 281.12 (§55); 284.7^2 (§66); 285.22 (§74); 286.5 (§76 with all others); 287.2 (§80); 291.22 (§99); 292.3 (§100); 293.8–9 (§106); 293.10 (§106); 294.5–6 (110); 294.18 (§113); 295.12–13 (§115); 296.14 (§120); 298.1–2 (§128); 298.20 (§133); 300.18 (§141); 302.20 (§150); 307.4 (§176).

5. *Where the Armenian Stands Alone at Times as an Odd or Corrupt Reading*

These do not always indicate corruption in the Greek exemplar but, more often than not, the translator's errors (rarely an inner-Armenian corruption); e.g., translating ὁμοίῳ wrongly, as if it were ὁμοιότατι (§104); δίκαια as if it were δικαιώματα (§107), the singular as plural and vice versa. However, certain rejections of the Armenian variants seem to be arbitrary, as some of the examples given below illustrate. Some show a degree of dynamism expressed in the translation; e.g., in §114, where the Armenian has γίνεσθαι instead of γίνεσθε (... զմարդ զգազանս ոմանս մարթիկ լինել; lit., "... men to become like certain beasts"). Other rejections are somewhat puzzling; e.g., the rejected addition of the word "Mosaic" in "There is an account recorded in the Mosaic story of the Creation..." (§97).

The following convey a great deal: 269.6 (§1 has ἐν τῇ προτέρᾳ συντάξει for ἐν ταῖς προτέραις συντάξεσι); 269.16 (§4 has ἀφ' οὗ for οὖν); 270.8 (§5 adds πρῶτον to ἴδιον); 270.24 (§10 has τοὺς μέλλοντας for τοῦ μέλλοντος); 271.19 (§14 has εὖ ἀσκηθέντας for ἐνασκηθέντας); 272.1 (§16 om. ἡμέρων due to *homoioteleuton*); 273.12–13 (§21 transp.); 275.2 (§29 transp.); 276.23 (§36 om. οὐ φονεύσεις due to *homoioteleuton*); 279.11 (§46, adds αὐτοῖς to ἐτρανοῦτο); 279.14 (§47 om. ὁρατὴν δὲ ὡς); 279.18 (§48 om. καί); 280.4 (§50 see discussion below); 281.14 (§56 om. τῷ λόγῳ); 281.15 (§56 corrupt. διχῆ to δύο); 282.11 (§60 adds ἄνθρωποι to ζῶντες); 283.3 (§63 om. στομάργῳ); 283.15 (§64 om. θεραπείᾳ); 285.18 (§74 om. μήτε δρῶντες due to *homoioarcton / homoioteleuton*); 290.16 (§94 om. οὔτε μητρός due to *homoioarcton / homoioteleuton*); 291.3 (§95 see discussion below); 291.10 (§97 adds Μωυσέως before κοσμοποιίαν); 291.15 (§98 om. ἡμέραις); 292.3 (§100 om. ἕν); 292.21 (§103 has ἡ for ἥν); 292.25 (§104 has ὁμοιότατι for ὁμοίῳ); 293.2 (§104 om. καὶ ἔτι); 293.11 (§107 has δικαιώματα for δίκαια); 294.7 (§110 corrupt. πρωτεῖα to πρεσβεῖα); 294.20 (§113 transp.); 295.3 (§113 om. ἐλπίδα); 295.4 (§114 has γίνεσθαι for γίνεσθε); 295.16 (§117 has ἡμεροῦντες for ἠρεμοῦντες); 295.17–18 (§117 has ἐπελαφρίζοντες for ἐπελαφριζόμενοι); 297.3 (§122 adds μεγίστας before οὐσίας); 297.6 (§123 transp.); 298.16 (§132 has ζώων for ζῶον); 300.2 (§138 has κόσμῳ for βίῳ); 300.12 (§140 corrupt. ἀδικεῖσθαι to ἐλέγχεσθαι); 300.14 (§140 corrupt. ψήφους to γνώμας); 300.16 (§141 has μετά for πρό); 301,7 (§142 om. μόνη); 302.5 (§148 adds εἰς before τὰ ὦτα); 302.14 (has προανεκριζωθείη for προανακρουσθείη); 302.15 (§150 has ἐπινεμόμενα for ἐπιθέοντα); 303.10 (§155 om. τῶν); 303.18 (§156 om. καὶ θεογονίαν due to *homoioarcton*); 304.1 (§159 has ἑβδομάδα for ἑβδόμην); 304.7 (§159 om. αὐτῶν); 304.15 (§161 has καί for κατά); 304.16 (§161 om. δυσίν due to *homoioarcton);* 304.21 (§161 om. ἱεράν due to *homoioteleuton);*[19] 305.6 (§163 om. χρησάμενας); 305.16 (has προπεπονθότες for πεπονθότες); 305,17[2] (§167 twice om. εἰς); 306.16 (§172 om. νόμοι); 306.16 (§172 has προσηκόντως for προσήκοντες); 306.17 (§173 has ἀνείργειν for ἀνεῖργον); 307.2–3 (§175 has ἀναπλάσας for ἀναπλήσας).

6. Where the Armenian Reading is Wrongly Indicated

It is not always feasible to determine with absolute certainty questionable readings in the Greek text of Philo by simply retranslating the Armenian, even when one is guided by its prevalent Greek syntax and equipped with Greek-Armenian and Armenian-Greek word-indices or concordances based on works of Philo which survive in both languages. Far more problematic are the attempts at retrospective translation with intent to reconstruct out of the Armenian text even a portion of a Philonic work the Greek of which is lost.[20] Dictionary-based methods have their limitations, especially when a single Armenian word renders a number of Greek synonyms and vice versa. I will illustrate this kind of difficulty here with just one expanded example from *De decalogo.* At §95 (PCW 4.291.3) Cohn notes that the Armenian has ἐκριζοῦν for κολάζειν. The Armenian verb is ի բաց խլել (*i bac' xlel,* "to prune"; "to cut out"; "to root out"; etc.) an infinitive agreeing with κολάζειν. The same verb (ի բաց խլել) is used in *Decal.* 12 as an equivalent to ὑπεξαιρέω, a verb found also in *Decal.* 150, but there the Armenian has զատեալ ի բաց (*zateal i bac').* Moreover, the same verb (ի բաց խլել) is used in *Decal.* 126 for the verbal adjective ἀνάστατος ("driven out [from one's house]" or "ravaged"; cf. ἀναστατόω). Without resorting to the implications of the use of κολάζω in *Spec.* 1.316 and 3.11[21] (κολαστέον in both, twice read as a verbal adjective by the translator, rendering it

---

[19] For a different explanation of this omission, see Paola Pontani, "Saying (Almost) the Same Thing. On Some Relevant Differences Between Greek-language Originals and Their Armenian Translations," in *Studies on the Ancient Armenian Version of Philo's Works,* p. 143.

[20] An excellent study by Romano Sgarbi, *Problemi linguistici e di critica del testo nel De vita contemplativa di Filone alla luce della versione armena,* Memorie, Instituto Lombardo—Classe Lettere, vol. 40 fasc. 1 (Milan: Instituto–Lombardo, 1992), shows how, if one were to translate the Armenian *De vita contemplativa* literally and apart from the Greek, the resultant translation would be considerably different from a literal translation of the Greek. See also his "Philo's Stylemes vs. Armenian Translation Stylemes," in *Studies on the Ancient Armenian Version of Philo's Works,* pp. 147–154.

[21] Parts of *Spec.* 1–4 where the same verb recurs (at *Spec.* 1.54; 2.37, 137, 232, 245, 246; 3.149, 152, 154, 156; 4.2) are not part of the Armenian *corpus Philoneum* (see above, n. 3).

uniformly as սատակէլի, *satakeli*), suffice to say that the Armenian has an accurate rendering of κολάζειν in *Decal.* 95 and need not be classified as a variant. As for ἐκριζοῦν, the synonymous equivalent conjectured by Cohn, purportedly the word behind the Armenian, it does not occur anywhere in the works of Philo. More examples follow.

275.7–8 (§30): τὰ ὦν οὐκ ἄνευ <πάντα>, χρόνον καὶ τόπον (text, emended by Cohn, following Mangey), adding "... ἄνευ χρόνου καὶ τόπου A Arm" in the *apparatus*. Actually, the Armenian has τὰ ὦν οὐκ ἄνευ ἀχρόνου καὶ ἀτόπου (յորոց ոչ է անժամանակ և անտեղի). It reduces the improper preposition ἄνευ, used with the redundant yet usual οὐκ and genitive adjectives,[22] to a simple preposition (յ- prefix) and seems to favor its meaning of "besides" over "without"; thus, "... besides those existences that are neither timeless nor placeless" (speaking of the last two of the ten categories of existence).

280.4 (§50) wrongly indicates the omission of προτέρα, which appears as a mistranslation in the text, corresponding to εἷς (մի in և մի հնգեակն).

290.20 (§95) wrongly indicates the omission of τὸ μὲν πρῶτον, which appears earlier in the sentence (իսկ սա զառաջին), in a rare instance where the translator deviates from the Greek syntax.

292.3 (§100) Arm. վեցերեակն չափ, corresponding to ἑξὰς μέτρον and agreeing with R (the palimpsest Vaticanus gr. 316),[23] is distinct from the other witnesses' reading of ἑξάμετρον and calls into question the emendation to ἑξαήμερον (Christophorson, followed by Mangey *et al.*).

296.1–2 (§117) wrongly indicates the omission of καὶ λαβόντες αὐτὸ καὶ ἀνταποδιδόντες (և ընդունելով զայս և փոխանակ հատուցանելով).

297.1 (§121) wrongly indicates μεγίστων as the Armenian reading, which is մեծ, in keeping with the Greek text (μέγιστον).

297.7 (§123) unnecessarily brackets τοῦ in the text, the inclusion of which is justified by the Armenian only (the suffix ն in այինն).

300.2 (§138) wonders (with a question mark) whether Arm. սրբագոյն agrees with ἱερώτερον (adopted reading on the basis of *lectio vulgata* [*v*]) or, as it does, with ἱερώτατον of the collectively rejected Greek witnesses—including the *Sacra Parallela* (D).

---

[22] On the grammatical correctness of such uses see Herbert W. Smyth, *Greek Grammar,* rev. by Gordon M. Messing (Cambridge, MA: Harvard University Press, 1956), §§1700, 2753.

[23] I owe this observation to James R. Royse, "The Text of Philo's *De Decalogo*" (paper presented at the annual meeting of SBL, San Diego, 25 November 2014).

301.14 (§144) unnecessarily brackets καί in the text, the inclusion of which is justified by the Armenian only (և).

302.5 (§148); 305,17² (§167) unnecessarily notes the addition of εἰς in one and the repeated omission of εἰς in the other. The prepositional use of εἰς is wanting in Armenian (ի, յ- when prefixed to a word beginning with a vowel), often implied by ellipsis. Note the Armenian text's omission of εἰς at 303.24 (§158, not noticed by Cohn).[24]

In instances where the Armenian reading stands alone, it seldom provides a convincing or preferred reading to emend the Greek; but where the latter's reading is called into question, there we stand to benefit from the Armenian version. Still, one has to look outside Cohn's *apparatus* for further merits of the Armenian text, in at least two areas: (a) where an Armenian reading could be decisive either on its own or alongside certain Greek witnesses—somehow overlooked by Cohn; and (b) where the Armenian agrees with the received Greek text and helps make a better sense when the latter appears to be somewhat ambiguous (even though the Armenian abounds in ambiguity especially when read apart from the Greek). To pursue these desiderata, a task that could help answer certain of the textual questions raised by Colson and Nikiprowetzky in the course of their respective translations,[25] is beyond the scope of this paper.

St. Nersess Armenian Seminary, NY
National Academy of Sciences, Armenia

---

[24] Likewise, the Armenian text omits the first ἐνί at 277.11 (§39, not noticed by Cohn).
[25] Colson, PLCL 7; Nikiprowetzky, PAPM 23.

The Studia Philonica Annual 27 (2015): 155–180

RHETORICAL TEXTURE AND PATTERN
IN PHILO'S *DE DECALOGO*

MANUEL ALEXANDRE JR.

According to Valentin Nikiprowetzky, this treatise is essentially an exegetical commentary on the Ten Commandments. Philo did not use lofty words and impressive thoughts to interpret them,[1] but philosophy and rhetoric can nevertheless be felt in the background of *De Decalogo*; philosophy shapes the thoughts that give Philo's commentaries substance, and rhetoric shapes the harmony and power of their expression. For Nikiprowetzky, Philo's style in this treatise was often admirable.[2] He knew how to treat the substance of the message he was expounding: "His real merit was to know… how to make an instrument of spiritual invention, and how to manage that instrument with an extreme ingenuity, an almost divinatory sense of analogy and symbol, a sort of visionary intensity that transfigures" every thing it touches.[3] His commentary is remarkable. The rhetorical

---

[1] "Les disciplines scolaires, et la philosophie grecque elle-même, ne fournissent à sa pensée qu'une langue conceptuelle très générale, dont il use précisément comme d'un langage, avec une franchise et une liberté telles qu'on a cru voir en lui un éclectique ou un professeur faisant 'sa classe de philosophie'" (Philon d'Alexandrie, *De Decalogo: Introduction, traduction et notes*, ed. Valentin Nikiprowetzky, PAPM 16 [Paris: Cerf, 1965], 32–33).

[2] There was a time when opinions were divided on this matter. For É. Herriot, *Philon le Juif. Essai sur l'École juive d'Alexandrie* (Paris: Librairie Hachette, 1898), 144, "Philon ne pratique pas l'art de composer… se soucie peu de la vraie logique, de la vraie méthode et de la rigueur dans les deductions." For G. Trotti, *Filone Alessandrino* (Rome: Istituto Poligrafico dello Stato, 1932), 10, "la manque d'ordre et de méthode dans l'exposition des commentaires… les longues et oiseuses digressions, les diverses contradictions et confusions" are more than evident. W. Völker censures his heavy style inclined to an excess of rhetorical symmetries, profuse images, capricious pieces of composition and unclearness (*Fortschritt und Volendung bei Philo von Alexandrien. Eine Studie zur Geschichte der Frömmigkeit* [Leipzig: J. C. Hinrichs, 1938], 5). But, with time, Philo's scholars like F. H. Colson, "Philo's Quotations from the Old Testament." *JTS* 41 (1940): 250; PLCL 7:ix-xxii, L. Massebieau, *Le Classement des oeuvres de Philon*, Bibliothèque de l'École des Autes Études, Sciences Religieuses [Paris: E. Loroux, 1889], 3) and many others have underlined the extraordinary articulation of his thought, and the art of his composition.

[3] Nikiprowetzky, *Philon d'Alexandrie, De Decalogo*, 33–34.

conventions that inform it are self-evident, not just in terms of eloquence or style.

Rhetorical categories of argumentation and interpretation were essential in the educational system of Philo's Alexandria, as intrinsic parts of intermediate and higher education. And Philo used these conventions abundantly in this treatise.

As "Heir and trustee of the Jewish thought of Alexandria" and a distinguished voice of Antiquity in the interpretation of Scripture,[4] Philo creatively used the compositional devices of rhetoric—oral patterns provided by the tradition,[5] as well as the strategies of argumentation he learned and practiced in the schools of *paideia*—to sharpen the interpretation of Scripture. These can help us not just to shed new light on interpretive difficulties, but also to better identify the line and focus of his arguments.[6] "After all, rhetoric is just this: the mastering and use of literary techniques to communicate one's ideas in various ways."[7]

Exploring the rhetorical texture of Philo's *De Decalogo* in its consistent variety of logical and qualitative reasoning, I found coherence and effectiveness in the discourse as a whole, and in the particular units of composition as well. My analysis brought to the surface types of argumentative topics, figures and elaborations which support my conviction that the essence of true rhetoric is pervasive in Philo, as a learned process of argumentation that "is more than a taxonomy of linguistic devices and persuasive strategies."[8] Philo used exegetical methods when expounding Scripture just like the rhetoricians of the Greco-Roman world in the interpretation of ancient texts, seeing "themselves first and foremost as pedagogues" in the context of their own *paideia*.[9]

---

[4] Nikiprowetzky, *Philon d'Alexandrie, De Decalogo*, 34.

[5] Eight categories of oral patterning are referred and analyzed by John D. Harvey, *Listening to the Text: Oral Patterning in Paul's Letters* (Grand Rapids, MI: Baker Books/ Leicester, UK: Apollos, 1998), 97–118: chiasmus, inversion, alternation, inclusion, ring-composition, word-chain, refrain, and concentric symmetry or extended chiasmus.

[6] See Harvey, *Listening to the Text*, 301–302.

[7] Hagit Amirav, *Rhetoric and Tradition: John Chrysostom on Noah and the Flood*, Traditio Exegetica Graeca (Leuven: Peeters, 2003), 33.

[8] Jennifer Richards, *Rhetoric: The New Critical Idiom* (London: Routledge, 2008), 13.

[9] Amirav, *Rhetoric and Tradition*, 221–223.

Argumentative Texture and Pattern

Philo's many reflections on secular education leave us no doubt that his formative years provided him the best of classical *paideia*, both in philosophy and rhetoric. His massive work proves it. He was trained in a large variety of argumentative strategies. From the simple enthymeme or rhetorical syllogism to the most expanded levels of thematic elaboration, he was qualified to apply them to each situation, be it related with oratorical speech or not. For, as Aristotle defines it, "rhetoric is not concerned with any single kind of subject, but is like dialectic, a useful art." It is rather "the power to detect the persuasive aspects of each matter and this is in line with all other skills."[10]

The most articulate patterns of argumentation taught in the schools of the time were: (1) two elaborations, as illustrated in the *Rhetorica ad Herennium*—"the most complete and perfect argument" (2.28–30), and an elaboration of a theme (4.55–58); also (2) the elaboration of a *chreia* or a maxim, as we find it in the *Progymnasmata*.[11] Each one of these exercises is similarly structured and developed, and what distinguishes them from the rhetorical syllogism, or the five parts of Ciceronian ratiocination is the enrichment of the argument after the proof has been established. In this particular case, if the matter proves to be too meager for amplification,

---

[10] Aristotle, *Rhet.* 1355b.

[11] "The term *progymnasmata* (προγυμνάσματα) or preparatory exercises denotes two important things: first, rhetorical *forms* (the chreia for instance is a *progymnasma*); and second, *techniques* for modifying these forms" (Alex Damm, *Ancient Rhetoric and the Synoptic Problem: Clarifying Markan Priority* [Peeters: Leuven, 2013], 19). These graded lessons on preliminary rhetorical exercises provided learning through memorization, imitation and practice as an introduction to the whole system of rhetorical theory and technique, and elaborations in argumentation as well. The elaboration that supports a chreia is the most complete rhetorical exercise, anticipating the thematic elaboration of a full judicial or deliberative speech. The educators who specifically wrote on the *Progymnasmata* were: Theon of Alexandria, in the first century CE; Hermogenes, in the second/third centuries; Aphthonius in the fourth century; and Nicolaus in the fifth century. "Although Quintilian does not author a treatise of *progymnasmata*, he recommends that pupils undertake *progymnasmata* like the chreia as part of their rhetorical education" (Damm, *Ancient Rhetoric*, 32). Among the basic texts that have appeared in recent years, I mention: Eugenio Amato, ed., *Severus Sophista Alexandrinus: Progymnasmata quae exstant omnia* (Berlin: de Gruyter, 2009); Craig A. Gibson, ed. and trans., *Libanius's* Progymnasmata: *Model Exercises in Greek Prose Composition and Rhetoric* (Atlanta: Society of Biblical Literature, 2008); George A Kennedy, trans., *Progymnasmata: Greek Textbooks of Prose Composition and Rhetoric* (Atlanta: Society of Biblical Literature, 2003); Ronald F. Hock and Edward N. O'Neil, eds., *The Chreia and Rhetoric: Classroom Exercises* (Atlanta: Society of Biblical Literature, 2002); Hermogène, "Les Exercices Préparatoires" in *L'Art Rhétorique*, trans. by Michel Patillon (Paris: L'Age de L'Homme et Les Belles Lettres, 1997).

statements from analogy, example, authority and other means should be added as needed. Theon of Alexandria suggests an even larger diversity of topics for the development of a theme or the proof of a thesis, used as needed and with no specific order. In both cases, however, the argumentation should be elegantly and completely developed, and the specific arguments be soberly used.[12]

These elaborations provided Philo with the keys for his writing as a rhetorical act, especially his exegetical commentaries. When he claims that "rhetoric, sharpening the mind to the observation of facts and training and exercising thought to interpretation and explanation, will make the human being a true master of words and thoughts," and that dialectic is the sister and twin of rhetoric,[13] Philo is apparently affirming that philosophy and rhetoric work together and complement each other in the task of interpreting and explaining the divine *Logos*. For him, rhetoric is then also a powerful tool to interpret Scripture and to direct the course of an exegetical exposition;[14] a meaning close to Perelman's, when he says that "Hermeneutics is another kind of rhetoric because you do not go from the speaker to the audience, but from the text written to the audience... The idea of looking for meaning is done now through the rhetorical method."[15]

As we know, Philo's "world was a rhetorician's world."[16] His rhetorical culture was characterized by a lively interaction between oral and written composition. Even "A number of philosophers developed a concept of oratory as it would be practiced by a true philosopher... The old Sophistic ideal of the well-trained man of public life devoted to action had never

---

[12] Cf. Damm, *Ancient Rhetoric*, 30–80.

[13] *Congr.* 17–18. Philo is reflecting here on the branches of preliminary studies—the ἐγκύκλιος παιδεία—as a road, which leads to virtue. Comparing rhetoric with dialectic, he refers to both as twin sisters and takes them as associates that lead humanity to the knowledge of the royal virtues. In other words, rhetoric and dialectic closely work together to reach the highest levels of consummate philosophy or wisdom, as it is well explained through the allegorical interpretation of the patriarchs Abraham, Isaac and Jacob, respectively representing virtue that comes through teaching, practice, and self-learned virtue (*Congr.* 18–38).

[14] The Greek text is clear: ῥητορικὴ δὲ καὶ τὸν νοῦν πρὸς θεωρίαν ἀκονησαμένη καὶ πρὸς ἑρμηνείαν γυμνάσασα τὸν λόγον καὶ συγκροτήσασα λογικὸν ὄντως ἀποδείξει τὸν ἄνθρωπον...

[15] Chaïm Perelman, "Old and New Rhetoric: An Address Delivered by Chaim Perelman at Ohio State University, November 16, 1982," in *Practical Reasoning in Human Affairs: Studies in Honor of Chaim Perelman*, ed. J. L. Golden and J. J. Pilotta (Dordrecht: D. Reidel Publishing Company, 1986), 11.

[16] George A. Kennedy, *The Art of Persuasion in Greece* (Princeton: Princeton University Press, 1963), 22.

entirely disappeared."[17] Aristotle, for instance, maintains that, "it is not sufficient to know what one ought to say, but one must also know how to say it."[18] Even Plato had to admit that the philosopher "plants and sows in a fitting soul intelligent words which are not fruitless but yield seed from which there spring up in other minds other words capable of continuing the process forever."[19]

We also know that, like all well-educated people in antiquity, Philo wrote his words to be heard. "All literature was written to be heard, and even when reading to himself a Greek read aloud."[20] In that predominantly oral world, authors "considered rhetorical techniques as important in persuading an audience as the evidence presented in their argument."[21] "There is an element of persuasiveness and understanding available only through *listening* to the text in its original language."[22] And we clearly see it in all his commentaries.

The Alexandrian interpreter of Scripture uses most of the argumentative patterns found in the rhetorical canons, as well as the topics or figures of argumentation that give these structures a logical or quasi-logical form.[23] A significant number of these elaborations contain a combination of statement, rationale and restatement, with or without a conclusion. But many are more expanded, either cohesively developing the basic thematic struc-

---

[17] Ibid., 21–22. "In a sense Cicero reverses the eloquent philosopher of the Greeks and substitutes a philosophical orator. There can be little question that this rhetorical ideal was more acceptable to the Romans than the figure of the sage" (Loc. Cit.).

[18] Aristotle, *Rhet.* 1403b (Freese, LCL).

[19] Plato, *Phaed.* 276e–277a (Fowler, LCL).

[20] Kennedy, *The Art of Persuasion in* Greece, 4.

[21] George A. Kennedy, *New Testament Interpretation through Rhetoric* (Chapel Hill: The University of North Carolina Press, 1984), 3.

[22] Michael R. Cosby, *The Rhetorical Composition and Function of Hebrews 11: In Light of Example Lists in Antiquity* (Macon, GA: Mercer University Press, 1988), 5. "The contemporary norm of silent reading... One should take the time to listen to the Greek words as if an ancient oral culture, recognizing that the author... considered the success of his message to be largely dependent on the way it sounded to his audience... To experience this is to add a new dimension to understanding and responding to his words" (p. 91).

[23] In a significant number of his exegetical commentaries the arguments are short and simple, having just a rationale that supports the proposition, theme or issue, as in Aristotle's enthymeme, or adding to the rationale a supporting argument to confirm it, as in Quintilian's *epichirema* and Cicero's *ratiocinatio*. Quintilian's *epichireme* is comprised of three parts, like the logical syllogism, but may present three or four premises (5.14.6): 1. *Propositio* (major premise); 2. *Assumptio* (minor premise); 3. *Conclusio* (conclusion). For Cicero's ratiocination, see Cicero, *Inv.* 1.67: Cicero divides the deductive argument ("argumentatio per ratiocinationem") in five parts: 1. *Propositio* (statement or thesis); 2. *Propositionis approbatio* (rationale); 3. *Assumptio* (restatement); 4. *Assumptionis approbatio* (rationale of the restatement); 5. *Complexio* (conclusion).

tures with a variety of supporting arguments, or plainly amplifying them with four major argumentative topics "especially effective in confirmation and embellishment": the arguments from opposite or contrary, from analogy, from example and from authority, namely the authority of Scripture.[24] In perfect alignment with these patterns of argumentation, thematic elaborations like a *chreia*[25] rhetorically incorporate a wide range of argumentative resources from textual and cultural traditions, with or without embellishments, pointing to a concluding application or exhortation.[26]

---

[24] The amplification of a theme according to the *Rhetorica ad Alexandrum,* includes: (1) a primary proof based on a list of eight argumentative topics; (2) a secondary proof accomplished with supporting arguments of analogy, example, contrary, citation of authority, etc. The amplified treatment of a theme according to [Cornificius], *Rhet. Her.* (4.55–58) contains seven parts: 1. *Res* (statement); 2. *Ratio* (rationale); 3. *Pronuntiatio* (restatement); 4. *Contrarium* (opposite); 5. *Simile* (analogy); 6. *Exemplum* (example); and 7. *Conclusio* (conclusion).

[25] *Chreia* is a brief saying or action or both with a pointed meaning, usually for the sake of something useful. Its rhetorical elaboration emerges in the form of a theme or thesis, whose meanings and meaning-effects unfold through argumentation as the unit progresses. The major topics or figures for the elaboration of this theme or issue are rationale, argument from the opposite, analogy, example, and authoritative testimony. See: Ronald F. Hock and Edward N. O'Neil, trans. and ed., *The Chreia and Ancient Rhetoric: Classroom Exercises* (Atlanta: Society of Biblical Literature, 2002).

[26] The two main references to this thematic elaboration are: (1) *the most complete and perfect argument,* according to *Rhet. Her.* 2.28–30; and (2) *the chreia elaboration,* according to Hermogenes and his followers Aphthonius and Nicolaus (George A. Kennedy, *Progymnasmata: Greek Textbooks of Prose Composition and Rhetoric* [Atlanta: Society of Biblical Literature, 2003] "Preliminary Exercises attributed to Hermogenes" [76–77]; "Preliminary Exercises of Aphthonius the Sophist" [97–99]; "Preliminary Exercises of Nicolaus the Sophist" [139–142]; "Commentary Attributed to John of Sardis" [193–196]).

The most complete and perfect argument is comprised of five parts, but the fourth includes at least four argumentative figures: 1. *Propositio* (proposition or thesis—what we intend to prove); 2. *Ratio* (rationale, reason—a brief explanation or justification); 3. *Confirmatio* (proof of the reason—corroborates the reason by means of additional arguments); 4. *Exornatio* (embellishment—adorns and enriches the argument after the proof has been established); and 5. *Complexio* (a brief conclusion). The basic argumentative figures in the *exornatio* are: 4.1. *Simile* (an analogy); 4.2. *Exemplum* (an example); 4.3. *Amplificatio* (amplification of the argument); 4.4. *Iudicatio* (a statement of authority).

The elaboration of a *chreia,* as mentioned in the previous note, is a complete argument consisting of eight argumentative topics on the whole: 1. Προοίμιον or *Encomium* (introduction, praise for the author); 2. Χρεία or *chria* (chreia or paraphrase of the chreia/thesis); 3. Αἰτίαι (statement of the rationale); 4. Ἐναντίον (statement of the contrary); 5. Παραβολή (analogy); 6. Παράδειγμα (example); 7. Κρίσις/Μαρτυρίαι (judgment or statement from authority); 8. Παράκλησις (conclusion or exhortation). As Vernon Robbins observes, the major characteristic of a thematic elaboration "is to bring a thesis and its rationale to the beginning of a unit... and to create a flow of argumentation out from the enthymematic beginning" ("Introduction: Using Rhetorical Discussions of the Chreia to Interpret

Philo's *De Decalogo* reveals then a wide range of rhetorical techniques, including typical forms of oral patterning. Traditional rhetoric drew on a broad range of oral patterns that were introduced into the organized system of conceptual rhetoric. Compositional devices like chiasmus and other concentric structures were supposed to perform rhetorical functions of emphasis, comparison and contrast. But the argumentative texture of each unit mainly involves a variation of devices well aligned with the patterns mentioned above. Some of his reasonings are logical, supporting or clarifying assertions through opposites and contraries. Others are developed in a more persuasive manner, using argumentative topics like analogies, examples and citations of authority.[27] Structure, elaboration and rhythm jointly concur to the harmony of their whole.[28]

De Decalogo's *Introduction*

This treatise is a harmonious whole in concentric structure [ABCB'A']. (1) It opens with four questions (2–49) and closes with one (176–178). (2) The commentary of the Ten Commandments in the middle is developed in two sets of five (52–120 and 121–153); (3) surrounded by an introductory summary of their particular contents (50–51) and a concluding synopsis on the general character of each of them (154–175).

The introductory four questions—on the desert in general (the first one), and on the Mount Sinai in particular (the remaining three)—reason on: (1) why the Law was given in the desert (2–17); (2) why the commands were ten (18–31); (3) how did God deliver the Ten Commandments (32–35); and (4) why was the singular number used (36–49). The concluding question of the treatise explains why God expressed these Ten Commandments as simple commands or prohibitions without laying down any penalty or punishment (176–178).

Philo knew how to adapt the weapons of his rhetoric to the public he wished to reach, and *De Decalogo*'s proem is no exception. His arguments are varied and harmoniously woven together. And the didactic-dialogical

---

Pronouncement Stories," *Semeia: An Experimental Journal for Biblical Criticism. The Rhetoric of Pronouncement* 64 [1993]: ix).

[27] Robbins, "The Rhetoric of Pronouncement," *Semeia* (1996): 21. See Burton L. Mack, and Vernon K. Robbins, "Elaboration of the Chreia in the Hellenistic Scholl," in *Patterns of Persuasion in the Gospels* (Sonoma, CA: Polebridge Press, 1989), 51.

[28] Figures like anaphora, asyndeton and polysyndeton, isocolon, rhetorical question, antithesis, etc.

strategies of argumentation used[29] were surely the best way to prepare his audience[30] for the commentary on the subject.[31] With varied degrees of development, the rationale that answers each question includes a variety of devices that rhetorically justify place, number and source of promulgation, as well as its mode of transmission. Their argumentative sequence moves from the desert in general to Sinai in particular in a variation of resources that involves sounds, vocabulary, rhythm, construction and persuasiveness.

To the first question, why was the Law given in the desert, four reasons are suggested: (1) cities are full of untold evils, namely pride and idolatry, and the desert marks a return to the law of nature (§2–9); (2) solitude promotes repentance, and purification from those evils was the preparatory step needed to receive the sacred laws (§10–13); (3) the desert was a preparation to grow familiar with the Law before full practice in their new home (§14); (4) the miraculous supply of food in the barren wilderness attested the divine origin of the Law (§15–18a).

Each of these reasoned forms of argumentation is justified and developed to show that the ideal learning environment for living well in accordance with nature was the desert. The rationale of the first two propositions and the fourth one is carefully ordered in five parts according to the Ciceronian model of ratiocination.[32] The third proposition is a

---

[29] They resemble the diatribe style used at the time, especially in a student-teacher relationship.

[30] Based on the exegetical nature of *De Decalogo*, Nikiprowetzky is inclined to defend a Hellenistic Jewish public as the obvious addressee of this treatise; he does not, however, omit the possibility of a universal audience due to the universal and absolute value of the Law (*Philon d'Alexandrie*, De Decalogo, 30–31). In the words of Perelman, "L'auditoire n'est pas nécessairement constitué par ceux que l'orateur interpelle expressément," but "l'ensemble de ceux sur lesquels l'orateur veut influer par son argumentation ;" the audience that he qualifies as "auditoire universel" (Chaïm Perelman, *L'Empire rhétorique: Rhétorique et argumentation* [Paris: Vrim, 1977], 29). And it makes even more sense in the case of Philo, since he wrote his commentary as a philosopher: "le discours adressé à un auditoire particulier vise à persuader, alors que celui qui s'adresse à l'auditoire universel vise a convaincre… Un discours convaincant est celui dont les prémisses et les arguments son universalisables, c'est-à-dire acceptables, en principe, par tous les membres de l'auditoire universel" (31).

[31] For Philo, "*De Decalogo* est, non une relation plus ou moins pittoresque de la Révélation des Dix Commandements, mais essentiellement un commentaire exégétique des textes de l'Écriture qui concernent l'une et les autres. La Loi était considérée comme la vérité absolue." Alexandrian Judaism installed "la Loi à la place de la philosophie. Philosopher, c'est étudier la Loi de Moïse et la mettre en pratique" (Nikiprowetzky, *Philon d'Alexandrie*, De Decalogo, 16–17).

[32] Cicero divides the deductive argument ("argumentatio per ratiocinationem") in five parts: (1) *Propositio* (Statement/Thesis); (2) *Propositionis approbatio* (Rationale); (3)

reasoned analogy that shows the importance of a thoughtful preparation for civic life "in harmony and fellowship of spirit."[33]

To the second question on why the commandments given by God Himself were ten (§18b-31), Philo descriptively justifies the excellences of the decad. Through enumerations in sequence, he shows that "ten" is the most comprehensive of all numbers, contains within it every kind of number and progression of numbers, and comprehends every proportion, harmony and symphony; that it represents the whole universe as the sum of 1 for the non extended point, 2 for the line, 3 for the surface, and 4 for the solid. In his argument as a whole, *omission* ends enumeration on the "infinite" virtues of number ten, and *climax* justifies its finale with a major

---

Assumptio (Restatement); (4) *Assumptionis approbatio* (Rationale of the restatement); (5) *Complexio* (Conclusion).

Philo's first, second and fourth reasons are developed accordingly. The first reason, as follows: 1. *Statement of thesis*: "the lawgiver gave his laws not in cities but in deep desert" (§2); 2. *Rationale*: "for most of the cities are full of unspeakable evils, and of acts of impiety towards God (§3); 3. *Restatement*: "Pride is the most insidious of foes" (§4a); 4. *Rationale of the restatement*: "Pride is admired and worshipped by some who add dignity to vain ideas..., is the cause of many other evils, such as insolence, arrogance and impiety..., brings divine things into utter contempt..." (§4b-8); 5. *Conclusion*: "This was the primary consideration which made him prefer to legislate away from cities" (§9). The second reason: 1. *Thesis*: "He who is about to receive the holy laws must first be cleansed and purified from all stains... contracted in cities..." (§10); 2. *Rationale*: His purification cannot be attained unless by dwelling apart from cities till the marks of his transgressions have disappeared (§11); 3. *Restatement*: Good physicians preserve their patients from food until they have removed the causes of their maladies (§12a); 4. *Rationale of restatement*: for thinking it unadvisable and for knowing that food is useless, even harmful, while diseases remain (§12b); 5. *Conclusion*: Therefore, having led his people from cities into the desert, that he might purify their souls, he began to bring them food for their minds, divine laws and words of God (§13). The fourth reason: 1. *Thesis*: "He led the nation a great distance away from cities into the depths of a desert" (§15b); 2. *Rationale*: For "it was necessary to establish a belief in their minds, that the laws were not the inventions of a man but quite clearly the oracles of God" (§15a); 3. *Restatement* :"they should no longer wonder whether the laws were actually the pronouncements of God... since they have been given the clearest evidence of the truth in the supplies which they had so unexpectedly received in their destitution (§16); 4. *Rationale of statement*: "For he who gave abundance of the means of life also bestowed the wherewithal of a good life..." (§17); 5. *Conclusion*: "These are the reasons suggested to answer the question under discussion" (§18a).

[33] The third reason compares Moses to men who equip themselves for a long voyage while still remaining on land, providing with time everything that will grant them success. The symmetric parallelism is developed as follows: A: *Just as* men who set out on a long voyage do not when they have embarked on board ship... B: *but while* still remaining on the land; A': *so in the same manner* Moses did not think it good that his people should just settle in cities and then go in quest of laws to regulate their civic life, B': *but rather* should first provide themselves with rules and be trained in them... and only then be settled down in their cities.

example of the ten so-called categories in nature.[34] These oracles are general laws directly given by God as well as the heads of the particular laws promulgated by the agency of his prophet Moses (§18b-19). And the perfection of the decad is the divine signature that seals them (§20–31).[35]

But how did God promulgate these laws (§32–35)? The answer to this question on the nature of the voice announcing the commandments is persuasively formulated as Ciceronian ratiocination. (1) *Thesis*: the ten laws were not delivered by the Father of all by his own utterance in the form of a voice (§32a); (2) *Rationale*: "for God is not as man needing mouth and tongue and windpipe" (§32b); (3) *Restatement*: "as it seems to me, God... wrought on this occasion a miracle of a truly holy kind, commanding an invisible sound to be created in the air, more marvelous than all instruments that ever existed... a rational soul full of clearness and distinctness which... sounded forth... an articulate voice so loud that it appeared to be equally audible to the farthest as well as to the nearest" (§33); (4) *Rationale of restatement*: "For the voices of men, if carried to a great distance, grow faint, so that those who are at a distance from them cannot arrive at a clear comprehension of them. But the miraculous voice was set in action and kept in flame by the power of God... which spread it abroad in every side and made it more illuminating in its ending than in its beginning..." (§34–35); **(5) *Conclusion*:** "This, then, may be enough to say about the divine voice" (§36a).

The reasons provided to answer, "Why was the singular number used when a multitude was present" are three. First, the singular emphasizes the value of the individual soul (§36–38); second, the personal appeal better secures obedience (§39); and third, not to despise the humblest is a real lesson to the powerful (§40–43).

These reasons are then expanded with references to the miraculous signs (44) and a visible voice from the midst of the fire flowing from heaven (§45–49). In the form of a most complete argument,[36] according to the *Rhetorica ad Herennium* 2:28–30, this thematic elaboration is comprised in five parts, the fourth being embellished with several topics of argumentation: (1) what we intend to prove; (2) its rationale; (3) a confirmation by means of additional arguments; (4) the persuasive enrichment of these logical developments with quasi-logical figures of argumentation after the proof has been established—example, analogy, amplification, and a citation

---

[34] These ten categories are substance, quality, quantity, relation, activity, passivity, situation, time, place and possession.

[35] Nikiprowetzky, *Philon d'Alexandrie*, De Decalogo, 35.

[36] The *"absolutissima et perfectissima argumentatio."*

of authority; and (5) a conclusion. This thematic elaboration is developed as follows:

1. *Thesis* (36b): Each of the Commandments was addressed in the singular number, not to several persons but to one, when so many thousands were present.

2. *Reason* (36–38): For each single person is equal in worth to a whole nation, or rather to all nations.

3. *Confirmation* (39): Commands and prohibitions are more impressive if addressed to each individual in the audience.

4. *Embellishment* in four topics: 4.1. *Amplification* (40–43): If God deigned to address himself to everyone of the mortals assembled before him, what right has the human king and tyrant to despise any of his subjects, even the meanest? 4.2. *Example* (44–46): miraculous signs and works on earth, all moved together to do him service when the power of God came among them; the people had kept pure in obedience to the warning of Moses; and the voice from the midst of the fire became articulate speech in a language familiar to the audience. 4.3. *Authority* (47): "And the law testifies to the accuracy of my statement, where it is written" that the voice of God is truly visible: "All people saw the voice (Exodus 20:18)... because whatever God says is not words but deeds;" 4.4. *Analogy* (48): "the voice proceeded from the fire, for the oracles of God have been refined and assayed *as gold is by fire.*"

5. *Conclusion* (49): "And God also intimates to us something of this kind by a figure: since it is the nature of fire both to give light and to burn, those who decide to be obedient to the sacred commandments will live forever as in unclouded light with the laws themselves as stars illuminating their souls... while all those who are rebellious will continue to be burnt by their inward lusts."

First and Fifth Commandments in De Decalogo

The Ten Commandments are thematically configured or expanded according to the social and historical phenomena entering the interactive world of the text. Their expository texture is always argumentative, even when Philo mixes narrative with persuasive patterns. With more or less elaboration, each commentary reflects the appropriate kind of inner reasoning exercised in a more logical or persuasive manner. Fully equipped with all the strategies of the rhetorical code, Philo easily adjusted its conventions to the exposition of his exegetical themes making the argument for each of them accordingly.

Close attention to the development of each commandment led me to the same conclusion: there is coherence and integrity in the whole work as well as in the argumentative texture of each unit, but the structures selectively vary to better serve the dynamic demands of each theme. The conjunction "reveals a studied and prepared display of rhetorical ability."[37]

The first and fifth commandments seemingly interact with each other, the arguments being chiastically[38] arranged as parts of an integrative unit. The internal coherence of this concentric structure is marked by common ideas and word-chains in both commands, connecting the beginning of the first law to the end of the fifth, and the end of the first law to the beginning of the fifth.

This circular construction may seem a coincidence, but the two arguments that shape it are similarly arranged as thematic elaborations that coherently develop the same ideas in inverted order. The mediating and connecting element at the center is *honor*: honor to God alone, and honor due to parents. Of twenty-two occurrences in the whole treatise, "honor" is repeated sixteen times plus synonyms,[39] as a linking keyword between the first five commands.[40]

A (52) – The transcendent source and the best of all things is *God*, and the source and the best of all virtues is *piety*.

B (53–57) – Some men *have deified* the four elements; others, the sun, moon, the stars fixed and the planets; others the heaven; others, the whole universe.

C (58–63) – This is to put the slave in the place of the Master, to honor the temporal as being the Eternal, the created in the place of the Creator.

---

[37] John R. Levison, "Did the Spirit Inspire Rhetoric? An Exploration of George Kennedy's Definition of Early Christian Rhetoric," in *Persuasive Artistry: Studies in New Testament Rhetoric in Honor of George A. Kennedy* (Sheffield: Sheffield Academic Press, 1991), 37–38.

[38] This type of concentric symmetry, often labeled "extended chiasmus," is a pattern that "involves multiple, inverse correspondences that extend over a considerable expanse of material and have a single element at the center" (Harvey, *Listening to the Text*, 104). This pattern is common in all sorts of ancient literature.

[39] Synonyms like: ἀποσεμνύνοντες, *exalt, magnify* (66); σεμνοποιέω, *glorify, confer dignity, exalt* (71).

[40] Linking first and second commandments: "acknowledge and *honor God*" (τιμᾶν, 65); "undoubtedly err by *magnifying* the subjects above the ruler" (ἀποσεμνύνοντες, 66). Linking second and third commands: "and called upon them *to honor* Him that truly is, not because He needed *that honor* should be paid to Him..." (τιμὴν, 81); "*honor* due to Him as such" (τιμῆς, 83). Linking fourth and fifth commands: "For these reasons and many others beside, *Seven is held in honor*" (τετίμηται, 105); "He gives the fifth commandment on *the honor due to parents*" (τιμῆς, 106).

D (64) – *Let us reject all these follies and not worship those who are our brothers by nature*, since the Father of them all is one, the Creator of the universe.

E (65) – Let us engrave deep in our hearts *this commandment as the holiest of all*, to acknowledge that there is but one God, and *to honor* him alone.

F – *Honor* to God alone, and *honor* due to parents

E′ (106) – *Honor* due to parents is the last of the sacred duties inculcated in the first table, in which *the most sacred duties* to the deity are enjoined.

D′ (107–112a) – *Let those who disregard parents* not fail to understand that in the courts of justice they are convicted, in the divine court of impiety and in the human court of inhumanity. "For *whom else will they show kindness to if they despise the closest of their kinsfolk* who have bestowed upon them the greatest boons" and to whom we owe what we can never repay?

C′ (112b–113) – "The greatest indignation is justified if *children* refuse to make even the slightest (return)" on behalf of *their parents*. "Wild beasts ought to become tame through association with them... for it is always good for *the inferior* to follow *the superior* in hope of improvement."

B′ (114–119) – Men who *disregard the natural obligation of honoring* their parents should imitate the beasts who repay the services bestowed upon them, house-dogs who protect their masters and gratefully die for them, and storks who put to shame sons who honor not their parents.

A′ (120) – A man who is impious towards his immediate and visible parents, cannot be pious towards his invisible Father. *God* is the uncreated maker of the world, and it is impossible that the invisible *God* can be *piously* worshipped by those who behave with *impiety* towards those who are visible and near to them.

I – *The First Commandment*

Philo develops the first commandment on the supreme honor due to God, following the pattern of a thematic elaboration as instructed by the author of the *Rhetorica ad Herennium* in 4.55–58, an elaboration in seven parts: (1) theme or statement; (2) reason or rationale; (3) theme or restatement in another form, with or without reasons; (4) an opposite or contrary; (5) an analogy or comparison; (6) an example; and finally (7) a conclusion or exhortation.

1. *Theme or Statement, Propositio (52b)*

After presenting the Ten Commandments as divided in two sets of five (50–51), Philo starts his commentary on the first Law with a thematic statement: God is the origin of all things as piety is the origin of all virtues. The best and the beginning of all things is God, and the best and the beginning of virtues is piety, but a grave error has taken possession of the majority of mankind.

ἀρχὴ δ᾽ ἀρίστη πάντων μὲν τῶν ὄντων θεός, ἀρετῶν δ᾽ εὐσέβεια· περὶ ὧν ἀναγκαιότατον πρῶτον διεξελθεῖν πλάνος τις οὐ μικρὸς τὸ πλεῖστον τῶν ἀνθρώπων γένος κατέσχηκε περὶ πράγματος, ὅπερ ἢ μόνον ἢ μάλιστα ἦν εἰκὸς ἀπλανέστατον ταῖς ἑκάστων διανοίαις ἐνιδρῦσθαι.[41]

2. *Rationale: Ratio, Contrarium and Amplificatio (53–57)*

In his reasoning on the follies of polytheism, namely the form of worship given to heavenly bodies, Philo develops his rationale with an amplified *contrarium*. He starts the argument and keeps it in balance tactfully composing two rhythmic periods to center the reader's attention in this essential point of his commentary.[42] The first rhythmic structure develops ratio enumerating those who have worshiped earth, water, air and fire, the sun, the moon, the stars and planets, and has six elements.

---

[41] "The transcendent source of all that exists is God, as piety is the source of the virtues, and it is very necessary that these two should be first discussed. A great delusion has taken hold of the larger part of mankind in regard to a fact which properly should be established beyond all question in every mind to the exclusion of, or at least above, all others."

On the role of piety in Philo see Gregory E. Sterling, "'The Queen of the Virtues': Piety in Philo of Alexandria," *SPhiloA* 18 (2006): 103–124.

[42] The choice of vocabulary and sentence structure is decisive in a rhetorical speech. But the rhythmic flow of the chosen words also has a notable effect on the persuasiveness and charm of what is being said. According to Aristotle, "The form of the diction should be neither fully metrical nor completely without rhythm... The speech must have rhythm, but not meter; otherwise it would be a poem." (*Rhet.* 1408b [3.8]). And Philo also knows how and where to put it to the service of his commentary.

ἐκτεθειώκασι γὰρ οἱ μὲν τὰς τέσσαρας ἀρχάς, | γῆν καὶ ὕδωρ καὶ ἀέρα καὶ πῦρ, | οἱ δ' ἥλιον καὶ σελήνην | καὶ τοὺς ἄλλους πλανήτας καὶ ἀπλανεῖς ἀστέρας, | οἱ δὲ μόνον τὸν οὐρανόν, | οἱ δὲ τὸν σύμπαντα κόσμον (53a).[43]

The second period is densely focused on the main theme of the command through an argument from the contrary, with seven elements integrated into the whole: a rhythmic period consisting of five longer parts called members or *cola*, and two shorter parts, each one called a *comma*.

τὸν δ' ἀνωτάτω καὶ πρεσβύτατον, ‖ τὸν γεννητήν, ‖ τὸν ἄρχοντα τῆς μεγαλοπόλεως, | τὸν στρατάρχην τῆς ἀηττήτου στρατιᾶς, | τὸν κυβερνήτην ὃς οἰκονομεῖ σωτηρίως ἀεὶ τὰ σύμπαντα, ‖ παρεκαλύψαντο ‖ ψευδωνύμους προσρήσεις ἐκείνοις ἐπιφημίσαντες ἑτέρας ἕτεροι (53b).[44]

The rationale is then strategically amplified in a similar tone. The objects above mentioned are represented by Greek deities whose names were handed down by mythmakers, each of them in accordance with their own character.

(54) καλοῦσι γὰρ οἱ μὲν τὴν γῆν Κόρην, Δήμητραν, Πλούτωνα, τὴν δὲ θάλατταν Ποσειδῶνα, δαίμονας ἐναλίους ὑπάρχους αὐτῷ προσαναπλάττοντες καὶ θεραπείας ὁμίλους μεγάλους ἀρρένων τε καὶ θηλειῶν, Ἥραν δὲ τὸν ἀέρα καὶ τὸ πῦρ Ἥφαιστον καὶ ἥλιον Ἀπόλλωνα καὶ σελήνην Ἄρτεμιν καὶ ἑωσφόρον Ἀφροδίτην καὶ στίλβοντα Ἑρμῆν· (55) καὶ τῶν ἄλλων ἀστέρων ἑκάστου τὰς ἐπωνυμίας μυθογράφοι παρέδοσαν, οἳ πρὸς ἀπάτην ἀκοῆς εὖ τετεχνασμένα πλάσματα συνυφήναντες ἔδοξαν περὶ τὴν τῶν ὀνομάτων θέσιν κεκομψεῦσθαι· (56) τόν τε οὐρανὸν εἰς ἡμισφαίρια τῷ λόγῳ διχῇ διανείμαντες, τὸ μὲν ὑπὲρ γῆς, τὸ δ' ὑπὸ γῆς, Διοσκόρους ἐκάλεσαν τὸ περὶ τῆς ἑτερημέρου ζωῆς αὐτῶν προστερατευσάμενοις διήγημα. (57) τοῦ γὰρ οὐρανοῦ συνεχῶς καὶ ἀπαύστως ἀεὶ κύκλῳ περιπολοῦντος, ἀνάγκη τῶν ἡμισφαιρίων ἑκάτερον ἀντιμεθίστασθαι παρ' ἡμέραν ἄνω τε καὶ κάτω γινόμενον ὅσα τῷ δοκεῖν· ἄνω γὰρ καὶ κάτω πρὸς ἀλήθειαν οὐδὲν ἐν σφαίρᾳ, πρὸς δὲ τὴν ἡμετέραν σχέσιν αὐτὸ μόνον εἴωθε λέγεσθαι τὸ μὲν ὑπὲρ κεφαλῆς ἄνω, κάτω δὲ τοὐναντίον.[45]

---

[43] "For some have deified the four elements, | earth, water, air and fire, | others the sun, moon, planets and fixed stars | | others again the heaven by itself, | others the whole world."

[44] "But the highest and the most august, | | the Begetter, | | the Ruler of the great World-city, | the Commander-in-Chief of the invincible host, | the Pilot who ever steers all things in safety, | | Him they have hidden from sight | | by the misleading titles assigned to the objects of worship mentioned above."

[45] "Different people give them different names: some call the earth Kore or Demeter or Pluto, and the sea Poseidon, and invent marine deities subordinate to him and great companies of attendants, male and female. They call air Hera and fire Hephaestus, the sun Apollo, the moon Artemis, the morning-star Aphrodite and the glitterer a Hermes, and each of the other stars have names handed down by the mythmakers, who have put together fables skilfully contrived to deceive the hearers and thus won a reputation for accomplishment in name-giving. So too in accordance with the theory by which they

3. Confirmation of the Rationale or Restatement, Pronuntiatio (58)

God gives this admirable and holy commandment to one who is determined to follow genuine philosophy and is devoted to guiltless and pure piety, not confusing parts of the world with their own Creator and worshiping them instead of the omnipotent God. To speak of God as not existing from all eternity is profanity.

(58) τῷ δὴ φιλοσοφεῖν ἀνόθως ἐγνωκότι καὶ ἀδόλου καὶ καθαρᾶς εὐσεβείας μεταποιουμένῳ κάλλιστον καὶ ὁσιώτατον ὑφηγεῖται παράγγελμα, μηδὲν τῶν τοῦ κόσμου μερῶν αὐτοκρατῆ θεὸν ὑπολαμβάνειν εἶναι· καὶ γὰρ γέγονε, γένεσις δὲ φθορᾶς ἀρχή, κἂν προνοίᾳ τοῦ πεποιηκότος ἀθανατίζηται, καὶ ἦν ποτε χρόνος, ὅτε οὐκ ἦν· θεὸν δὲ πρότερον οὐκ ὄντα καὶ ἀπό τινος χρόνου γενόμενον καὶ μὴ διαιωνίζοντα λέγειν οὐ θεμιτόν.[46]

4. Argument from the Contrary with Reasons, Contrarium (59–60)

Those whose views are affected with such folly regard not only the above-mentioned objects as gods, but also each of them as the greatest and primal God. Either because of ignorance or indifference and no desire to learn, they persist in their supposed idea that there is no invisible or intelligible cause outside what the senses perceive. Though living, planning and doing everything in life with their soul, they cannot see it with the eyes of the body; much less to apprehend the uncreated, the eternal, the invisible guide and ruler of the universe by themselves.

(59) ἀλλὰ γὰρ ἔνιοι περὶ τὰς κρίσεις ἀπονοίᾳ τοσαύτῃ κέχρηνται, ὡς οὐ μόνον τὰ εἰρημένα θεοὺς νομίζειν, ἀλλὰ καὶ ἕκαστον αὐτῶν μέγιστον καὶ πρῶτον θεόν, τὸν ὄντα ὄντως ἢ οὐκ εἰδότες ἀδιδάκτῳ τῇ φύσει ἢ οὐ σπουδάζοντες μαθεῖν, ἕνεκα τοῦ μηδὲν ἔξω τῶν αἰσθητῶν ἀόρατον καὶ νοητὸν αἴτιον ὑπολαμβάνειν εἶναι, καίτοι σαφεστάτης ἐγγὺς παρακειμένης πίστεως. (60) ψυχῇ γὰρ ζῶντες καὶ βουλευόμενοι καὶ πάνθ' ὅσα κατὰ τὸν ἀνθρώπινον βίον δρῶντες οὐδέποτε ψυχὴν

divided the heaven into two hemispheres, one above the earth and one be low it, they called them the Dioscuri and invented a further miraculous story of their living on alternate days. For indeed as heaven is always revolving ceaselessly and continuously round and round, each hemisphere must necessarily alternately change its position day by day and become upper or lower as it appears, though in reality there is no upper or lower in a spherical figure, and it is merely in relation to our own position that we are accustomed to speak of what is above our heads as upper and the opposite to this as lower."

[46] "Now to one who is determined to follow a genuine philosophy and make a pure and guileless piety his own, Moses gives this truly admirable and religious command that he should not suppose any of the parts of the universe to be the omnipotent God. For the world has become what it is, and its becoming is the beginning of its destruction, even though by the providence of God it be made immortal, and there was a time when it was not. But to speak of God as 'not being' at some former time, or having 'become' at some particular time and not existing for all eternity is profanity."

ὀφθαλμοῖς σώματος ἴσχυσαν θεάσασθαι, καίτοι φιλοτιμηθέντες ἂν πάσας φιλοτιμίας, εἴ πως ἰδεῖν οἷόν τε ἦν τὸ ἄγαλμα τὸ πάντων ἱεροπρεπέστατον, ἀφ' οὗ κατὰ μετάβασιν εἰκὸς ἦν ἔννοιαν τοῦ ἀγενήτου καὶ ἀιδίου λαβεῖν, ὃς ἅπαντα τὸν κόσμον ἡνιοχῶν σωτηρίως ἀόρατος ὢν κατευθύνει.[47]

5. *Argument from Analogy, Simile (61)*

This is to put the slave in the place of the master, to honor the temporal as if it were the eternal, the created as the Creator; just as anyone who were to assign to the subordinate satraps the honors due to the Great King, appearing to be not only the most ignorant and senseless of men, but also the most foolhardy.

(61) καθάπερ οὖν τοῦ μεγάλου βασιλέως τὰς τιμὰς εἴ τις τοῖς ὑπάρχοις σατράπαις ἀπένειμεν, ἔδοξεν ἂν οὐκ ἀγνωμονέστατος μόνον ἀλλὰ καὶ ῥιψοκινδυνότατος εἶναι χαριζόμενος τὰ δεσπότου δούλοις, τὸν αὐτὸν τρόπον ἂν τοῖς αὐτοῖς εἴ τις γεραίρει τὸν πεποιηκότα τοῖς γεγονόσιν, ἴστω πάντων ἀβουλότατος ὢν καὶ ἀδικώτατος, ἴσα διδοὺς ἀνίσοις οὐκ ἐπὶ τιμῇ τῶν ταπεινοτέρων ἀλλ' ἐπὶ καθαιρέσει τοῦ κρείττονος.[48]

6. *Argument from Example with Amplification, Exemplum (62–63)*

There are some who exceed in impiety, not giving the Creator and the creature even equal honor, but assigning to the latter all honor and respect and reverence, and refusing to the former the commonest tribute of remembering Him. These men are so possessed with an insolent and free-spoken madness that they venture to blaspheme the Godhead and to vex

---

[47] "But there are some whose views are affected with such folly that they not only regard the said objects as gods but each of them severally as the greatest and primal God. Incapacity for instruction or indifference to learning prevents them from knowing the truly Existent because they suppose that there is no invisible and conceptual cause outside what the senses perceive, though the clearest possible proof lies ready at their hand. For while it is with the soul that they live and plan and carry out all the affairs of human life, they can never see the soul with the eyes of the body, though every feeling of ambition might well have been aroused in the hope of seeing that most august of all sacred objects, the natural stepping stone to the conception of the Uncreated and Eternal, the invisible Charioteer who guides in safety the whole universe."

[48] "So just as anyone who rendered to the subordinate satraps the honors due to the Great King would have seemed to reach the height not only of unwisdom but of foolhardiness, by bestowing on servants what belonged to their master in the same way anyone who pays the same tribute to the creatures as to their Maker may be assured that he is the most senseless and unjust of men in that he gives equal measure to those who are not equal, though he does not thereby honor the meaner many but deposes the one superior."

the pious. This is the great engine of the unholy, by which alone they bridle the mouths of those who love God.

(62) εἰσὶ δ᾽ οἳ καὶ προσυπερβάλλουσιν ἀσεβείᾳ μηδὲ τὸ ἴσον ἀποδιδόντες, ἀλλὰ τοῖς μὲν τὰ πάντα τῶν ἐπὶ τιμῇ χαριζόμενοι, τῷ δ᾽ οὐδὲν νέμοντες ἀλλ᾽ οὐδὲ μνήμην, τὸ κοινότατον· ἐπιλήθονται γὰρ οὗ μόνον μεμνῆσθαι προσῆκον ἦν, ἐπιτηδεύοντες οἱ βαρυδαίμονες ἑκούσιον λήθην. (63) ἔνιοι δὲ καὶ στομάργῳ κατεχόμενοι λύττῃ τὰ δείγματα τῆς ἐνιδρυμένης ἀσεβείας εἰς μέσον προφέροντες βλασφημεῖν ἐπιχειροῦσι τὸ θεῖον, ἀκονησάμενοι κακήγορον γλῶτταν, ἅμα καὶ λυπεῖν ἐθέλοντες τοὺς εὐσεβοῦντας, οἷς ἄλεκτον καὶ ἀπαρηγόρητον εὐθὺς εἰσδύεται πένθος τὴν ὅλην πυρπολοῦν ψυχὴν δι᾽ ὤτων· ἡ γὰρ τῶν ἀνοσίων ἑλέπολις τοῦτ᾽ ἐστίν, ᾧ μόνῳ τοὺς φιλοθέους ἐπιστομίζουσι νομίζοντας ὑπὲρ τοῦ μὴ παροξύνειν ἐν τῷ παρόντι κάλλιστον ἡσυχίαν.[49]

7. Conclusion, Conclusio (64–66a)

Bringing his arguments to a close, Philo uses three times a similar exhortatory expression *in crescendo*: *Let us reject* these follies of the impious and not worship those who are our brothers by nature, since the Father of them all is one, the creator of the universe; *Let us gird* ourselves to the service of that Being who is the uncreated and everlasting, and the maker of the universe; *Let us deeply engrave* in our hearts the first and holiest of the commandments to acknowledge and honor the one, the most high God.

(64) πᾶσαν οὖν τὴν τοιαύτην τερθρείαν **ἀπωσάμενοι** τοὺς ἀδελφοὺς φύσει μὴ προσκυνῶμεν, εἰ καὶ καθαρωτέρας καὶ ἀθανατωτέρας οὐσίας ἔλαχον ἀδελφὰ δ᾽ ἀλλήλων τὰ γενόμενα καθὸ γέγονεν, ἐπεὶ καὶ πατὴρ ἁπάντων εἷς ὁ ποιητὴς τῶν ὅλων ἐστίν, ἀλλὰ καὶ διανοίᾳ καὶ λόγῳ καὶ πάσῃ δυνάμει τῇ τοῦ ἀγενήτου καὶ ἀιδίου καὶ τῶν ὅλων αἰτίου θεραπείᾳ σφόδρα εὐτόνως καὶ ἐρρωμένως **ἐπαποδυώμεθα**, μὴ ὑποκατακλινόμενοι μηδ᾽ ὑπείκοντες ταῖς τῶν πολλῶν ἀρεσκείαις, ὑφ᾽ ὧν καὶ οἱ δυνάμενοι σῴζεσθαι διαφθείρονται. (65) πρῶτον μὲν οὖν παράγγελμα καὶ παραγγελμάτων ἱερώτατον **στηλιτεύσωμεν** ἐν ἑαυτοῖς, ἕνα τὸν ἀνωτάτω νομίζειν τε καὶ τιμᾶν θεόν· δόξα δ᾽ ἡ πολύθεος μηδ᾽ ὤτων ψαυέτω καθαρῶς καὶ ἀδόλως ἀνδρὸς εἰωθότος ζητεῖν ἀλήθειαν (66) ἀλλ᾽ ὅσοι μὲν ἡλίου καὶ σελήνης καὶ τοῦ σύμπαντος οὐρανοῦ τε καὶ κόσμου καὶ τῶν ἐν

---

[49] "And there are some who in a further excess of impiety do not even give this equal payment, but bestow on those others all that can tend to honor, while to Him they refuse even the commonest of all tributes, that of remembering Him. Whom duty bids them remember, if nothing more, a Him they forget, a forgetfulness deliberately practiced to their lasting misery. Some again, seized with a loud-mouthed frenzy, publish abroad samples of their deep-seated impiety and attempt to blaspheme the Godhead, and when they whet the edge of their evil-speaking tongue they do so in the wish to grieve the pious who feel at once the inroad of a sorrow indescribable and inconsolable, which passing through the ears wastes as with fire the whole soul. For this is the battery of the unholy, and is in itself enough to curb the mouths of the devout who hold that silence is best for the time being to avoid giving provocation."

αὐτοῖς ὁλοσχερεστάτων μερῶν ὡς θεῶν πρόπολοί τε καὶ θεραπευταί, διαμαρτάνουσι μὲν – πῶς γὰρ οὔ;[50]

This commandment forms a type of inclusion that involves the whole argument in a chiastic construction of four elements: ABB'A':

A – The best and the beginning of all things is God, and of all virtues is piety;
> B – But a great error has taken possession of the majority of mankind honoring the created instead of the Creator;
> B' – Let us reject these follies of the impious, and engrave in our hearts the first and holiest of the commandments;
A' – Let us acknowledge and honor the most high God.

A correspondence in wording frames the whole section, opening and closing the argument. The final expressions διαμαρτάνουσι and ἥττων δὲ τῶν ἄλλων ἀδικοῦσι (66) respond to the initial πλάνος τις οὐ μικρός (52).[51] The repetition of τιμή *honor*, ten times in five paragraphs, is the expression of an important word-chain pattern in this commandment.

II – *The Fifth Commandment*

The fifth commandment concerns the honor due to parents as the concluding law of the first table. Its commentary is developed in eight parts on the rhetorical form of a *chreia* elaboration, and the first words define the

---

[50] "*Let us* then reject all such imposture and refrain from worshipping those who by nature are our brothers, even though they have been given a substance purer and more immortal than ours, for created things, in so far as they are created, are brothers, since they have all one Father, the Maker of the universe. *Let us* instead in mind and speech and every faculty gird ourselves up with vigor and activity to do the service of the Uncreated, the Eternal, the Cause of all, not submitting nor abasing ourselves to do the pleasure of the many who work the destruction even of those who might be saved. *Let us*, then, engrave deep in our hearts this as the first and most sacred of commandments, to acknowledge and honor one God Who is above all, and let the idea that gods are many never even reach the ears of the man whose rule of life is to seek for truth in purity and guilelessness. But while all who give worship and service to sun and moon and the whole heaven and universe or their chief parts as gods most undoubtedly err by magnifying the subjects above the ruler."

[51] The difference between *inclusio* and ring-composition is as follows, according to Harvey: "inclusion is the use of the same word or words to begin and end a discussion, or the use of 'a nominal form of a word in one place and a cognate verbal form in the other'; ring-composition 'differs from inclusion in that the framing is done with sentences rather than single words' marking a correspondence between them" (Harvey, *Listening to the Text*, 102–103). Cf. Aristotle, *Rhet.* 1361a, 1376b.

speech situation, placing honor due to parents in the center of its action. As Vernon Robbins said, "Elaboration is not simply an expansion or amplification of a narrative. Rather, a theme or issue emerges in the form of a thesis or *chreia* near the beginning of a unit, and meanings or meaning-effects of this theme or issue unfold through argumentation as the unit progresses."[52] Here, the thesis is immediately given and the rationale that follows logically converges to directly prove the initial thesis. The remaining argumentative topics of analogy, example and authority lead the elaboration to a better point of understanding and completion.

1. *Theme/Praise, Προοίμιον* (106a)

The fifth commandment concerns the honor due to parents. It is placed on the borderline between the two sets of five; as the last command of the first and most important table, but as part of the set in which the most *sacred duties* are enjoined. Procreation is akin to creation.

μετὰ δὲ τὰ περὶ τῆς ἑβδόμης παραγγέλλει πέμπτον παράγγελμα τὸ περὶ γονέων τιμῆς τάξιν αὐτῷ δοὺς τὴν μεθόριον τῶν δυοῖν πεντάδων.[53]

2. *Thesis/Chreia Paraphrasis, Χρεία* (106b)

Because parenthood assimilates human beings to God, this commandment is the last of the first table in which the most sacred duties to the deity are given, and it adjoins the second table that contains the duties of human being to human being.

τελευταῖον γὰρ ὂν τῆς προτέρας, ἐν ᾗ τὰ ἱερώτατα προστάττεται, συνάπτει καὶ τῇ δευτέρᾳ περιεχούσῃ τὰ πρὸς ἀνθρώπους δίκαια.[54]

3. *Rationale with Amplification, Αἰτίαι* (107–110a)

And the reason is as follows: Parents by their nature stand on the borderline between the mortal and the immortal side of existence; the mortal because of their kinship with men and other animals on account of the

---

[52] Vernon K. Robbins, *Exploring the Texture of Texts: A Guide to Socio-Rhetorical Interpretation* (Valley Forge, PA: Trinity Press International, 1996), 52.

[53] "After dealing with the seventh day, He gives the fifth commandment on the honor due to parents. This commandment He placed on the border-line between the two sets of five."

[54] "It is the last of the first set in which the most sacred injunctions are given and it adjoins the second set which contains the duties of man to man."

perishable nature of the body; the immortal because the act of generation assimilates them to God, the Father of the Universe.

The rationale is then amplified to show how subtly easy it is to be associated with one of two sides neglecting the other. Some devote their lives exclusively to piety and to the service of God, renouncing all other concerns. Others concentrate themselves wholly in human causes, based on the idea that there is no good outside doing justice to men. Both come but halfway in virtue, neglecting the other side of their duty as human beings.

(107) αἴτιον δ' ὡς οἶμαι τόδε· τῶν γονέων ἡ φύσις ἀθανάτου καὶ θνητῆς οὐσίας ἔοικεν εἶναι μεθόριος, θνητῆς μὲν διὰ τὴν πρὸς ἀνθρώπους καὶ τὰ ἄλλα ζῷα συγγένειαν κατὰ τὸ τοῦ σώματος ἐπίκηρον, ἀθανάτου δὲ διὰ τὴν τοῦ γεννᾶν πρὸς θεὸν τὸν γεννητὴν τῶν ὅλων ἐξομοίωσιν, (108) ἤδη μὲν οὖν τινες τῇ ἑτέρᾳ μερίδι προσκληρώσαντες ἑαυτοὺς ἔδοξαν τῆς ἑτέρας ὀλιγωρεῖν· ἄκρατον γὰρ ἐμφορησά- μενοι τὸν εὐσεβείας πόθον, πολλὰ χαίρειν φράσαντες ταῖς ἄλλαις πραγματείαις ὅλον ἀνέθεσαν τὸν οἰκεῖον βίον θεραπείᾳ θεοῦ, (109) οἱ δ' οὐδὲν ἔξω τῶν πρὸς ἀνθρώπους δικαιωμάτων ἀγαθὸν ὑποτοπήσαντες εἶναι μόνην τὴν πρὸς ἀνθρώπους ὁμιλίαν ἠσπάσαντο, τῶν τε ἀγαθῶν τὴν χρῆσιν ἐξ ἴσου πᾶσι παρέχοντες διὰ κοινωνίας ἵμερον καὶ τὰ δεινὰ κατὰ δύναμιν ἐπικουφίζειν ἀξιοῦντες, (110) τούτους μὲν οὖν φιλανθρώπους, τοὺς δὲ προτέρους φιλοθέους ἐνδίκως ἂν εἴποι τις, ἡμιτελεῖς τὴν ἀρετήν· ὁλόκληροι γὰρ οἱ παρ' ἀμφοτέροις εὐδοκιμοῦντες.[55]

4. *Argument from the Contrary Logically Amplified,* Ἐναντίον (110b–114a)

In either case these men are convicted in one court of justice, human or divine. Some of them are content with performing their duties towards God, and others with accomplishing their duties towards other humans. But all who neither attend to their duties towards humans nor cling to piety and holiness towards God may be thought to be transformed into the nature of wild beasts. They stand convicted in the two courts: in the divine court, of impiety; in the human court, of inhumanity.

[55] "The reason I consider is this: we see that parents by their nature stand on the border-line between the mortal and the immortal side of existence, the mortal because of their kinship with men and other animals through the perishableness of the body; the immortal because the act of generation assimilates them to God, the generator of the All. Now we have known some who associate themselves with one of the two sides and are seen to neglect the other. They have drunk of the unmixed wine of pious aspirations and turning their backs upon all other concerns devoted their personal life wholly to the service of God. Others conceiving the idea that there is no good outside doing justice to men have no heart for anything but companionship with men. In their desire for fellow- ship they supply the good things of life in equal measure to all for their use, and deem it their duty to alleviate by anything in their power the dreaded hardships. These may be justly called lovers of men, the former sort lovers of God. Both come but halfway in virtue; they only have it whole who win honor in both departments."

This statement of the contrary[56] works together with the previous rationale to support the initial thesis, and is amplified with two other forceful arguments in the form of an *interrogatio*[57] in order to enhance the grievous effects of such ingratitude and justify the indignation it conveys. This expanded rationale on how much children owe to their own parents, closes with an incisive call to gratitude: "You men who disregard this natural obligation of honor and obedience towards your parents should imitate wild beasts that repay the services bestowed upon them."

(110b) ὅσοι δὲ μήτ' ἐν τοῖς πρὸς ἀνθρώπους ἐξετάζονται, συνηδόμενοι μὲν ἐπὶ τοῖς κοινοῖς ἀγαθοῖς, συναλγοῦντες δ' ἐπὶ τοῖς ἐναντίοις, μήτ' εὐσεβείας καὶ ὁσιότητος περιέχονται, μεταβεβληκέναι δόξαιεν ἂν εἰς θηρίων φύσιν· ὧν τῆς ἀγριότητος οἴσονται τὰ πρωτεῖα οἱ γονέων ἀλογοῦντες, ἑκατέρας μερίδος ὄντες ἐχθροὶ καὶ τῆς πρὸς θεὸν καὶ τῆς πρὸς ἀνθρώπους (111) ἐν δυσὶν οὖν δικαστηρίοις, ἃ δὴ μόνα ἐστὶν ἐν τῇ φύσει, μὴ ἀγνοείτωσαν ἑαλωκότες, ἀσεβείας μὲν ἐν τῷ θείῳ, διότι τοὺς ἐκ τοῦ μὴ ὄντος εἰς τὸ εἶναι παραγαγόντας καὶ κατὰ τοῦτο μιμησαμένους θεὸν οὐ περιέπουσι, μισανθρωπίας δ' ἐν τῷ κατ' ἀνθρώπους (112) τίνα γὰρ ἕτερον εὖ ποιήσουσιν οἱ τῶν συγγενεστάτων καὶ τὰς μεγίστας παρασχομένων δωρεὰς ὀλιγωροῦντες, ὧν ἔνιαι δι' ὑπερβολὴν οὐδ' ἀμοιβὰς ἐνδέχονται; πῶς γὰρ ἂν ὁ γεννηθεὶς ἀντιγεννῆσαι δύναιτο τοὺς σπείραντας, κλῆρον ἐξαίρετον τῆς φύσεως χαρισαμένης πρὸς παῖδας γονεῦσιν εἰς ἀντίδοσιν ἐλθεῖν οὐ δυνάμενον; ὅθεν καὶ σφόδρα προσῆκεν ἀγανακτεῖν, εἰ μὴ πάντα ἔχοντες ἀντιχαρίζεσθαι μηδὲ τὰ κουφότατα ἐθελήσουσιν. (113) οἷς δεόντως ἂν εἴποιμι· τὰ θηρία πρὸς ἀνθρώπους ἡμεροῦσθαι δεῖ· καὶ πολλάκις ἔγνων ἡμερωθέντας λέοντας, ἄρκτους, παρδάλεις, οὐ μόνον πρὸς τοὺς τρέφοντας διὰ τὴν ἐπὶ τοῖς ἀναγκαίοις χάριν, ἀλλὰ καὶ πρὸς τοὺς ἄλλους, ἕνεκά μοι δοκῶ τῆς πρὸς ἐκείνους ὁμοιότητος· καλὸν γὰρ ἀεὶ τῷ κρείττονι τὸ χεῖρον ἀκολουθεῖν διὰ βελτιώσεως ἐλπίδα. (114a) νυνὶ δ' ἀναγκασθήσομαι τἀναντία λέγειν· μιμηταὶ θηρίων ἐνίων, ἄνθρωποι, γίνεσθε. τοὺς ὠφελήκοτας ἀντωφελεῖν ἐκεῖνα οἶδε καὶ πεπαίδευται.[58]

---

[56] A statement of the contrary is used to test the validity of an argument, and is not easily refuted (*Rhet. Her.* 4.18.25–26).

[57] A double question is included in this speech as a device of pathos, as a means of sharpening the line of thought here flowing in crescendo. The answer is supposed to be self-evident, not expected, and the emotive couching of the statement is intended to humiliate such ungrateful children (cf. Quintilian, *Inst.* 9.2.8).

[58] "But all who neither take their fit place in dealings with men by sharing the joy of others at the common good and their grief at the reverse, nor cling to piety and holiness, would seem to have been transformed into the nature of wild beasts. In such bestial savagery the first place will be taken by those who disregard parents and are therefore the foes of both sides of the law, the Godward and the manward. Let them not then fail to understand that in the two courts, the only courts which nature has, they stand convicted; in the divine court, of impiety because they do not show due respect to those who brought them forth from non-existence to existence and in this were imitators of God; in the human court, of inhumanity. For to whom else will they show kindness if they despise the closest of their kinsfolk who have bestowed upon them the greatest boons, some of them far exceeding any possibility of repayment? For how could the begotten beget in his turn

5. *Argument from analogy,* παραβολή (114b-115a)

If house-dogs protect and die for their masters when any danger suddenly overtakes them, if sheep-dogs fight on behalf of the flocks and endure till they conquer or die in order to keep the herdsmen unscathed, how much more a human being, the most civilized of living creatures, ought to be grateful and obediently honor his parents?

(114b) κύνες οἰκουροὶ προασπίζουσι καὶ προαποθνήσκουσι τῶν δεσποτῶν, ὅταν κίνδυνός τις ἐξαπιναίως καταλάβῃ· τοὺς δ' ἐν ταῖς ποίμναις φασὶ προαγωνιζο- μένους τῶν θρεμμάτων ἄχρι νίκης ἢ θανάτου παραμένειν ὑπὲρ τοῦ διατηρῆσαι τοὺς ἀγελάρχας ἀζημίους. (115) εἶτ' οὐκ αἰσχρῶν ἐστιν αἴσχιστον, ἐν χαρίτων ἀμοιβαῖς ἄνθρωπον ἡττηθῆναι κυνός, τοῦ θηρίων θρασυτάτου τὸ ἡμερώτατον ζῷον;[59]

6. *Argument from Example,* Παράδειγμα (115b–118)

The rhetorical questions are used here as dialogic devices to sharpen the argumentative line of thought being developed with the example.[60] In a word, men who neglect their parents should cover their faces from shame, and reproach themselves for disregarding those things that they ought to have cared for alone. For the children have nothing of their own which does not belong to their parents.

ἀλλ' εἰ μὴ τοῖς χερσαίοις ἀναδιδασκόμεθα πρὸς τὴν πτηνὴν καὶ ἀεροπόρον μετίωμεν φύσιν ἃ χρὴ παρ' αὐτῆς μαθησόμενοι. (116) τῶν πελαργῶν οἱ μὲν γηραιοὶ καταμένουσιν ἐν ταῖς νεοττιαῖς ἀδυνατοῦντες ἵπτασθαι, οἱ δὲ τούτων παῖδες ὀλίγου δέω φάναι γῆν καὶ θάλατταν ἐπιποτώμενοι πανταχόθεν ἐκπορίζουσι τοῖς γονεῦσι τὰ ἐπιτήδεια· (117) καὶ οἱ μὲν ἀξίως τῆς ἡλικίας ἡρεμοῦντες ἐν ἀφθονίᾳ

---

those whose seed he is, since nature has bestowed on parents in relation to their children an estate of a special kind which cannot be subject to the law of 'exchange'? And therefore the greatest indignation is justified if children, because they are unable to make a complete return, refuse to make even the slightest. Properly, I should say to them, 'beasts ought to become tame through association with men.' Indeed I have often known lions and bears and panthers become tame, not only with those who feed them, in gratitude for receiving what they require, but also with everybody else, presumably because of the likeness to those who give them food. That is what should happen, for it is always good for the inferior to follow the superior in hope of improvement. But as it is I shall be forced to say the opposite of this, 'You men will do well to take some beasts for your models.' They have been trained to know how to return benefit for benefit."

[59] "Watch-dogs guard and die for their masters when some danger suddenly overtakes them. Sheep-dogs, they say, fight for their charges and hold their ground till they conquer or die, in order to keep the herdsmen unscathed. Is it not, then, a very scandal of scandals that in returning kindnesses a man should be worsted by a dog, the most civilized of living creatures by the most audacious of brutes?"

[60] Cf. Quintilian, *Inst.* 9.2.7, 8.

διατελοῦσι τῇ πάσῃ τρυφῶντες, οἱ δὲ τὰς εἰς τὸν πορισμὸν κακοπαθείας ἐπελαφριζόμεν τῷ εὐσεβεῖν καὶ τῷ προσδοκᾶν ἐν γήρᾳ τὰ αὐτὰ πείσεσθαι ὑπὸ τῶν ἐκγόνων ἀναγκαῖον ὄφλημα ἀντεκτίνουσιν ἐν καιρῷ καὶ λαβόντες αὐτὸ καὶ ἀνταποδιδόντες ὅτ' οὐδέτεροι τρέφειν αὐτοὺς δύνανται, παῖδες μὲν ἐν ἀρχῇ τῆς γενέσεως, γονεῖς δ' ἐπὶ τελευτῇ τοῦ βίου· ὅθεν αὐτοδιδάκτῳ τῇ φύσει νεοττοτροφηθέντες γηροτροφοῦσι χαίροντες. (118) ἆρ' οὐκ ἄξιον ἐπὶ τούτοις ἀνθρώπους, ὅσοι γονέων ἀμελοῦσιν, ἐγκαλύπτεσθαι καὶ κακίζειν ἑαυτούς, ὠλιγωρηκότας ὧν ἢ μόνων ἢ πρὸ τῶν ἄλλων ἀναγκαῖον ἦν πεφροντικέναι, καὶ ταῦτ' οὐ διδόντας μᾶλλον ἢ ἀποδιδόντας; παίδων γὰρ ἴδιον οὐδέν, ὃ μὴ γονέων ἐστίν, ἢ οἴκοθεν ἐπιδεδωκότων ἢ τὰς αἰτίας τῆς κτήσεως παρασχομένων.[61]

7. Argument from Authority, Κρίσις/μαρτυρίαι (119–120a)

Piety and holiness are the queens among the virtues. A man who is impious towards his immediate and visible parents cannot be pious towards his invisible Father. For parents are the servants of God for the task of begetting children, and he who dishonors the servant dishonors also the Lord. The truth of these values is confirmed by the argument of authority that climactically supports the thesis initially enunciated: "Some bolder spirits, glorifying the name of parenthood, say that a father and a mother are in fact gods revealed to sight who copy the Uncreated in his work as the Framer of life. He, they say, is the God or Maker of the world, but the others (human parents) only of those children whom they have begotten."[62]

---

[61] "But, if we cannot learn from the land animals, let us turn for a lesson in right conduct to the winged tribe that ranges the air. Among the storks the old birds stay in the nests when they are unable to fly, while their children fly, I might almost say, over sea and land, gathering from every quarter provision for the needs of their parents; and so while they in the inactivity justified by their age continue to enjoy all abundance of luxury, the younger birds making light of the hardships sustained in their quest for food, moved by piety and the expectation that the same treatment will be meted to them by their offspring, repay the debt which they may not refuse—a debt both incurred and discharged at the proper time—namely that in which one or other of the parties is unable to maintain itself, the children in the first stage of their existence, the parents at the end of their lives. And thus without any teacher but their natural instinct they gladly give to age the nurture which fostered their youth. With this example before them may not human beings, who take no thought for their parents, deservedly hide their faces for shame and revile themselves for their neglect of those whose welfare should necessarily have been their sole or their primary care, and that not so much as givers as repayers of a due? For children have nothing of their own which does not come from their parents, either bestowed from their own resources or acquired by means which originate from them."

[62] This form of argumentation shows that recognized authorities support the proposition being advanced, and that the expression "Bolder spirits," sage or wise men, suggest that. Stoic sages are shown to be exemplary authorities. "One such is Hierocles, the Stoic quoted by Stobaeus (Meineke iii. 96), ...The ordinary Stoic view is given by Diogenes Laertius 7.120, that parents, brothers and sisters are to be reverenced next to the gods" (F. C. Colson, PLCL 7:612 [§ 120]).

(119) εὐσέβειαν δὲ καὶ ὁσιότητα, τὰς ἀρετῶν ἡγεμονίδας, ἆρά γ' ἐντὸς ὅρων ἔχουσι τῶν ψυχῶν; ὑπερορίους μὲν οὖν ἀπεληλάκασι καὶ πεφυγαδεύκασι· θεοῦ γὰρ ὑπηρέται πρὸς τέκνων σποράν οἱ γονεῖς· ὁ δ' ὑπηρέτην ἀτιμάζων συνατιμάζει καὶ τὸν ἄρχοντα, (120a) τῶν δ' εὐτολμοτέρων ἀποσεμνύνοντες τὸ γονέων ὄνομά φασί τινες, ὡς ἄρα πατὴρ καὶ μήτηρ ἐμφανεῖς εἰσι θεοί, μιμούμενοι τὸν ἀγένητον ἐν τῷ ζῳοπλαστεῖν· ἀλλὰ τὸν μὲν εἶναι τοῦ κόσμου θεόν, τοὺς δὲ μόνων ὧν ἐγέννησαν.[63]

8. Conclusion or Exhortation, Παράκλησις (120b–121a)

In repeating conceptual language of the two opening statements, and praising the table of the first five commandments, the rationale strengthens the conclusion with an implicit exhortation to worship God through honoring parents.

As said, it is with these wise words about the honor to be paid to parents that God/Moses closes the one and more divine table of the first five commandments. For a man who is impious towards his immediate and visible parents cannot be pious and piously worship God, his invisible Father.

(120b) ἀμήχανον δ' εὐσεβεῖσθαι τὸν ἀόρατον ὑπὸ τῶν εἰς τοὺς ἐμφανεῖς καὶ ἐγγὺς ὄντας ἀσεβούντων. (121a) τοσαῦτα καὶ περὶ γονέων τιμῆς φιλοσοφήσας τέλος ἐπιτίθησι τῇ ἑτέρᾳ καὶ θειοτέρᾳ πεντάδι.[64]

Rhetorical criticism is being recognized anew as a necessary tool for the interpretation of specific texts of the past. And this essay may somehow suggest that rhetoric is an important key to the analysis and interpretation of Philo's commentaries of Scripture.

My analysis of *De Decalogo* brought to the surface a variety of rhetorical strategies in its argumentative texture; strategies that show the pervasiveness of true rhetoric in Philo, and integrate a learned process of argumenta-

---

[63] "Piety and religion are the queens among the virtues. Do they dwell within the confines of such souls as these? No, they have driven them from the realm and sent them into banishment. For parents are the servants of God for the task of begetting children, and he who dishonors the servant dishonors also the Lord. Some bolder spirits, glorifying the name of parenthood, say that a father and a mother are in fact gods revealed to sight who copy the Uncreated in His work as the Framer of life. He, they say, is the God or Maker of the world, they of those only whom they have begotten."

[64] "And how can reverence be rendered to the invisible God by those who show irreverence to the gods who are near at hand and seen by the eye? With these wise words on honoring parents He closes the one set of five which is more concerned with the divine."

tion that is more than a taxonomy of linguistic devices and persuasive strategies.

Seen together, this commentary is in fact a nice display of rhetorical elaboration. Argumentative structures are modeled according to the conventions of the time, as well as its coherence and effectiveness. The introduction and commands analyzed help us to better see how rhetorical form and content determine meaning, and how much these patterns reflect the rhetorical codes found elsewhere in Hellenistic culture.

As we know, Philo did not write his treatises to be read as literature. But they are rich in thought and elaboration. The thread of his discourse varies from simplicity to complexity. Like a piece of tapestry, it may look sometimes redundantly complex, though unified enough in its diversity to be minimally understood. Ring-composition, inclusion and concentric structures are rhetorical devices he subtly and cleverly uses to enclose the elaboration of his themes or sets of ideas in the diverse typologies of his commentary. But persuasive argumentation and thematic elaboration were the exegetical techniques he most used according to the rhetorical conventions of the time; neither as slavish imitator nor as groundbreaking pioneer, but rather as an effective user of the features he found most adequate to each unit of the commentary, be it allegorical or literal.[65]

Not to get lost in reading his treatises, we need then to take into account those patterning features, as well as to understand each particular piece as part of an integrative whole, with its teleological horizon in perspective. Once the biblical text is mentioned and the theme announced, the arguments flow with their diversity and density adjusted to each exegetical case, sometimes in clusters, the conclusion of one being the thesis of the other, and usually with impeccable coherence in between.

University of Lisbon
Portugal

---

[65] Harvey, *Listening to The Text*, 292. What Harvey says about Paul's letters can be said even better about the writings of Philo.

* The texts in translation are from F. H. Colson.

BIBLIOGRAPHY SECTION

PHILO OF ALEXANDRIA
AN ANNOTATED BIBLIOGRAPHY 2012

D. T. Runia, K. Berthelot, E. Birnbaum, A. C. Geljon, H. M. Keizer,
J. Leonhardt-Balzer, J. P. Martín, M. R. Niehoff, S. J. K. Pearce,
T. Seland

2012[1]

M. Alesso, 'El sumo sacerdocio en Filón y la lectura de Clemente Alejandrino,' *Circe de clásicos y modernos* 16 (2012) 27–42.

The paper offers a brief exploration of the characteristics of the High Priest in the Old Testament and summarizes how this figure is presented in the works by Philo. The High Priest appears in the Philonic texts under three features: (1) as a mediator (*Fug.* 108–115); (2) as completely sinless (*Fug.* 117–118; *Spec.* 1.80–81); (3) symbolizing the four elements (*Mos.* 2.117–130; *Spec.* 1.84–96). As a mediator, he is directly related to his people and identifies with them in the atonement. The sacred garments of the High Priest are the Logos and contain many ornaments that relate to the intelligible and sense-perceptible powers (*Migr.* 102). The allegory of the priestly garments in terms of the elements of the universe demonstrates the correspondence of the macrocosm to the microcosm, because it relates to the mixture of earth, water, air and fire of the human body (*Opif.* 146; *Her.* 152–153). A century and a half later, Clement of Alexandria will project onto Jesus Christ the symbolic features of the High Priest of Israel that Philo had awarded to Moses. (JPM)

---

[1] This bibliography has been prepared by the members of the International Philo Bibliography Project under the leadership of D. T. Runia (Melbourne). The principles on which the annotated bibliography is based have been outlined in *SPhA* 2 (1990) 141–142, and are largely based on those used to compile the 'mother works,' R-R, RRS and RRS2 (on the inclusion of works in languages outside the scholarly mainstream see esp. RRS2 xii). The division of the work this year is as follows: material in English (and Dutch) by D. T. Runia (DTR), E. Birnbaum (EB), A. C. Geljon (ACG) and S. J. K. Pearce (SJKP); in French by K. Berthelot (KB); in Italian by H. M. Keizer (HMK); in German by Jutta Leonhardt-Balzer (JLB); in Spanish and Portuguese by J. P. Martín (JPM); in Scandinavian languages (and by Scandinavian scholars) by T. Seland (TS); and in Hebrew and by Israeli scholars by M. R. Niehoff (MRN). This year too assistance has been derived from the related bibliographical labours of L. Perrone (Bologna) and his team in the journal *Adamantius* (studies on the Alexandrian tradition). Other scholars who have given assistance this year are Zoltán Adorjáni, Marta Alesso, Manuel Alexandre Jr., Giovanni Benedetto, Courtney Friesen, Scott Mackie, Jean-Claude Loba-Mkole, Gregory Sterling. This year once again I owe much to my former Leiden colleague M. R. J. Hofstede, who laid a secure foundation for the

M. ALEXANDRE, 'La culture grecque servante de la foi. De Philon d'Alexandrie aux Pères grecs,' in A. PERROT (ed.), *Les chrétiens et l'hellénisme. Identités religieuses et culture grecque dans l'Antiquité tardive,* Études de littérature ancienne 20 (Paris 2012) 31–59.

The article deals with the place of *paideia* in Philo's thought and that of the Greek Church Fathers. The author focuses on *Congr.*, while also taking into account other Philonic treatises. In Philo's view, the desire for *paideia* leads to the contemplation of the world and the interpretation of the Law, but in *Congr.* the main point is that the encyclical sciences (τὰ ἐγκύκλια) such as grammar, geometry and music represent a path toward virtue. Precisely this issue is discussed by Seneca in his *Ep.* 88, as well as by Maximus of Tyre. There is no clear-cut, unique philosophical background behind Philo's discourse, but his allegory of Sarah and Hagar is clearly related to the allegorical reading of Penelope and her servants. In Philo's view, several elements of the Greek *paideia* need to be corrected, a fact reflected in Hagar's necessary submission to Sarah. The influence of Philo's conception of *paideia* in *Congr.* is first felt in the work of Clement of Alexandria, who uses it to show that the encyclical sciences and philosophy are necessary to understand the Christian doctrines, even if faith can develop without them. Clement, however, is as critical and careful as Philo in his appreciation of the *enkyklia* and of philosophy. A further theme that the author explores is the dependency of Origen and the Cappadocian Fathers on Philo. In the end, most Christian authors adopt Philo's subordination of both the *enkyklia* and philosophy to Wisdom (or Theology), a religious reinterpretation of the Platonic subordination of the *enkyklia* to philosophy. (KB)

Y. AMIR and M. R. NIEHOFF. פילון האלכסנדרוני. כתבים. כרך חמישי. ירושלים. הוצאת ביאליק והאקדמיה הלאומית הישראלית למדעים [*Philo of Alexandria Writings.* Part V, Allegorical Exegesis on Genesis 12–41] (Jerusalem 2012).

The latest volume thus far of Philo's writings in Hebrew contains the books from the *Allegorical Commentary* treating Gen 12–41. It opens with obituaries of Yehoshua Amir and Susanne Daniel-Nataf, the initiators of the Hebrew translation project, written by J. Cohen-Yashar. This is followed by the following Philonic treatises: *The Migration of Abraham* (translated by Y. Amir), *Who is the Heir* (by Y. Amir), *On the Preliminary Studies* (by Eva Shor), *On Flight and Finding* (by Y. Amir), *On the Change of Names* (by Eva Shor), and *On Dreams* (by J. Cohen-Yashar). Each treatise receives an introduction and full annotation in the form of notes at the bottom of the page. (MRN)

---

bibliography through his extremely thorough electronic searches. However, the bibliography remains inevitably incomplete, because much work on Philo is tucked away in monographs and articles, the titles of which do not mention his name. Scholars are encouraged to get in touch with members of the team if they spot omissions (addresses below in 'Notes on Contributors'). In order to preserve continuity with previous years, the bibliography retains its own customary stylistic conventions and has not changed to those of the Society of Biblical Literature used in the remainder of the Annual. Investigations continue in relation to the possibility of making an online version of the Bibliography which will cover the entire history of Philonic scholarship, including the material included in G-G.

H. W. ATTRIDGE, 'Creation and Sacred Space: the Reuse of Key Penta-teuchal Themes by Philo, the Fourth Evangelist, and the Epistle to the Hebrews,' in A. MORIYA and G. HATA (eds.), *Pentateuchal Traditions in the Late Second Temple Period: Proceedings of the International Workshop in Tokyo, August 28–31, 2007,* Supplements to the Journal for the Study of Judaism 158 (Leiden 2012) 243–255.

Philo uses the Pentateuch not to score individual points but as the object of a compre-hensive interpretation. Thus the Logos is developed throughout the allegorical treatises in a variety of metaphors, inviting not only a cognitive recognition but a response from the reader. Familial, ethnic and liturgical themes are explored (Sonship: *Conf.* 41, 62, 146; High Priest: *Fug.* 53–116). These develop the concept that the Logos is present in every human being, but in its highest form it is present in the Torah. (JLB)

R. BAUCKHAM, 'Moses as "God" in Philo of Alexandria: a Precedent for Christology?,' in I. H. MARSHALL, C. BENNEMA and V. RABENS (eds.), *Spirit and Christ in the New Testament and Christian theology: Essays in Honor of Max Turner* (Grand Rapids Mich. 2012) 246–265.

This article discusses the question of Moses 'as God' in Philo and its relevance for Christology. Among scholars there are two rather contrasting views. Some authors argue that Philo speaks about a real deification of Moses. In this way Philo's Moses is a precedent for Christianity, which gives the divine status to Jesus. In contrast other scholars under-stand Philo's use of the term 'god' for Moses as figurative or metaphorical. The author underlines that Philo's usage is above all exegetical. In the LXX Moses is called 'god' in Exod 7:1, and in referring to Moses as 'god' Philo is always echoing the biblical text. Philo quotes or makes an allusion to Exod 7:1 at least ten times, among which *Prob.* 43–44 and *Mos.* 1.158 are prominent. These two passages are discussed in detail. The author con-cludes that Philo's use of the term 'god' in his interpretation of Exod 7:1 differs from the meaning he usually gives the word. In this context he takes 'god' to mean 'ruler' or 'king.' The implications for New Testament Christology are negative. 'Philo's use of the word 'god' with reference to Moses provides no precedent for the attribution of divine nature or status to Jesus (p. 264).' (ACG)

K. BERTHELOT, 'Philo and the Allegorical Interpretation of Homer in the Platonic tradition (with an Emphasis on Porphyry's *De Antro Nympharum*),' in M. R. NIEHOFF (ed.), *Homer and the Bible in the Eyes of Ancient Interpreters,* Jerusalem Studies in Religion and Culture 16 (Leiden 2012) 155–174.

The article first argues that Philo's relationship to Homer is to some extent similar to that shown by the Platonist school in the Roman period, insofar as: (1) he defends Homer against his 'adversaries'; (2) he uses Homeric verses in order to support or corroborate his interpretation of Scriptures (while the Neoplatonists did the same in connection with Plato's writings); (3) he has a good knowledge of Greek allegorical explanations of Homer, including ones in the Platonist tradition. Second, there are many similarities between Philo's allegorical exegesis of the Bible and the allegorical interpretation of the Homeric corpus in Neoplatonic writings. The most striking convergence between Philo and that tradition lies in the existence of an overall reading of the biblical narrative or the Homeric epic in terms of a mystical allegory pertaining to the journey of the soul. Philo knew this reading—which apparently already existed in some form in the first century CE—and adapted it to the biblical texts. (KB)

M. Bettini, *Vertere. Un'antropologia della traduzione nella cultura antica*, Piccola Bibliotheca Einaudi 573 (Turin 2012).

The last chapter, entitled 'In search of the perfect translation,' of this monograph on translation in antiquity concentrates on the Septuagint as thematised in the *Letter of Aristeas*, Philo, Irenaeus, Pseudo-Justin (*Cohortatio*), Epiphanius, Augustine and Jerome. Applying an anthropological approach, the book studies the cultural metaphors on which the Romans—and to a lesser extent the Greeks—have based their concept of the act of translating (p. xv). The last chapter addresses the question: how is translation possible if the author of the original text is God? It starts with an analysis of how the *Letter of Aristeas* presents the origin and nature of the LXX translation (the work of intellectually, socially and morally authoritative translators who apply a refined philological method of establishing the correct original, confronting possible interpretations, and then defining the most accurate translation). The author then discusses Philo and underlines the difference between his view of the LXX and that of Aristeas: for Philo the LXX has the nature of a sacred revelation (the translators were ἐνθουσιῶντες; there is a perfect correspondence between the original and its translation; God himself has produced the translation). An appendix contains 'some observations on passages in the *Letter of Aristeas* of difficult or controversial interpretation; Philo and the perfect translation according to the Wassersteins.' (HMK)

R. Bloch, 'Alexandria in Pharaonic Egypt: Projections in *De Vita Mosis*,' *The Studia Philonica Annual* 24 (2012) 69–84.

The author argues that Philo's *Mos.* contains autobiographical elements and that the treatise can be connected with the troubles in Alexandria in 38 CE. There are parallels between the description of the sufferings of the Jews in *Legat.* and *Mos.* Furthermore, Philo presents Moses as a mirror image of himself. Just like Moses, Philo had enjoyed a secular education, the so-called *enkyklios paideia*, but after this education both went their own ways and turned to their ancestral traditions. Philo was member of the Jewish delegation that was sent to Rome, and he pleaded with the Roman emperor just as Moses pleaded with the Pharaoh. Philo was unwilling to leave his philosophical life behind and to get involved in political maters just as Moses was hesitant when God calls him from Midian back to Egypt. Because of the parallels and connections between *Legat.* and *Mos.* it is likely that they were written around the same time, in Philo's maturity and old age. (ACG)

P. M. Blowers, *Drama of the Divine Economy: Creator and Creation in Early Christian Theology and Piety* (Oxford 2012).

Chapter 3 of this broadly ranging study discusses the most important legacies of Hellenistic Jewish cosmology for early Christian doctrine on God as Creator and his creation. The two most influential sources are the Wisdom of Solomon and Philo. Discussing Philo's ideas the author underlines that Philo incorporates three key elements: (1) technical, philosophical, and theological concerns; (2) an attention to 'wisdom' as inspired knowledge of things sensible and intelligible; (3) a focus on spiritual psychagogy. Having set out Philo's view on God, the Logos, and the creation of the world, he concludes that many early Christian thinkers recognized in Philo and the Wisdom of Solomon an integration of scriptural ideas on creation with philosophical (especially Platonic and Stoic) notions relating to the divine mediation of the creation, the providence working in creation, and the ordered nature of the cosmos. Both Philo and the Wisdom of Solomon believe in a creation of the world by God from pre-existent matter. An important legacy is Philo's model of a 'double' creation, which influenced several Patristic theologians. Another legacy is the notion of Wisdom or Logos as guiding the pious to righteousness and sanctity. The Church fathers, however, reject the notion of eternity of matter. See also the review of this study by R. R. Cox, *SPhA* 26 (2014) 247–253. (ACG)

F. BORCHARDT, 'The LXX Myth and the Rise of Textual Fixity,' *Journal for the Study of Judaism* 43 (2012) 1–21.

Borchardt explores what he names the 'myth' of the origin of the LXX as presented in the *Letter of Aristeas*, Philo's *Mos.*, and in Josephus's *Jewish Antiquities*. He focuses in particular on the ways in which these sources treat the topic of the 'textual fixity' of the LXX and more broadly how they contribute to knowledge of ideas about the textual form of scriptural texts. A brief discussion of Philo's presentation of LXX origins concludes that, comparatively speaking, the Alexandrian shows 'a marked increase in the extent to which textual fixity is important for scripture' (p. 17). (SJKP)

F. CALABI, 'Il giardino delle delizie e la storia delle origini secondo Filone di Alessandria,' in F. CALABI and S. GASTALDI (eds.), *Immagini delle origini — la nascità della civiltà e delle culture nel pensiero antico*, Contributions to Classical Political Thought 5 (Sankt Augustin 2012) 173–194.

The article re-narrates and illustrates Philo's allegorizing account in the Allegorical Commentary and *QG* of the origins of humankind under the following headings: Adam, the introduction of duality (with the creation of Eve), leaving Eden, mortality, Cain and Abel, the flood, a new generation, the tower of Babel, arts and crafts. The concluding section, entitled 'temporality,' highlights that in an allegorical reading temporality is irrelevant, since the events receive a meaning that is valid always and everywhere. At the same time, however, for Philo the events in Genesis are historical facts: each story is to be taken both literally (embedded in time and succession) and metaphorically or typologically (as an a-temporal image). (HMK)

F. CALABI, 'La trasgressione di Adamo e la torre di Babele nella rilettura di Filone di Alessandria,' in E. MANICARDI and L. MAZZINGHI (eds.), *Genesi 1–11 e le sue interpretazioni canoniche: un caso di teologia biblica. XII Settimana Biblica Nazionale (Roma, 6–10 Settembre 2010)*, Ricerche Storico-Bibliche (Bologna 2012) 155–170.

A discussion of Philo's 're-reading' of Adam's fall in *Opif.* and of the tower of Babel in *Conf.* Adam and Eve represent the intellect and the sensations respectively. The serpent (pleasure) succeeds in persuading Eve by using a human voice and speech; the original unity of reality and speech is broken by the serpent's duplicity. The tower of Babel stands for another unity of speech, which consists in a common will to do wrong rather than in a common language. The construction of the tower represents pride, φιλαυτία, and rebellion against the order of the cosmos and its Maker. The article explores exegetical details, allegorical meanings and the (very limited) weight Philo attributes to a literal reading of the fall and the tower. (HMK)

F. Calabi, 'Filone di Alessandria e l'*Epinomide*,' in F. Alesse and F. Ferrari (eds.), *Epinomide: studi sull'opera e la sua ricezione*, Elenchos 60.1 (Naples 2012) 235–261.

Philo more than once uses the term *Epinomis* to indicate what may be a part of the book of Deuteronomy or a compendium of the Law. There can be no doubt that, in using this name, Philo also alludes to the Platonic *Epinomis*, but the exact relationship with this text is an issue of scholarly debate. The article points out possible influences of the *Epinomis* on Philo's discussion of astral theology, his description of the 'universal legislator' (Moses), his demonology, and in particular his use of the word, ἀγαλματοφορέω (with reference to the intellect) and ποικίλλω. It is concluded that influences of the *Epinomis* on Philo are far from impossible, but they were probably indirect (through an intermediary source) rather than direct. (HMK)

S. Chepey, 'Is the Timing Respecting Paul and the Four Men under a Vow in Acts 21:23–27 Plausible? Possible Implications from Josephus and Philo on the Nazirite Vow and First-fruits,' *Criswell Theological Review* 9 (2012) 69–75.

The author focuses on the timing of the four men under a vow and Paul; that is, Acts 21 locates this event to the Pentecost. Though Acts does not use the term 'Nazirite' here, the view that the vows of the four men were Nazirite vows is supported by other Jewish sources. The problem, however, is the timing (at Pentecost). Chepey argues that late Second Temple Jewish sources, particularly Josephus (*Ant.* 4.70–72) and Philo (*Spec.* 1.247–254), indicate that at least some Jews made an association between Nazirite vows and the annual giving of the First-fruits, which took place at Pentecost. (TS)

G. Collier, *Scripture, Canon and Inspiration: Faith in Pursuit of Conversation* (Coverdale Ind. 2012), esp. 199–204.

The aim of the book as a whole is to challenge all its readers to think seriously and even to reconsider some widely held opinions about the Bible. The author argues that the ancient Jewish and Christian usage of the term γραφή, often translated as 'scripture' implies the inspiration of a document as a 'holy writing,' but did not imply 'canon' and certainly not 'closed canon.' In this context he examines the occurrence of the term in Philo's writings. Of the 56 instances in total, only 22 denote 'the holy writings.' A closer examination of these texts leads to the conclusion that Philo does not clearly use the term without a qualifier (i.e. ἱερός, sacred) to refer to holy writings. He concludes (p. 204) that 'although it is widely assumed and stated that, in Philo, both the singular and plural of the word 'scripture(s)' are interchangeable and refer to 'scripture in its entirety,' this case is not established and cannot be taken for granted.' (DTR)

M. D. Cooper, *The Johannine Jesus as the Interpretive Basis for the Johannine Logos in Light of Philo's Logos* (M.A. thesis New Orleans Baptist Theological Seminary 2012).

Because of the clear link between John's use of Logos and that presented by Philo of Alexandria, Philo serves as the best possible background for understanding John's Logos. The thesis seeks to examine various themes within the Gospel proper and their relationship to the Philonic Logos. After discussing various background topics, in the main body of the thesis similarities are explored between the prologue's Logos and Philo's. Once an explicit link has been established, the various thematic parallels between the self-proclamations of Jesus and Philo's Logos are examined. The conclusion argues that the author of the Gospel could have used the teachings within the Gospel proper to base the Logos Christology in the prologue, which in turn is based upon a relationship to another first century Logos theology. (DTR; based on the author's abstract)

D. CREESE, 'Rhetorical Uses of Mathematical Harmonics in Philo and Plutarch,' *Studies in History and Philosophy of Science* 43 (2012) 258–269.

The first securely datable use of the term κανονικὴ θεωρία is found in Philo (*Opif.* 96) as part of the lengthy account of features of the hebdomad. This science combines harmonics and mathematics and is named from the single-stringed instrument, the κανών (monochord). The article first discussed the context of the text at some length, with special emphasis on the role of arithmology in Philo's account. Harmonics is included in the praise of the seven at least in part because it plays a key role in establishing the order of the cosmos. Most of Philo's account of harmonics in *Opif.* 95–96 is straightforward and correct, but he appears to make a curious mistake. He praises the ratio 5:2, but it is in fact discordant and has no special harmonic status. The article discusses this mistake at some length, asking whether it was deliberate in order to fit the exegetical context, or whether it was on the basis of a genuine belief that it was harmonic. Other Philonic texts suggest that his knowledge of musical theory was sufficient to recognize the anomaly of this particular ratio. But he also may have derived it from an anterior arithmological source. The author concludes that it is likely that Philo introduced the reference to harmonic theory as a rhetorical smokescreen in order to hide the inconsistency in his analysis of the powers of the hebdomad. It is a good example of use of technical scientific terms for non-scientific purposes. (DTR)

M. CUTINO, 'Réemploi de Philon d'Alexandrie et typologies épistolaires dans la correspondance d'Ambroise de Milan,' in A. CANELLIS (ed.), *La correspondance d'Ambroise de Milan*, Centre Jean Palerne. Mémoires 33 (Saint-Étienne 2012) 201–236.

The article demonstrates Ambrose's heavy dependence upon Philo in several of his letters, arguing that in some cases it nearly amounts to plagiarism. This dependency is particularly evident in *Ep.* 1.1–2 (*Her.*), 2.7 (*Prob.*), 6.29, 31, 34 (*Opif.*), 8.55 (*Fug.*). On the one hand, Ambrose uses these Philonic works to find the *exempla* that he needs for the theological issues he is dealing with (such as freedom in 1 Cor in *Ep.* 2.7). On the other hand, in the letters in which he follows Philo's development most closely, Ambrose seeks to highlight the specificity of Christian exegesis and of Christian moral values, in opposition to the Jewish ones. The presence of Philo's work in several of Ambrose's letters leads to a reconsideration of the idea that there was a 'Philonic period' followed by an 'Origenian one' in Ambrose's exegetical and theological thought. (KB)

J. M. Dillon, *The Platonic Heritage. Further Studies in the History of Platonism and Early Christianity*, Variorum Collected Studies Series CS 1008 (Abingdon 2012).

In this third collection of articles in the series by the distinguished scholar of the Platonist tradition (see also RRS 9014 and RRS2 9716) two articles focus on Philo specifically: 'The Pleasures and Perils of Soul-gardening,' summarized in RRS2 9719; and '*Asômatos*: Nuances of Incorporeality in Philo,' summarized in RRS2 9841. Reference is also made to Philo in the article on 'Thrasyllus and the Logos,' published in 1996 (see pp. 100–101). (DTR)

L. Doering, *Ancient Jewish Letters and the Beginnings of Christian Epistolography*, Wissenschaftliche Untersuchungen zum Neuen Testament 1.298 (Tübingen 2012).

Philo does not often employ the epistolary mode in his writings. Only very few letters are embedded in his treatises, such as the alleged letter of the gymnosophist Calanus to Alexander (*Prob.* 95) and the summarized correspondence regarding the crisis around Gaius' plans to erect his statue in the Temple (*Legat.* 199–203, 207, 248, 259–260, 330–334), and most notably Agrippa's letter to the Emperor (276–323). The letters advance Philo's narrative. Probably even Agrippa's letter is a literary fiction, as it displays more of Philo's concerns than references to Gaius' historical concerns. The existence of the narrative features of *exordium, narratio, argumentatio* and *peroratio* does not indicate so much that these existed in every letter, but rather that these features shaped Philo's literary style in general. The fact that the letter does not have any preface or epistolary conclusion seems to indicate that it was optional to reproduce these features. (JLB)

T. Faia, 'Fílon de Alexandria, *De vita Mosis* 1.83–44: Moisès e os arquètipos das palavras,' *Euphrosyne* 40 (2012) 349–354.

This short article analyses the relation between the interpretation that Philo makes of Moses and Aaron as representatives of two different kinds of logos, as well as the history of this interpretation and of its Greek interpretative models, particularly as found in Plato. (JPM)

C. Fraenkel, *Philosophical Religions from Plato to Spinoza: Reason, Religion, and Autonomy* (Cambridge 2012), esp. 24–32, 100–122.

The aim of this wide-ranging study is to present the development of the philosophical religion which commences with Plato and continues through to the Enlightenment. Philosophy here is not the handmaid of religion, but the other way around, with religion serving to promote a life of reason among non-philosophers. The frequently stated antithesis between Athens and Jerusalem is seen as not very useful except in the strictly historical sense. In fact the Alexandrian philosophers such as Philo, Clement and Origen were strongly influenced by the Platonic heritage in their interpretation of Jerusalem, i.e. the laws, stories, exhortations and practices of worship that make up Judaism and Christianity (p. 31). Philo's thought is studied in more depth as part of the chapter on 'Moses, Christ and the universal rule of reason in antiquity.' It is simplistic to describe philosophers such as Philo, Clement and Origen as primarily 'apologists' of their religious tradition. They were just as concerned to defend philosophy and show how it aligns with the pedagogical-political ideals that they attribute to Moses and Christ. These ideals focus on the role of reason. Because human beings have reason, they are created in God's image. This means that in a community of perfect Platonic philosophers there is no need for the laws, stories and worship of religious tradition, but these are valuable because they can give non-philosophers a share in the philosophical life. Philo's presentation of Judaism as a philosophical religion centres on the figure of Moses. The Law of Moses does not teach philosophy but it does contain philosophical doctrines on the allegorical level. However, 'the Law of Moses ... is not the kind of book whose study can lead to wisdom' (p. 117). This has to be learnt elsewhere, either through the study of non-Jewish sources or through divine inspiration. Thus the portrait of Moses as an accomplished philosopher-ruler and of the Divine Law as a pedagogical-political program for non-philosophers provides the frame-work for Philo's reinterpretation of Jewish beliefs, practices and institutions. But as long as human beings are embodied, they are also tied to the body of the Law for the reasons that Philo gives in the well-known passage at Migr. 89–93. See further the review by Scott Mackie in *SPhA* vol. 26, pp. 237–244. (DTR)

P. FRICK, 'Monotheism and Philosophy: Notes on the Concept of God in Philo and Paul (Romans 1:18–21),' in S. E. PORTER and A. W. PITTS (eds.), *Christian Origins and Hellenistic Judaism: Social and Literary Contexts for the New Testament*, Texts and Editions for New Testament Study 10—Early Christianity in Its Hellenistic Context 2 (Leiden 2012) 237–258.

The focus of this study is a comparison of the Apostle Paul's theology of the concept of God vis-à-vis the notion of God in Philo of Alexandria. The author first presents a sketch of Philo's formal concept of God (pp. 239–243); then he discusses whether or how the Philonic notion of God sheds light on Paul's presentation of God in Rom 1.18–21 (pp. 244–255), followed by a brief comparative assessment. The main focus is thus on the theology of Paul. In dealing with Philo, the author draws especially on *Opif.* 172, focusing on issues as Philo's monotheism, divine transcendence, the distinction between the existence and essence of God and the theological consequences of Philo's notion of God. He concludes this section by stating that in Philo we have a concept of God who is utterly unique and transcendent, inaccessible to the human mind and cognition. However, these notions are philosophically mediated via his doctrine of the logos and the powers, while theologically he has recourse to some anthropomorphic designations, the via negativa and even positive descriptions. (TS)

A. GALIMBERTI, 'Gli Ebrei e la storiografia giudaica nella *Methodus* di Jean Bodin,' in G. ZECCHINI and A. GALIMBERTI (eds.), *Storici antichi e storici moderni nella* Methodus *di Jean Bodin* (Milan 2012) 9–25.

Jean Bodin (1529–1596) in chapters VI and XI of his *Methodus ad facilem historiarum cognitionem* (1566) outlines a political and constitutional history of ancient Israel and identifies a historical-political—as well as religious—paradigm in the organisation of the Hebrew state (monarchy and aristocracy). Bodin was well acquainted with the Talmud, and with Josephus and Philo. The latter is for him an important source in matters of chronology and numerology, and in considerations about the best form of government (monarchy) as well as about Moses as lawgiver and king. (HMK)

E. L. GALLAGHER, *Hebrew Scripture in Patristic Biblical Theory*, Supplements to Vigiliae Christianae 114 (Leiden 2012).

Philonic evidence is frequently utilized in this meticulous study on how the Hebrew scriptures were regarded in Greek-speaking Judaism and the Church Fathers. Philo, who is the first writer to state explicitly that the translators of the Pentateuch were inspired, based his conception of the miracle of its translation on the conviction that the underlying Hebrew text was correct and authoritative. We note also the discussion of Philo's purported authorship of the Wisdom of Solomon on p. 43. (DTR)

E. S. GRUEN, 'Caligula, the Imperial Cult, and Philo's *Legatio*,' *The Studia Philonica Annual* 24 (2012) 135–147.

In this article, Gruen examines the historical reliability of Philo's portrayal of the emperor Gaius in *Legat*. According to Gruen, Philo's account is implausible in many respects, but particularly so with respect to two fundamental points. Firstly, Philo's claim about Gaius's hatred of the Jews, which Philo connects directly to the emperor's plans for a statue in the Jerusalem temple, has no support in any other ancient source, including Philo's other version of events in *Flacc*. According to Gruen, the idea of Gaius's hatred of the Jews is 'a mere Leitmotif for Philo's drama' (p. 141) of the triumph of virtue over vice and the hatred of virtue. Secondly, Gruen questions Philo's account of the emperor's convictions about his personal divinity. Other ancient sources have plenty to say about this latter topic, but they do not interpret Gaius's attempts to impersonate the gods as a serious claim to divine status. Nor do the coins, inscriptions and archaeology of Italy give any hint that the worship of the emperor was officially acknowledged or demanded there. Philo, on the other hand, attributes Gaius's behavior as driven by the emperor's ambition for superhuman power and his plan for a statue in the temple as inspired by hatred of the Jews who rejected the emperor's claims to divinity. In Gruen's analysis, Philo's construction of the motives behind the emperor's plans for the Jerusalem temple is not to be trusted. The emperor did not cultivate a deliberate policy of hostility against the Jews; his plan for a statue in the temple was a misjudgment, not an act of war. Whatever other vices we may attribute to Gaius Caligula, hatred of the Jews should not be counted among them. (SJKP)

M. HADAS-LEBEL, *Philo of Alexandria: a Thinker in the Jewish Diaspora*, Studies in Philo of Alexandria 7 (Leiden 2012).

This is a translation of the French original, *Philon d'Alexandrie: un penseur en diaspora* (see RRS2 20361), which was also translated into Hebrew in 2006 (see RRS2 20633). Unlike the earlier editions, the English translation contains an expanded bibliography and indices of ancient authors and texts and of Philonic passages. As stated in the Preface, 'this book seeks to explain [Philo's] personality in the context of the first major synthesis of Hellenism and Judaism' (p. xiii). To this end, the author draws upon a careful reading of Philonic texts and a wide range of other sources to present a lively and engaging account of Philo's Alexandria: his Jewish beliefs, practices, and exegesis; his philosophy; and his later reception among Christians and Jews. Specific chapters include: 'Alexandria 'on the Edge' of Egypt,' 'Being Jewish in Alexandria in Philo's Day,' 'Philo's Cultural World,' 'Amid Political Turmoil,' 'Judaism according to Philo: Practice and Ethics,' 'The Biblical Commentary,' 'Philo and Philosophy,' 'Philo's Doctrine,' and 'Philo, 'Father of the Church *Honoris Causa*'. (EB)

H. Hägg Fiskå, 'Kunnskap og frelse i aleksandrinsk teologi og filosofi. Filon og Klemens [Norwegian: Knowledge and Salvation in Alexandrian Theology and Philosophy: Philo and Clement],' in B. Ekman and H. Rydell Johnsén (eds.), *Soteria och gnosis. Frälsning och kunskap i den tidiga kyrkan. Föreläsningar hållna vid Nordiska patrisikermôtet i Lund 18–21 augusti 2010 [Swedish: Soteria and gnosis. Salvation and Knowledge in the Early Church. Papers given at the Nordic Patristi Conference in Lund 18–21 August 2010]* (Skellefteå 2012) 85–104.

After having provided a brief review of the Alexandrian context and Philo's life and work (pp. 85–90), the author deals with Philo's view of 'knowledge of God' and 'salvation.' At the end there is a brief comparison of Philo and Clement (pp. 99–101 plus bibliography). Concerning Philo's view of 'knowledge of God,' the author emphasizes that God as he really is, is transcendent and unknowable, but because God has revealed himself, he is knowable in his manifestations. Furthermore, salvation is in the end to 'see God'; salvation is thus a relationship with God based upon knowledge and contemplation. The author then finds that Clement is very much influenced by Philo. A major difference, however, is that for Clement the Logos is to be identified as Jesus Christ. (TS)

M. Hillar, *From Logos to Trinity: the Evolution of Religious Beliefs from Pythagoras to Tertullian* (Cambridge 2012).

This monograph discusses the concept of the Logos from Greek philosophy via Christian thinkers (Justin Martyr, Tertullian) up to the Middle Ages (Thomas Aquinas). Chapter 2 is devoted to the Logos in Judaism. Having first discussed the Hebrew concept of *davar* and Jewish wisdom literature, the author then turns to Philo. In this treatment he discusses several aspect of Philo's thought (ethics, doctrine of creation, mysticism, his view on the contemplative life). The doctrine of the Logos is set out in some detail. In his logos theory Philo combines biblical concepts of the Hebrew Logos and Hebrew wisdom with the Platonic notion of the Forms and the Stoic notion of the logos as all-pervading element. The Logos is the second hypostasis after the supreme God and is a mediator between God and the world. It is neither uncreated like God nor created like human beings. The Logos was used as an instrument by God creating the cosmos. Creation is seen as an eternal process. The supreme God is the Father and the Logos is metaphorically described as God's Son. Other names with which the Logos is associated are the eldest of God's angels, the great archangel, the Authority, the name of God, man according to God's image, and 'he who sees' (Israel). Philo also regards the Logos as the divine Mind, as the Form of Forms, the Idea of Ideas, or the sum total of Forms. Because the reasoning part in human beings is part of the Logos, they have some likeness with the Father. Finally it is noted that occasionally Philo brings to the fore the Stoic notion of an immanent Logos which binds all things in the universe together. (ACG)

M. S. B. H. Ishak, 'Allegorical Interpretation of the Role of Philosophy in the Discourse of Philo and Ibn Rushd,' *Al-Masaq: Islam & the Medieval Mediterranean* 24 (2012) 253–264.

Instead of dismissing traditional mythology and poetry as heresies, Greek philosophy introduced a methodology of understanding known as allegory. Philo was one of the first whose writings survived in the Christian tradition to employ allegory for understanding religious scriptures. In the Arab world, the philosopher Ibn Rushd (Averroes, 520–595/1126–1198) initiated the same method of commentary with his demonstration of the essential harmony between philosophy properly understood and scripture properly interpreted. The essay posits that Greek philosophy laid down a common tool for understanding the scriptures which exist in the Christian and Muslim traditions. (DTR; based on author's abstract)

S. J. JOSEPH, *Jesus, Q, and the Dead Sea Scrolls: a Judaic Approach to Q (on Qumran and the Essenes)*, Wissenschaftliche Untersuchungen zum Neuen Testament 2.333 (Tübingen 2012), esp. 94–123.

A revision of a Claremont Graduate University Ph.D. (2010), this study aims to open up a new understanding of the New Testament's Q source and new models for interpreting the contexts within which Jesus and the Jesus tradition can be located in first-century Judaism. In the third chapter entitled 'Qumran, the Essenes, and the Dead Sea Scrolls,' the author includes brief comments on Philo, together with other ancient authors, as a source for information about the Essenes (see pp. 95–97, 108–113). (SJKP)

F. J. KING, 'Ice-cold in Alex: Philo's Treatment of the Divine Lover in Hellenistic Pedagogy,' in H. TARRANT and M. JOHNSON (eds.), *Alcibiades and the Socratic Lover-Educator* (Bristol 2012) 164–179.

Paper presented in the context of a conference on Socrates and the lover-educator motif well-known from Plato's dialogues. Mention of this theme in Philo is only found in passages highly critical of homosexual behaviour (notably *Spec.* 3.37–42, *Contempl.* 59–63). Of the two elements of masculinity in Greco-Roman culture in Philo's time, dominance and self-restraint, Philo does not refer to the former in his critique. The latter is taken up, but it is attributed to Judaism rather than Greek culture, which is strongly criticized in its acceptance of same-sex masculine behaviour. This critique must be seen as rooted in a highly contentious social and political context. The final part of the article looks at the legacy of Philo's views in emerging Christianity. (DTR)

A. KORCZAK, 'Alegoreza Filona z Aleksandrii [Polish: Allegoresis of Philo of Alexandria],' *Przeglad Religioznawczy (Warsaw)* 243 (2012) 3–17.

After first discussing three of Philo's predecessors in the allegorical interpretation of the Bible, the author outlines the most important aspects of Philo's allegorical method. These are intuitive allegoresis, etymology, Platonic and Pythagorean features. He then shows the purpose of the method. Philo reveals an intellectual approach towards Greek culture, while at the same time remaining loyal to Jewish culture. (DTR; based on author's summary)

J. L. KUGEL, '*Jubilees*, Philo and the Problem of Genesis,' in N. DÁVID, A. LANGE, K. DE TROYER and S. TZOREF (eds.), *The Hebrew Bible in Light of the Dead Sea Scrolls*, Forschungen zur Religion und Literatur des Alten und Neuen Testaments 239 (Göttingen 2012) 295–311.

A challenging question in antiquity was why Genesis was included in the Pentateuch, considered primarily a source of laws. In *Jubilees*, Kugel discerns two explanations. According to the first, put forward by the original author, Genesis showed that despite the later political vicissitudes of the people of Israel, these vicissitudes did not signify that Israel had lost God's favor expressed in His covenant with them at Sinai. Instead God had adopted Israel on the sixth day of creation and forged a strong connection with Israel's earliest ancestors. They, in turn, even before the Sinai covenant, spontaneously observed practices that were later presented there as laws. A second explanation was introduced by a subsequent, deterministic interpolator, who understood the early ancestors' apparently spontaneous practices of later laws as evidence that these laws had always existed, inscribed on an eternal set of 'heavenly tablets'—which, consciously or not, Israel's ancestors followed. Like *Jubilees*, Philo responded to the question of Genesis by explaining that the early figures 'spontaneously did what was later to be embodied in the laws promulgated at Sinai' (p. 306). His approach differs, however, in that he does not, like *Jubilees*, specify particular laws that the patriarchs followed. Also, in *Abr.* he offers two rationales not found in *Jubilees*, i.e., that 'the Torah's laws are enacted first in the lives of the patriarchs ... to show that these laws are 'not inconsistent with nature'' (p. 308) and that it is not problematic to observe them. Reflecting on the similarity between *Jubilees* and Philo, Kugel suggests that given that *Jubilees* may have been well-known, travelers from Judea to Alexandria may possibly have imparted ideas there that appealed to Philo. (EB)

J. L. KUGEL, '*Jubilees*, Philo and the Problem of Genesis,' in IDEM (ed.), *A Walk through Jubilees: Studies in the •Book of Jubilees and the World of its Creation*, Supplements to the Journal for the Study of Judaism 156 (Leiden 2012) 391–405.

This study, the same as that in the previous entry, is included in this volume along with an exegetical commentary on *Jubilees* and other studies pertaining to *Jubilees* and to its relationship to other Second Temple writings (see the Preface, p. ix). (EB)

V. LAURAND, 'La contemplation chez Philon d'Alexandrie,' in T. BÉNA-TOUÏL and M. BONAZZI (eds.), *Theoria, Praxis, and the Contemplative Life after Plato and Aristotle*, Philosophia Antiqua 131 (Leiden 2012) 121–138.

The paper is a chapter in a volume on the theme of contemplation in Greek philosophy after Plato and Aristotle. Its starting-point is Philo's treatise on the Therapeutae with the title *De vita contemplativa*. It appears in this treatise as if one cannot penetrate to the heart of Philo's metaphysics except for the description of love and desire for the divine in §12–13. There follows a discussion on the two kinds of life (βίος), the active and the contemplative. Joseph is an ambiguous representative of the former. From his double treatment in *Somn.* and *Ios.* it can be concluded that contemplation always involves an exile from the body and the world, as seen in the case of the Therapeutae. But there is another relevant Philonic classification, the types of life (ζωή), of which the mixed life relates to the life of human beings. Human life is only live fully when turned towards God. This is illustrated by the life of Abraham, turning from Chaldea through Haran to the desert. It ends in recognition of human nothingness (οὐδένεια), that is, in searching for oneself, one finds Another. It is in the desert or at least outside the city that the process of discovery takes place. The final section of the article examines texts mainly from *Somn.* and its account of Jacob. An allegorical reading of scripture reveals the defeat of both sensation and intelligence until help comes from the Other. In this way the lost soul finds itself in quiet study of the law and celebration of the Sabbath, just as practised by the Therapeutae. (DTR)

J. LEONHARDT-BALZER, 'Priests and Priesthood in Philo: Could He Have Done without Them?,' in D. R. SCHWARTZ and Z. WEISS (eds.), *Was 70 CE a Watershed in Jewish History? On Jews and Judaism Before and after the Destruction of the Second Temple,* Ancient Judaism and Early Christianity 78 (Leiden 2012) 121–147.

Priests for Philo are the main agents of the Temple worship, receiving the offerings of the people and performing the sacrifices (*Mos.* 2.141–143; *Spec.* 1.167). They must be pure, as exemplified in the rationality of their worship. The validity of the Temple worship depends on their worthiness and trustworthiness when performing the sacrifices. The priests also help the people in their worship (*Spec.* 2.217–219). The Temple service is the inheritance of the priests as descendants of Levi (*Spec.* 2.222); God shares his own dues with them (*Spec.* 1.131,152). Outside the Temple priests occasionally are invited to teach in the synagogues (*Hyp.* 7.13–14). The High Priest focuses the worship of God in a particular way, representing the nation to God and, through the Logos, who is also called High Priest, God to the nation (*Her.* 82; *Spec.* 3.131–132; *Ebr.* 129–131; *Legat.* 306). By extension, he brings the whole universe before God (*Somn.* 1.214–215; *Spec.* 1.93–96). Even the people can occasionally have the status of priests, exceptionally on Passover (*Spec.* 2.145–148), metaphorically through the Nazirite vow when they dedicate themselves to God, their abstinence symbolizing priestly purity (*Somn.* 1.252–253). Indeed ultimately the Jews also function as priests for the pagan world (*Spec.* 2.162–175). Yet nowhere does Philo declare the basic distinction between priests and lay people irrelevant. There is no indication that he would have taken the loss of the Temple lightly. Like the heartbeat of the body, for Philo the Diaspora Jew the Temple service was essential in order to keep the nation alive, even if one is not aware of it most of the time. (JLB)

C. LÉVY, 'Quelques remarques sur le problème de la traduction dans l' Antiquité: Philon et Cicéron,' in B. BERNARD-PRADELLE and C. LECHEVA-LIER (eds.), *Traduire les anciens en Europe du Quattrocento à la fin du XVIIIe siècle: d' une renaissance à une révolution?* (Paris 2012) 17–30.

The author reflects on the parallel encounters between Israel and Rome on the one hand, and Greek language and culture on the other, through the examples of two outstanding intellectuals, Philo and Cicero. First, he contrasts the Jewish Alexandrian tradition exemplified by the *Letter of Aristeas* and Philo, for which the Greek translation of the Bible was as inspired as the Hebrew original and could replace it, with the rabbinic tradition, which is generally very critical of the translation. Whereas it remains impossible to state with certainty that Philo did not know Hebrew, the fact is that he only uses the Greek text of the Bible. In the end, the Philonic or, more generally, Jewish Alexandrian stance on the use of Greek ended in disaster. In the second part of the paper, Lévy argues that Cicero shares the optimism of the Alexandrian Jews concerning the possibility for the translation to match the quality of the original, but that he is far more penetrating than they in recognising the power relationship involved in the use of languages and in the act of translating. In the end, and to a large extent thanks to Cicero's innovative work with the Latin language, translation into Latin became an instrument of imperial domination. (KB)

S. D. MACKIE, 'Seeing God in Philo of Alexandria: Means, Methods, and Mysticism,' *Journal for the Study of Judaism* 43 (2012) 147–179.

This article discusses three aspects of the seeing of God, which is the pinnacle of Philo's spiritual experience. First, the effectual means of the vision is examined. In this question Philo's attitude is ambiguous. He consistently emphasizes that the *visio Dei* depends entirely on the self-manifestation of God. It is only possible to see God through God. On the other hand, there are many texts in which he underlines the role of human striving in the vision. Secondly, the methods that Philo employs in the noetic ascent are discussed. Platonic contemplative philosophy and the allegorical exegesis of scripture are connected with the ascent, but the pursuit and practice of a virtuous life is also a requisite for the seeing of God. The joining together of reading scripture, noetic ascent, and the seeing of God is found in his description of the Therapeutae. Finally, the author denies that Philo's texts have to be read metaphorically, whereby 'seeing' is equivalent to 'knowing' (i.e. 'achieving a rational awareness of God's existence'). Philo's passages are based on actual, mystical visual encounter with the Existent One. (ACG)

P. W. MARTENS, '*On the Confusion of Tongues* and Origen's Allegory of the Dispersion of Nations,' *The Studia Philonica Annual* 24 (2012) 107–127.

This article examines Origen's allegorical treatment of the Babel narrative on the dispersion of nations (Gen 11:1–9) and the extent to which the Patristic theologian, one of the most important of early Christian readers of Philo, may have been influenced by Philo's understanding of the same episode in his treatise *Conf*. In her fundamental study of Origen's use of Philo, Annewies van den Hoek identified six passages in which Origen borrows from *Conf*. Through the study of the interpretation of Babel presented in this article, Martens aims to add to the identifiable cases in which Origen draws on Philo's treatise. Martens begins by examining Origen's most extended allegorical treatment of Babel, which appears in Book 5 of the *Against Celsus* and aims to reveal the hidden teaching within the Genesis narrative, including such topics as the primordial fall of souls and their later embodiment, and also the work of angelic powers in this transformation. The second part of Martens' study emphasizes seven key similarities between the interpretations of Babel in *Conf*. and *Against Celsus*, two of which (the interpretation of Gen 11:7 on angelic punishment and the theme of peace) are likely to reflect Origen's direct knowledge of Philo's treatise. (SJKP)

J. P. MARTÍN (ed.), *Filón de Alejandría Obras Completas* Vol. 3 (Madrid 2012).

The third volume of the Philo's complete works in Spanish translation contains the last part of the Allegorical Commentary from *Conf*. to *Mut*. The titles and the text of each treatise follow the edition of Cohn and Wendland, although the reader is informed about noteworthy textual variations in the manuscripts. The general editor José Pablo Martín has been assisted by Marta Alesso in producing the volume. The treatment of each treatise consists of an introduction, translation and notes. Francisco García Bazán, senior research-er of the Argentinian National Research Council, is responsible for *Conf*. and *Migr*. Marco Antonio Santamaría, Philosophy Professor in Salamanca, has taken care of *Her*. Marcela Coria, Professor of Greek at the Universidad Nacional de Rosario, was entrusted with *Congr*. Marta Alesso, Professor of Greek at the Universidad Nacional de La Pampa, was responsible for *Fug*. Maria Victoria Spottorno, member of the Research Council of Spain, was entrusted with *Mut*. The treatment of the Allegorical Commentary in this edition is concluded with the translation and commentary on the fragment *De deo* by Martín, based on the transliteration from Greek into Armenian by Folker Siegert, with the assistance of Pablo Torrijano for the underlying Armenian text. The volume is brought to a close with indices of biblical and Philonic passages, of ancient and modern authors, of Greek and Hebrew languages and of subjects. (JPM)

O. McFARLAND, 'Whose Abraham, Which Promise? Genesis 15.6 in Philo's *De Virtutibus* and Romans 4,' *Journal for the Study of the New Testament* 35 (2012) 107–129.

This article explores the ways in which Philo and Paul meet and depart from each other in understanding the faith of the patriarch Abraham, based on their respective interpretations of Gen 15:6 ('And because he put his trust in the Lord, He reckoned it to his merit'). According to McFarland, both authors treat Abraham as a representative figure or model; but they also develop their interpretations of Abraham in strikingly different ways. McFarland seeks to explain their differing approaches by showing that Philo focuses on Abraham as a model for the attainment of virtue by one who overcame a godless past, while Paul emphasizes Abraham's faith in Christian perspective as emerging from a context of universal godlessness and as representing the unworthiness of the human being who is graciously pardoned by God. With regard to Philo's treatment of Gen 15:6, McFarland focuses on *Virt*. 212–219 in which Abraham is represented as an example of nobility arising from ignoble origins, characterized by Abraham's faith in the God of Israel and abandonment of the godlessness of his ancestral Chaldean family. For Philo, Abraham believes and is rewarded by God for this faith with the gift of virtue. (SJKP)

J. MORE, 'On Kingship in Philo and the Wisdom of Solomon,' in J. COOK and H.-J. STIPP (eds.), *Text-Critical and Hermeneutical Studies in the Septuagint*, Vetus Testamentum Supplements 157 (Leiden 2012) 409–425.

The article explores a three-way comparison between the Wisdom of Solomon, Philo's *Mos*. and Pythagorean tracts *On Kingship*. These last-named writings only survive as fragments in Stobaeus and probably go back in their content to the Hellenistic period. It emerges from the analysis that both Philo and the author of Wisdom have drawn on Jewish as well as Greco-Roman traditions in their portrayals of Moses and Solomon as kings. No direct relationship with the Pythagorean Περὶ βασιλείας writings can be proven, but certainly dependence on a common pool of ideas is demonstrable. However, the various themes examined illustrate differences between the two Jewish authors. Philo's ideas on kingship show similarities with the Pythagorean texts which are absent or have been suppressed in Wisdom. An explanation may lie in the different audiences envisaged for the two works. Philo's biography seems to have been written for 'outsiders,' whereas Wisdom is possibly written for an audience more familiar with scriptural traditions and has a less apologetic tone. (DTR)

R. Ngozo, *The One God and the Many Gods: Monotheism and Idolatry in 1 Cor 8:1–11.1 in Light of Philo's Writings* (diss. School of Mission and Theology, Stavanger, Norway 2012).

The main objective of this thesis prepared under the supervision of Prof. Torrey Seland is to 'provide a historical study of monotheism and the danger of idolatry.' This undertaking is also motivated by a pastoral concern about idolatrous practices among Gbaya Christians from Meiganga in Adamaoua Region, Cameroon. The goals of the thesis include a description of Paul and Philo in their social contexts, examination of Paul's view on the One God illuminated by that of Philo, and their practical exhortations on issues regarding monotheism and idolatry. The dissertation is divided into three chapters: Some Relevant aspects on Paul's and Philo's Greco-Roman World, Monotheism and Idolatry in Paul and Philo, and Monotheism and Idolatry in 1 Cor 8:1–11.1. With regard to the method of research, the candidate has chosen to use socio-rhetorical criticism, following the steps advocated by Vernon. K. Robbins in terms of intertexture, social and cultural texture and ideological texture. Accordingly, the first chapter makes use of 'intertexture, social and cultural texture to scrutinize Paul's and Philo's social and cultural contexts.' In the second chapter he makes 'appeal to Jewish texts represented by Philo's writings to shed more light on Paul's view of One God.' Finally, the third chapter which is largest part of this work, applies the method of innertexture (1 Cor 9:1–27) and intertexture (1 Cor 8:1–11.1) to explore Paul's Christological monotheism. (TS; based on a summary by Jean-Claude Loba-Mkole)

M. R. Niehoff (ed.), *Homer and the Bible in the Eyes of Ancient Interpreters*, Jerusalem Studies in Religion and Culture 16 (Leiden 2012).

Hitherto interpretations of Homer and the Bible have largely been studied in isolation, even though both texts became foundational for Western civilisation and were often commented upon in the same cultural context. The present collection of articles redresses this imbalance by bringing together original contributions of scholars from different fields, who cross traditional boundaries and interpret Biblical and Homeric interpreters in light of each other. The picture which emerges from these studies is highly complex: Greek, Jewish and Christian readers were concerned with similar literary and religious questions, often defining their own position in dialogue with others. Special attention is given to four central corpora: the Alexandrian scholia, Philo, Platonic writers of the Imperial Age, rabbinic exegesis. See also the papers by Berthelot and Niehoff summarised elsewhere in this bibliography. (MRN)

M. R. Niehoff, 'Philo and Plutarch as Biographers: Parallel Responses to Roman Stoicism,' *Greek, Roman, and Byzantine Studies* 52 (2012) 361–392.

This article argues for Philo's significance as a biographer. Preceding Plutarch by a generation, he was the first to explore the biographical genre for moral purposes. He is shown to have been inspired by Stoic notions of character, which helped him to shape the biblical material in the form of a biography. In addition, his concerns and techniques are compared to Plutarch's and shown to anticipate him in significant ways. Examples are taken both from his exegetical treatises (esp. *Mos.*) and his portrait of Gaius in *Legat*. (MRN)

M. R. NIEHOFF, 'Philo and Plutarch on Homer,' in M. R. NIEHOFF (ed.), *Homer and the Bible in the Eyes of Ancient Interpreters*, Jerusalem Studies in Religion and Culture 16 (Leiden 2012) 128–153.

This article argues for Philo's significance as an interpreter of Homer. He is the first Platonist to overcome Plato's harsh criticism of the Homeric epics and argue for their moral value. In this respect Philo significantly anticipates Plutarch. (MRN)

M. R. NIEHOFF, 'Commentary Culture in the Land of Israel from an Alexandrian Perspective,' *Dead Sea Discoveries* 19 (2012) 442–463.

This article investigates the development of commentary culture in the Land of Israel from an Alexandrian perspective, using Philo as an important witness to Alexandrian exegesis, both in his own right and as a polemicist against other Jewish Bible interpreters. While both the rabbis and the exegetes at Qumran developed forms of systematic commentary, they differ in important respects. The article argues that there are significant similarities between rabbinic exegesis and the commentary culture of Alexandria, both Homeric and biblical, while Qumranic exegesis can be characterized as prophetic. The Alexandrians and the rabbis explained their canonical text from within itself and appreciated it as a literary work. This means that a human author with a distinct style is assumed and that problems of contradictions as well as verisimilitude are explicitly addressed. The particular form of rabbinic exegesis, which is novel in the Land of Israel, thus seems to have resulted from a lively engagement with Hellenistic culture. In Qumran, on the other hand, prophetic forms of commentary were prevalent. The exegete does not inquire into the biblical text from within itself, but assumes prophetic authority, which enables him to reveal the 'secrets' of the text and gain direct access to God's wisdom. Biblical lemmata are directly applied to contemporary events, while textual problems or literary questions are not explicitly addressed. (MRN)

C. S. O'BRIEN, 'The Middle Platonist Demiurge and Stoic Cosmobiology,' *Horizons: Seoul Journal of the Humanities* 3 (2012) 19–39, esp. 31–33.

The Platonic demiurge was not of major importance in the Old Academy, but certainly exerted influence on Stoic cosmobiology in the form of the creative Logos, which combines technological imagery with influences derived from Aristotelian biological theory. Philo is the earliest witness to a renewal of the demiurgic model. Stoic influence clearly emerges in Philo's designation of his demiurgic entity as the Logos, who is immanent and pervades the parts of the cosmos where it would be beneath God's dignity to go. The continuous activity of the Logos also answers the Aristotelian objection against demiurgic theory, namely the question as to what God was doing before he created the cosmos. Despite these modifications, Philo uses his adaptation of Platonic demiurgy in order to explain Genesis. (DTR)

E. PARKER, and A. TREIGER, 'Philo's Odyssey into the Medieval Jewish World: Neglected Evidence from Arab Christian Literature,' *Dionysius* 30 (2012) 117–146.

The article commences by pointing out, contrary to what is often thought by scholars, Arabic literature does not fall outside the Christian tradition. In fact most Arabic translation of philosophical works from Greek into Arabic were made by Christians. In the first part it surveys scholarship on possible Arabic translations of Philonic treatises, beginning with Harkavy's suggestion made in 1894 that 'the Alexandrian' referred to by the Karaite Jewish author Qirqisānī was Philo and ending with the confirmation of his identification by Bruno Chiesa in 1998 (see summary in RRS2 a96102). Unfortunately, however, Chiesa's reconstruction of the two crucial chapters in Qirqisani's work have not yet been published. In the article's second part it examines the presence of Philo in Arab Christian literature, about which scholarship has hitherto been completely silent. Recently Treiger discovered a number of Philonic passages from *Contempl.* preserved in an appendix to the Arabic translation of the Dionysian corpus by Ibn Sahqūq in 1009. These passages go back to much earlier Greek scholia appended to the Greek text, probably by John of Scythopolis in the 6th century. They do not come from the original Philonic work but are taken from the extracts in Eusebius' *Ecclesiastical History*. An English translation of these passages from Ibn Sahqūq's version is then given (the Arabic text and the Eusebian original are printed at the end of the article). There are also other references to Philo in Arab Christian literature, for example in the historians Agapius of Manbij and Bar Hebraeus, and also in florilegia. The authors conclude by affirming that there is evidence of Arabic transmission of Philonic material. This demonstrates that, as in Late antiquity, so also in the early Islamic period it was the Christians who were the custodians of the Philonic legacy. In fact it is clear that contacts between Middle-Eastern Jews and Christians hold the key to many unresolved puzzles of intellectual history. Since as much as 90 percent of Christian literature in Arabic remains unpublished, it is even possible that translations of Philo may be discovered. (DTR)

P. A. PATTERSON, *Visions of Christ: The Anthropomorphite Controversy of 399 CE,* Studien und Texte zu Antike und Christentum 68 (Tübingen 2012).

The vision of God for Philo is only possible through the Logos. Philo's Logos doctrine must be seen in the context of Middle Platonism. God is the transcendent being and cannot be perceived by humankind (*Post.* 168). The only visible aspect of God is the Logos (*Somn.* 1.65–71, 230), visible that is only to the mind, not the eyes of the body (*Migr.* 5). In this sense, he is part of God, the archetypal idea of the world (*Opif.* 16–24), God's image and intermediary to the world (*Her.* 231; *Leg.* 3.96; *Spec.* 1.81; 3.83, 207). The Philonic Logos, however, is occasionally also seen as distinct from God (*QG* 2.62), an 'agent of creation' (p. 124), described with anthropomorphic attributes (*Opif.* 20; *Agr.* 51; *Conf.* 95–96, 145–147). The difference between the two concepts results from two different layers of tradition. Philo's exegesis of Gen 1–2 as the creation of the intelligible and then the sense perceptible man, of species and specimen (*Opif.* 134; *Leg.* 1.31) influenced some of the Nag Hammadi texts, in which the primordial light of Gen 1:3–4 is described in anthropomorphic terms and identified with the Logos (*Opif.* 31; *Somn.* 1.75). The author argues that this influence does not need to have occurred by direct interaction with Philo's writings: Logos theories were common among Jews of the time and can be traced to the Targumim and even to Memra concepts in the rabbinic writings. (JLB)

S. J. K. PEARCE, 'Philo and Roman Imperial Power: Introduction,' *The Studia Philonica Annual* 24 (2012) 129–133.

Brief Introduction to three studies (see summaries of Gruen, Schwartz, and Yoder in this volume) on the theme of 'Philo and Roman Imperial Power,' based on papers given at the Society of Biblical Literature Annual Meeting (Atlanta) in 2010. (SJKP)

S. J. K. Pearce, 'Philo and the *Temple Scroll* on the Prohibition of Single Testimony,' in N. Dávid, A. Lange, K. De Troyer and S. Tzoref (eds.), *The Hebrew Bible in Light of the Dead Sea Scrolls*, Forschungen zur Religion und Literatur des Alten und Neuen Testaments 239 (Göttingen 2012) 321–336.

By way of an exercise in studying Philo's works in the light of the Dead Sea Scrolls, this short study compares the treatment of the Torah's prohibition of single testimony (Deut 17:2–7; 19:15; and Num 35:30) in Philo's *Spec.* (4.53–54) and in its formulation in the *Temple Scroll* (col. 61). Philo's interpretation of the prohibition exhibits some similarities with that found in the *Temple Scroll* in bringing together laws on 'false utterances.' This finding may help to situate Philo's organisation of the 'special laws' in the wider context of Jewish exegesis in the Greco-Roman world. (SJKP)

V. Rabens, 'Johannine Perspectives on Ethical Enabling in the Context of Stoic and Philonic Ethics,' in J. van der Watt and R. Zimmerman (eds.), *Rethinking the Ethics of John: 'Implicit Ethics' in the Johannine Writings (Kontexte und Normen neutestamentlicher Ethik / Contexts and Norms of New Testament Ethics III)*, Wissenschaftliche Untersuchungen zum Neuen Testament 1.291 (Tübingen 2012) 114–139.

The main question dealt with in this article is: how is religious-ethical life empowered in John's gospel? The author first discusses the possible impact from Stoicism, which he denies; then he works out his concept of empowerment in the Gospel of John and describes it as enabled through the experience of divine love in an intimate relationship to Jesus and the Father. He also suggests that there are some Jewish traditions representing distinct parallels to this view, and on pp. 134–139 he discusses relational empowering in Philo (esp. *Post.* 12–13; *Legat.* 4–5; *QE* 2.7; *Mos.* 1.175 etc.). Here he finds that the Spirit of God has a definite place in the context of relational empowering for ethics. Hence, while he does not claim that John had read Philo, there is evidence in Philo demonstrating that there are Jewish traditions that knew the transforming and empowering effect of an intimate relationship to the divine, and also of the role of the Spirit in this empowering. (TS)

I. L. E. Ramelli 'Philo as Origen's Declared Model: Allegorical and Historical Exegesis of Scripture,' *Studies in Christian-Jewish Relations* 7 (2012) 1–17.

Philo influenced Origen in several ways, especially in the allegorical interpretation of Scripture and in the conviction that Scripture and Platonism were 'inspired by the same Logos' (p. 5). Both exegetes had to defend their approach against internal attacks on the very practice of allegoresis and external denials that Scripture held any profound philosophical meaning. Origen often refers to Philo indirectly in his homilies as one of his predecessors and names Philo or one of his writings explicitly in *Against Celsus*, in 'points that are crucial to his [Origen's] Scriptural allegorical method,' a practice that 'strongly suggests that Philo was his main inspirer for the very technique of philosophical allegoresis of Scripture' (p. 6). For both interpreters the literal and spiritual meaning corresponded, respectively, to the body and soul of Scripture. In contrast to Stoic and 'pagan' Middle and Neoplatonic allegorists, Origen and Philo affirmed both the literal and the allegorical meaning. The one exception is in the case of the Genesis creation account, for which both exegetes were inspired by the myths of Plato, especially in the *Timaeus*, and also for the story of Paradise and Eden. Although Origen denounces the literal meaning as 'Jewish,' he does so primarily in the homilies, for rhetorical purposes. He well knew that some Christians were literalists and some Jews—like the predecessors he cites—interpreted Scripture allegorically. Indeed Origen preferred the spiritual interpretations of these Jewish predecessors to the Gnostics and Marcionites, who wished to separate the Old Testament from the New and did not understand the Old Testament allegorically. (EB)

J. M. Rogers, *Didymus 'the Blind' and his use of Philo of Alexandria in the 'Tura Commentary on Genesis'* (diss. Hebrew Union College – Jewish Institute of Religion, Cincinatti 2012).

The dissertation prepared under the supervision of Adam Kamesar and Matthew Kraus discusses Philo's influence on the Tura commentaries of Didymus the Blind. In the commentaries found at Tura the name of Philo appears a total of ten times. Seven of these can be located in the Commentary on Genesis, which serves as the focus of the present work. After a brief introduction the first chapter discussed Didymus' place in the Alexandrian 'school' of biblical interpretation. The next chapter presents a survey of Philo's influence on Alexandrian Christianity. Chapter three treats the Jewish sources of Didymus, first his use of Philo outside the Genesis commentary, then of other writers including Josephus. Chapter four discusses explicit reference to Philo in the Genesis commentary. The final chapter moves on to Didymus's unacknowledged borrowings from Philo in the same work, with specific focus on etymologies, arithmological doctrines and general exegetical and philosophical themes. On the basis of his research the author concludes that there are up to three hundred possible borrowings from Philo in the Commentary. The distribution of these indicate that Didymus had access to a range of treatises in the Philonic corpus. In addition the exegetical tools used by Didymus are similar to those of Philo. The author concludes that it is impossible to deny that Didymus was influenced by Philo. It may also be assumed that the exegete's audience did not feel scandalized by this usage. Indeed it appears not to have viewed Philo as a Jew, but as a respected trail-blazing exegete who combined Greek erudition with biblical interpretation. (DTR)

T. A. Rogers, 'Philo's Universalization of Sinai in *De Decalogo* 32–49,' *The Studia Philonica Annual* 24 (2012) 85–105.

In this article it is argued that in his description of the giving of the Law on Mount Sinai in *Decal.* 32–49, Philo universalizes it in order to present the law as not being exclusive for Jews but as applicable for all people. For this reason he does not mention the name Sinai, omits the description of the people as Jews, and does not refer to covenantal and cultic elements. At the same time he underlines elements in the story that show the universal character of the giving of the Law. The cosmic elements of the theophany indicate that the revelation of the Law goes beyond a specific location. He spends a good deal of time describing the anomalous voice, which he takes to be God speaking to the souls of all rational beings. It should be noted, however, that in universalizing the presentation of the Law, he does not intend to compromise the distinctiveness and superiority of the Jewish Law, manner of living, and God. In fact he is so intent on presenting the law's exceptionalness that he presents it as universally applicable. (ACG)

J. R. Royse, 'Philo of Alexandria, *Quaestiones in Exodum* 2.62–68: Critical Edition,' *The Studia Philonica Annual* 24 (2012) 1–68.

First modern critical edition of a small section of the Greek text of the *Quaestiones* which remarkably was preserved in the manuscript tradition and not as an excerpted fragment. It is found in the 14th century ms. Vaticanus Graecus 379. The editor first describes its location in the manuscript and then its treatment at the hand of Philonic scholars. First published by Angelo Mai in 1831, the text has since then been edited on five occasions. Nevertheless it has suffered neglect in studies on Philo and this comprehensive critical edition, which takes into account all the details of both the Greek and the Armenian manuscript traditions, is a landmark in Philonic scholarship. After comments on the Greek text and the Armenian version and an explanation of the edition's format, the text is presented in a double page format, with the Greek text and critical apparatus on the left hand page and the Armenian text and an English translation of the Greek text on the right hand page. The final section presents copious and detailed notes on the text, with frequent references to earlier editors. (DTR)

D. T. Runia, 'Philon d'Alexandrie,' in R. Goulet (ed.), *Dictionnaire des philosophes antiques* (Paris 2012) 5.362–390.

Eight philosophers with the name Philo are included in this magnificent French reference work on ancient philosophers, the first volume of which was published in 1989 and which is now nearing completion. Philo of Alexandria (no. P148) receives extensive treatment. After a brief introductory resumé, the article is divided into 35 unnumbered sections each dealing with a separate topic related to Philo's life, writings, thought and *Umwelt* (with an emphasis on philosophy). The basic method is to present summaries of the chosen topics interspersed with copious references to scholarly literature, which are numbered in sequence (in total 235 bibliographical items). The sections begin with introductory studies and bibliographical aids, before treating topics on Philo's life and background. Next his writings and their contents are presented, followed by discussion of his methods of biblical interpretation and how these vary between his different kinds of writings. Attention is then given to his so-called philosophical treatises, followed by discussion of his relation to the various philosophical schools of his time. The article concludes with his *Nachleben* (or lack thereof) in Judaism and early Christianity and the beginnings of modern scholarship on his legacy. (DTR)

D. T. Runia, 'Jewish Platonism (Ancient),' in G. A. Press (ed.), *The Continuum Companion to Plato* (London 2012) 267–269.

Brief general article on Platonic influence on Hellenistic Judaism, commencing with the incidence of philosophical terms in the LXX, but focusing mainly on the writings and thought of Philo. (DTR)

D. T. Runia, 'God the Creator as Demiurge in Philo of Alexandria,' *Horizons: Seoul Journal of the Humanities* 3 (2012) 41–59.

The paper was presented as part of a conference on the figure of the Demiurge in the Platonic tradition from Plato's *Timaeus* to Marsilius Ficino in the Renaissance. Sedley's book on creationism and its critics in Antiquity only tell half the story. An equally important contribution was made by Jewish and Christian authors. Philo's mission was to show that the books of Moses were superior to Greek wisdom. From this perspective the creation account in Genesis was a trump card. The article focuses on his presentation in *Opif*. It first outlines the main features of his use of the demiurgic metaphor, including terminology and its basis in the biblical text. The metaphor is particularly prominent in the account of the creation of the human being. Key questions that the interpretation raises are the role of matter and the nature of time. The second part of the paper reflects on the consequences of the metaphor for Philo's interpretation. Some elements of the biblical account are better accounted for than others, the role of matter remaining particularly difficult. (DTR)

D. T. Runia, *Philo of Alexandria: an Annotated Bibliography 1997–2006 with Addenda for 1987–1996*, Supplements to Vigiliae Christianae 109 (Leiden 2012).

Further continuation of the series of Annotated bibliographies published in 1989 (RRS 1201) and 2000 (RRS2 1214). The work is based on the annual bibliographies published in *The Studia Philonica Annual* by the members of the International Philo Bibliography Project in the years 2000 to 2009. The names of the participating scholars are listed on the title page, 15 in all including the editor David Runia, who is the convenor of the Project. The introduction outlines the method of the project and of this work, which scarcely deviates from that of the previous volume RRS. Because of the advent of the new millennium in 2000 (strictly speaking 2001, but the problems already emerge in the previous year) a new numbering system had to be devised. In all the volume contains 1092 items (953 for the previous volume) and 38 extra items for the years 1987–1996. A section of Corrigenda and Addenda for 1987–1996 follows, succeeded by extensive indices. For further details see the review by G. E. Sterling at *SPhA* vol. 24, pp. 269–273. (DTR)

D. T. Runia, K. Berthelot, A. C. Geljon, H. M. Keizer, J. Leonhardt-Balzer, J. P. Martín, M. R. Niehoff, S. J. K. Pearce, and T. Seland, 'Philo of Alexandria: an Annotated Bibliography 2009,' *The Studia Philonica Annual* 24 (2012) 183–242.

The yearly annotated bibliography of Philonic studies prepared by the members of the International Philo Bibliography Project covers the year 2009 (118 items), with addenda for the years 2007–2008 (8 items), and provisional lists for the years 2010–12. (DTR)

D. T. Runia and G. E. Sterling (eds.), *The Studia Philonica Annual*, Vol. 24 (Atlanta 2012).

The twenty-fourth volume of the Journal dedicated to Philonic studies contains four articles, a Special section on Philo and Roman Imperial Power containing an introduction and three articles, the usual bibliography section (see summary below), and ten book reviews. These are followed by a section of News and Notes on recent events in Philo studies, Notes on contributors and Instructions for contributors. The articles are summarised elsewhere in this bibliography. (DTR)

K.-G. SANDELIN, *Attraction and Danger of Alien Religion: Studies in Early Judaism and Christianity*, Wissenschaftliche Untersuchungen zum Neuen Testament 1.290 (Tübingen 2012).

This volume represents the second collection of Prof. Karl-Gustav Sandelin's articles previously published in various journals and books; the first volume entitled *Sophia och hennes värld* (Åbo 2008) contained articles in the Swedish language. Its contents relating to Philo were reviewed in *SPhA* vol. 23, pp. 129–131. The present volume contains 10 studies and a summarizing essay in English; of these studies two have not been previously published, and four deal with issues of idolatry in 1 Corinthians, not drawing much on Philo. Furthermore, one study deals with the Revelation of John ('Attraction and Danger of Alien Religion in the Revelation of John,' pp. 169–191, not previously published); and one deals with 'The Jesus-Tradition and Idolatry' (pp. 161–168, published in 1996). This leaves us with another four studies, all dealing with issues of idolatry in the works of Philo ('The Danger of Idolatry according to Philo of Alexandria,' published 1991, see *SPhA* vol. 6, p. 139; 'Philo's Ambivalence towards Statues,' published in 2001, see *SPhA* vol 16, p. 255; 'Philo and Paul on Alien Religion: a Comparison,' published in 2005, see *SPhA* vol 20, p. 184, and 'Jews and Alien Religious Practices During the Hellenistic Age,' published 2006, the latter containing just a few references to Philo. See further the review elsewhere in this volume of *SPhA*. (TS)

L. DE LOS SANTOS GRANADOS, 'Aportaciones filosóficas de Filón, san Teófilo y san Ireneo al concepto de pecado original,' *Anuario de historia de la Iglesia* 21 (2012) 511–519.

The article is a summary of a thesis defended at the University of Navarra. Philo's name is linked with two Christian authors, although without citing specific texts (with the exception of a passing reference to *Leg.* 2.70). In Theophilus and Irenaeus, as in Philo, Adam was νήπιος and ἄλογος. For Philo, the fault committed by Adam and Eve was the action of an intermediate intellect. (JPM)

L. SAUDELLI, *Eraclito ad Alessandria. Studi e ricerche intorno alla testimonianza di Filone*, Monothéismes et Philosophie 16 (Turnhout 2012).

This book on 'Heraclitus in Alexandria: studies and researches on Philo's testimony' is the commercial publication of the author's thorough doctoral dissertation (with a slightly variant title) defended in 2008. The bibliography has additions up to 2011. See the summary in *SPhA* vol. 23, p. 131 and the review by D. T. Runia elsewhere in this volume. (HMK)

G. SCHÖLLGEN (ed.), *Reallexikon für Antike und Christentum* Band 24 (Stuttgart 2012).*

C. Tornau, art. Materie, 346–410, esp. 370–373 (Matter); M. Durst, R. Amedick, E. Enss, art. Meer 505–609, esp. 549–552 (Sea); S. Rebenich, art. Monarchie, 1112–1196, esp. 1164–1166 (Monarchy). (DTR)

---

* Only lemmata are noted which have a sub-section explicitly naming Philo in its title. Other lemmata under the titles Judaism or Hellenistic Judaism often refer to him.

D. R. SCHWARTZ, 'Philo and Josephus on the Violence in Alexandria in 38 CE,' *The Studia Philonica Annual* 24 (2012) 149–166.

In this article, Schwartz explores different ancient perspectives on the violence between Jews and non-Jews in Alexandria in 38 CE by comparing what Philo has to say about this in his treatises *Flacc.* and *Legat.* with Josephus's main account of the same events in his *Ant.* 18.257–60. In this context, Josephus gives little space to the experience of the Jews of Alexandria. According to Schwartz, Josephus's primary concern in recounting Alexandrian events of this era is focused—reflecting his own status as a Jerusalem priest—on the attempt by the emperor Gaius to install a statue in the Jerusalem temple. Furthermore, Josephus's comments in *Ant.* 18.257 suggest that he wishes to present the persecution of Alexandrian Jewry as an example of the impious ideology which had inspired Gaius to form his idolatrous plans for the Jerusalem temple. Schwartz identifies three main areas in which Josephus's account of events differs from Philo's reports: (1) Philo blames non-Jews for starting the troubles in Alexandria, while Josephus does not offer a view on this issue; (2) Philo argues for the defense of the Alexandrian Jews' religious and political rights, while Josephus presents the conflict only in terms of the Jews' right to practice ancestral customs; (3) in contrast to Philo, who never describes the Jews' Alexandrian enemies as 'Greeks,' Josephus has no hesitation in assigning this name to local forces hostile to the Jews of Alexandria, reflecting a Roman perspective on negative values associated with the 'Greek' label. Philo and Josephus represent two very different areas of concern in their interpretations of the same events: Philo's passionate interest in the defense of Alexandria's Jews; and Josephus's focus on the defense of Jerusalem and Gaius's plans for its temple. (SJKP)

G. E. STERLING, '"Prolific in Expression and Broad in Thought": Internal References to Philo's Allegorical Commentary and Exposition of the Law,' *Euphrosyne* 40 (2012) 55–76.

The article examines the internal cross-references in two of Philo's biblical commentaries (the *Quaestiones* are not dealt with). It first looks at internal indications that might help us determine the relationship between the Allegorical Commentary and the Exposition of the Law and concludes that it is likely that the Allegorical Commentary is the earlier of the two works. It then looks at each of the two large works and examines the evidence that they give about their extent and their structure. This evidence consists of (a) internal cross-references, and (b) the use of prefatory statements, usually at the beginning and end of individual treatises. In the case of both works Philo has planned his sets of commentaries as unified treatments of the biblical text. He works his way through the biblical text in sequence and expects his reader to do so to in reading his commentaries. The summaries that he gives on three occasions of the structure of the Exposition of the Law are of particular interest. They suggest a writing sequence of *Abr.*, *Mos.* and *Praem.* This also raises the question of the status of *Mos.* in relation to the Exposition. Sterling agrees with A. Geljon that its genre is that of the philosophical *bios*, but interprets it as an introduction to the Exposition rather that to the corpus of exegetical works as a whole. In the case of both commentaries their sequences are interrupted for us by the loss of some of their contents, as can again be reconstructed from cross-references and introductory comments. As large as the corpus is, it is not nearly as large as it once was. (DTR)

G. E. STERLING, 'Which Version of the Greek Bible Did Philo Read?,' in A. MORIYA and G. HATA (eds.), *Pentateuchal Traditions in the Late Second Temple Period: Proceedings of the International Workshop in Tokyo, August 28–31, 2007*, Supplements to the Journal for the Study of Judaism 158 (Leiden 2012) 89–127.

The author poses the question: which text of the Greek Bible did Philo read? In order to answer this question the author examines the main biblical texts in *Leg.* A complicating factor is the manuscript tradition: the three books of *Leg.* are transmitted in different manuscripts. The author then offers an overview of the readings of the main biblical texts in *Leg.*, also giving the text of the MT and the LXX and including in his discussion the quotations found in *QG*. He concludes that Philo was acquainted with a text of the LXX that was different from the LXX text as we know it. This text is preserved in the treatises of some Philonic manuscripts. In others the text has been changed into a more literal reading. Because there are differences between the biblical citations in *Leg.* and *QG* it is clear that Philo was aware of some variants but it was not a matter of great concern for him. (ACG)

G. E. STERLING, 'The Interpreter of Moses: Philo of Alexandria and the Biblical Text,' in M. HENZE (ed.), *A Companion to Biblical Interpretation in Early Judaism* (Grand Rapids Mich. 2012) 415–435.

The article is a thorough introduction to Philo's interpretation of scripture, making copious reference to the results of recent scholarship. How he used scripture in his commentaries can be seen from the different methods use in his three great exegetical works, each of which appear to have had a different reading public in mind. The extent of what he regarded as scripture can be deduced from his quotations of and references to the Hebrew Bible. Extensive statistics are cited in order to show that there is an overwhelming concentration on the Pentateuch. However, there are at least four texts which show that Philo recognized sacred writings beyond the Pentateuch. The final part of the article examines the text of Philo's scripture. It is certainly the Greek text. But the fact that Philo's text is not always identical to the transmitted text of the Septuagint has given rise to a number of different theories. A number of examples of Philo's quotations of scripture (Gen 3:19, 2:16, 15:18) are examined. Although these are far too limited to allow firm conclusions, they do provide evidence to support the view of Katz (cf. R-R 5007) that scribes altered the biblical quotations in Philo's text to bring them more in line with a literal translation of the Pentateuch. Although Philo's statement at the beginning of *Opif.* is hyperbolic, its spirit is genuine: his admiration for Mosaic scripture was such that he devoted his life to its interpretation. He had a special fondness for the book Genesis for two reasons: it lent itself so well to the allegory of the soul and it could illustrate the life enjoined by the law through the examples of the Patriarchs. But the scope of his work was broader. Eusebius was right to describe Philo as 'prolific in expression and broad in thought ... lofty in his perspectives on the divine writings' (*Hist. eccl.* 2.18.1). (DTR)

G. E. STERLING, 'When the Beginning is the End: the Place of Genesis in the Commentaries of Philo,' in C. A. EVANS, J. N. LOHR and D. L. PETERSEN (eds.), *The Book of Genesis: Composition, Reception, and Interpretation*, Vetus Testamentum Supplements 152 (Leiden 2012) 427–446.

Genesis was the most significant biblical book for Philo. He composed 43 treatises on it in his three commentary series and the citations or echoes of of this book constitute over half of his citations or echoes of all biblical books combined. Why did Philo find Genesis so worthy of his attention? Before turning to this question, Sterling briefly describes the content, form, and features of Philo's three sets of commentaries: *The Questions and Answers on Genesis and Exodus*, The Allegorical Commentary, and Exposition of the Law. He then offers three main explanations for why Philo regarded Genesis as so important: First, unlike other Pentateuchal books, Genesis is a narrative. This feature allowed Philo to draw upon Stoic models of allegorical and etymological treatments of narratives produced by Homer and Hesiod and to develop his own allegory of the soul, which illustrated the soul's progress towards virtue and the divine. Second, the lives of the ancestors in Genesis gave Philo the opportunity to present these ancestors in biographies, which, like those of Plutarch, highlighted the virtues of these early figures and presented them as models to be emulated. Third, Philo argued that Moses opened his legislation with accounts of creation and the lives of the ancestors to show that Mosaic law and natural law were equivalent and that the ancestors embodied the law of nature. By focusing so much on Genesis with its narratives that preceded the giving of the Mosaic law, Philo was able to present Judaism not as a narrow, ethnic religion but rather 'as an understanding of God that is open to all who live a rational life' (p. 444). (EB)

G. E. Sterling, "The Image of God': Becoming like God in Philo, Paul, and Early Christianity,' in S. B. Myers (ed.), *Portraits of Jesus: Studies in Christology*, Wissenschaftliche Untersuchungen zum Neuen Testament 2.321 (Tübingen 2012) 157–173.

The author examines the exegetical traditions of the interpretation of creation in the image of God (Gen 1:27) in *Opif*. In his discussion he observes several Platonic traditions that Philo accepted. Two important Platonic frameworks for creation are attested: the distinction between the creation of the intelligible world on 'day one' and the creation of the sense-perceptible world on the other days. Another tradition places this distinction between the accounts in Gen 1 and in Gen 2. Furthermore, Philo offers three different interpretations of the phrase 'the image of God.' He identifies God's image with the Logos, with the human mind, and with the idea of humankind. The author concludes that Philo has subsumed these interpretations within the framework of his thought, implicitly harmonizing the three interpretations. This shows that Philo was willing to let tensions stand in his text. (ACG)

G. J. Steyn, 'Can We Reconstruct an Early Text Form of the LXX from the Quotations of Philo of Alexandria and the New Testament: Torah Quotations Overlapping between Philo and Galatians as a Test Case,' in S. Kreuzer, M. Meiser and M. Sigismund (eds.), *Die Septuaginta— Entstehung, Sprache, Geschichte*, Wissenschaftliche Untersuchungen zum Neuen Testament 1.286 (Tübingen 2012) 444–464.

The author re-examines Philo's 'aberrant' quotations of the LXX. In his study on the LXX quotations in Hebrews he had found that they all agree with Philo's text, even where it disagrees with the MT and the LXX. The Pauline LXX quotations, particularly those in Galatians, are now compared with Philo. From the eight LXX quotations in Galatians, six have parallels in Philo. In one case the two agree with each other (Gal 3:12; *Congr.* 86) against LXX Lev 18:5. For LXX Gen 15:6 Steyn finds complete agreement between the variations in *Mut.* 177, Rom 4:3 and James 2:23. There are cases where Philo has the LXX text and Paul has a variation (LXX Gen 12:3 and 26:4–5: *Migr.* 1, 118, 122; *Her.* 8; Gal 3:8; LXX Gen 13:15; 17:8; 25:7; 28:12–15: *Somn.* 1.3; Gal 3:16) and others where Paul has the LXX text and Philo paraphrases (LXX Deut 21:23; Gal 3:13; *Post.* 26). Sometimes both vary in different ways (LXX Gen 21:10; Gal 4:30; *Cher.* 9). Thus there is some, but quite scant, evidence for another (not necessarily earlier) text form, which would need to be verified by other material such as from the Dead Sea Scrolls. (JLB)

J. E. Taylor and D. M. Hay, 'Astrology in Philo of Alexandria's "De vita contemplativa",' *ARAM Periodical* 24 (2012) 293–309.

In *Contempl.* Philo uses the verb θεραπεύω in a cultic sense to indicate those who serve God. In contrast to the Jewish example of those who serve the true God, in *Contempl.* 3–9 he lists five categories of those who serve 'inferior and quite laughable things' (p. 296). The focus of the article is on his mention in *Contempl.* 5 of those who honor 'the completed created entities—sun, moon, and other stars, wandering or fixed, or both the entire sky and adornment.' This category follows the listing of those who serve the four elements (*Contempl.* 3–4). In *Decal.* 52–57, Philo links those who worship the elements with those who honor sun, moon, planets, and stars and unlike in *Contempl.* 5, he associates some of these bodies specifically with Greco-Roman deities (e.g., sun with Apollo; moon with Artemis; morning star with Aphrodite). Philo's works in general are 'a little-used resource for evidence of astral understandings in Hellenistic Egypt that have otherwise not been much preserved' (p. 300). His ideas, however, are associated more with Babylonia or 'Chaldea' than with Greek astronomy. In several places Philo speaks of Chaldea as representative of ideas that Abraham abandoned or moved away from. Sometimes Philo presents these ideas as scientific and simply inferior to Moses's ethical philosophy, but sometimes he connects them to equation of the physical world with the deity and thus to false worship. In Alexandria specifically, it appears that 'the cult of Serapis integrated Chaldean star worship and the cult of the sun' (p. 307), although Philo himself does not explicitly name this cult when he disparages false beliefs and worship. (EB)

C. Termini, 'L'immortalità tradita. La rilettura di Gen 2–3 in Filone di Alessandria (*Opif.* 151–152),' in E. Manicardi and L. Mazzinghi (eds.), *Genesi 1–11 e le sue interpretazioni canoniche: un caso di teologia biblica. XII Settimana Biblica Nazionale (Roma, 6–10 Settembre 2010)* (Bologna 2012) 129–153.

After a reflection on Philo's nuanced position with regard to the myth-like character of Gen 2–3, the article analyses Philo's interpretation of this passage and finds that the first encounter between man and women is given an almost romantic and erotising, not a demonising exegesis. Not because of amorous desire (πόθος) but as a result of the intervention of pleasure (ἡδονή), symbolized by the serpent, has woman become the ἀρχή of sin (ἀρχή in the temporal rather than the causal sense). The author discusses Philo's complex, even oscillating views on the status of sensation (closely related to pleasure and sin) in creation. For Philo, the fall of the first couple is paradigmatic, without a causative or originating force; their sin consists not in the transgression of a prohibition, but in the choice and inclination to prefer carnal satisfaction above a deep relationship with the living God. (HMK)

A. Timotin, *La démonologie platonicienne. Histoire de la notion de daimôn de Platon aux derniers néoplatoniciennes,* Philosophia Antiqua 128 (Leiden 2012) esp. 100–112.

This substantial study claims to be the first synthesis of the concept of δαίμων as it developed in the Platonic tradition from Plato himself to the later Neoplatonists. Philo's views are discussed in the section on Middle Platonist authors which has the general title 'The theologization of demonology: reading the *Timaeus* in the light of the *Symposium*.' In three texts (*Gig.* 6–18, *Somn.* 1.134–143, *Plant.* 12–14) Philo presents a demonological theory based on the relation between the τάξις of living beings and the elements. The argument that each part of the cosmos needs to be inhabited by a class of living beings goes back to Aristotle, while the theory that the air must have a species of divine beings, i.e. δαίμονες, is already found in the *Epinomis*. It would appear that in the Old Academy there were two ways of conceiving the disposition of living beings in the cosmos, the one naturalistic based on Plato *Tim.* 39e–40a, the other theological developed by the *Epinomis* and Xeno-crates. Philo's argument draws on the latter tradition. His originality derives from the connection that he makes with the biblical text and can be seen in his assimilation of δαίμονες with the ἄγγελοι of scripture and his explanation of ἄγγελοι πονηροί (cf. Ps 77:49) in terms of wicked souls. The role assigned to providence in his theory is found in Middle Platonist texts (esp. Plutarch). Philo can link it to the doctrine of the angels of the nations (Deut 32:8). The section ends with a brief discussion of the role of messenger ascribed to δαίμονες and ἄγγελοι in the Greek and biblical traditions respectively. (DTR)

S. Weisser, 'Why Does Philo Criticize the Stoic Ideal of *Apatheia* in *On Abraham* 257? Philo and Consolatory Literature,' *Classical Quarterly* 62 (2012) 242–259.

Although Philo elsewhere views the Stoic ideal of *apatheia*, or eradication of passions, as superior to the Platonic-Aristotelian concept of *metriopatheia*, or moderation of passions, in *Abr.* 257 Philo rejects the ideal of *apatheia* and attributes to Abraham the 'second-rank virtue' of *metriopatheia* (p. 242). After reviewing the various ways in which scholars have explained this apparent inconsistency, Weisser argues that in *Abr.* 245–261, Philo is following the conventions of the genre of consolation literature, which favors *metriopatheia*. A significant but no longer extant work of this genre was produced by Crantor of Soli (c. 335–276/5 BCE) and other examples are found in Cicero and Seneca. Usually in the form of letter to a bereaved individual, consolatory literature is marked by similarities in structure, stories about model grievers, and—especially important—consolatory argu-ments. Features of Philo's description of Abraham's grief that accord with consolation literature include the eulogy of Sarah and several consolatory arguments. The latter presents the following themes: the strength of grief and the power of reason to control it, condemnation of excessive grieving and the need to prepare oneself for the inevitability of death, the understanding that life is a loan, and belief in survival of the soul after death. Although Seneca generally rejects the passion of grief, he occasionally praises moderation of passions, a position that Weisser attributes to his conformity with the norms of consola-tion literature. Likewise, in *Abr.* Philo's seemingly inconsistent advocacy of *metriopatheia*, which is also supported by Gen 23:1–3, can best be understood as his adherence to the norms of this same genre. (EB)

M. R. Whitenton, 'Rewriting Abraham and Joseph: Stephen's speech (Acts 7:2–16) and Jewish Exegetical Traditions,' *Novum Testamentum* 54 (2012) 149–167.

Taking up the suggestion of C. R. Holladay to consider Acts in relation to its Hellenistic-Jewish environment, the author focuses on Acts 7:2–16 and related treatments of Abraham and Joseph in the LXX, *Jubilees*, Philo, *Liber antiquitatum biblicarum*, Josephus's *Jewish Antiquities*, *Genesis Rabbah*, and *Targum Pseudo-Jonathan*. After surveying these treatments, the author comments on the rhetorical method of Stephen's speech and its traditional content in relation to three motifs: 'Called from Chaldea,' 'Timing of the death of Terah,' and 'Joseph the wise sage.' Unlike the Hebrew Bible and LXX, which situate the call to Abraham to leave his home in Haran, Acts—like Philo (*Abr.* 62, 67) and Josephus (*Ant.* 1.154)—understands the call as coming to him in Chaldea, or Mesopotamia. Stephen also specifies that Abraham left Haran only after the death of his father, Terah, a detail that does not agree with the Hebrew or LXX but does conform to Philo's *Migr.* 177 and the Samaritan Pentateuch. Underlying this difference may have been the concern to preserve Abraham's reputation as not dishonoring his father by leaving before his death. Finally, Stephen attributes wisdom to Joseph, a quality named only in Philo (*Ios.* 106, 269), Josephus (*Ant.* 2.63, 65, 80, 87), *Jubilees* (40:5), and Artapanus (Fr. 2.1 = Eus. *P.E.* 9.23.1). The similarities between Acts and these Jewish exegetical traditions suggest a promising avenue for further research. (EB)

J. Yoder, 'Sympathy for the Devil? Philo on Flaccus and Rome,' *The Studia Philonica Annual* 24 (2012) 167–182.

In this article, Yoder argues that Philo's treatise *Flacc.* portrays the eponymous subject of this work, the Roman prefect of Alexandria in 38 CE, in strikingly varied ways. Thus, Philo represents Aulus Avilius Flaccus as a tyrant who plans and executes harm against the Jews of Alexandria. But he also treats Flaccus as a victim of political events and in this respect at least, Yoder argues, appears to show some sympathy for the Roman. Based on an examination of the different dimensions of Philo's multivalent portrait of Flaccus in this treatise, Yoder concludes that *Flacc.* shows that Philo's attitude towards the Roman Empire is very complex and cannot be reduced to a straightforward dichotomy between 'pro-Roman' and 'anti-Roman' views. (SJKP)

Extra items from before 2012

Z. ADORJÁNI, 'Alexandriai Philón: *Quod omnis probus liber sit* – aki igaz, az szabad is 75–91 fordítása [Hungarian: Philo of Alexandria—*Who is good is also free* 75–91. Translation],' *Református Szemle [Reformed Review] (Cluj, Rumania)* 98 (2005) 449–506.

Translation into Hungarian of one of Philo's two accounts of the Essenes. It is difficult to know how he obtained this information. Perhaps it occurred on a pilgrimage that he made to Jerusalem. As the treatise *Contempl.* shows, he had an interest in such pious communities. The translation is accompanied by extensive notes. (DTR; based on author's abstract)

Z. ADORJÁNI, 'Philo, Pro Judaeis defensio. Euszebiosz: Praeparatio evangelica VIII. 11,1–8 fordítása [Hungarian: Philo, *Pro Judaeis defensio*. Eusebius of Caesaria: *Praeparatio evangelica* VIII. 11,1–18. Translation],' *Református Szemle [Reformed Review] (Cluj, Rumania)* 98 (2005) 597–607.

Translation into Hungarian of Philo's other account of the Essenes in his apologetic treatise on the Jews preserved by Eusebius. The Greek text used is based on A. Adam (ed.), *Antike Berichte über die Essener*, Kleine Texte für Vorlesungen und Übungen 182 (Berlin 1961) 5–7 (see R-R 6101). The translation is accompanied by notes with references to parallel texts. (DTR; based on author's abstract)

Z. ADORJÁNI, 'Alexandriai Philón: *De opificio mundi* 87–107 fordítása. [HUNGARIAN: Philo of Alexandria *De opificio mundi* 87–107. Translation],' *Református Szemle [Reformed Review] (Cluj, Rumania)* 99 (2006) 139–150.

Translation into Hungarian of a section of Philo's treatise on the Mosaic creation account where he shows his interest in and knowledge of Pythagorean arithmology, which he uses to explain Jewish traditions. (DTR; based on author's summary)

Z. ADORJÁNI, 'A therapeuták himnuszéneklése Philón *De vita contemplativa* című munkája alapján [Hungarian: Psalm-singing in the community of Therapeutae based on *De vita contemplativa* by Philo of Alexandria],' *Református Szemle [Reformed Review] (Cluj, Rumania)* 99 (2007) 408–417.

The Therapeutae's ascetic devotion is characterized not only by searching the scriptures, meditation and prayer but also by the singing of hymns and psalms. The article examines their practice and compares it with that of the Essenes in Palestine. The singing of psalms by the two communities is based first of all on their common Jewish origin. However, these religious communities had a different self-identity from that of normative Jews and this identity explains the special practices associated with their psalm-singing, i.e. festive occasions in the case of the Essenes and cultic dance in the case of the Therapeutae. (DTR; based on author's summary)

Z. ADORJÁNI, *Alexandriai Philón: De vita contemplativa*. Simeon könyvek.
A Simeon Kutatóintézet (Pápa) könyvsorozata. Vol. 6. Pápai Református
Teológiai Akadémia és a L'Harmattan Könyvkiadó és Terjesztő Kft.
(Budapest 2008).

First translation into Hungarian of the Philonic treatise (and only the second ever, after
the translation of *Mos.* by János Bollók, Budapest 1994). The book begins with an introductory study addressing the following topics: The philosopher as ambassador to Rome;
Philo, the philosopher and therapeut? *De vita contemplativa* among Philo's works (pp. 9–
29). This introduction is followed by a translation of *Contempl.* (pp. 31–50) and the most
substantial part of the book, the philological notes and commentaries (pp. 51–157). The
notes and descriptive analyses attached to a fluent translation provide the necessary background information to grasp the significance of the Therapeutae in their ancient Jewish
and wider intercultural context. It hardly requires any substantial effort to contextualise
their contemplative spirituality in our world, which means that Philo's work has much to
say for the current reader as well. (DTR; based on author's summary)

Z. ADORJÁNI, 'A χάρισμα és a δύναμις fogalma Alexandriai Philón
műveiben [The concepts χάρισμα and δύναμις in the works of Philo of
Alexandria],' *Református Szemle [Reformed Review] (Cluj, Rumania)* 101 (2008)
16–34.

Comparison of the semantic field of the term χάρισμα as it appears in the works of
Philo with the use of the term in the New Testament shows that the Philonic meaning
(often in a wider or narrower sense) is a parallel for its use in the letters of Paul and in 1
Peter. Philo, whose thought is based on the Old Testament, developed a complex, almost
confusing, doctrine of the Logos. His doctrine of God's δύναμις is closely linked with early
Christian concepts of the service of Jesus Christ and the coming kingdom. God's power is
revealed in Christ's person (Matt 28:18, Rom 8:35–39, Phil 2:9–10, Rev 5:12, 12:10, 1 Pet
3:22). (DTR; based on author's summary)

Z. ADORJÁNI, 'Női tagság és szüzesség az egyiptomi therapeuták
közösségében [Women Membership and Chastity in the Community of
Therapeutae], '*Studia Doctorum Theologiae Protestantis (Cluj, Rumania)* 1
(2010) 57–74.

Most scholars adopt the view that the Essenes' feast had sacral character and that it
replaced the feast connected to offering a sacrifice. The Therapeutai community on Lake
Mareotis, which was considered by Philo to be 'most admirable' can be compared above
all to the Essenes of Qumran. On this site there lived women who took a vow of chastity,
leading the same way of life as men. This phenomenon proves that the Hellenistic entou-
rage accepted feminine perfection if women disdained the pleasures of the flesh and they
assumed chastity not only of their free will but also due to their devotion to wisdom, so
that they 'gave birth' not to mortals but to spiritual successors: spiritual and immortal fruit
bestowed on God's beloved servants (§68). Engagement to God, that is chastity offered to
God, was not strange to Jewish mystics. This mysterious union was thus not exclusive to
men. We read in Philo's *Cher.* that Sarah, Lea, Rebecca and Zipporah also shared in this
and therefore they too can be considered chaste (§§40–52). This community with its

monastic character raised the level of genuine devotion not only to celibacy but also founded the institution of female chastity. (DTR; based on author's abstract)

J. ANNAS, 'Virtue and Law in Plato,' in C. BOBONICH (ed.), *Plato's Laws: a Critical Guide* (Cambridge 2010) 71–91, esp. 80–84, 89–90.

In his final work, the Laws, Plato argues that in order to become virtuous and happy the citizens of his ideal state must not only live under a system of laws but should also regard themselves as having the deeply deferential attitude to them as slaves. Philo's presentation of the Mosaic law can help us understand the direction of Plato's thought. For Philo the laws are not ethically self-standing, i.e. as mere rules to be followed. Living according to the law of Moses produces a character in which reasoning, feeling and decision are harmoniously intergrated. Obedience to the laws enable us to structure our practices so that we become virtuous in doing them. For Plato law is divine reason. Given this theocratic approach it is not surprising to see analogies between Platonic and Philonic thought, despite the differences in their actual theologies. (DTR)

A. D. BAKER, *Diagonal Advance: Perfection in Christian Theology*, Veritas Series (London 2011).

The book presents a new theory of perfection which argues for a radical revision in Christian thinking on the purpose of human life. Perfection is neither a vertical drop from the divine, nor a horizontal progression through social and personal development. It is rather a diagonal advance into the divine perfections through the making perfect of life in the world. The first part of the book is entitled 'First Movement: Inceptions,' and contains chapters on perfection in Athens and in Jerusalem. The second part entitled 'Second Movement: Emergence' studies the New Testament and the Church Fathers. In between these two parts is a section entitled 'First Interlude: Yahwistic Deification in Philo of Alexandria,' which contains reflections on Philo's understanding of the theme of divine and human perfection. The basis of the analysis is a number of Philonic texts on Moses and his ascent on Mt. Sinai (especially *Mos.* 1.158–159), the giving of the Law, the making of the Tabernacle, the creation of the cosmos and the institution of the Sabbath as a day of rest for human beings (but not for God). Via Judaism Philo makes God more perfect than the gods in the Hellenic tradition or the Demiurge in Plato. But he then suggests that human participation is either cut off from God (because God is unknowable in his essence) or cut off from humanity (because being alienated from human nature means that the human being is annihilated in divine perfection). Moses must either accept imperfectibility or become divine and leave his human nature behind. In both cases perfection is defeated. (DTR)

J. M. G. BARCLAY, 'Paul and Philo on Circumcision: Romans 2.25–29 in Social and Cultural Context,' in J. M. G. BARCLAY (ed.), *Pauline Churches and Diaspora Jews*, Wissenschaftliche Untersuchungen zum Neuen Testament 1.275 (Tübingen 2011) 61–79.

Reprint of 1998 article, summarized in RRS2 9808, as part of a collection of studies examining the relation of the churches established by Paul and their context in Diaspora Judaism. (DTR)

G. Bensussan, *Qu'est-ce que la philosophie juive?* (Paris 2003), esp. 21–64.

This book is a general introduction to Jewish philosophy, structured chronologically around three moments: the encounter with Greek philosophy (this moment corresponds to the work of Philo); the encounter with Arabic philosophy (mainly through the work of Maimonides); and the encounter with German philosophy (from Mendelssohn to Levinas). The first part thus deals with Philo and represents an introduction to his thought. After a brief presentation of Philo's Alexandrian context, the author first tackles different aspects of Philo's literal and allegorical reading of Scripture. Then he presents Philo's doctrine of the Logos and the Divine powers, as well as its connections with Sophia and Hokhmah, emphasizing parallels and convergences between Philo's philosophical views and the discourse of the rabbis (around notions like *memra* or *middot*). He then presents Philo's doctrine of creation (in general, and that of human beings in particular). Finally, he addresses the issue of God as a transcendent and unknowable entity and of the unending quest of the soul. (KB)

P. Bilde, 'Der Konflikt zwischen Gaius Caligula und den Juden über die Aufstellung einer Kaiserstatue im Tempel von Jerusalem,' in A. Lykke and F. T. Schipper (eds.), *Kult und Macht, Religion und Herrschaft im syro-palästinensischen Raum. Studien zu ihrer Wechselbeziehung in hellenistisch-römischer Zeit*, (Tübingen 2011) 9–48.

Per Bilde (1939–2014) was Professor at Aarhus University, Denmark and an expert on Josephus, on whom he published several books and articles. In the present article he deals with the conflict between Gaius Caligula and the Jews over the establishment of a statue of the emperor in the Jerusalem temple. His intention and aim is to study the interpretations and the reconstructions of the episode narrated by Philo in *Flacc.* and *Legat.*, and by Josephus in *BJ* 2.184–203 and *Ant.* 18.261–309. After a brief review of the available sources (pp. 11–12), he deals with the interpretation in recent research (pp. 12–14). He then discusses the problems in understanding the Caligula crisis, and provides a comparative paraphrase of the main sources (pp. 15–22). Next he tries to work out the tendencies of the main sources and provide a critical analysis of the sources and a reconstruction of the historical event (pp. 22–31). He also provides a brief comparison of this crisis with other conflicts in antiquity (p. 31–44). Methodologically he looks for the tendencies and redactions of the various ancient authors in order to arrive at a historically plausible description of the events. As a result he is rather critical of the expositions inherent in the works of both Philo and Josephus. They are so apologetic that they are in need of an 'Entapolo-getisierung.' As to the 'was eigentlich geschehen ist' (what really happened), he concludes that the 'Caligula-crisis' must be seen as the threat of war between Rome and the Jewish Palestine. The so-called crisis was a Jewish uproar that began with the damaging of the altar for the emperor in Jamna, an event to which Caligula and Rome responded with the project of establishing a statue in the Jerusalem temple and by mobilizing the great army in Syrian Antioch (p. 30). Hence Bilde can characterize the conflict as a confrontation between two peoples, the Roman and the Jews, and also as a conflict between two religions, or rather, between two 'religionspolitischen Mächten' (religious-political powers, p. 46). (TS)

J. Bollók, *Alexandriai Philón: Mózes élete*, Atlantisz Könyvkiadó (Budapest 1994).

The significance of this publication is that it makes known the two books Philo's *Life of Moses* to a broader circle of educated Hungarian readers. The work is by no means easy reading, since Philo's way of thinking is quite foreign for today's reading public. With this in mind the author has prefaced the translation with an introduction on Philo and his work (pp. 7–17). In addition he has added extensive notes to the translation (pp. 147–155). (DTR; based on the summary by Z. Adorjáni)

W. K. Gilders, 'Jewish Sacrifice: Its Nature and Function (according to Philo),' in J. Wright Knust and Z. Varhelyi (eds.), *Ancient Mediterranean Sacrifice* (New York 2011) 94–105.

Philo is unique in his focus on interpreting ritual sacrifice symbolically. He understood the sacrificial animal as analogous to the human soul and prescriptions for sacrifice, such as examining the animal for blemishes or pouring out the blood in a circle, as corresponding to internal preparations of the soul in its devotion to God. Although sacrifice was a common practice in the ancient Mediterranean world, Philo understood Jewish sacrifice as perfect in establishing a relationship between human and divine. For him the real purpose of sacrifice lay in the motivations of the sacrificer rather than in the act itself. Philo's approach fits in well with modern theories about sacrifice, which understand its symbolic meaning to be essential. It is important to recognize, however, that such meaning is not inherent but is instead conventional, that ritual does not have *only* symbolic meaning, and that different cultures and different people within those cultures may have different understandings of sacrifice's symbolic or functional meaning. It is also important to distinguish between symbolic or functional meanings offered by native informants and by scholarly interpreters. While Philo may represent the approach of an intellectual elite among Diaspora Jews, other texts, like the Dead Sea Scrolls, show interest in 'the definition and elaboration of correct practice' (p. 101). (EB)

R. E. Heine, *Origen: Scholarship in the Service of the Church* (Oxford 2011).

Philo is constantly drawn upon as an important precursor of and influence on Origen and particularly his methods as a biblical commentator. This influence was much stronger in the author's view while Origen was still working in Alexandria than after he moved to Caesarea, even though then he came into much more contact with Jews and living Judaism. See further the review by D. T. Runia in *SPhA* vol. 25, pp. 240–241. (DTR)

M. R. Niehoff, 'Philons Beitrag zur Kanonisierung der griechischen Bibel,' in E.-M. Becker and S. Scholz (eds.), *Kanon in Konstruktion und Dekonstruktion: Kanonisierungsprozesse religiöser Texte von der Antike bis zur Gegenwart. Ein Handbuch* (Berlin 2011) 329–343.

Philo developes two distinct concepts of canonization. In his Allegorical Commentary, which he wrote at the beginning of his career and is directed towards Jewish readers in Alexandria, he distinguishes between the Greek Bible and the Homeric epics, using the methods of Homeric text interpretation to show that Moses' work can stand up to this kind of critique of style and content. Philo's argumentation can be seen as dialectical in that he interprets apparent literary shortcomings as indications of deeper allegorical intentions, thereby reinforcing the conviction of the infallibility of scriptural truth. On the other hand, in the Exposition of the Law, which is directed to a wider reading public, he presents Mosaic scripture as a perfect work which is far superior in its philosophical content than other legal codes. Here Philo's argumentation is not dialectical, but linear. (MRN)

M. J. REDDOCH, 'Philo of Alexandria's Use of Sleep and Dreaming as Epistemological Metaphors in Relation to Joseph,' *The International Journal of the Platonic Tradition* 5 (2011) 283–302.

Plato uses the image of dreaming and awaking in an epistemological context: someone who has an uncertain kind of knowledge is dreaming, whereas he who has true knowledge is awake. Philo takes over this imagery in his presentation of Joseph in *Somn.* 1–2 and *Ios.* In *Somn.* 1–2 Joseph is primarily presented in negative terms as a dreamer and as unable to have true knowledge. He is fixated on a number of vices. In *Ios.* Philo underlines his role as an interpreter of dreams and thus presents him more positively. In the context of dreaming Philo uses the language of mystery religion and this suggests that Joseph as an interpreter of dreams can be compared with Moses as a mystagogue who leads the reader into a deeper meaning of Scripture. Joseph had undergone a transformation from ignorance to knowledge, which is expressed in terms of waking up. According to the author the analysis of the imagery of sleeping and dreaming shows that there is no contradiction between the presentation of Joseph in *Somn.* and *Ios.* (ACG)

D. T. RUNIA, 'Philo of Alexandria (Subject: Biblical Studies),' in *Oxford Bibliographies* (Oxford University Press 2010).

Bibliography of Philonic studies presented using the distinctive method of the Oxford Bibliographies Online database (http://www.oxfordbibliographies.com). This bibliography was commissioned as part of the section on Biblical Studies. It consists of twenty sections, with a maximum of eight bibliographical items in each section. Every section and every item is briefly annotated. Most items are quite recent and in the English language, but some older works and studies in other languages are also included. The bibliography was revised in 2015. See further the note on this and two other Philo bibliographies in the same database in News and Notes elsewhere in this volume. (DTR)

SUPPLEMENT

A Provisional Bibliography 2013–2015

The user of this supplemental Bibliography of the most recent articles on Philo is reminded that it will doubtless contain inaccuracies and red herrings because it is not in all cases based on autopsy. It is merely meant as a service to the reader. Scholars who are disappointed by omissions or are keen to have their own work on Philo listed are strongly encouraged to contact the Bibliography's compilers (addresses in the section 'Notes on Contributors').

2013

A. AFTERMAN, 'From Philo to Plotinus: the Emergence of Mystical Union,' *Journal of Religion* 93 (2013) 177–196.

M. ALESSO, 'Filón como fuente de la identificacíon del sumo sacerdote con Jesús en Clemente Alejandrino,' in Á. HERNÁNDEZ, S. VILLALONGA and P. CINER (eds.), *La identidad de Jesús: unidad y diversidad en la época de la Patrística. Actas del I Congreso Internacional de Estudios Patrísticos, Universidad Católica de Cuyo* (San Juan 2013) 167–198.

M. ALESSO, 'Poder y potencias en los textos de Filón alejandrino,' in M. ELIZALDE (ed.), *Debates y perspectivas de la Investigación en las Ciencias Humanas y Sociales. Actas de las XX Jornade de Investigación de la Facultad de Ciencias Humanas,* (Santa Rosa 2013) 35–44.

R. M. BERCHMAN, 'Arithmos and Kosmos: Arithmology as an Exegetical Tool in the *De Opificio Mundi* of Philo of Alexandria,' in K. CORRIGAN and T. RASIMUS (eds.), *Gnosticism, Platonism and the Late Antique World. Essays in Honour of John D. Turner* (Brill 2013) 167–198.

E. BIRNBAUM, 'The Biblical Interpretations of Philo: *On the Life of Abraham,*' in L. H. FELDMAN, J. L. KUGEL and L. H. SCHIFFMAN (eds.), *Outside the Bible: Ancient Jewish Writings Related to Scripture* (Lincoln, NE 2013) 916–950.

U. BITTRICH, 'Die drei Formen des Weisheitserwerbs bei Philo von Alexandrien und ihre Wurzeln in der aristotelischen Ethik,' in M. HIRSCHBERGER (ed.), *Jüdisch-hellenistische Literatur in ihrem interkulturellen Kontext* (Frankfurt am Maim 2013) 72–90.

M. BÖHM, 'Philo und die Frage nach den jüdischen Identitat in Alexandria,' in M. ÖHLER (ed.), *Religionsgemeinschaft und Identität. Prozesse jüdischer und christlicher Identitätsbildung im Rahmen der Antike,* Biblisch Theologische Studien 142 (Neukirchen-Vluyn 2013) 69–112.

P. Borgen, 'The Biblical Interpretations of Philo: *On the Migration of Abraham*,' in L. H. Feldman, J. L. Kugel and L. H. Schiffman (eds.), *Outside the Bible: Ancient Jewish Writings Related to Scripture* (Lincoln, NE 2013) 951–958.

S. C. Byers, *Perception, Sensibility, and Moral Motivation in Augustine: a Stoic-Platonic Synthesis* (Cambridge 2013).

F. Calabi, *Filone di Alessandria*, Pensatori 32 (Roma 2013).

N. G. Cohen, 'The Biblical Interpretations of Philo: *On the Decalogue*,' in L. H. Feldman, J. L. Kugel and L. H. Schiffman (eds.), *Outside the Bible: Ancient Jewish Writings Related to Scripture* (Lincoln, NE 2013) 1033–1133.

M. Colazingari, *Il concetto di Logos in Filone in relazione alla Philosophie der Offenbarung di Schelling [Elektronische Ressource]* (diss. Katholische Universität Eichstätt-Ingolstadt 2013).

B. Cook, *Pursuing Eudaimonia: Re-appropriating the Greek Philosophical Foundations of the Christian Apophatic Tradition*, Liverpool Hope University Studies in Ethics Series 10 (Newcastle upon Tyne 2013).

M. B. Cover, *Lifting the Veil: 2 Corinthians 3:7–18 in Light of Jewish Homiletic and Commentary Traditions* (diss. University of Notre Dame 2013).

F. Damgaard, *Recasting Moses: The Memory of Moses in Biographical and Autobiographical Narratives in Ancient Judaism and 4th Century Christianity*, Early Christianity in the Context of Antiquity 13 (Frankfurt am Main 2013).

D. De Brasi, '„Uno principe, pertanto, debbe consigliarsi sempre" (Machiavelli, *Il Principe* XXIII): Fürstenspiegel in der jüdisch-hellenistischen politischen Philosophie?,' in M. Hirschberger (ed.), *Jüdisch-hellenistische Literatur in ihrem interkulturellen Kontext* (Frankfurt am Maim 2013) 51–71.

D. J. DeVore, 'Eusebius' Un-Josephan History: Two Portraits of Philo of Alexandria and the Sources of Ecclesiastical Historiography,' in M. Vinzent (ed.), *Studia Patristica: Papers Presented at the Sixteenth Internaitonal Conference on Patristic Studies held in Oxford 2011* (Leuven 2013) 14.161–180.

M. J. Edwards, *Image, Word and God in the Early Christian Centuries*, Ashgate Studies in Philosophy and Theology in Late Antiquity (Farnham UK 2013), esp. 61–68.

L. H. Feldman, J. L. Kugel, and L. H. Schiffman (eds.), *Outside the Bible: Ancient Jewish Writings Related to Scripture*, 3 vols. (Lincoln, NE 2013).

C. Fraenkel, 'Philo of Alexandria, Hasdai Crescas, and Spinoza on God's Body,' in R. S. Boustan, K. Herrmann, R. Leicht, A. Y. Reed and G. Veltri (eds.), *Envisioning Judaism: Studies in Honor of Peter Schäfer on the Occasion of his Seventieth Birthday* (Tübingen 2013) 809–819.

P. Frick, 'Monotheism and Philosophy: Notes on the Concept of God in Philo and Paul (Romans 1:18–21),' in S. E. Porter and A. W. Pitts (eds.), *Christian Origins and Hellenistic Judaism: Social and Literary Contexts for the New Testament*, Texts and Editions for New Testament Study 10 (Leiden 2013) 237–258.

F. García Martínez, H. Najman and E. Tigchelaar (eds.), *Between Philology and Theology: Contributions to the Study of Ancient Jewish Interpretation*, Supplements to the Journal for the Study of Judaism 162 (Leiden 2013).

F. García Martínez, 'Divine Sonship at Qumran and in Philo,' in F. García Martínez (ed.), *Between Philology and Theology. Contributions to the Study of Ancient Jewish Interpretation*, Supplements to the Journal for the study of Judaism 162 (Leiden 2013) 83–97.

A. C. Geljon and D. T. Runia, *Philo On Cultivation: Introduction, Translation and Commentary*, Philo of Alexandria Commentary Series 4 (Leiden 2013).

Y. Green, 'Who Knows Seven?,' *Jewish Bible Quarterly* 41 (2013) 255–261.

J. Greenberg, *'Agoniasomen': Philo Judaeus, a Voice of a Colonized Nation* (M.A. thesis University of Colorado at Boulder 2013).

D. M. Hay†, 'Philosophical Treatises of Philo: *On the Contemplative Life*,' in L. H. Feldman, J. L. Kugel and L. H. Schiffman (eds.), *Outside the Bible: Ancient Jewish Writings Related to Scripture* (Lincoln, NE 2013) 2481–2500.

W. Helleman-Elgersma, 'Augustine and Philo of Alexandria's 'Sarah' as a Wisdom Figure (*De Civitate Dei* XV 2f.; XVI 25–32),' in M. Vinzent (ed.), *Studia Patristica: Papers Presented at the Sixteenth International Conference on Patristic Studies held in Oxford 2011* (Leuven 2013) 18.105–116.

S. Honigman, '"Jews as the Best of All Greeks": Cultural Competition in the Literary Works of Alexandrian Judaeans of the Hellenistic Period,' in E. Stavrianopoulou (ed.), *Shifting Social Imagineries in the Hellenistic period. Narrations, Practices, and Images*, Mnemosyne Supplements 363 (Leiden 2013) 207–232.

W. Horbury, 'Biblical Interpretation in Greek Jewish Writings,' in J. Carleton Paget and J. Schaper (eds.), *The New Cambridge History of the Bible: From the Beginnings to 600* (Cambridge 2013) 289–320, esp. 311–316.

J. Jay, 'The Problem of the Theater in Early Judaism,' *Journal for the Study of Judaism* 44 (2013) 218–253.

M. Jones, 'Philo Judaeus and Hugo Grotius's Modern Natural Law,' *Journal of the History of Ideas* 74 (2013) 339–359.

L. Kerns, 'Soul and Passions in Philo of Alexandria,' in M. Vinzent (ed.), *Studia Patristica: Papers Presented at the Sixteenth International Conference on Patristic Studies held in Oxford 2011* (Leuven 2013) 11.141–154.

M. KISTER, 'Allegorical Interpretations of Biblical Narratives in Rabbinic Literature, Philo, and Origen: Some Case Studies,' in G. A. ANDERSON, R. A. CLEMENTS and D. SATRAN (eds.), *New Approaches to the Study of Biblical Interpretation in Judaism of the Second Temple Period and in Early Christianity.* [*Proceedings of the Eleventh International Symposium of the Orion Center for the Study of the Dead Sea Scrolls and Associated Literature, 9–11 January, 2007*], Studies on the Texts of the Desert of Judah 106 (Leiden 2013) 133–183.

E. KOSKENNIEMI, 'Philo and the Sophists,' in L. ROIG LANZILLOTTA and I. MUÑOZ GALLARTE (eds.), *Greeks, Jews, and Christians. Historical, Religious and Philological Studies in Honor of Jesús Peláez del Rosal,* Estudios de Filología Neotestamentaria 10 (Córdoba 2013) 253–279.

R. A. LAYTON, 'Moses the Pedagogue: Procopius, Philo, and Didymus on the Pedagogy of the Creation Account,' in L. JENOTT and S. K. GRIBETZ (eds.), *Jewish and Christian Cosmogony in Late Antiquity,* Texts and Studies in Ancient Judaism 155 (Tübingen 2013) 167–192.

C. LÉVY, 'L'étrange monsieur Aquilius,' *Bulletin de l'Association Guillaume Budé,* No.1 (2013) 202–213.

V. LIMONE, *Inizio e Trinità. Il neoplatonismo giovanneo nell'ultimo Schelling,* Philosophica 114 (Pisa 2013), esp. 99–104.

D. LINCICUM, *Paul and the Early Jewish Encounter with Deuteronomy* (Baker Academic 2013).

D. LINCICUM, 'Philo and the Physiognomic Tradition,' *Journal for the Study of Judaism* 44 (2013) 57–86.

D. LINCICUM, 'Aeschylus in Philo, *Anim.* 47 and *QE* 2.6,' *The Studia Philonica Annual* 25 (2013) 65–68.

D. LINCICUM, 'A Preliminary Index to Philo's Non–Biblical Citations and Allusions,' *The Studia Philonica Annual* 25 (2013) 139–167.

W. LOADER, *Making Sense of Sex: Attitudes Towards Sexuality in Early Jewish and Christian Literature* (Grand Rapids 2013).

O. W. MCFARLAND, *The God who Gives: Philo and Paul in Conversation* (diss. Durham University 2013).

J. P. MARTÍN, 'Las esperanzas mesiánicas de Filón de Alejandría, un judío contemporáneo de Jesús,' in Á. HERNÁNDEZ, S. VILLALONGA and P. CINER (eds.), *La identidad de Jesús: unidad y diversidad en la época de la Patrística* (San Juan 2013).

O. MUNNICH, 'Δορυφορεῖν, δορυφόρος: l'image de la «garde» chez Philon d'Alexandrie,' *The Studia Philonica Annual* 25 (2013) 41–63.

M. R. NIEHOFF, 'A Jewish Critique of Christianity from Second-Century Alexandria: Revisiting the Jew Mentioned in *Contra Celsum*,' *Journal of Early Christian Studies* 21 (2013) 151–175.

M. R. Niehoff, 'Jüdische Bibelinterpretation zwischen Homerforschung und Christentum,' in T. Georges, F. Allbrecht and R. Feldmeier (eds.), *Alexandria*, Civitatum Orbis Mediterranei Studia 1 (Tübingen 2013) 341–360.

M. R. Niehoff, 'The Emergence of Monotheistic Creation Theology in Hellenistic Judaism,' in L. Jenott and S. K. Gribetz (eds.), *Jewish and Christian Cosmogony in Late Antiquity*, Texts and Studies in Ancient Judaism 155 (Tübingen 2013) 85–106.

M. R. Niehoff, 'Biographical Sketches in Genesis Rabbah,' in R. S. Boustan, K. Herrmann, R. Leicht, A. Y. Reed and G. Veltri (eds.), *Envisioning Judaism: Studies in Honor of Peter Schäfer on the Occasion of his Seventieth Birthday* (Tübingen 2013) 265–286.

M. R. Niehoff, 'The Biblical Interpretations of Philo: *Allegorical Interpretation* 1.31–62,' in L. H. Feldman, J. L. Kugel and L. H. Schiffman (eds.), *Outside the Bible: Ancient Jewish Writings Related to Scripture* (Lincoln, NE 2013) 902–915.

M. R. Niehoff, 'The Biblical Interpretations of Philo: *On the Life of Moses*,' in L. H. Feldman, J. L. Kugel and L. H. Schiffman (eds.), *Outside the Bible: Ancient Jewish Writings Related to Scripture* (Lincoln, NE 2013) 959–988.

F. Oertelt, 'Gender, Religion und Politik bei Philo von Alexandria,' in U. E. Eisen, C. Gerber and A. Standhartinger (eds.), *Doing Gender — Doing Religion. Case Studies on Intersectionality in Early Judaism, Christianity and Islam*, Wissenschaftliche Untersuchungen zum Neuen Testament 1.302 (Tübingen 2013) 227–250.

J. Otto, 'Philo, Judaeus? A Re-evaluation of Why Clement Calls Philo "the Pythagorean",' *The Studia Philonica Annual* 25 (2013) 115–138.

A. Pasquier, 'Parole intérieure et parole proférée chez Philon d'Alexandrie et dans l'*Évangile de la Vérité* (NH I,3),' in K. Corrigan and T. Rasimus (eds.), *Gnosticism, Platonism and the Late Antique World. Essays in Honour of John D. Turner* (Brill 2013) 199–208.

S. Pearce, 'Rethinking the Other in Antiquity: Philo of Alexandria on Intermarriage,' in P. J. Burton (ed.), *Culture, Identity and Politics in the Ancient Mediterranean World. Papers from a Conference in Honour of Erich Gruen*, = *Antichthon* vol. 47 (Melbourne 2013) 140–155.

S. J. K. Pearce, *The Words of Moses: Studies in the Reception of Deuteronomy in the Second Temple Period*, Texts and Studies in Ancient Judaism 152 (Tübingen 2013).

S. J. Pearce, 'The Biblical Interpretations of Philo: *On the Decalogue*,' in L. H. Feldman, J. L. Kugel and L. H. Schiffman (eds.), *Outside the Bible: Ancient Jewish Writings Related to Scripture* (Lincoln, NE 2013) 989–1032.

R. Penna, 'Il vino nele nozze di Cana (Gv 2,1–11) e in Filone Alessandrino,' in D. Chrupcala (ed.), *Rediscovering John. Essays on the Fourth Gospel in Honour of Frédéric Manns*, Analecta 80 (Milan 2013) 371–381.

L. Pérez, 'El homicidio es robo de templos (ἱεροσυλία) según Filón: explicación metafórica de un mandamiento bíblico,' in R. Braicovich, R. Andrea and R. De Angelis (eds.), *Actas del Primer Simposio Internacional de Filosofía Helenística* (Rosario 2013) 109–118.

S. E. Porter and A. W. Pitts (eds.), *Christian Origins and Hellenistic Judaism: Social and Literary Contexts for the New Testament*, Texts and Editions for New Testament Study 10 (Leiden 2013).

V. Rabens, 'Philo's Attractive Ethics on the "Religious Market" of Ancient Alexandria,' in P. Wick and V. Rabens (eds.), *Religious Formation, Transformation and Cross-Cultural Exchange between East and West*, Dynamics in the History of Religions 5 (Leiden 2013) 333–356.

T. Rajak, 'Text, Prophesy, and the Individual in Hellenistic Judaism: Texts from Philo and Josephus,' in J. Rüpke (ed.), *The Individual in the Religions of the Ancient Mediterranean* (New York 2013) 298–314.

M. J. Reddoch, 'Enigmatic Dreams and Onirocritical Skill in *De Somniis* 2,' *The Studia Philonica Annual* 25 (2013) 1–16.

C. M. Rios, *O próprio e o comum: rastros de interculturalidade na escrita de Fílon de Alexandría* (diss. Universidade Federal de Minas Gerais 2013).

J. R. Royse, 'Did Philo Publish his Works?,' *The Studia Philonica Annual* 25 (2013) 75–100.

D. T. Runia, 'Philo and the Gentiles,' in D. S. Sim and J. S. McLaren (eds.), *Attitudes to Gentiles in Ancient Judaism and Early Christianity* (London 2013) 28–45.

D. T. Runia, 'The Writings of Philo,' in L. H. Feldman, J. L. Kugel and L. H. Schiffman (eds.), *Outside the Bible: Ancient Jewish Writings Related to Scripture* (Lincoln, NE 2013) 11–17.

D. T. Runia, 'The Biblical Interpretations of Philo: On the Creation of the World,' in L. H. Feldman, J. L. Kugel and L. H. Schiffman (eds.), *Outside the Bible: Ancient Jewish Writings Related to Scripture* (Lincoln, NE 2013) 882–901.

D. T. Runia, K. Berthelot, E. Birnbaum, A. C. Geljon, H. M. Keizer, J. Leonhardt Balzer, J. P. Martín, M. R. Niehoff, S. J. K. Pearce and T. Seland, 'Philo of Alexandria: an Annotated Bibliography 2010,' *The Studia Philonica Annual* 24 (2013) 169–224.

D. T. Runia and G. E. Sterling (eds.), *The Studia Philonica Annual*, Vol. 25 (Atlanta 2013).

B. J. S. Ryu, *Knowledge of God in Philo of Alexandria with Special Reference to the Allegorical Commentary* (diss. Oxford 2013).

G. Schöllgen (ed.), *Reallexikon für Antike und Christentum*, Band 25 (Stuttgart 2013).

A. Lehnart, art. Mose I (literarisch), 58–102, esp. 74–75 (Moses); P. Mueller-Jourdan, art. Mystagogie, 404–422, esp. 414–415 (initiation); H. Crouzel and C. Mühlenkamp, art. Nachahmung Gottes, 525–565, esp. 538–541 (imitation of God); P. Terbuyken, art. Noe, 938–969, esp. 947–948 (Noah); K.-W. Niebuhr, art. Nomos, 978–1106, esp. 1025–1028 (Law). (DTR)

J. Schröter and J. K. Zangenberg (eds.), *Texte zur Umwelt des Neuen Testaments (3rd edition)* (Tübingen 2013).

D. R. Schwartz, 'Humbly Second-Rate in the Diaspora? Philo and Stephen on the Tabernacle and the Temple,' in R. S. Boustan, K. Herrmann, R. Leicht, A. Y. Reed and G. Veltri (eds.), *Envisioning Judaism: Studies in Honor of Peter Schäfer on the Occasion of his Seventieth Birthday* (Tübingen 2013) 81–89.

T. Seland, 'Philo and the New Testament,' in J. B. Green and L. M. McDonald (eds.), *The World of the New Testament: Cultural, Social, and Historical Contexts* (Grand Rapids 2013) 405–412.

P. M. Sherman, *Babels tower Translated. Genesis 11 and Ancient Jewish Interpretation*, Biblical interpretation series 117 (Leiden 2013).

G. E. Sterling, 'Philo's Ancient Readers: an Introduction,' *The Studia Philonica Annual* 25 (2013) 69–73.

G. E. Sterling, '"A Man of the Highest Repute": Did Josephus Know the Writings of Philo?,' *The Studia Philonica Annual* 25 (2013) 101–113.

G. E. Sterling, 'Philo Judaeus,' in R. Bagnall, K. Brodersen, C. B. Champion, A. Erskine and S. R. Huebner (eds.), *The Encyclopedia of Ancient History* (Malden, MA 2013) 9.5268–5270.

G. E. Sterling, 'Different Images or Emphases? The Image of God in Philo's *De opificio mundi*,' in G. A. Anderson, R. A. Clements and D. Satran (eds.), *New Approaches to the Study of Biblical Interpretation in Judaism of the Second Temple Period and in Early Christianity* [*Proceedings of the Eleventh International Symposium of the Orion Center for the Study of the Dead Sea Scrolls and Associated Literature 9–11 January, 2007*], Studies on the Texts of the Desert of Judah 106 (Leiden 2013) 41–56.

G. E. Sterling, 'Philosophical Treatises of Philo: *Hypothetica*,' in L. H. Feldman, J. L. Kugel and L. H. Schiffman (eds.), *Outside the Bible: Ancient Jewish Writings Related to Scripture* (Lincoln, NE 2013) 2501–2522.

G. J. Steyn, 'A Comparison of the Septuagint Textual Form in the Torah Quotations Common to Philo of Alexandria and the Gospels of Mark and Matthew,' in *XIV Congress of the IOSCS. Helsinki 2010*, Septuagint and Cognate Studies 59 (Atlanta 2013) 605–623.

G. J. Steyn, 'The Text Form of the Torah Quotations Common to the Corpus Philonicum and Paul's Corinthian Correspondence,' in S. Moise and

J. Verheyden (eds.), *The Scriptures of Israel in Jewish and Christian Tradition: Essays in Honour of Maarten J.J. Menken,* Supplements to Novum Testamentum 148 (Leiden 2013) 193–210.

G. J. Steyn, 'Torah Quotations Common to Philo of Alexandria and the Acts of the Apostles,' *Acta Theologica* 33 (2013) 164–181.

G. J. Steyn, 'Elements of the Universe in Philo's *De Vita Mosis*: Cosmological Theology or Theological Cosmology?,' *In die Skriflig/In Luce Verbi (South Africa)* 47 (2013) 9 pages.

H. Svebakken, *Philo of Alexandria's Exposition on the Tenth Commandment,* Studia Philonica Monographs 6 (Atlanta 2013).

N. L. Tilford, '"After the Ways of Women": the Aged Virgin in Philo's Transformation of the Philosophical Soul,' *The Studia Philonica Annual* 25 (2013) 17–39.

T. H. Tobin, S.J., 'The Importance of Hellenistic Judaism for the Study of Paul's Ethics,' in J. W. van Henten and J. Verheyden (eds.), *Early Christian Ethics in Interaction with Jewish and Greco-Roman Contexts,* Studies in Theology and Religion 17 (Leiden 2013).

A. Topchyan and G. Muradyan, 'The Biblical Interpretations of Philo: *Questions and Answers on Genesis and Exodus,*' in L. H. Feldman, J. L. Kugel and L. H. Schiffman (eds.), *Outside the Bible: Ancient Jewish Writings Related to Scripture* (Lincoln, NE 2013) 807–881.

L. Troiani, 'Filone di Alessandria nella *Storia Ecclesiastica* di Eusebio,' in O. Andrei (ed.), *Caesarea Maritima e la scuola orgieniana. Muticulturalità, forme di competizione culturale e identità cristiana,* Supplementi di Adamantius 3 (Brescia 2013) 211–215.

M. Vogel, 'Modelle jüdischer Identitätsbildung in hellenistisch-römischer Zeit,' in M. Öhler (ed.), *Religionsgemeinschaft und Identität. Prozesse jüdischer und christlicher Identitätsbildung im Rahmen der Antike,* Biblisch Theologische Studien 142 (Neukirchen-Vluyn 2013) 69–112.

W. T. Wilson, 'Philosophical Treatises of Philo: *On the Virtues* (51–174),' in L. H. Feldman, J. L. Kugel and L. H. Schiffman (eds.), *Outside the Bible: Ancient Jewish Writings Related to Scripture* (Lincoln, NE 2013) 2447–2480.

B. Wyss, 'Philon und die Pentas. Arithmologie als exegetische Methode,' in T. Georges, F. Allbrecht and R. Feldmeier (eds.), *Alexandria,* Civitatum Orbis Mediterranei Studia 1 (Tübingen 2013) 361–379.

B. Wyss, 'Philon und der Sophistendiskurs,' in M. Hirschberger (ed.), *Jüdisch-hellenistische Literatur in ihrem interkulturellen Kontext* (Frankfurt am Maim 2013) 89–105.

S. Yli-Karjanmaa, *Reincarnation in Philo of Alexandria* (diss. Åbo Akademi University 2013).

2014

E. Albano, *I silenzi delle sacre scritture: Limiti e possibilità di rivelazione del Logos negli scritti di Filone, Clemente e Origene*, Studia ephemeridis Augustinianum 138 (Rome 2014).

M. von Albrecht and R. Feldmeier (eds.), *The Divine Father: Religious and Philosophical Concepts of Divine Parenthood in Antiquity* (Leiden 2014).

M. Alesso, 'El concepto de dýnamis en la teología de Filón alejandrino y sus proyecciones en la Patrología,' in S. Filippi and M. Coria (eds.), *La identidad propia del pensamiento patrístico y medieval: ¿Unidad y pluralidad?* (Rosario 2014) 25–34.

F. Avemarie, 'Image of God and Image of Christ: Developments in Pauline and Ancient Jewish anthropology,' in J.-S. Rey (ed.), *The Dead Sea scrolls and Pauline literature*, Studies on the Texts of the Desert of Judah 102 (Leiden 2014) 209–235.

P. J. Bekken, 'Philo's Relevance for the Study of the New Testament,' in T. Seland (ed.), *Reading Philo: a Handbook to Philo of Alexandria* (Grand Rapids, MI 2014) 226–267.

P. J. Bekken, *The Lawsuit Motif in John's Gospel from New Perspectives. Jesus Christ, Crucified Criminal and Emperor of the World*, Supplements to Novum Testamentum 158 (Leiden 2014).

E. Birnbaum, 'Philo's Relevance for the Study of Judaism,' in T. Seland (ed.), *Reading Philo: a Handbook to Philo of Alexandria* (Grand Rapids MI 2014) 200–225.

E. Birnbaum, 'Philo at Yale,' *Adamantius* 20 (2014) 632–635.

E. Bons, R. Brucker, and J. Joosten, *The Reception of Septuagint Words in Jewish-Hellenistic and Christian Literature*, Wissenschaftliche Untersuchungen zum Neuen Testament 2.367 (Tübingen 2014).

P. Borgen, *The Gospel of John: More Light from Philo, Paul and Archaeology: The Scriptures, Tradition, Exposition, Settings, Meaning*, Novum Testamentum Supplements 154 (Leiden 2014).

P. Borgen, 'Philo—An Interpreter of the Laws of Moses,' in T. Seland (ed.), *Reading Philo: a Handbook to Philo of Alexandria* (Grand Rapids, MI 2014) 75–101.

F. E. Brenk, 'Philo and Plutarch on the Nature of God,' *The Studia Philonica Annual* 26 (2014) 79–92.

L. Brisson, 'Alexandrie, berceau du néoplatonisme. Eudore, Philon, Ammonios et l'école d'Alexandrie,' in C. Méla and F. Möri (eds.), *Alexandrie la divine* (Geneva 2014) 354–363.

J. Brumberg-Kraus, 'Contrasting Banquets: a Literary Commonplace in Philo's *On the Contemplative Life* and Other Greek and Roman Symposia,' in S. Marks and H. Taussig (eds.), *Meals in Early Judaism: Social Formation at the Table* (New York 2014) 139–162.

B. G. Bucur, 'Clement of Alexandria's Exegesis of Old Testament Theophanies,' *Phronema* 29 (2014) 61–79.

M. Cover, 'The Sun and the Chariot: the *Republic* and the *Phaedrus* as Sources for Rival Platonic Paradigms of Psychic Vision in Philo's Biblical Commentaries,' *The Studia Philonica Annual* 26 (2014) 151–167.

F. Damgaard, 'Philo's Life of Moses as "Rewritten Bible",' in J. Zsengellér (ed.), *Rewritten Bible after Fifty Years: Texts, Terms, or Techniques: A Last Dialogue with Geza Vermes*, Supplements to the Journal for the Study of Judaism 166 (Leiden 2014) 233–248.

J. Daniélou, *Philo of Alexandria*, Translated by James G. Colbert (Eugene, OR 2014).

J. Dillon, 'Pythagoreanism in the Academic Tradition: the Early Academy to Numenius,' in C. A. Huffmann (ed.), *A History of Pythagoreanism* (Cambridge 2014) 250–273, esp. 263–266.

R. Feldmeier, *Der Höchste: Studien zur hellenistischen Religionsgeschichte und zum biblischen Gottesglauben*, Wissenschaftliche Untersuchungen zum Neuen Testament 1.330 (Tübingen 2014).

S. D. Fraade, 'Between Rewritten Bible and Allegorical Commentary: Philo's Interpretation of the Burning Bush,' in J. Zsengellér (ed.), *Rewritten Bible after Fifty Years: Texts, Terms, or Techniques? A Last Dialogue with Geza Vermes*, Journal for the Study of Judaism 166 (Leiden 2014).

D. A. Giulea, *Pre-Nicene Christology in Paschal Contexts. The Case of the Divine Noetic Anthropos*, Supplements to Vigiliae Christianae 122 (Leiden 2014), esp. 56–60, 273–283.

M. Hadas-Lebel, *Une histoire du Messie* (Paris 2014), esp. 136–138.

G. Holtz, 'Von Alexandrien nach Jerusalem. Überlegungen zur Vermittlung philonisch-alexandrinischer Tradition an Paulus,' *Zeitschrift für die neutestamentliche Wissenschaft und die Kunde der älteren Kirche* 105 (2014) 228–263.

P. W. van der Horst, *Studies in Ancient Judaism and Early Christianity*, Ancient Judaism and Early Christianity 87 (Leiden 2014).

J. Joosten, 'Mixed blessings: the Biblical Notion of Blessings in the Works of Philo and Flavius Josephus,' in E. Bons, R. Brucker and J. Joosten (eds.), *The Reception of Septuagint Words in Jewish-Hellenistic and Christian Literature*, Wissenschaftliche Untersuchungen zum Neuen Testament. 2.367 (Tübingen 2014) 105–115.

M. Klinghardt, 'The Ritual Dynamics of Inspiration: the Therapeutae's Dance,' in S. Marks and H. Taussig (eds.), *Meals in Early Judaism: Social Formation at the Table* (New York 2014) 139–162.

E. KOSKENNIEMI, 'Philo and Classical Education,' in T. SELAND (ed.), *Reading Philo: a Handbook to Philo of Alexandria* (Grand Rapids, MI 2014) 102–128.

J. LEONHARDT-BALZER, 'Vorstellungen von der Gegenwart Gottes bei Philo von Alexandrien,' in B. JANOWSKI and E. E. POPKES (eds.), *Das Geheimnis der Gegenwart Gottes. Zur Schechina-Vorstellung in Judentum und Christentum,* Wissenschaftliche Untersuchungen zum Neuen Testament 1.318 (Tübingen 2014) 103–118.

D. LINCICUM, 'Philo's Library,' *The Studia Philonica Annual* 26 (2014) 99–114.

M. D. LITWA, 'The Deification of Moses in Philo of Alexandria,' *The Studia Philonica Annual* 26 (2014) 1–27.

M. D. LITWA, *Iesus Deus: The Early Christian Depiction of Jesus as a Mediterranean God* (Minneapolis 2014).

W. LOADER, 'Same-sex Relationships: a 1st-century Perspective,' *HTS Teologiese Studies / Theological Studies* 70 (2014) 9 pages.

S. D. MACKIE, 'The Passion of Eve and the Ecstasy of Hannah: Sense Perception, Passion, Mysticism, and Misogyny in Philo of Alexandria, *De ebrietate* 143–152,' *Journal of Biblical Literature* 133 (2014) 141–163.

M. McGLYNN, 'The Politeuma: Guardian of Civil Rights or Heavenly Commonwealth in Ptolemaic and Roman Egypt,' *Biblische Notizen* 161 (2014) 77–98.

A. B. McGOWAN, 'The Food of the Therapeutae: a Thick Description,' in S. MARKS and H. TAUSSIG (eds.), *Meals in Early Judaism: Social Formation at the Table* (New York 2014) 129–138.

A. K. MOORTHY, *A Seal of Faith: Rereading Paul on Circumcision, Torah, and the Gentiles* (diss. Columbia University 2014).

C. MORESCHINI, 'Further Considerations on the Philosophical Background of *Contra Eunomium* III,' in J. LEEMANS and M. CASSIN (eds.), *Gregory of Nyssa Contra Eunomium III: an English Translation with Commentary and Supporting Studies,* Supplements to Vigiliae Christianae 124 (Leiden 2014) 595–612, esp. 598–601.

M. R. NIEHOFF, 'Les juifs d'Alexandrie à l'école de la critique textuelle des païen,' in C. MÉLA and F. MÖRI (eds.), *Alexandrie la divine* (Geneva 2014) 733–740.

M. R. NIEHOFF, 'Philo of Alexandria (Section: Jewish Studies),' in *Oxford Bibliographies* (Oxford 2014)

P. NIETO HERNÁNDEZ, 'Philo and Greek Poetry,' *The Studia Philonica Annual* 26 (2014) 135–149.

F. OERTELT, *Herrscherideal und Herrschaftskritik bei Philo von Alexandria. Eine Untersuchung am Beispiel seiner Josephsdarstellung in De Josepho und De somniis II,* Studies in Philo of Alexandria (Leiden 2014).

A. PAUL, *Éros enchanté. Les chrétiens, la famille et le genre* (Paris 2014).

V. RABENS, *The Holy Spirit and Ethics in Paul: Transformation and Empowering for Religious-Ethical Life*, 2nd ed (Minneapolis 2014).

T. RAJAK, 'Philo's Knowledge of Hebrew: the Meaning of the Etymologies,' in J. K. AITKEN and J. CARLETON PAGET (eds.), *The Jewish-Greek Tradition in Antiquity and the Byzantine Empire* (Cambridge 2014) 173–187.

I. RAMELLI 'Philo's Doctrine of Apokatastasis: Philosophical Sources, Exegetical Strategies, and Patristic Aftermath,' *The Studia Philonica Annual* 26 (2014) 29–55.

M. J. REDDOCH, 'Cicero's *De Divinatione* and Philo of Alexandria's Criticism of Chaldean Astrology as a Form of Artificial Divination,' *Dionysius* 32 (2014) 54–70.

A. REINHARTZ, 'Philo's Exposition of the Law and Social History: Methodological Considerations,' in T. SELAND (ed.), *Reading Philo: a Handbook to Philo of Alexandria* (Grand Rapids, MI 2014) 180–199.

J. RIST, 'Il 'Logos' nella Tarda Antichità,' *Acta Philosophica: Pontificia Universita della Santa Croce* 23 (2014) 43–54.

J. M. ROGERS, 'The Philonic and the Pauline: Hagar and Sarah in the Exegesis of Didymus the Blind,' *The Studia Philonica Annual* 26 (2014) 57–77.

D. T. RUNIA, 'Philo in the Patristic Tradition: a List of Direct References,' in T. SELAND (ed.), *Reading Philo: a Handbook to Philo of Alexandria* (Grand Rapids, MI 2014) 268–286.

D. T. RUNIA, K. BERTHELOT, E. BIRNBAUM, A. C. GELJON, H. M. KEIZER, J. LEONHARDT BALZER, J. P. MARTÍN, M. R. NIEHOFF, S. J. K. PEARCE, T. SELAND and S. WEISSER, 'Philo of Alexandria: an Annotated Bibliography 2014,' *The Studia Philonica Annual* 25 (2014) 169–216.

D. T. RUNIA and G. E. STERLING (eds.), *The Studia Philonica Annual*, Vol. 26 (Atlanta 2014).

M. L. SAMUEL, *Torah from Alexandria: Philo as a Biblical Commentator. Volume 1 Genesis* (New York 2014).

M. L. SAMUEL, *Torah from Alexandria: Philo as a Biblical Commentator. Volume 2 Exodus* (New York 2014).

K.-G. SANDELIN, 'Philo as a Jew,' in T. SELAND (ed.), *Reading Philo: a Handbook to Philo of Alexandria* (Grand Rapids, MI 2014) 19–46.

L. SAUDELLI, 'Loi de Moïse et philosophies grecque: le judaïsme Alexandrie,' in C. MÉLA and F. MÖRI (eds.), *Alexandrie la divine* (Geneva 2014) 726–731.

F. SCHMIDT, 'The Plain and Laughter: the Hermeneutical Function of the Sign in Philo of Alexandria,' in J. K. AITKEN and J. CARLETON PAGET (eds.), *The Jewish-Greek Tradition in Antiquity and the Byzantine Empire* (Cambridge 2014) 188–199.

G. Schöllgen (ed.), *Reallexikon für Antike und Christentum*, Lieferungen 203–205 (Stuttgart 2014).

R. J. Daly, Art. Opfer, 143–206, esp. 169–170 (sacrifice); C. Neuber, Art. Orakel, 206–350, esp. 312–313 (oracle); A. Fürst, Art. Origenes, 460–567, esp. 490–491 (Origen). (DTR)

T. Seland (ed.), *Reading Philo: a Handbook to Philo of Alexandria* (Grand Rapids, MI 2014).

T. Seland, 'Philo as a Citizen: Homo Politicus,' in T. Seland (ed.), *Reading Philo: a Handbook to Philo of Alexandria* (Grand Rapids, MI 2014) 47–74.

T. Seland, 'Why Study Philo? How?,' in T. Seland (ed.), *Reading Philo: a Handbook to Philo of Alexandria* (Grand Rapids, MI 2014) 157–179.

M. Sheridan, '"God is not as Man" (Num 23:19): the Theological Critique of the Scripture by Early Christian Writers,' American Benedictine Review 65 (2014) 242–256.

F. Siegert, 'Die theoretischen Bewaltigung des Bösen bei Philon,' in F. Jourdan and R. Hirsch-Luipold (eds.), *Die Würzel allen Übels: Vorstellungen über die Herkunft des Bösen und Schlechten in der Philosophie des 1.–4. Jahrhunderts*, Studien und Texte zu Antike und Christentum 91 (Tübingen 2014) 69–86.

G. E. Sterling, 'Philo's Hellenistic and Hellenistic-Jewish Sources,' *The Studia Philonica Annual* 26 (2014) 93–97.

G. E. Sterling, 'From the Thick Marshes of the Nile to the Throne of God: Moses in Ezekiel the Tragedian and Philo of Alexandria,' *The Studia Philonica Annual* 26 (2014) 115–133.

G. E. Sterling, '"The Jewish Philosophy": Reading Moses via Hellenistic Philosophy according to Philo,' in T. Seland (ed.), *Reading Philo: a Handbook to Philo of Alexandria* (Grand Rapids, MI 2014) 129–154.

G. E. Sterling, 'The People of the Covenant or the People of God: Exodus in Philo of Alexandria,' in T. B. Dozeman, C. A. Evans and J. N. Lohr (eds.), *The Book of Exodus: Composition, Reception, and Interpretation*, Vetus Testamentum Supplements 164 (Leiden 2014) 404–439.

G. J. Steyn, 'Some Observations on Philo of Alexandria's Sensitivity to Strangers,' in J. Kok, T. Nicklas, D. T. Roth and C. M. Hays (eds.), *Sensitivity to Outsiders. Exploring the Dynamic Relationship Between Mission and Ethics in the New Testament and Early Christianity*, Wissenschaftliche Untersuchungen zum Neuen Testament. 2.364 (Tübingen 2014) 59–78.

H. Taussig, 'The Pivotal Place of the Therapeutae in Understanding the Meals of Early Judaism,' in S. Marks and H. Taussig (eds.), *Meals in Early Judaism: Social Formation at the Table* (New York 2014) 117–128.

S. Torallas Tovar, 'Philo of Alexandria's Dream Classification,' *Archiv für Religionsgeschichte* 15 (2014) 67–82.

2015

S. A. Adams and S. M. Ehorn (eds.), *Composite Citations in Antiquity: Jewish, Graeco-Roman, and Early Christian Uses*, Library of New Testament Studies (London 2015).

R. Bloch, 'Philo and Jeremiah in Egypt,' in H. Najman and K. Schmid (eds.), *Jeremiah's Scriptures* (Leiden 2015).

R. Bloch, 'Leaving Home: Philo of Alexandria on the Exodus,' in T. E. Levy, T. Schneider and W. H. C. Propp (eds.), *Israel's Exodus in Transdisciplinary Perspective – Text, Archaeology, Culture, and Geoscience* (Cham 2015) 357–364.

C. J. P. Friesen, 'Hannah's 'Hard Day' and Hesiod's 'Two Roads': Poetic Wisdom in Philo's *De ebrietate*,' *Journal for the Study of Judaism* 45 (2015) 44–64.

C. J. P. Friesen, *Reading Dionysus: Euripides' Bacchae and the Cultural Contestations of Greeks, Jews, Romans, and Christians*, Studies and Texts in Antiquity and Judaism 95 (Tübingen 2015), esp. chapters 6 and 13.

K. Gibbons, 'Moses, Stateman and Philosopher: the Philosophical Background of the Ideal of Assimilating to God and the Methodology of Clement of Alexandria's *Stromateis* 1,' *Vigiliae Christianae* 69 (2015) 157–185.

O. Kaiser, *Philo von Alexandrien: Denkender Glaube—eine Einführung*, Forschungen zur Religion und Literatur des Alten und Neuen Testaments 259 (Göttingen 2015).

K. Metzler, *Prokop von Gaza Eclogarum in libros historicos Veteris Testamenti epitome. Teil 1: Der Genesiskommentar*, Die griechischen christlichen Schriftsteller der ersten Jahrhunderte NF 22 (Berlin 2015).

M. R. Niehoff (ed.), *Philo of Alexandria Writings. Vol. IV Part Two: Allegorical exegesis and Philosophical Treatises* (Jerusalem 2015).

C. S. O'Brien, *The Demiurge in Ancient Thought: Secondary Gods and Divine Mediators* (Cambridge 2015).

D. T. Runia, 'Cosmos, Logos, and Nomos: the Alexandrian Jewish and Christian Appropriation of the Genesis Creation Account,' in P. Derron (ed.), *Cosmologies et cosmogonies dans la littérature antique* (Vandœuvres-Geneva 2015) 179–209.

M. L. Samuel, *Torah from Alexandria: Philo as a Biblical Commentator. Volume 3 Leviticus* (New York 2015).

BOOK REVIEW SECTION

Y. Amir and M. R. Niehoff, פילון האלכסנדרוני. כתבים. כרך חמישי. ירושלים.
הוצאת ביאליק והאקדמיה הלאומית הישראלית למדעים [*Philo of Alexandria: Writings.
Part V: Allegorical Exegesis on Genesis 12–41*]. Jerusalem: Bialik Institute
and Israel Academy of Sciences and Humanities, 2012. ISBN 978-965-
342-928-4. 416 pages. Price NIS 136 ($35). (hb)

This is the first part of the fifth volume of the five volume series which will
provide the first complete translation of Philo's works in modern Hebrew.
The translation covers Philo's allegorical interpretations of Gen 12–41 and
contains *On the Migration of Abraham*; *Who is the Heir of Divine Things*; *On
Mating with the Preliminary Studies*; *On Flight and Finding*; *On the Change of
Names*; as well as the surviving two books from *On Dreams*.

In addition to the translations, introductions, and notes written by
Yehoshua Amir, Chava Schur, and Yochanan Cohen-Yashar, the book contains a short foreword by Cohen-Yashar, in memory of Yehoshua Amir and
Suzanne Daniel-Nataf in which he describes the intellectual and geographical journey of these scholars, as well as their important contribution to the
study of Philo in Israel.[1] Although Amir passed away more than a decade
ago, many of the translations presented in this volume are his handiwork,
his typewritten translations and manuscript notes having been reviewed by
Maren Niehoff. In addition, the book contains a list of Philo's works in
Latin and Hebrew, as well as six appendices to *On Dreams,* written by
Cohen-Yashar.

Every modern translation of an ancient work should not only be
evaluated on the basis of its scientific quality *per se*, but also on the basis of
the function it fulfills. In these two respects, the present volume deserves
much praise.

I will start with the second aspect. As it is well known, the study of
Philo belongs to many disciplines: Ancient History, Classics, Ancient

---

[1] On the history of the study of Philo in Israeli universities see Maren Niehoff,
"Does the Israeli Academia need Hellenistic Judaism? [in Hebrew]," *Zmanim* 117 (2012),
52–57.

Philosophy, New Testament, Patristics, Gnosticism and of course, Judaism.[2] In all these fields, Philo's historical, exegetical and philosophical works have an incontestable value and therefore they should be made easily accessible to any scholar and student working in these disciplines. In a country in which the study and the teaching of Judaism, in all its aspects and in all its periods, has such a prime importance, it is crucial to offer the Hebrew readership easy access to Philo's complete corpus.

After a twelve year break since the last published volume and the present one,[3] and thanks to the sustained effort of Maren Niehoff, who has taken the leadership of the project, the series is approaching completion. Vol. 4, part 2 has just been published (2015), and thereby the important lacuna in the study of Philo in Israel is about to be filled soon.[4]

In the general introduction of the series, Suzanne Daniel-Nataf explains the pedagogical principle that has guided the arrangement of Philo's works in the present series, which proposes a "gradual immersion" into Philo's thought and method, from the more accessible historical treatises, to the more complex allegorical ones.[5] The present translation will thus make Philo's allegorical interpretations accessible to many students and impact them at an early stage of their career. Indeed, despite their great interest in the subject, many students of the Israeli universities have been discouraged by the somewhat outdated English translations of the Loeb Classical Library.[6] In making Philo's exegetical enterprise accessible to scholars, students, and non-specialists alike, the volume helps to reclaim Philo's place in the study of Jewish thought in Israel and to introduce the Israeli readership with an often neglected facet of its cultural heritage.

The excellent scientific quality of the work should also be stressed. Philo's elaborate and expressive prose is not always easy to translate. His allegorical interpretations unfold through long sentences, expressed in a rich philosophical and technical vocabulary, and resort to many rhetorical

---

[2] See David Runia, "Why Philo of Alexandria is an Important Writer and Thinker" in S. Inowlocki and B. Decharneux (eds.) *Philon D'Alexandrie: Un penseur à l'intersection des cultures gréco-romaine, orientale, juive et chrétienne* (Turnhout: Brepols, 2011), 13–33.

[3] S. Daniel-Nataf (ed.), *Philo of Alexandria. Writings*, vol. 3. *The Exposition of the Law* (Jerusalem: Bialik Institute and Israel Academy of Sciences and Humanities, 2000).

[4] The remaining works to be published are the philosophical treatises *On Providence I* and *II* and *Alexander* as well as the *Questions and Answers* (the planned volume 5, part 2).

[5] S. Daniel-Nataf and Y. Amir (eds.), *Philo of Alexandria. Writings*, Vol. 1: *Historical Writings* (Jerusalem: Bialik Institute and Israel Academy of Sciences and Humanities, 1986), 22–24.

[6] The Philo of Alexandria's Commentary Series, published by Brill and edited by G. Sterling and D. T. Runia, is gradually replacing the translations of Colson, Whitaker and Marcus of the Loeb Classical Library.

devices. The translations capture faithfully the Greek original, while making it intelligible and easily readable. Furthermore, the division of the text into chapters makes the intricate structure of Philo' exegesis more accessible.

The translation is accompanied by numerous footnotes, often of a philological nature or referring to parallel passages in other Philonic works. As the series addresses a Hebrew readership more familiar with the Masoretic text of the Torah, the notes systematically guide the reader into the retroversion of the Greek Pentateuch. One could perhaps question the use of Greek alphabet in the notes, in keeping with the procedure adopted in the previous volumes, as the non-specialist or beginner readers would have benefitted more from the use of Latin transcriptions. One could also regret the few references to modern studies on Philo, or the regular absence of precise reference to Greek sources. For instance, a reference to Plato's *Cratylus* 400c (or *Gorgias* 493a; *Phaedrus* 250 c) in *Migr.* 16, would have helped the reader to understand the platonic background of the motive of the body as a sepulcher.

With the exception of the introduction to *On dreams*, in which Cohen-Yashar notes the parallels between Philo and Rabbinical Judaism as well as the influence of Greek thought and culture, the introductions are succinct and present the reader with the general framework and content of the work.

A last concern touches upon the lack of consistency in the translations of philosophical terms into Hebrew—a remark which is unfortunately applicable to many modern translations of Philo. Although this lack of consistency is evidently more understandable when happening between different translators, it is not restricted to these cases only. Thus, for instance, *pathos* and the plural *pathē* (emotion or passion) are sometimes translated by ריגוש (*Mut.* 261), at other times by היפעלויות (*Migr.* 143), רגשות (*Somn.* 2.255), or יצר (*Congr.* 31). *Eupatheia* appears most of the time as ריגוש טוב (*Migr.* 120; *Congr.* 36) but is also translated by הנאה (*Congr.* 174). I doubt whether the reader of the exposition on the human intellect (*nous*) in *Somn.* 1.25–40, translated there as שכל, will understand that it is to the same concept that Philo refers in other places, where it is translated as תבונה (*Migr.* 77). Concerning the same passage of *Somn.* 1.25–40, I would question Cohen-Yashar's affirmation, in the second appendix, that when Philo argues that the voice originates from the *dianoia* (translated here as בינה; *Somn.* 1.28), he undoubtedly recalls Aristotle's words in the *De anima* 420b6. It seems to me that it reflects a Stoic tenet, formulated by Diogenes of Babylon (Galen, *PHP* 2.5.9–13 and 15–20). I would moreover question the translation of *dianoia* as תודעה which, in *Migr.* 3, falsely gives the impression that Philo upheld a concept of "irrational conscience." More problematic in my view is the translation of the term *logismos* by רוח (*Fug*. 92), יסוד תבוני (*Fug*. 72), יכולת להגות (*Fug*. 121) or כושר שכלי (*Somn*. 1.122). More consistency in the philosophical vocabulary used by Philo, complemented by precise reference to the Greek and Latin corpus of philosophical texts, would certainly have helped to highlight the philosophical anchorage of Philo's exegesis.

Of course, these are points of detail, which are inevitable in light of the scale of the task. These remarks do not diminish the significance and quality of this work. The meticulous and careful labor of all the scholars involved in this project should be commended. We should be most thankful to the translators and editors for the opportunity to read, and to be insightfully guided into, an elegant and accurate translation of Philo's works.

Sharon Weisser
Tel Aviv, Israel

FRANCESCA CALABI, *Filone di Alessandria*. Pensatori 32. Carrocci editore: Roma, 2013. 203 pages. ISBN 978 88 430 6796 1. Price €19.

Calabi's book is a monograph that throws light on the figure and in particular on the thought of Philo of Alexandria. The author first looks at Philo's position in the cultural cross-roads of Alexandria, with its many cultural, Jewish, Greek, and Roman influences. She then focuses her attention on the exegetical character of Philo's writings, affirming that exegesis and philosophy coincide, because his exegetical work is so constitutive of his thought that theory and interpretation are hard to separate (p. 26). For Philo, the inspired Mosaic books cover the whole structure of reality, describe the law that governs the cosmos and human conduct, and need to be interpreted both literally and allegorically because they reveal hidden ethical, noetic, and ontological truths to the intelligent reader. In the second chapter, the author shows how Philo applies his two-level reading both to Moses' account on origins (Gen 1–9), in which the biblical narrative shows a superficial resemblance to the Greek mythological tales, and to the story of Joseph (in *De Iosepho*) and to the life of Moses (*De vita Moysis*), which do not display these mythical aspects. However, Philo pursues divergent exegetical strategies: in interpreting Gen. 1-9 he tends to cut down on literal analysis and expand on allegorical meanings. Whereas in *De Iosepho* he follows a more balanced double approach, while in *De vita Mosis* he devotes the first book to biographical narrative and the second to a philosophical-moral explanation of the preceding exposition.

Chapters three and four deal with complex theological and cosmo-logical issues. For Calabi, Philo sees the creation not as *creatio ex nihilo*, but as a passage from formless matter to an ordered cosmos. It is a *creatio simul-tanea*, inasmuch as the intelligible world—the model existing in the divine mind and corresponding to the first day of the Genesis account—and the sensible world are realized at the same time (*Opif.* 13). The divine act cannot be described as *creatio aeterna* or *temporalis*, but rather as *creatio con-tinua* and therefore the cosmos, although generated, will not be destroyed, because the Creator watches over his work with vigilant and benevolent providence so as to save it from dissolution. The author dedicates a number of densely packed pages to Philo's understanding of God, emphasizing that Philo combines an image of God that remains close to the biblical text with the necessity of thinking God in more rigorous philosophical terms such as unknowable, incomprehensible, ineffable, immutable, totally transcendent and so on (pp. 73–84). The introduction of the powers serves to bridge this gap: Calabi does not situate the logos and the powers in the context of Middle Platonist philosophical categories as an ontologically subordingate level of the divine (cf. Eudorus, Alcinous and Numenius of Apamea). Rather she states that *a parte dei* they are modes of God's being, names through which he manifests himself and acts, and that *a parte hominis* they are different levels of knowledge of God, so that man is able progressively to understand partial aspects of God, grasp his being in his action, but not fathom his mysterious essence. In line with Middle Platonist demonology, which develops the intermediary notion of the *daimôn* found in *Symposium* 202, Philo accepts the existence of souls, *daimones*, angels, invisible beings who dwell in the air, who play a mediating role and who bear different names according to their functions. Some of these souls may also enter bo-dies, whereas others dedicate themselves only to God and are called angels.

Chapter five discusses the relation between the active and the con-templative life. For Philo, human beings must become like God to find the good life and divine action in the week of creation, culminating in the Sabbath rest, serves as a model for human activity by exemplifying the need to alternate theoretical activities and practical life. Moses pre-eminently typifies how contemplation and action constantly interpenetrate, but Philo also cites the examples of the mainly contemplative Therapeutae and the more active Essenes. Taking up a conceptual thread that leads from Plato to Seneca and also to Plutarch and to the authors of the Pseudo-Pythagorean treatises on kingship, Philo regards God's kingship as arche-typical: the foundation of every power resides in the divine will and because God is the guarantor of order and justice, the king, by analogy, must respect the law and indeed embody the law as a model of virtue for his subjects. Moses embodies perfect kingship, but Abraham too can be defined as a king, because he is perfectly free and wise. As Calabi rightly points out in chapter six, there are two types of kingship in Philo, one of Platonic, Pythagorean and biblical origin, the other of Stoic extraction according to which only the wise man is king. In chapter seven, the author links the two triads of patriarchs (Enos, Enoch, Noah and Abraham, Isaac, Jacob) to the different levels of moral perfection achievable by human beings and carefully examines the complex system of etymologies proposed by Philo, the richness of his exegetical levels, and the network of his philosophical influences. She also discusses important issues such as the theme of death and immortality, the relation between encyclical studies and wisdom and between the passions and the hierarchy of virtues. The volume concludes with an overview of Philo's reception in the pagan Platonic tradition, Patristic authors, and Judaism, a catalogue of Philonic works divided per genre, and a bibliography listed per chapter.

Due to its mainly descriptive character, Calabi's book forms a good introduction to the most important themes of Philo of Alexandria's thought and is eminently useful for non-specialists. The important points of the exposition also allow such readers to grasp, in essential outlines, the substance of the scholarly debate both past and present, and in fact it would have been difficult to accommodate a more penetrating approach within the volume's scope and character. What is perhaps lacking is a more in-depth evaluation of the historical, religious, and cultural position of Philo in the Alexandrian diaspora, one that evaluates the type of Judaism which he represents within the variegated picture of Middle Judaism, specifying the methods and goal of his appropriation of Greek culture and examining the relations with the Roman world. Such an evaluation would make it possible to bury the persistent idea that Philo was a singular and isolated phenomenon.

Cristina Termini
Pontificia Università Lateranense
Rome, Italy
(translated by Anthony P. Runia)

Torrey Seland, ed. *Reading Philo: A Handbook to Philo of Alexandria.* Grand Rapids: William B. Eerdmans, 2014. xvi + 345 pages. ISBN 978-0-8028-7069-8. Price $45.

This book now joins the ranks of general introductions to Philo by E. R. Goodenough, Samuel Sandmel, Jean Daniélou, and more recently by Peder

Borgen, Kenneth Schenck, and Adam Kamesar. The project was born in Scandinavia with four of the key authors in the volume, and then branched out to include well-known Philo researchers from other parts of the globe. The result is perhaps the best contemporary introduction to Philo for individuals with an introductory knowledge of the first century Mediterranean world.

"The intended readership is M.A. and Ph.D. students who are just embarking on a study of Philo" (p. 3). The book hits this target extremely well. It is more advanced than Kenneth Schenck's *Brief Guide to Philo* and yet not as demanding as the *Cambridge Companion to Philo* edited by Adam Kamesar. One of the most distinctive features of the book is its clarity. While the book may become more demanding in one or two places, the ability of this team of advanced scholars to present the salient points of Philo's *oeuvre* in a clear, concise, yet comprehensive way is truly impressive. In keeping with its target audience, most of the chapters helpfully suggest possible avenues for future research. Readers thus not only get a sense of where scholarly discussion stands currently, but also where they themselves might take it going forward. This feature of the book, perhaps more than any other, makes it commendable to the student contemplating scholarly engagement with Philo as a career.

The book is divided into two parts. After an Introduction by Torrey Seland, the first five chapters survey Philo in his overlapping identities: Philo the Jew, Philo the citizen, Philo the exegete, Philo and classical education, and Philo the philosopher. The remaining five chapters examine Philo from the perspective of contemporary disciplines of study. Seland once again leads off this second half with the basic question of how and why to study Philo in general. Then follow chapters on Philo and social history, Philo and Judaism, Philo and the New Testament, and finally Philo in relation to the patristic tradition.

Seland's Introduction to the entire book does exactly what is expected of an introduction. He gives us a brief sense of who Philo was as a person and where he stood against the backdrop of his world. Then Karl-Gustav Sandelin expands on "Philo as a Jew" in the first context chapter. (As an aside, the idea for the book grew out of a larger project initiated by Sandelin and then modified by Seland.) Sandelin considers Philo in relation to topics like circumcision, Sabbath observance, dietary laws, sexuality, and the biblical canon. He leans toward Philo being a law-observant Jew and rightly emphasizes the fact that Philo accepted the literal interpretation of passages in addition to the allegorical. A brief comparison of Philo with Essenes, Pharisees, and Sadducees is included. One point where I would question Sandelin's presentation is where he follows Burton Mack in associating wisdom with a higher realm than the Logos. It seems to me that Mack here (and Sandelin) are systematizing imagery from different parts of Philo that should not be combined.

Seland himself then writes the second chapter on Philo's context: "Philo as a Citizen: *Homo politicus*." All of Seland's chapters in the book are written with great clarity. He is judicious in presenting the spectrum of positions on the state of Jews in Alexandria at the time of Philo. He also gives us a brief taste of Philo's political theory and the treatises you would want to study to go further into the subject. One conspicuous aspect of the chapter is the way E. R. Goodenough dominates it. Some more recent sources are mentioned at the end, but Seland does not engage them greatly.

Peder Borgen writes the third context chapter: "Philo—An Interpreter of the Laws of Moses." This chapter focuses primarily on the exegetical techniques, forms, and hermeneutical assumptions Philo uses and displays in his expository treatises (as opposed to his historical or apologetic treatises). Borgen also compares Philo briefly to other interpreters in his context. In my opinion, Borgen has a tendency to present details in a way that may require some effort for someone trying to grasp the larger picture, such as someone just beginning to study Philo. In that respect, this chapter may be a little more difficult for the uninitiated. It is, nonetheless, a helpful collection of exegetical "tastes" from Philo, and the beginning student can be easily guided through it.

The chapter by Erkki Koskenniemi on "Philo and Classical Education" was a great surprise and very well written. The person who might only be acquainted with H. I. Marrou's 1948 classic will be delighted to come up to speed with the debates that have transpired in recent years. Easy assumptions about both the form and content of Hellenistic education are questioned and problematized, including what took place in the Hellenistic *gymnasion* and the extent of Philo's involvement with the one in Alexandria. This is a chapter full of potential for students currently looking for an area of Philo to explore at the graduate level.

Then Gregory Sterling ends the first half of the book with a chapter entitled, "'The Jewish Philosophy': Reading Moses via Hellenistic Philosophy according to Philo." Sterling does not disappoint with another chapter that is written with great clarity while covering all the essential features of Philo in relation to Hellenistic philosophy. While Philo was primarily an exegete of Scripture, he read Scripture through Plato and an eclectic collection of philosophical lenses. More importantly, Philo was well acquainted with the writings and teachings of the philosophy of his day. Sterling systematically and skillfully discusses Philo's antecedents in Alexandria, as well as the various philosophical schools with which he engaged.

The second half of the book then launches with another clear and extremely useful chapter by Seland himself. He not only presents the basic "why" to study Philo but in a short space, he brings the modern researcher of Philo into the twenty-first century. We get an introduction to key books to begin the study of Philo, and we are introduced to electronic resources and sources available on the web. In the tradition of Goodenough, he suggests a helpful order in which to read through Philo's works.

Then begin the chapters that engage Philo from a disciplinary standpoint. The first by Adele Reinhartz is another well-written surprise titled, "Philo's *Exposition of the Law* and Social History: Methodological Considerations." Along with Koskenniemi, this chapter may be the most generative for students of Philo looking for a potential area of research in which to specialize. While various elements of social history have been explored in an *ad hoc* way—Philo's thought in relation to topics like the family or social groupings in Alexandria—what is distinctive about Reinhartz's chapter is the way that she sets out a cogent *method* for such investigations. She ends the chapter with some generative examples relating to infanticide among Jews and the difficulties faced by orphaned daughters in relation to inheritance.

Ellen Birnbaum writes the chapter on "Philo's Relevance for the Study of Jews and Judaism in Antiquity," while Per Jarle Bekken covers "Philo's Relevance for the Study of the New Testament." Birnbaum ably addresses what we might learn from Philo about Jewish practices, beliefs, and community institutions, as well as Philo's own specific interactions and attitudes with both Jews and non-Jews. Just as in other chapters, she does an excellent job of suggesting fruitful avenues of future investigation, such as how Philo might further illuminate the nature of ancient Jewish communal institutions.

My reaction to Bekken's chapter is more mixed. On the one hand, numerous potential insights are scattered throughout this longest of chapters in the book. One finds a host of specific textual comparisons not only between Philo and the New Testament, but also with rabbinic literature. Some of these are potentially generative, such as his comparison between Philo and Paul on "proselytes" and Gentile believers. In many other cases, however, the parallels seem much less substantial, perhaps even superficial. The overly detailed nature of the comparisons perhaps makes this chapter less introductory and more a collection of potential articles. Still more glaring is the omission of key areas of comparison such as Hebrews, which is barely mentioned in the chapter. The potential relevance of Philo for the development of New Testament Christology is entirely omitted.

In the final chapter, David Runia catalogs the explicit mentions of Philo in Christian literature up to 1000 CE. Since he has written extensively elsewhere on the subject, Runia's introductory remarks are rather brief. Nevertheless, he makes clear the significant impact that Philo had on the Christians of the first few centuries, as well as the fact that we would not have Philo's works today if Christians had not preserved them.

On the whole, we must consider this handbook by Seland and the other contributors a great success. It is clearly written, covers the spectrum of Philonic topics well, and extensively introduces the reader to a wide range of Philo scholars. This will surely become a standard text for graduate seminars on Philo for years to come.

Kenneth Schenck
Indiana Wesleyan University
Marion, Indiana

LUCIA SAUDELLI, *Eraclito ad Alessandria. Studi e ricerche intorno alla testimonianza di Filone.* Monothéismes et Philosophie. Turnhout: Brepols, 2012. 488 pages. ISBN 978-2-503-54339-0. Price €90.

This monograph is the commercial edition of the doctoral dissertation completed in 2008 at the Sorbonne in Paris under the supervision of Professor Carlos Lévy. Its aim is to investigate Philo's use of the book and the thought of the early Ionian philosopher Heraclitus and what it can teach us about the tradition of its interpretation and ultimately about the philosopher himself. It is the first book-length study devoted to Philo's evidence on an author earlier than Plato. Heraclitus is an excellent choice, since it emerges from the results of the research that he is utilized by Philo more than any other early Greek philosopher writing prior to the dramatic turn in Greek philosophy brought about by the Athenian philosophers Socrates and Plato.

The study is very properly conscious of its method, which proceeds in three stages. First the Philonic evidence is examined. The various quotations and allusions are clustered in five main themes: the first three, under the heading 'Nature,' are Nature which hides itself, the Unity of contraries, and the Cosmic god; the final two, under the heading 'the Soul,' are the Cycle of the soul and the Cycle of human existence. In her analysis the author undertakes to separate quotations from allusions, to isolate elements of Heraclitus' doctrine from the interpretation they are given in the context of Philo's own beliefs and the specific nature of his writings, and to separate out the information on Heraclitus from the Philonic context of argumentation. Next she examines all the passages in other authors which cite or refer to the same Heraclitan fragments. Thirdly she draws together her results on each theme and determines what they might tell us about Heraclitus' thought. Before the final summary of the results of the project there is also an Appendix in which Philo's references to other Presocratic authors are briefly outlined. The main other author here is Empedocles but he is utilized much less than Heraclitus.

It emerges from Saudelli's research that Philo occupies a crucial place in the extant record of the reception of Heraclitus' book. In the case of many fragments he is the first witness and his evidence is taken as demonstrating a break between the earlier reception in the classical and Hellenistic periods and the subsequent reception in later antiquity. She argues that Heraclitus' thought was rediscovered in 1st century BCE Alexandria and there may be a connection with an increase in doxographical activity at this time in the same city. Philo himself may have had direct access to Heraclitus' book. An important result of the research is the identification of a considerable number of Philonic texts which contain clear allusions to Heraclitan pronouncements, but have not been included in the collections of fragments of Marcovich and Mouraviev (see the list on p. 362 n. 3).

The decisive turn in the reception of Heraclitus is brought about by the rise of Middle Platonism in this and the following two centuries, which exerted a strong influence on the way the philosopher's thought was under-stood and utilized. This Platonizing interpretation, though strongly present in the Philonic evidence, should not be identified with his own appropria-tion, which has many particular Hellenistic-Jewish aspects. Far from being uniform and coherent, it is in fact "unfaithful and opportunistic" (p. 365), not only coloured by apologetic themes (Heraclitus stealing from Moses, cf. *QG* 3.5, *Her.* 214) but also combined with motifs based on Stoic and other school doctrines.

Examples of specifically Philonic interpretations of Heraclitus' doctrines abound. Remarkably he is the first witness to the seminal pronouncement that nature loves to keep itself concealed (φύσις κρύπτεσθαι φιλεῖ, fr. 123 DK). Philo broadens the intent of the saying so that it refers not only to the nature and truth of every thing, but also to God and crucially to the revelation of divine truth in scripture, which must be accessed through the allegorical method. Another fine example is Heraclitus' doctrine of the unity of contraries. Saudelli claims that Philo is the only explicit witness to this key doctrine. For Philo it can be linked to the divine activity in creation and especially the process of division initiated in Gen 1:3. But Philo resists the link to the Heraclitan logos (which also engages in division, fr. 1) because he recognizes that its operation is confined to the human sphere and is not compatible with biblical creationism. Similarly the role of division is recognized in the interpretation of the holocaust (esp. *Spec.* 1.208), but Philo, here reading Heraclitus through a Stoic lens, polemicizes against the failure to recognize divine transcendence. Whereas for Heraclitus the one *is* all (ἕν τὸ πᾶν, *Leg.* 3.7), for Philo God is one (masculine) *and* all (εἷς καὶ τὸ πᾶν, *Leg.* 1.44). It is plausibly argued that this is a deliberate variation on the Heraclitan formula. In the numerous allusions to Heraclitus' views on the soul Philo cannot accept his naturalism (the death of the soul) but reinterprets it in terms of the soul as πνεῦμα (Gen 2:7) and the Middle Platonist doctrine of the soul's immortality, as for example in the interpretation of Jacob's ladder in *Somn.* 1.153–156. Following the research of J. Mansfeld and D. Zeller, Saudelli recognizes the passage at *Leg.* 1.105–108 on the soul's death as a cento incorporating themes of diverse provenance, but she rightly notes that Philo prioritizes Heraclitus' pronouncement (fr. 62), not only citing his words in a slightly adapted form also found in the Neoplatonist author Hierocles, but also making an allusion to the saying on corpses in fr. 96. Philo means us to understand that there is a special affinity in some cases between Heraclitus and the biblical record, but that it always needs to be seen in the right perspective.

These are just some examples of the many Heraclitan themes which Philo refers to and adapts for his own purposes. Saudelli has collected the texts and woven them into a rich tapestry of analysis and interpretation. Where her study is most ambitious is in the thesis that Philo's evidence not only provides valuable material for reconstructing the tradition and transmission of Heraclitus' sayings, but also allows a fresh examination of problems related to the interpretation of particular fragments and to his general conception of the universe and the place of the human being within it. It is to be recognized that she has done all she possibly could to separate out the various layers of interpretation that have been laid over the original words of the philosopher. I am less optimistic, however, about Philo's ability to help us penetrate through to the original intentions and central thrust of Heraclitus' philosophy. To my mind the earlier Presocratics will always remain opaque and open to multiple interpretations, not only because of the fragmentary nature of the evidence, but also because they were writing at a stage when philosophical concepts and tools were still being developed and had not reached the precision that would be attained in later times. For this reason it was inevitable that a tradition of interpretation would develop, which must necessarily cast a veil over the original text.

The author and the supervisor of her doctoral studies are to be warmly congratulated on the high quality of the research that forms the basis of this monograph. Saudelli has mastered the complexities of the Philonic corpus and also the many twists and turns of the interpretation of Heraclitus in the philosophical tradition. As the extensive bibliography shows, she has taken into account all the relevant primary and secondary literature. The book is highly recommended reading for all scholars who wish to increase their knowledge of Philo's use and adaptation of the tradition of ancient philosophy. Unfortunately the fact that the book is published in Italian will be an obstacle for many Anglophone readers. It would be highly desirable if an English version could be made available. Readers can consult the article published in this journal in 2007, but it only treats a small part of the much larger subject covered in this excellent study.

David T. Runia
The University of Melbourne

DAVID LINCICUM, *Paul and the Early Jewish Encounter with Deuteronomy*. Wissenschaftliche Untersuchungen zum Neuen Testament 2. Reihe 284. Tübingen: Mohr Siebeck, 2010. xiii + 289 pages. ISBN 978-3-16-150386-3. Price €64.

David Lincicum's monograph is a revised version of his doctoral thesis, produced under the supervision of Professor Markus Bockmuehl and defended at Oxford in 2009. The subject of the study deals with the role played by Deuteronomy in Paul's letters and early Jewish literature, primarily from the period of the Second Temple. As such, the book adds to the stream of recently published monographs that have addressed various aspects of the way Deuteronomy is appropriated by Paul within a Jewish context.

After an introductory chapter, locating the approach of the study within the state of art, the book proceeds in two parts, followed by a conclusion, an appendix, a bibliography, and indices. Part I (chapter 2) surveys "the Liturgical Deuteronomy in the Second Temple Period," while part II (chapters 3–8) contains a scrutiny of the relevant Jewish texts.

More specifically, part I evidences aspects of a Jewish cultural context, which provides glimpses of how the material and the practical functions of Deuteronomy were woven into the very fabric of Jewish society and institutions, such as, e.g., the material exigencies of books, public recitation of the Torah in worship, and the practices of *tefillin* and *mezuzot*. Its purpose is to broaden the liturgical field of reception in which Paul is one instantiation in the Jewish encounter of Deuteronomy. I concur with the author's claim that this chapter provides a historical sketch or prolegomena that

might broaden our imagination of how Paul came to encounter Deuteronomy as *a whole*, but I would have appreciated if Lincicum had elaborated
more on how this context of "Torah as practice, institution, and things" (an
expression applied by the Swedish scholar Birger Gerhardsson on Torah as
practiced Laws) sheds light on Paul's and other Jewish contemporaries'
way of "living" with Deuteronomy as part of the Torah. In addition to the
appendix on the Biblical passages in *tefillin, mezuzot,* and excerpted texts, I
would, for example, have liked to see a similar survey and additional notes
with regard to behavioral, institutional, and material traditions reflected in
the Pauline texts.

Part II investigates the influence of Deuteronomy in various Jewish
writings from the Second Temple period, such as at Qumran, in the
Apocrypha and Pseudepigrapha, the works of Philo of Alexandria, Paul's
letters, and the writings of Josephus. The author has also added a chapter
on midrashic works from Tannaitic and Amoraic times, namely *Sifre to
Deuteronomy* and the Aramaic Targums. The purpose is to chart a series of
trajectories, in which Paul's reception of Deuteronomy might shed light on
his Jewish contemporaries and vice versa. For reasons of space and scope of
this journal, I shall proceed with brief comments on Lincicum's reading of
Philo's and Paul's appropriation of Deuteronomy, and with an eye also to
some of the comparative observations Lincicum provides on these two
authors.

Lincicum investigates the variety of ways Deuteronomy is applied in
the works of Philo of Alexandria. Besides being aware of its delimited role
and existence, most probably in the form of a scroll, Philo refers to Deuteronomy's different sub-units such as the blessings and curses (Deut 27–30),
the Song (Deut 32), and Blessing of Moses (Deut 33). These sub-units,
highlighting Moses' last actions and words, demonstrate Philo's practice as
an exegete. Thus, Philo interprets Deuteronomy as part of the particular
and cosmic Torah, combining both the cosmic aspects of biblical and historical events and the time perspectives of past, present, and future. Lincicum
correctly emphasizes Deueteronomy as a book of theological and ethical
authority for Philo, and offers some thoughts on the hermeneutical grids
applied in Philo's exegesis, such as, e.g., the distinction drawn between the
Ten Commandments and the Special Laws, conceived like "the heads
summarizing the particular laws" (*Decal.* 19). I miss, however, some more
reflections on Philo's hermeneutic in order to understand the various levels,
namely the concrete, the cosmic and ethical, and the divine level, that often
determine his expositions of Deuteronomy as relevant both to his own time
and for the future eschatological age to come. Hence, for example, I think
Lincicum could have paid more attention to the way the principles of Law

in Deuteronomy are applied to Philo's interpretation of the conflicts involved in the historical treatise *Against Flaccum* and the eschatological expectations conveyed in *On Rewards and Punishments*. I also wonder whether such a distinction of various expository levels might have clarified in a better way how Deuteronomy is applied in the Allegorical Commentary on Genesis. Very often Philo interprets the Torah, with Deuteronomy as no exception, on different levels: on its concrete level as texts of the past, or on a figurative level as texts which points to ethical conflicts and struggles either within humanity itself or within a pagan and Egyptian context, and sometimes on a divine level referring to the relationship between God and human beings. In general, even when Philo's application of Scripture from a modern perspective might seem arbitrary, it can often be shown that he conforms to hermeneutic conventions, exegetical methods, and terminology of his day.

Without discussing in detail the influence of Deuteronomy in Paul's letters, Lincicum has made a fine synthesis of the data, setting out Paul's appropriation within a wide range of cases, from quotations to allusions and echoes. In his scrutiny of the relevant Pauline passages, however, Lincicum has limited himself to the more explicit encounters with Deuteronomy. As the outcome of such an analysis, he has categorized the way Paul works with Deuteronomy in three ways; as both an ethical and a theological authority, as well as providing the lens through which Paul read Israel's history.

Among the issues of ethical authority, Lincicum deals with Paul's use of the Ten Commandments in Rom 7:7 and 13:6–8. In the latter text, Paul seems to presuppose the distinction between the Ten Commandments summarizing the particular laws of the Torah in a way similar to Philo. Here Paul finds that the second table of the Decalogue is summarized and restricted to the love command of Lev 19:18, leaving behind the rest of the special laws of Moses. Such a distinction also has an analogy in Paul's distinction between observance of the *whole* law (Gal 5:3) and the fulfilment of the *entire* Law, summarized by the ethical virtue and principle of love commanded in Lev 19:18 (referred to in Gal 5:14) as well as other ethical virtues (supported by the Law, cf. Gal 5:22–23). As for Paul's interpretation of the Tenth Commandment of Deut 5:21 in Rom 7:7, it exhibits what it forbids, namely excessive desire. Over against this the good Law is powerless, since it has been hijacked by "sin." At this point as well, Paul seems to presuppose a thought evidenced by Philo, viz. that the observance of the Special Laws might promote the fulfilment of the Ten Commandment, prescribing the virtue of self-control and in this way replacing the desire proscribed by the commandment. Thus, further research and comparison with Philo beyond Lincicum's observations might give a better Jewish perspective on the function of the Law that Paul seems to oppose in both Rom 7:7 and 13:6–8.

With regard to the category of theological axioms anchored in Deuteronomy, Lincicum points out that much of Paul's theological motifs, not least his view on the *Shema* and universal monotheism, have their referential background in Deuteronomy. Thus, it is a bit surprising that Lincicum does not discuss Rom 3:29–30 and the tension between God as the Creator of all humankind and as the ethnic God for the Jewish people in contrast to how Deuteronomy (cf. 4:37–39; 14:2) resolved this matter by means of the motif of election.

As to Paul's "rewriting" of Deuteronomy as the lens of Israel's history, Lincicum offers noteworthy observations on texts such as Romans 2, 10, 15 and Galatians 3. These chapters represent in many ways Paul's christological re-interpretation of Deuteronomy in the light of Christ's death and resurrection. In his interpretation of some of the relevant Pauline passages, I wish that Lincicum had taken more into account Philo's eschatological appropriation of the Law in order to strenghten and encourage its observance by the Jewish people as a condition for bringing about their future hopes. In my view, Paul's encounter with Deuteronomy and his reconfiguration of the relation between Christ, the Law, and the cosmic role of the Jewish people vis-à-vis other nations is comprehensible and becomes more coherent within such a Jewish cultural context.

To sum up, David Lincicum achieves to some extent his goal to place Paul's application of Deuteronomy in its broader Jewish context.

Per Jarle Bekken
University of Nordland

PEDER BORGEN, *The Gospel of John: More Light from Philo, Paul and Archaeology: The Scriptures, Tradition, Settings, Meaning.* Supplements to Novum Testamentum 154. Leiden: Brill 2014. ISBN 978-900-424-790-1. 329 pages. Price €125, $162 (hb).

In this volume Peder Borgen collects eight previously published contributions, works them together, and adds new material, thus drawing on the research of 55 years to create a monograph which argues a coherent thesis. In addition to an introductory chapter, the book has five parts: Part 1, "Research and Debate," consisting of two chapters: chapter 1: "The Scriptures and Works of Jesus," including a response by M. Labahn (both previously published in 2010); and chapter 2: "Debates on Method and

Form" (previously published in 1983). Part 2, "John, Philo, Paul and the Hellenistic World," contains a chapter on John and Philo (chapter 3, previously published in 2003), one on methods and structures in the study of John and the Synoptics (chapter 4), and one on "John and Hellenism" (chapter 5, previously published in 1996). Part 3 "From John and the Synoptics to John within Early Gospel Traditions" compares the gospels regarding the passion narrative (chapter 6, previously published in 1959), the relationship between Synoptic material in John and Paul (chapter 7, previously published in 1990), and John's independence from the Synoptics (chapter 8). Part 4 on "God's agent in Johannine Exposition" begins with a chapter on God's agent in John (chapter 9, previously published in 1968), then it studies the Sabbath Controversy (John 5:1–18) in comparison with a similar controversy in Philo (chapter 10, previously published in 1991), God's agent in John 5-10 and the historical Jesus (chapter 11), and John as witness in the prologue (chapter 12). The concluding Part 5 addresses "Challenge and Response." It compares Philo's historical writings (*In Flaccum; Legatio*) with John (chapter 13), looks at Thomas as witness to the truth (chapter 14), and summarizes the results of the monograph (chapter 15). Borgen emphasises that John needs to be seen in the context of Hellenistic Jewish witnesses such as Philo, is independent of the Synoptics, and has more similarity with Paul than with them. This last is not because of direct dependence but because of John's use of earlier, oral traditions, which Borgen argues could even have been written down before 70 CE (chapter 15, esp. 290–292).

Regarding the Jewish background, Philo of Alexandria is seen as an important witness to the kind of Hellenistic Judaism in which Borgen situates John. Although he also emphasises the Palestinian setting of John, he hardly uses any texts of Palestinian provenance. The bread from heaven motif in John 6:31–59 is an important focus of Borgen's interaction with Johannine thought. He sees it as the development of the Scriptural manna tradition. This was already the topic of a note in the *ZNW* in 1959 as well as his 1965 book on the subject. Borgen develops how Philo represents another example of an exegetical tradition based on this motif. The Jesus traditions, Borgen argues, were similarly treated, as can already be seen in the Pauline letters. Just as in the case of the manna motif, the Johannine idea of divine agency is related to Jewish traditions, and Borgen focuses on Philonic ideas of agents and intermediaries and develops their relationship to Johannine Christological concepts. The Jewish Hellenistic context is also relevant in relation to such themes as ascent/descent and visions of God, being equal to God, as well as wisdom and Logos and dualism (chapter 5). Borgen argues that further Christological themes, such as "Father and Son," "Son of Man," "Messiah" can be traced traced against the same background of the divine agent (chapters 9–12). Unlike in his monograph *Bread from Heaven* Borgen no longer sees docetism, the denial of Jesus' humanity, as the main problem in the Christological debate, but rather it is the denial of his divinity, the idea that "a human being can be divine and 'come down from heaven'" (p. xii).

Regarding the Christian background to John, Borgen sees Paul as more useful, although there is no direct dependence. With the Synoptics, Borgen does not find any direct relationship either, but postulates that John uses oral traditions which explain any similarities. Borgen summarises his results in three points as answer to "challenges": (1) John is not dependent on Mark; (2) extensive theological/ideological elaboration of John can be combined with the specific geographical, historical and social awareness and interest using such contemporary texts as Philo and Paul; and (3) the confession of Thomas in John reflects the confession of the church as mentioned in Pliny's letter (xiv, chapter 15). Woven into this are chapters on Philo's historical treatises as indicating how Philo's view on the Law of Moses influences his view on history (chapter 13).

As Labahn's response to chapter 1 already indicates, Borgen's research clashes with what has crystallized as a consensus of recent research on John. This is the case not only with Borgen's argument that John 5:19–6:71 comprises one single literary unit, but especially with his emphasis that John did not use and did not even know about the Synoptics. Labahn also points out that the details of early Christian transmission of traditions regarding rites and liturgies are not well known, therefore the comparison with Paul, while methodologically sensible, is not straightforward. Beyond Labahn's comments, Borgen's main use of Philo in making comparisons with John is fraught with problems, as there is a serious debate about how representative Philo is for the Judaism of his time. Of course he gives insights into many areas of Jewish life, but his perspective is specific, probably representative of certain streams of Diaspora Judaism, but not of Judaism as a whole. The more Borgen emphasises the Palestinian background of John, the more methodologically difficult is his exclusive focus on Philo as witness for Judaism, even if the alternative between a so-called "Palestinian (normative) Judaism and Hellenistic Judaism" (p. 82) is rightly rejected. Certainly, the focus on Philo offers many creative perspectives on John, but the comparison needs to take into account that both are literary documents. Conclusions regarding history need to be methodologically reflected. In this context, the archeological and historical insights promised in the title turn out to be a weak spot. There are no original archaeological or historical insights offered in the monograph, and their treatment consists solely (as the author himself admits on p. x) of the summary of other scholars covering four pages, esp. J. Charlesworth, U. von Wahlde, and M. Hengel. (p. 275–278). The use of Philo's historical treatises offers not so much historical but rather literary aids for the understanding of John. Also the link to Pliny does not offer insights into the historical Jesus but to the situation of the early Church in Asia Minor. And the chapter on the historical Jesus (chapter 11) does not provide convincing evidence for historical sayings of Jesus. It works with literary themes, rather than historical evidence, even where it applies social themes, such as familial concepts in the language of "Father and Son" or the use of the witness and the agent. Borgen does not take into account that these social themes in John are used as literary motifs rather than socio-historical evidence of actual proceedings.

Without doubt Peder Borgen has been a highly influential scholar in Philonic as well as Johannine studies. The book gives an overview of important trajectories of his work over more than half a century. Two of the main points of the book, the importance of Paul and Philo as background to John are undisputed, and Borgen offers many detailed, stimulating, creative and highly useful observations on these topics. As for his conclusions regarding John and the Synoptics and the historical placement of John, these are much more open to debate.

Jutta Leonhardt-Balzer
University of Aberdeen

KARL-GUSTAV SANDELIN, *Attraction and Danger of Alien Religion: Studies in Early Judaism and Christianity*, Wissenschaftliche Untersuchungen zum Neuen Testament 1. Reihe 290. Tübingen: Mohr Siebeck, 2012. xiii + 270 pages. ISBN 978-3-16-151742-6. Price €94. (pb)

Karl-Gustav Sandelin (b. 1940), was Lecturer of Exegetics and the Languages of the Bible at the Åbo Akademi University, Åbo, Finland from 1975 to 1995; then Professor of New Testament Exegetics at the same institution until he retired in 2006. A Bibliography of his works 1973–2008 is available in the volume mentioned below, *Sophia och hennes värld*, pp. 303–304.

The present volume represents the second collection of Prof. Sandelin's articles published in various journals and books; the first volume (*Sophia och hennes värld. Exegetiska uppsatser från fyra årtionden* (Åbo 2008)) contains 19 articles in the Swedish language, and was summarized in this journal, vol. 23, pp. 129–131. Some of these articles also deal with Philo. The present volume contains ten other studies and a summarizing essay, all in English; of these studies four deal with issues of idolatry in 1 Corinthians, not drawing much on Philo. Furthermore, one study deals with the Revelation of John ("Attraction and Danger of Alien Religion in the Revelation of John," pp. 169–191, not previously published); and one deals with "The Jesus-Tradition and Idolatry" (pp. 161–168, published in 1996). This leaves us with four more studies, all dealing with issues of idolatry in the works of Philo: "The Danger of Idolatry according to Philo of Alexandria," published 1991; "Philo's Ambivalence towards Statues," published 2001; "Philo and Paul on Alien Religion: A Comparison," published in 2005, and "Jews and Alien Religious Practices During the Hellenistic Age," published 2006, the latter containing just a few references to Philo. Due to the focus of the Annual, I will primarily deal with his studies related to Philo.

In many ways, the study on "The Danger of Idolatry according to Philo" is the primary one both with regard to date of publication and importance, as it lays the groundwork for many issues dealt with in the other studies. However, in the present volume this article is proceeded by another, drawing a more general picture of "Jews and Alien Religious Practices During the Hellenistic Age" (pp. 1–26), and this arrangement allows the latter to function as a fine introduction to the whole book. In this study, Sandelin deals with the Jews' daily confrontation with the complex phenomenon labeled "Hellenistic Religion." He poses the question: how much is documented regarding how non-Jewish religious activities attracted Jews in the Hellenistic world and in the early Roman Empire? In response, he deals with Jewish participation in such activities in both Eretz Israel and in the Diaspora, considering both indirect and direct documentation. Concerning Jewish participation in Eretz Israel, he deals with *direct* statements by focusing on the first two Books of the Maccabees. As *indirect* documentation, he offers a few remarks on the possible evidence found in the Epistle of Jeremiah. The largest part of the article then deals with the Diaspora. Here he first suggests that public life in antiquity could imply participation in various milieus that were associated with religious rituals such as performances in the theatres and especially in gymnasial education. Then he deals with '*direct* documentation' of participation in Greco-Roman cults. Relevant material includes inscriptions in Greece and Asia Minor as well as in Egypt. Furthermore, there are some examples of a very high degree of assimilation of Jews to non-Jewish culture and religious behavior: he mentions here Dositheos (2 Macc 1:3) who is possibly also the same Dositheos mentioned in a papyrus dated to 222 BCE. It is conjectured that Dositheos might have wanted to be both a Jew and a Greco-Egyptian priest. Then Sandelin uses three pages to discuss the case of Tiberius Julius

Alexander, the nephew of Philo (pp. 15–18), finding that he completely distanced himself from Jewish monotheism and corresponding behavior. And reading 3 Maccabees and Josephus, Sandelin suggests that there is some evidence indicating that Jews could at times be forced to attend alien religious activities, thus unwillingly compromising their Jewish principles.

As *indirect evidence* for Jewish participation in Greco-Roman cults, Sandelin draws upon Deut 23:18 and the paraphrasing addition in the Septuagint indicating the temptation of the mystery rites (cf. also Wis 14:12–16). The works of Philo are then treated as an indirect witness to Jewish participation as he does not explicitly mention Jewish individuals participating in non-Jewish religious practices. He reads *Praem.* 162–165 as describing how certain Jews had become estranged from Judaism. *Spec.* 1.319 and other texts are adduced as evidence that the warning of Deut 13:1–11 was felt as very relevant, and Philo's presentations of the Phinehas episode (Num 24), and of how Balaam instructed Balak, etc. are interpreted in the same way (*Mos.* 1.296–302, cf. Josephus *A.J.* 4.126–141).

The next study, "The Danger of Idolatry according to Philo" (pp. 27–59), represents what to me is the major study in this volume on the attraction and danger of alien religion for Philo. Some of the issues mentioned in the preceding study reappear here, and one particular issue, the problem of religious statues, is further investigated in the next study. Sandelin states his own purpose thus: "I want to study how Philo understands idolatry as a phenomenon, how he sees it as a danger to faith, what should be said about the social contexts in which he was confronted with it, and finally, the way he as an exegete tries to combat its manifestations" (p. 29). It goes without saying that such a broad range of questions is hard to deal with in a review. But we shall here bring into relief some of what Sandelin emphasizes. The article has four main sections: The Phenomenon of Idolatry; The Threat of idolatry in its different forms; Philo's experience of idolatry as a concrete reality; and Exegetical Actualizations.

The phenomenon of idolatry as such is to Philo primarily a deification of the created. Philo might describe it as 'ignorance' (*Ebr.* 108–110; *Conf.* 144), or he can emphasize that the deification of the whole universe has the effect that God himself is forgotten (*Virt.* 212; *Migr.* 178–179). There might also be an association between idolatry and passions. In *Ebr.* 36–64, according to Sandelin, we may observe how Philo sees the body, the senses, and the passions as intertwined, and he states that in several passages we can see parallels of focus on the body with its passions on the one hand and idolatry on the other (*Migr.* 64–69; *Conf.* 144; *Mos.* 1.263–318; *Post.* 158–164).

The threat of idolatry can be encountered in several ways. Sandelin here deals with polytheistic creeds and images of gods (*Praem.* 162). To

Philo the statues of gods are to be held as gods on hearsay only; but he nevertheless thinks they might have seductive power through their beauty. The seriousness of idolatry can also be read from the ways Philo treats OT passages like Num 25:12–13 (on Phinehas) and Deut 13:2–12 (on false prophets) in *Spec.* 1.54–57 and 1.316. Both of these Philonic passages seem to argue for punishment by death on the spot.

How then did Philo experience idolatry as a concrete reality (pp. 40–47)? One issue, which Sandelin surmises might have been especially tempting to elite Jews, is the danger of idolatry in striving for glory. Tiberius Julius Alexander is one example from Philo's own family. Sandelin here comments further upon various cultural activities as sport, theater, club-meetings, and education. He admits that we do not know much about how Philo himself reacted when he happened to be a witness to a pagan ritual performance. What we do have, however, is that in his teaching on the Bible Philo took a stand against idolatry as he observed it in the world of Alexandria.

In the final section of this study, called Exegetical Actualizations (pp. 47–57), he focuses on three aspects of social life, and deals with them in light of some particular text passages or episodes from the Scriptures. The first deals with *Idolatry proper: the episode with the Golden Calf.* This episode of Exod 32 is dealt with in several of Philo's works. First, Philo presents the golden calf as a manifestation of Egyptian religion (the Apis bull). This makes the story relevant for his Alexandrian readers as the worship of the Apis bull still existed at that time. Then Philo interprets the episode of the golden calf as an expression of deifying created things. Thirdly, he also sees the golden calf as a symbol for those who make a god of the body (*Ebr.* 95).

The second issue he deals with is *Idolatry in a transferred sense: the Character of Joseph.* It is well known that in the *Allegorical Commentary*, Philo depicts Joseph mostly in negative terms. Philo can, for instance, see Joseph as a mind "which loves the body and the passions" (*Deus* 111). Joseph also symbolizes, according to Philo, the type of man who forms ties of fellowship with the "mixed multitude," comparable to Lot's actions which had a negative effect upon his soul. Furthermore, the role of a politician is also given negative interpretations in the allegorical commentaries. Hence Sandelin opines that the description of Joseph as a politician "seems to be an actualization of dangers confronting people belonging to a stratum of people such as Philo himself or his nephew Tiberius Julius Alexander" (p. 53).

The third and final issue focused upon by Sandelin is *Encyclical Dangers: the cases of Jethro and Rachel.* This aspect is mostly taken from Philo's *De*

Ebrietate. Jethro here becomes a polytheist, and Philo's ways of describing Jethro may be read as an attack on the aspects of the encyclia which contain polytheistic ideas. Furthermore, to Philo Rachel means encyclical education in contrast to Leah, who stands for philosophy. Laban wanted Jacob to take Leah before Rachel; that is, philosophy before the encyclical education. Sandelin surmises that inherent in the retelling of this story, Philo probably describes the fate of many an Alexandrian Jew who was brought up in Jewish traditions, but who later become interested in the culture of the surrounding society.

The volume's last major study dealing with Philo and idolatry focuses on "Philo's Ambivalence toward Statues" [pp. 60–76]. At the outset, Sandelin states that his purpose in the article is to "address an area in Philo's world of religious ideas which might also be illustrative for the struggle in his mind between 'conflicting patterns of thought,' i.e. his view of statues" [p. 60]. Sandelin is then able to demonstrate that there is a certain ambivalence in Philo towards statues of gods. On the one hand, his general attitude towards statues of the gods is that of denouncement (*Dec.* 72–74; *Mos.* 2.205). On the other hand, he can also evaluate them positively, as when he mentions the statues made by Phidias (*Ebr.* 89); that is, he has also an eye for the beauty of handmade statues. Hence, in Philo's ways of handling statues, Sandelin opines that Philo demonstrates his own difficulty to balance on the one hand his commitment to his Jewish heritage and on the other hand his fondness for the culture of the Greco-Roman world. Furthermore, Sandelin argues that when Philo sometimes offers positive evaluations of statues, he shows some indebtedness to Platonism. Hence, there exists in Philo's mind a conflict between Jewish and Greek ideas which are hard to reconcile.

Then follow four studies on Paul, on which I offer just a few comments here. The two first essays deal with 1 Cor 10:1–14 ("Does Paul argue against Sacramentalism and Over-Confidence in 1 Cor 10:1–14" [pp. 77–93]; "Do not become Idolaters!" (*1 Cor 10:7*) [pp. 94–108]). Their main thesis is that Paul does here not argue against over-confidence, especially as based on the effects of the sacraments, but warns against participation in idolatrous practices. To strengthen this interpretation, Sandelin draws, inter alia, on Philo's warnings against idolatry. The next essay ("Drawing the Line: Paul on Idol food and Idolatry in 1 Cor 8:1–11:1" [pp. 109–122]), deals with two questions much discussed in research on this letter: did Paul react against actual participation by Corinthian Christians at banquets in the temple precincts? And where does Paul draw the line between acceptable and unacceptable Christian behavior concerning consumption of food offered to idols? Sandelin points to the fact that in 1 Cor 8:10 Paul uses a conditional sentence to address the issue of participation, and in 1 Cor 10:7 and 14 he uses imperatives to forbid the Corinthians to become idolaters and orders them to flee idolatry. Hence these aspects could point more to what might happen in the future than to actual and past events. As to where the line is to be drawn, Sandelin suggests that Paul draws the line around the whole temple precinct, not only at the altar. In the last essay on Paul, Sandelin deals with the question: "Does Paul warn the Corinthians not to Eat Demons?" The primary text discussed here is 1 Cor 10:14–22. The answer is that the issue is not that Paul warns the Corinthians against eating demons, but that he does not want the Christians, who are a community of the blood and body of Christ, to become a community of demon-worship.

The studies on Philo and on Paul and their discussions of the influence of alien religion is rounded off by an essay comparing Philo and Paul: "Philo and Paul on Alien Religion: A Comparison" (pp. 133–160). To a large extent this essay is a summary of the conclusions reached in the previous chapters on Philo and Paul, and a comparison of these two with regard to similarities and differences, paying due attention to their different settings.

The last two essays deal with idolatry and the attraction of alien religion in the Jesus traditions and in the Revelation of John, respectively. Finally, the volume has a 41 page bibliography, indices of references, of modern authors, and of subjects and names.

This volume should prove interesting and helpful to students of both the works of Philo and of Paul. Karl-Gustav Sandelin is an expert reader of both these two ancient writers, as scholars in the field well know. And here we are presented with some important studies of the influence of alien religion as well as the temptations felt and dangers perceived of idolatry by both Philo and Paul. Furthermore, it is nice to have these studies—published in a variety of journals and books—available in one volume. The reader will soon discover that there also are several repetitions and overlaps from essay to essay, while at the same time they also each bring in new perspectives. As the essays are examples of tightly knit arguments, some repetitions can hardly be avoided; otherwise the author would have had to indulge in some heavy editing and re-arranging of his material. As it is now, the studies previously published are kept in their original form. This collection of these articles in one volume is highly recommended for those who want to see how Philo and Paul coped with the pluralistic societies of their time.

Torrey Seland,
Drammen, Norway

The Studia Philonica Annual 27 (2015): 255–261

NEWS AND NOTES

The Philo of Alexandria Group of the Society for Biblical Literature

At the 2014 Annual Meeting of the Society of Biblical Literature in San Diego, California, the Philo of Alexandria Seminar (formerly Group) met, for the first time as a Seminar, in two separate sessions. (For details on the Group's renewal as a Seminar, please see *SPhiloA* 26 [2014] 259–261). The first session, held Sunday, November 23, and presided over by Ellen Birnbaum (Cambridge, Massachusetts), was devoted to "Philo's Legal Exegesis." Speakers and topics included Maren R. Niehoff (The Hebrew University of Jerusalem), "Philo's Rationalisation of the Jewish Law in Greco-Roman Context"; Yedidya Etzion (University of California–Berkeley), "Philo's Sabbath: A Study in Philo's Jewish Law"; Daniel R. Streett (Durham University), "Philo's Exegesis of the Biblical Festival Laws: Arithmology, Askesis, and *Imitatio Dei*"; Michael Francis (University of Notre Dame), "Wasted Seed and Sins of Intent: Sexual Ethics in *Spec.* 3.34–36 in the Case of Infertile Marriage"; and Horacio Vela (University of Notre Dame), "A New Command: Philo as Lawgiver and Interpreter in the Case of the Egyptian Blasphemer."

This session was intended as a companion to the next one, on Philo's *De Decalogo*, held on Tuesday, November 25, and presided over by Ronald Cox (Pepperdine University). Sarah J. Pearce (University of Southampton), who is preparing a translation and commentary on this treatise for the Philo of Alexandria Commentary Series, presented her paper "Philo of Alexandria on the Second Commandment," to which Hindy Najman (Yale University) responded. The remaining speakers and topics included James R. Royse (Claremont, California), "The Text of Philo's *De Decalogo*"; Abraham Terian (National Academy of Sciences/Armenia), "The Armenian Textual and Interpretive Traditions of Philo's *De Decalogo*"; and Manuel Alexandre, Jr. (Universidade de Lisboa, Portugal), "*Rhetorical Texture and Pattern in Philo of Alexandria's De Decalogo*." Presentations at both sessions stimulated questions, comments, and lively discussion. Readers can find copies of these papers at the following site, graciously maintained by Torrey Seland (Norway): http://torreys.org/philo_seminar_papers/ (a number of them have been published in the present volume of *The Studia Philonica Annual*).

A business meeting, at which future plans were discussed, concluded the second session. Ellen Birnbaum was acknowledged for completing her six-year term as the Group/Seminar's Co-Chair and Ron Cox will continue to serve as Chair. One evening, several session participants and friends of the Philo Seminar enjoyed each other's company over dinner at Acqua Al 2 in San Diego's Gaslamp District.

Ellen Birnbaum, Cambridge MA
Ronald Cox, Pepperdine University

Session on Philo at Christian Scholars Conference

For the first time since its inception in 1981, the 2015 Thomas H. Olbricht Christian Scholars Conference hosted a session wholly devoted to Philo of Alexandria. The conference, an interdisciplinary gathering of scholars from around North America, took place at Abilene Christian University in Abilene, Texas, June 3–5. The Philo of Alexandria session, held on Friday, June 5, was presided over by Ronald Cox (Pepperdine University) and was intended to highlight the importance of Philo for understanding Judaism and Christianity in the early imperial and late antique worlds. Speakers and topics included Zane McGee (Emory, University); "Slave to the Servant: The Allegorical Interpretation of Hagar and Sarah by Philo and Paul"; Gregory Sterling (Yale Divinity School), "'A Law to Themselves': Limited Universalism in Paul and Philo of Alexandria"; and Justin Rogers (Freed Hardeman University), "Origen in the Likeness of Philo: Eusebius of Caesarea's Portrait of the Model Scholar." The session concluded with a response by Cox to the three papers and a general discussion.

Ronald Cox
Pepperdine University

Papers on Philo at General Meeting of the Studiorum Novi Testamenti Societas (SNTS)

The 70th General Meeting of the *Studiorum Novi Testamenti Societas* (SNTS) was this year held at the VU University Amsterdam, 29 July to 1 August, with ca. 300 participants. The meeting has no fixed annually held seminar dedicated to Philo of Alexandria, but the seminar this year on *Early Jewish*

Theologies and the New Testament, led by Profs. Jens Herzer and Gerben Oegema, had three papers directly linked to Philo.

Professor emeritus Otto Kaiser (Marburg) was supposed to present the first paper, dealing with "Philos Hochschätzung der Freundschaft—Im Kontext der hellenistisch-römischen Philosophie beurteilt." Kaiser, who was able to celebrate his ninetieth birthday last year, and who this very year had an introductory volume published on Philo (*Philo von Alexandrien. Denkender Glaube—Eine Einführung* (Göttingen; Vandenhoeck & Ruprecht, 2015), was, alas, not able to participate because of illness. The session was not cancelled, however, as Prof. Karl-Wilhelm Niebuhr (Friedrich-Schiller-Universität Jena) was able to step in and presented a paper on *Die Sapientia Salomonis im Kontext hellenistisch-römischer Philosophie*.

Then, in the following two sessions, Prof. Thomas H. Tobin (Loyola University, Chicago), presented a paper on *Reconfiguring Apocalyptic Imagery: The Examples of Philo of Alexandria and Paul*, and Gregory E. Sterling (Yale University), on *"A Law to Themselves": Limited Universalism in Philo and Paul*.

The papers were sent out to the participants in advance, and were thus only summarized in the sessions. The seminar was attended by some 15 participants, and the papers evoked some good discussions, not at least concerning the sections dealing with Philo. A revised version of Sterling's paper will appear in a forthcoming issue of *ZNW*. The next General Meeting of the SNTS is scheduled to be held in Montreal, Canada on 2–5 August 2016.

Torrey Seland
Drammen, Norway

Philo in Africa

Torrey Seland reports that his Ph.D. student Ruben Ngozo from Cameroon had his public disputation in Stavanger in August 2012 on his thesis "The One God and the Many Gods: Monotheism and Idolatry in 1 Cor 8:1–11:1 in Light of Philo's Writings." A summary of the thesis will be found in the Bibliography section. In fact, Ruben is the first African ever to get a Ph.D. in Norway, and according to his external examiner Jean-Claude Loba-Mkole (Kenya), he was even the first African to write a Ph.D. thesis on Philo! On his return to Cameroon he was appointed Bishop of the Eglise Evangélique Luthérienne au Cameroun (EELC), demonstrating how Philonic studies can lead to very rapid ecclesiastical advancement. Another African scholar, Jean-Claude Loba Mkole (Catholic University of Eastern Africa, Kenya), is undertaking a PhD project entitled "Inter-cultural and Re-construction Paradigms in Philo's *Legatio*" under the supervision of Prof. Jan G. van der Watt at the Radboud University, Nijmegen, Netherlands.

National Endowment for the Humanities Grant to Philo Project

We are pleased to report that the Scholarly Editions and Translations Program of the National Endowment for the Humanities has awarded a grant to Yale University for a project entitled, "*On the Life of Abraham*, by Philo of Alexandria: A New Introduction, Translation, and Commentary." The Project Director is Gregory E. Sterling, General Editor of the Philo of Alexandria Commentary Series (PACS) and the PACS volume on *De Abrahamo* is being prepared by Ellen Birnbaum (Cambridge MA) and John Dillon (Trinity College Dublin).

Hebrew Translation of Philo

Maren Niehoff writes from Jerusalem: "I am delighted to share with you the good news that another volume of Philo's writings in Hebrew has just been published by the Israeli Academy of Sciences and Humanities and the Bialik Institute. It is Part 2 of Volume IV and contains Allegorical exegesis and Philosophical treatises. All of Philo's treatises available in Greek have thus been translated. The Armenian treatises will take a bit longer, but I trust that they will also appear in Hebrew before too long. It would be great if you can encourage your library to order the new volume and thus help distribute Israeli scholarship, especially the notes, which contextualize Philo in the Jewish (and Greek) tradition. For more information see www. bialik-publishing.co.il. The ISBN is 978-965-536-146-9." Maren modestly declines to write that she herself is the editor of this volume.

Loeb Classical Library Online

The best complete English translation of Philo remains the one published in the Loeb Classical Library, even though it was commenced nearly a century ago and badly needs to be updated or superseded. Philonists may be interested to know that the Library's publisher, Harvard University Press, has now placed the entire Library online, including the twelve volumes of Philo. The online version replicates each page of the text and translation, including all notes and is fully searchable. Further information at www.loebclassics.com.

Oxford Bibliographies Online

It is now five years since Oxford Bibliographies Online started their project to publish authoritative digital bibliographies on subjects and authors in the Humanities. There are now 38 subject areas with more than 8000 separate bibliographies. Each bibliography uses a fixed method, dividing its subject into headings, for each of which up to eight bibliographic items must be selected and briefly commented on. Authors are encouraged to present up-to-date surveys of research, but also to include important older works and works written in languages other than English (although predictably there is a heavy bias towards English-language publications). More information, including how to subscribe, can be found at www.oxford bibliographies.com.

The programme does not hesitate to commission multiple bibliographies on the same subject, if the subject belongs to more than one subject area. Philo scholars will therefore soon have three bibliographies to choose from. In the subject area Biblical Studies, a bibliography on Philo of Alexandria by David Runia has been available since 2010 (and was revised in 2015). In the subject area Jewish Studies, Maren Niehoff has prepared a bibliography on Philo, which has been available since 2014. And in the subject area of Classics Gregory E. Sterling has submitted a bibliography which will soon be available. Philonic connoisseurs will be able to compare the three and discern subtle differences of approach. Numerous other bibliographies will be of interest to Philonists. I give a small sample: Hellenistic Judaism (subject area: Biblical Studies) by Lester Grabbe; Hellenistic Jewish Literature by the same scholar in the subject area of Jewish Studies; Middle Platonism (Classics) by Mauro Bonazzi; Alexandria (Biblical Studies) by Joan Taylor; Hellenistic and Roman Egypt (Classics) by Caitlin E. Barrett.

David Runia
Melbourne, Australia

Abbreviations in the SBL Handbook of Style

The second edition of *The SBL Handbook of Style* was published by SBL Press in 2014. It replaces the earlier edition, which first saw the light of day in 1999. The first edition did not contain an abbreviation for *The Studia Philonica Annual* but did give *SPhilo* for its predecessor *Studia Philonica*. The second edition prescribes the abbreviation SPhiloA for *The Studia Philonica Annual*. The lack of italics with the abbreviation is, we are informed, an error that will be corrected in future printings. The abbreviation *SPhA*, which our Instructions to Contributors have hitherto used for the *Annual*, is now assigned to the book series Studies in Philo of Alexandria published by Brill, Leiden (not italicized). In light of these developments, in the Instructions to Contributors below we will now list the abbreviation for *The Studia Philonica* Annual as *SPhiloA* (retaining the italics), while the abbreviation for The Studia Philonica Monograph Series will change to SPhiloM (not in italics).

Outside the Bible Project

This massive project was first conceived by the Jewish Publication Society in the final years of the previous century. It aimed to bring together a modern group of "the seventy," emulating the translators of the Septuagint. Their task was to present a truly comprehensive collection of the extra-biblical texts of Jewish antiquity, making the available to both scholars and lay readers. The project started in earnest in 2005, when it received a substantial NEH grant. Originally it was called The Lost Bible Project, but when in 2011 the Society began a collaboration with the University of Nebraska Press, the name was changed to *Outside the Bible*. After many years of preparation the work was finally published in three volumes at the end of 2013 as *Outside the Bible: Ancient Jewish Writings Related to Scripture*. The editors were Louis Feldman, James L. Kugel and Lawrence H. Schiffman.

Two substantial sections of the work are devoted to Philo. The first is entitled The Biblical Interpretations of Philo and contains the following:

Questions and Answers on Genesis and Exodus, by Aram Topchyan and Gohar Muradyan
On the Creation of the World, by David T. Runia
Allegorical Interpretation 1.31–62, by Maren R. Niehoff
On the Migration of Abraham, by Peder Borgen
On the Life of Moses, by Maren R. Niehoff

On the Decalogue, by Sarah Judith Pearce
On the Special Laws 1–4, by Naomi G. Cohen.

The second section is entitled Philosophical Treatises of Philo and consists of:

On the Virtues (51–174), by Walter T. Wilson
On the Contemplative Life, by David M. Hay
Hypothetica, by Gregory E. Sterling.

The publication of the chapter on *Contempl.* by David Hay is particularly poignant, since it was the last scholarly publication that he worked on before his untimely death in 2006.

The three volumes are magnificently presented and cover a remarkably range of ancient Jewish writings in modern translations with copious annotation. The writings are prefaced by five brief introductory chapters, one of which focuses on Philo (by David T. Runia). The entire set is highly recommended, but *caveat emptor*. The volumes, which are priced at $275, contain 3361 pages and weigh more than eight kilos, as I know from bitter experience after lugging them all the way from Baltimore to Melbourne.

David Runia
Melbourne, Australia

NOTES ON CONTRIBUTORS

MANUEL ALEXANDRE JR is Professor of Classics Emeritus at the University of Lisbon, Faculty of Letters, Portugal, and Senior Research fellow of the Center of Classical Studies at the same University. His postal address is Rua Joly Braga Santos, Lote E - 3 Dto., Lisbon 1600-123, PORTUGAL; his electronic address is malex@fl.ul.pt.

PER JARLE BEKKEN is Professor of Religion at the Faculty of Professional Studies, University of Nordland. His postal address is Faculty of Professional Studies, University of Nordland, N-8049 Bodø, NORWAY; his electronic address is Per.Jarle.Bekken@uin.no.

KATELL BERTHELOT is currently appointed at the Centre Paul-Albert Février at the University of Aix-Marseille, Aix-en-Provence. Her postal address is Maison Méditerranéenne des Sciences de l'Homme, 5 rue du château de l'horloge, BP 647, 13094 Aix-en-Provence Cedex 2, FRANCE; her electronic address is katell.b@free.fr.

ELLEN BIRNBAUM has taught at several Boston-area institutions, including Boston University, Brandeis, and Harvard. Her postal address is 78 Porter Road, Cambridge, MA 02140, U.S.A.; her electronic address is ebirnbaum78@gmail.com.

RONALD R. COX is Blanche E. Seaver Professor of Religion in Pepperdine University's Seaver College. His postal address is Religion and Philosophy Division, Pepperdine University, Malibu, CA 90263-4352, U.S.A.; his electronic address is ronald.cox@pepperdine.edu.

MICHAEL FRANCIS holds a Postdoctoral Fellowship in the College of Arts and Letters at the University of Notre Dame. His postal address is 130 Malloy Hall, Notre Dame, IN 46556, U.S.A.; his electronic address is mfranci2@nd.edu.

ALBERT C. GELJON teaches classical languages at the Christelijke Gymnasium in Utrecht. His postal address is Gazellestraat 138, 3523 SZ Utrecht, THE NETHERLANDS; his electronic address is ageljon@xs4all.nl.

Arco J. den Heijer graduated in Classics at the Radboud University, Nijmegen [and is currently finishing his Master of Theology at the Theological University of Apeldoorn]. His postal address is Lankforst 2207, 6538 GJ Nijmegen, The Netherlands; his electronic address is arcodenheijer@gmail.com.

Heleen M. Keizer is Dean of Academic Affairs at the Istituto Superiore di Osteopatia in Milan, Italy. Her postal address is Via Guerrazzi 3, 20900 Monza (MB), Italy; her electronic address is h.m.keizer@virgilio.it.

Jutta Leonhardt-Balzer is Senior Lecturer at the University of Aberdeen, UK. Her postal address is King's Quadrangle, University of Aberdeen, Aberdeen AB24 3UB, United Kingdom. Her electronic address is j.leonhardt-balzer@ abdn.ac.uk.

José Pablo Martín is Professor Consultus at the Universidad Nacional de General Sarmiento, San Miguel, Argentina, and Senior Research fellow of the Argentinian Research Organization (CONICET). His postal address is Azcuenaga 1090, 1663 San Miguel, Argentina; his electronic address is josepablomartinb@gmail.com.

Orrey McFarland is Visiting Professor of New Testament and Historical Theology at Knox Theological Seminary. His postal address is 1919 E. 2nd St., Apt. 484, Edmond, OK 73034, U.S.A.; his electronic address is orreymac@gmail.com.

Maren R. Niehoff is Professor in the Department of Jewish Thought at the Hebrew University, Jerusalem. Her postal address is Department of Jewish Thought, Hebrew University, Mt. Scopus, Jerusalem 91905, Israel; her electronic address is msmaren@mscc.huji.ac.il.

Sarah J. K. Pearce is Ian Karten Professor of Jewish Studies at the University of Southampton. Her postal address is Department of History, Faculty of Humanities, Avenue Campus, Highfield, Southampton SO17 1BF, United Kingdom; her electronic address is sjp2@soton.ac.uk.

Benjamin Pollock is Associate Professor of Religious Studies at Michigan State University, and of Jewish Thought at the Hebrew University of Jerusalem. His electronic address is pollockbenjamin14@gmail.com.

JAMES R. ROYSE is a Visiting Scholar at the Claremont School of Theology. His postal address is P.O. Box 567, Claremont, CA 91711-0567, U.S.A.; his electronic address is jamesrroyse@hotmail.com.

DAVID T. RUNIA is Master of Queen's College and Professorial Fellow in the School of Historical and Philosophical Studies at the University of Melbourne. His postal address is Queen's College, 1–17 College Crescent, Parkville 3052, AUSTRALIA; his electronic address is runia@queens.unimelb.edu.au.

KENNETH L. SCHENCK is Professor of New Testament in the School of Theology and Ministry at Indiana Wesleyan University. His postal address is Noggle Christian Ministries Building, Indiana Wesleyan University, 4201 S. Washington St., Marion, IN 46953-4972, U.S.A.; is electronic address is ken.schenck@indwes.edu.

TORREY SELAND is Professor Emeritus of The School of Mission and Theology, Stavanger, Norway. His postal address is Milorgveien 41, 3035 Drammen, NORWAY; his electronic address is torreys@gmail.com.

GREGORY E. STERLING is the Lillian Claus Professor of New Testament and the Reverend Henry L. Slack Dean of the Yale Divinity School. His postal address is 409 Prospect Street, New Haven, CT 06511, U.S.A.; his electronic address is gregory.sterling@yale.edu.

ABRAHAM TERIAN retired in 2008 as Professor Emeritus of Early Christianity and Armenian Patristics at St. Nersess Armenian Seminary. His postal address is 5478 N. Ferger Ave., Fresno, CA 93704, U.S.A.; his electronic address is terian@stnersess.edu.

CRISTINA TERMINI teaches at the Pontifical Lateran University, Rome. Her postal address is Via Caio Manilio 30, 00174 Roma, ITALY; her electronic address is cristermini@gmail.com.

SHARON WEISSER is Lecturer at the Department of Philosophy, Tel Aviv University. Her postal address is The Department of Philosophy, Tel-Aviv University, P.O.B. 39040, Ramat Aviv, Tel-Aviv 69978, ISRAEL; her electronic address is weisser@post.tau.ac.il.

The Studia Philonica Annual 27 (2015): 265–271

INSTRUCTIONS TO CONTRIBUTORS

Articles and Book reviews can only be considered for publication in *The Studia Philonica Annual* if they rigorously conform to the guidelines established by the editorial board. For further information see also the website of the Annual:

http://divinity.yale.edu/philo-alexandria

1. *The Studia Philonica Annual* accepts articles for publication in the area of Hellenistic Judaism, with special emphasis on Philo and his *Umwelt*. Articles on Josephus will be given consideration if they focus on his relation to Judaism and classical culture (and not on primarily historical subjects). The languages in which the articles may be published are English, French and German. Translations from Italian or Dutch into English can be arranged at a modest cost to the author.

2. Articles and reviews are to be sent to the editors in electronic form as email attachments. The preferred word processor is Microsoft Word. Users of other word processors are requested to submit a copy exported in a format compatible with Word, e.g. in RTF format. Manuscripts should be double-spaced, including the notes. Words should be italicized when required, not underlined. Quotes five lines or longer should be indented and may be single-spaced. For texts in Greek only Unicode fonts can be accepted. Authors are requested to use **a different font for Greek text**, e.g. SBL Greek (available at no cost from the SBL website), as compared to Roman text. For Hebrew the font provided on the SBL website is recommended. If the manuscript contains Greek or Hebrew text, a PDF version of the document must be sent together with the word processing file. No handwritten Greek or Hebrew can be accepted. Authors are requested not to vocalize their Hebrew (except when necessary) and to keep their use of this language to a reasonable minimum. It should always be borne in mind that not all readers of the Annual can be expected to read Greek or Hebrew. Transliteration is encouraged for incidental terms.

3. Authors are encouraged to use inclusive language wherever possible, avoiding terms such as "man" and "mankind" when referring to humanity in general.

4. For the preparation of articles and book reviews the Annual follows the guidelines of the *SBL Handbook of Style*, Second Edition, Atlanta: SBL Press, 2014. Here are examples of how a monograph, a monograph in a series, an edited volume, an article in an edited volume and a journal article are to be cited in notes (different conventions apply for bibliographies):

> Joan E. Taylor, *Jewish Women Philosophers of First-Century Alexandria—Philo's 'Therapeutae' Reconsidered* (Oxford: Oxford University Press, 2003), 123.
>
> Ellen Birnbaum, *The Place of Judaism in Philo's Thought: Israel, Jews, and Proselytes*, BJS 290; SPhiloM 2 (Atlanta: Scholars Press, 1996), 134.
>
> Gerard P. Luttikhuizen, ed., *Eve's Children: The Biblical Stories Retold and Interpreted in Jewish and Christian Traditions*, Themes in Biblical Narrative 5 (Leiden: Brill, 2003), 145.
>
> G. Bolognesi, "Marginal Notes on the Armenian Translation of the *Quaestiones et Solutiones in Genesim* by Philo," in *Studies on the Ancient Armenian Version of Philo's* Works, ed. Sara Mancini Lombardi and Paola Pontani, Studies in Philo of Alexandria 6 (Leiden: Brill, 2011) 45–50.
>
> James R. Royse, "Jeremiah Markland's Contribution to the Textual Criticism of Philo," *SPhiloA* 16 (2004): 50–60.

Note that abbreviations are used in the notes and also in bibliographies. Numbers should be given in full for ancient texts, e.g. *Aet.* 107–110; in references to modern publications the conventions of the *SBL Handbook of Style* should be followed (see p. 18). When joining up numbers in all textual and bibliographical references, the en dash should be used and not the hyphen, i.e. 50–60, not 50-60. For publishing houses only the first location is given. Submissions which do not conform to these guidelines will be returned to the authors for re-submission.

5. The following abbreviations are to be used in both articles and book reviews.

(a) Philonic treatises are to be abbreviated according to the following list. Numbering follows the edition of Cohn and Wendland, using Arabic numbers only and full stops rather than colons (e.g. *Spec.* 4.123). Note that *De Providentia* should be cited according to Aucher's edition, and not the LCL translation of the fragments by F. H. Colson.

Abr.	*De Abrahamo*
Aet.	*De aeternitate mundi*
Agr.	*De agricultura*
Anim.	*De animalibus*
Cher.	*De Cherubim*
Contempl.	*De vita contemplativa*
Conf.	*De confusione linguarum*
Congr.	*De congressu eruditionis gratia*
Decal.	*De Decalogo*
Deo	*De Deo*
Det.	*Quod deterius potiori insidiari soleat*

Deus	*Quod Deus sit immutabilis*
Ebr.	*De ebrietate*
Flacc.	*In Flaccum*
Fug.	*De fuga et inventione*
Gig.	*De gigantibus*
Her.	*Quis rerum divinarum heres sit*
Hypoth.	*Hypothetica*
Ios.	*De Iosepho*
Leg. 1–3	*Legum allegoriae* I, II, III
Legat.	*Legatio ad Gaium*
Migr.	*De migratione Abrahami*
Mos. 1–2	*De vita Moysis* I, II
Mut.	*De mutatione nominum*
Opif.	*De opificio mundi*
Plant.	*De plantatione* '
Post.	*De posteritate Caini*
Praem.	*De praemiis et poenis, De exsecrationibus*
Prob.	*Quod omnis probus liber sit*
Prov. 1–2	*De Providentia* I, II
QE 1–2	*Quaestiones et solutiones in Exodum* I, II
QG 1–4	*Quaestiones et solutiones in Genesim* I, II, III, IV
Sacr.	*De sacrificiis Abelis et Caini*
Sobr.	*De sobrietate*
Somn. 1–2	*De somniis* I, II
Spec. 1–4	*De specialibus legibus* I, II, III, IV
Virt.	*De virtutibus*

(b) Standard works of Philonic scholarship are abbreviated as follows:

G-G   Howard L. Goodhart and Erwin R. Goodenough, "A General Bibliography of Philo Judaeus." In *The Politics of Philo Judaeus: Practice and Theory* ed. Erwin R. Goodenough (New Haven: Yale University Press, 1938; repr. Georg Olms: Hildesheim, 1967), 125–321.

PCH   *Philo von Alexandria: die Werke in deutscher Übersetzung*, ed. Leopold Cohn, Isaac Heinemann *et al.*, 7 vols. Breslau: M & H Marcus Verla (Berlin: Walter de Gruyter, 1909–1964).

PCW   *Philonis Alexandrini opera quae supersunt*, ed. Leopoldus Cohn, Paulus Wendland et Sigismundus Reiter, 6 vols. (Berlin: Georg Reimer, 1896–1915).

PLCL   *Philo in Ten Volumes (and Two Supplementary Volumes)*, English translation by F. H. Colson, G. H. Whitaker (and R. Marcus), 12 vols. Loeb Classical Library; London: William Heinemann (Cambridge, Mass.: Harvard University Press, 1929–1962).

PACS   Philo of Alexandria Commentary Series

PAPM   *Les œuvres de Philon d'Alexandrie*, French translation under the general editorship of Roger Arnaldez, Jean Pouilloux, and Claude Mondésert (Paris: Cerf, 1961–1992).

R-R	Roberto Radice and David T. Runia, *Philo of Alexandria: an Annotated Bibliography 1937–1986* VCSup 8 (Leiden: Brill 1988).
RRS	David T. Runia, *Philo of Alexandria: an Annotated Bibliography 1987–1996* VCSup 57 (Leiden: Brill 2000).
RRS2	David T. Runia, *Philo of Alexandria: an Annotated Bibliography 1997–2006* VCSup 109 (Leiden: Brill 2012).
SPhA	Studies in Philo of Alexandria
SPhilo	*Studia Philonica*
SPhiloA	*The Studia Philonica Annual*
SPhiloM	Studia Philonica Monographs

(c) References to biblical authors and texts and to ancient authors and writings are to be abbreviated as recommended in the *SBL Handbook of Style* §8.2–3. Note that biblical books are not italicized and that between chapter and verse a colon is placed (but for non-biblical references colons should not be used). Abbreviations should be used for biblical books when they are followed by chapter or chapter and verse unless the book is the first word in a sentence. Authors writing in German or French should follow their own conventions for biblical citations.

(d) For giving dates the abbreviations BCE and CE are preferred and should be printed in regular large caps.

(e) Journals, monograph series, source collections, and standard reference works are to be be abbreviated in accordance with the recommendations listed in *The SBL Handbook of Style* §8.4. The following list contains a selection of the more important abbreviations, along with a few abbreviations of classical and philosophical journals and standard reference books not furnished in the list.

ABD	*The Anchor Bible Dictionary*, 6 vols. New York, 1992
AC	*L'Antiquité Classique*
ACW	Ancient Christian Writers
AGJU	Arbeiten zur Geschichte des antiken Judentums und des Urchristentums
AJPh	*American Journal of Philology*
AJSL	*American Journal of Semitic Languages*
ALGHJ	Arbeiten zur Literatur und Geschichte des hellenistischen Judentums
ANRW	*Aufstieg und Niedergang der römischen Welt*
APh	*L'Année Philologique*
BDAG	Bauer, W., F. W. Danker, W. F. Arndt, and F. W. Gingrich. *A Greek-English Lexicon of the New Testament and Other Early Christian literature*. 3rd ed. Chicago: University of Chicago Press, 1999
BibOr	Bibliotheca Orientalis
BJRL	*Bulletin of the John Rylands Library*
BJS	Brown Judaic Studies
BMCR	*Bryn Mawr Classical Review* (electronic)

BZAW	Beihefte zur Zeitschrift für die alttestamentliche Wissenschaft
BZNW	Beihefte zur Zeitschrift für die neutestamentliche Wissenschaft
BZRGG	Beihefte zur Zeitschrift für Religions- und Geistesgeschichte
CBQ	*The Catholic Biblical Quarterly*
CBQMS	The Catholic Biblical Quarterly. Monograph Series
CC	Corpus Christianorum, Turnhout
CIG	*Corpus Inscriptionum Graecarum*. Edited by A. Boeckh, 4 vols. in 8. Berlin, 1828–1877
CIJ	*Corpus Inscriptionum Judaicarum*. Edited by J. B. Frey, 2 vols. Rome, 1936–1952
CIL	*Corpus Inscriptionum Latinarum*. Berlin, 1862–
CIS	*Corpus Inscriptionum Semiticarum*. Paris, 1881–1962
CPh	*Classical Philology*
CPJ	*Corpus Papyrorum Judaicarum*. Edited by V. Tcherikover and A. Fuks, 3 vols. Cambrige Mass., 1957–64
CQ	*The Classical Quarterly*
CR	*The Classical Review*
CRINT	Compendia Rerum Iudaicarum ad Novum Testamentum
CPG	*Clavis Patrum Graecorum*. Edited by M. Geerard, 5 vols. and suppl. vol. Turnhout, 1974–1998
CPL	*Clavis Patrum Latinorum*. Edited by E. Dekkers. 3rd ed. Turnhout, 1995
CSCO	Corpus Scriptorum Christianorum Orientalium
CWS	Classics of Western Spirituality
DA	Dissertation Abstracts
DBSup	*Dictionnaire de la Bible*, Supplément. Paris, 1928–
DPhA	R. Goulet (ed.), *Dictionnaire des philosophes antiques*, Paris, 1989–
DSpir	*Dictionnaire de Spiritualité*, 17 vols. Paris, 1932–1995
EncJud	*Encyclopaedia Judaica*, 16 vols. Jerusalem, 1972
EPRO	Études préliminaires aux religions orientales dans l'Empire romain
FrGH	*Fragmente der Griechische Historiker*. Edited by F. Jacoby et al. Leiden, 1954–
FRLANT	Forschungen zur Religion und Literatur des Alten und Neuen Testaments
GCS	Die griechischen christlichen Schriftsteller, Leipzig
GLAJJ	M. Stern, *Greek and Latin Authors on Jews and Judaism*, 3 vols. Jerusalem, 1974–1984
GRBS	*Greek, Roman and Byzantine Studies*
HKNT	Handkommentar zum Neuen Testament, Tübingen
HNT	Handbuch zum Neuen Testament, Tübingen
HR	*History of Religions*
HThR	*Harvard Theological Review*
HUCA	*Hebrew Union College Annual*
JAAR	*Journal of the American Academy of Religion*
JAOS	*Journal of the American Oriental Society*
JAC	*Jahrbuch für Antike und Christentum*
JBL	*Journal of Biblical Literature*
JHI	*Journal of the History of Ideas*
JHS	*The Journal of Hellenic Studies*
JJS	*The Journal of Jewish Studies*
JQR	*The Jewish Quarterly Review*
JR	*The Journal of Religion*

JRS		*The Journal of Roman Studies*
JSHRZ		Jüdische Schriften aus hellenistisch-römischer Zeit
JSJ		*Journal for the Study of Judaism in the Persian, Hellenistic and Roman Periods*
JSJSup		Supplements to the Journal for the Study of Judaism
JSNT		*Journal for the Study of the New Testament*
JSNTSup	Journal for the Study of the New Testament. Supplement Series
JSOT		*Journal for the Study of the Old Testament*
JSOTSup	Journal for the Study of the Old Testament. Supplement Series
JSP		*Journal for the Study of the Pseudepigrapha and Related Literature*
JSSt		*Journal of Semitic Studies*
JThS		*The Journal of Theological Studies*
KBL		L. Koehler and W. Baumgartner, *Lexicon in Veteris Testamenti libros*, 3 vols. 3rd ed. Leiden, 1967–1983
KJ		*Kirjath Sepher*
LCL		Loeb Classical Library
LSJ		*A Greek-English Lexicon.* Edited by H. G. Liddell, R. Scott, H. S. Jones. 9th ed. with revised suppl. Oxford, 1996
MGWJ		*Monatsschrift für Geschichte und Wissenschaft des Judentums*
Mnem		*Mnemosyne*
NCE		*New Catholic Encyclopedia*, 15 vols. New York, 1967
NETS		New English Translation of the Septuagint. Edited by Albert Pietersma and Ben Wright, New York: Oxford University Press, 2007
NHS		Nag Hammadi Studies
NT		*Novum Testamentum*
NTSup		Supplements to Novum Testamentum
NTA		*New Testament Abstracts*
NTOA		Novum Testamentum et Orbis Antiquus
NTS		*New Testament Studies*
ODJ		*The Oxford Dictionary of Judaism.* Edited by R.J.Z. Werblowsky and G. Wigoder, New York 1997
OGIS		*Orientis Graeci inscriptiones selectae*
OLD		*The Oxford Latin Dictionary.* Edited by P. G. W. Glare. Oxford, 1982
OTP		*The Old Testament Pseudepigrapha.* Edited by J. H. Charlesworth. 2 vols. New York–London, 1983–1985
PAAJR		*Proceedings of the American Academy for Jewish Research*
PAL		*Philon d'Alexandrie: Lyon 11–15 Septembre 1966.* Éditions du CNRS, Paris, 1967
PG		Patrologiae cursus completus: series Graeca. Edited by J. P. Migne. 162 vols. Paris, 1857–1912
PGL		*A Patristic Greek Lexicon.* Edited by G. W. H. Lampe. Oxford, 1961
PhilAnt		Philosophia Antiqua
PL		Patrologiae cursus completus: series Latina. Edited by J. P. Migne. 221 vols. Paris, 1844–1864
PW		Pauly-Wissowa-Kroll, *Real-Encyclopaedie der classischen Altertumswissenschaft.* 49 vols. Munich, 1980
PWSup		Supplement to PW
RAC		*Reallexikon für Antike und Christentum*
RB		*Revue Biblique*
REA		*Revue des Études Anciennes*
REArm		*Revue des Études Arméniennes*

REAug	*Revue des Études Augustiniennes*
REG	*Revue des Études Grecques*
REJ	*Revue des Études Juives*
REL	*Revue des Études Latines*
RGG	*Die Religion in Geschichte und Gegenwart*, 7 vols. 3rd edition Tübingen, 1957–1965
RhM	*Rheinisches Museum für Philologie*
RHR	*Revue de l'histoire des religions*
RQ	*Revue de Qumran*
RSR	*Revue des Sciences Religieuses*
Str-B	H. L. Strack and P. Billerbeck, *Kommentar zum Neuen Testament aus Talmud und Midrasch*, 6 vols. Munich, 1922–1961
SBLDS	Society of Biblical Literature Dissertation Series
SBLMS	Society of Biblical Literature Monograph Series
SBLSCS	Society of Biblical Studies Septuagint and Cognate Studies
SBLSPS	Society of Biblical Literature Seminar Papers Series
SC	Sources Chrétiennes
Sem	*Semitica*
SHJP	E. Schürer, *The History of the Jewish People in the Age of Jesus Christ*. Revised edition, 3 vols. in 4. Edinburgh, 1973–1987
SJLA	Studies in Judaism in Late Antiquity
SNTSMS	Society for New Testament Studies. Monograph Series
SR	*Studies in Religion*
STAC	Studies and Texts in Antiquity and Judaism
SUNT	Studien zur Umwelt des Neuen Testaments
SVF	*Stoicorum veterum fragmenta*. Edited by J. von Arnim. 4 vols. Leipzig, 1903–1924
TDNT	*Theological Dictionary of the New Testament*. 10 vols. Grand Rapids, 1964–1976
THKNT	Theologischer Handkommentar zum Neuen Testament, Berlin
TRE	*Theologische Realenzyklopädie*, Berlin
TSAJ	Texte und Studien zum Antike Judentum
TU	Texte und Untersuchungen zur Geschichte der altchristlichen Literatur, Berlin
TWNT	*Theologisches Wörterbuch zum Neuen Testament*, 10 vols. Stuttgart 1933–1979.
TZ	*Theologische Zeitschrift*
VC	*Vigiliae Christianae*
VCSup	Supplements to Vigiliae Christianae
VT	*Vetus Testamentum*
WMANT	Wissenschaftliche Monographien zum Alten und Neuen Testament
WUNT	Wissenschaftliche Untersuchungen zum Neuen Testament
YJS	*Yale Jewish Studies*
ZAW	*Zeitschrift für die alttestamentliche Wissenschaft*
ZKG	*Zeitschrift für Kirchengeschichte*
ZKTh	*Zeitschrift für Katholische Theologie*
ZNW	*Zeitschrift für die neutestamentliche Wissenschaft*
ZRGG	*Zeitschrift für Religions- und Geistesgeschichte*

www.ingramcontent.com/pod-product-compliance
Lightning Source LLC
Chambersburg PA
CBHW020403100426
42812CB00001B/186